Exploring the Fusion of Quantum Computing and Machine Learning

Minu R.I.
SRM Institute of Science and Technology, India

Nagarajan G.
Sathyabama Institute of Science and Technology, Chennai, India

Martin Margala
University of Louisiana at Lafayette, USA

Siva Shankar S.
KG Reddy College of Engineering and Technology, India

Logashanmugam E.
Sathyabama Institute of Science and Technology, Chennai, India

IGI Global
Scientific Publishing
Publishing Tomorrow's Research Today

Vice President of Editorial	Melissa Wagner
Director of Acquisitions	Mikaela Felty
Director of Book Development	Jocelynn Hessler
Production Manager	Mike Brehm
Cover Design	Phillip Shickler

Published in the United States of America by
IGI Global Scientific Publishing
701 East Chocolate Avenue
Hershey, PA, 17033, USA
Tel: 717-533-8845
Fax: 717-533-7115
Website: https://www.igi-global.com E-mail: cust@igi-global.com

Library of Congress Cataloging-in-Publication Data

LCCN: 2024054380 (CIP Data Pending)
ISBN13: 9798369362259
Isbn13Softcover: 9798369362266
EISBN13: 9798369362273

British Cataloguing in Publication Data
A Cataloguing in Publication record for this book is available from the British Library.

Table of Contents

Detailed Table of Contents

This chapter explores the transformative potential of quantum computing in various domains, particularly focusing on its applications in machine learning and data management. Utilizing a comprehensive literature review and case studies, the research examines the execution speed and accuracy of quantum algorithms compared to classical methods, highlighting the advantages of quantum feature mapping. Key findings indicate that quantum computing can significantly enhance processing efficiency and problem-solving capabilities in complex datasets, particularly in finance and healthcare. The study concludes that integrating quantum computing into existing frameworks can lead to more resilient and efficient systems, paving the way for innovative solutions in emerging technologies. The implications of this research underscore the necessity for interdisciplinary collaboration to harness the full potential of quantum advancements.

This chapter delves into how ML and QC combine in the development of the theory of quantum systems. With an increase in system complexity, traditional approaches to quantum system analysis suffer from extremely vast computational limitations. Incorporation of ML algorithms along with the frameworks of quantum computation allows for novel solutions in quantum system classification, optimization, and noise mitigation. We present key ML techniques; both supervised and unsupervised learning, and their synthesis with quantum algorithms, such as the Quantum Approximate Optimization Algorithm (QAOA), the Variational Quantum Eigensolver, among others. The latter will also focus on their application in real-world activities like quantum chemistry, cryptography, and material science, as their synergy increases efficiency with better accuracy. This work gives a comprehensive roadmap for harnessing ML and QC to revolutionize the analysis of quantum systems and solve previously intractable problems by addressing current challenges and outlining future directions.

Quantum computing provides the transformative capability to take advancements in AI in medicine several notches ahead. Building on the principles of quantum mechanics, quantum computing can supply computational speed and efficiency that leave the limitations of classical computers far behind, especially as they deal with complex data sets in medicine. As such, this chapter provides a look at the frontier areas of intersection between quantum computing and AI in medicine, particularly in drug discovery, genomics, precision medicine, and medical imaging. The accelerated simulation of molecular interactions would promise quantum algorithms to find therapeutic targets quickly and to optimize treatment pathways. Quantum machine learning also promises breakthroughs in diagnostic accuracy and predictive analytics, which will provide personalized care. This chapter explores the potential of quantum computing in medical advancement, focusing on hardware scalability, algorithm development, data privacy, and ethical considerations.

QML is the quantum machine learning, a new approach to explore the potential of quantum computation allowing us to discover solutions that otherwise would be hard for a classical computer to find. A variety of applied QML areas will be highlighted in the following chapter such as optimization problems NLP, drug discovery. Some foundations of quantum- superposition and entanglement- are designed to provide more efficient approach- towards higher fidelity in all data driven pipelines. This chapter gives some practical use cases for integration of quantum algorithms into pipelines of machine learning as well as some main challenges (i.e., regarding noise, scalability and algorithm selection) concerning it. Hybrid quantum-classical schemes are thought as the key for progress towards practicality on currently available noisy intermediate-scale quantum hardware. In this chapter, we will address QML viewpoints of the operational strategy and future, including potential QML disruptive effects and the future adoption insights of QML.

Quantum Error Correction (QEC) is essential for overcoming the fragility of qubits, enabling reliable and scalable quantum computing by mitigating the effects of noise, decoherence, and operational errors. This chapter explores QEC's foundational principles, including error types, noise impact, and syndrome measurement techniques for identifying and correcting errors. It covers key codes such as Shor and Steane, which provide basic error protection, and advanced codes like concatenated codes, surface codes, and quantum Low-Density Parity-Check (LDPC) codes. Concatenated codes employ hierarchical encoding to exponentially reduce logical error rates, while surface codes, including Toric codes, utilize topological properties of qubits arranged on a 2D lattice to detect and correct errors with high fault tolerance and scalability. Quantum LDPC codes leverage sparse parity-check matrices to offer efficient and scalable error correction, closely approaching theoretical performance limits. The chapter concludes by exploring current research efforts to optimize QEC codes.

This study delves into quantum simulation, exploring its foundational principles and potential applications. On the one hand, the classic methods of energy computation were used. On the other hand, the link between molecular dynamics (MD) and machine learning (ML) was also investigated. In the first part dedicated to adiabatic and diabatic potential energy curve (PEC), we examine quantum simulation techniques, including diabatization using neural networks to capture complex molecular dynamics. For the KFr molecule, we present novel adiabatic and diabatic potential energy curves. In the second part related to molecular dynamics simulation based on machine learning, the link between MD and ML was highlight to overcome difficulties of the classic simulation methods. This research aims to develop new approaches to molecular dynamics beyond the Born-Oppenheimer approximation and to explore the potential of machine learning, particularly interpretable neural networks, for efficient and interpretable simulations.

This chapter discusses the transformative effect of Machine Learning on medical marketing strategies. With the healthcare landscape becoming increasingly data-driven, ML provides innovative solutions for enhancing patient engagement, optimizing marketing efforts, and improving outcomes. The integration of ML technologies in

This chapter discusses the means whereby QML can revolutionize and transform online marketing and business practices. QML is a derivative from the principles of quantum computation and machine learning, such that tremendous volumes of data may be processed at unprecedented velocities, hence advanced analytics in terms of customer behavior being made possible, and also that of hyper-personalized marketing campaigns. Some of the key QML techniques discussed in terms of increasing the efficiency of marketing, reducing costs, and improving return on investments include techniques in quantum algorithms for clustering, classification, and optimization. It explores the potential of quantum technology in business intelligence, including real-time customer segmentation, predictive analytics, and dynamic pricing models, and predicts future trends and adoption roadmaps in the digital economy.

In this literature survey, we seek after the manner in which the idea of boundlessness adjusts the universe of money. Utilizing bibliometric information of around 37 examination articles from the Scopus data set alongside different books on Quantum finance and the development of money, this survey reveals insight into the main writers, nations, organizations, outlets, articles, and subjects of different logical ways to deal with get into the quantum domain of money involving Vastness as the center base that gives us numerous ways of characterizing our ongoing economy and how it can change and adjust to the ongoing situation and how we can manage future possibilities of reforming Money in general. Discoveries of this audit recommend that there is a roundabout connection among money and boundlessness. Future exploration headings for The Job of Endlessness in Molding Monetary Reality finish up this survey.

N. Nithiyanandam, Department of Computing Technologies, SRM Institute of Science and Technology, Kattankulathur, India
G. K. Sandhia, Department of Computing Technologies, SRM Institute of Science and Technology, Kattankulathur, India
K. Vijiyakumar, Department of Computing Technologies, SRM Institute of Science and Technology, Kattankulathur, India

This research presents a new architecture for structured picture categorization problems called Hierarchical Fused Quantum Fuzzy Neural Network (HFQ-FNN). It combines the ideas of quantum computing with fuzzy logic and neural networks. With an accuracy of 84.04%, the suggested HFQ-FNN beats CNN and FDNN, two industry standards, on the Dirty-MNIST dataset, by a margin of 2.9% and 1.4%, respectively. Also, on the 15-Scene dataset, HFQ-FNN achieves an accuracy of 74.27% and shows a considerably higher F1 value, which is 3.0% better than DNN and 0.6% better than FDNN. The robustness analysis shows that HFQ-FNN is resilient against quantum noise, with a fidelity of 0.95 at a 0.1 noise probability. These findings show that HFQ-FNN is a powerful tool for improving picture classification accuracy through the use of quantum computing, which could lead to major developments in the field of complicated data classification.

S. Sony Priya, SRM Institute of Science and Technology, India
R. I. Minu, SRM Institute of Science and Technology, India

The convolutional neural network (CNN) is a widely recognized model in computer vision due to its capability to utilize data correlation effectively. However, CNNs often face challenges when training on large datasets or dimensions. To address this, the Quantum Convolutional Neural Network (QCNN) introduces an innovative solution for CNN-based problems, specifically within quantum computing frameworks. By integrating CNN architecture into quantum environments, QCNN enhances the model's overall efficiency and functionality. This approach marks an initial effort to propose a solution for classification challenges in quantum physics and chemistry. Furthermore, the study highlights a computational method utilizing the Multi-scale Entanglement Renormalization Ansatz (MERA) with logarithmic depth O(log(n)). Experiments conducted using the TensorFlow Quantum platform on the

Foreword

The union of quantum computing and machine learning marks a turning point in our technological journey, heralding a new era of computation and problem-solving. These two transformative fields, independently remarkable, combine to form an intersection that promises unprecedented advancements. As we stand at the threshold of this new frontier, *Exploring the Fusion of Quantum Computing and Machine Learning* emerges as a timely and indispensable contribution to the scientific community.

Quantum computing, with its ability to process information at an atomic level, has the potential to solve complex problems far beyond the reach of classical computers. Machine learning, on the other hand, continues to reshape how we analyze data, make predictions, and derive actionable insights. Together, these technologies hold the key to breakthroughs in areas as diverse as healthcare, finance, physics, and artificial intelligence.

This book brings together a wealth of knowledge from leading experts, offering a comprehensive exploration of this fusion. Its 12 meticulously crafted chapters span a range of topics, from quantum systems analysis and error correction to cutting-edge applications in business, medical advancements, and beyond. By balancing theoretical depth with practical relevance, the book caters to a diverse audience, including researchers, academicians, and R&D professionals in industry.

In an era where interdisciplinary collaboration is paramount, this book serves as a beacon, encouraging readers to think beyond traditional boundaries. It invites us to envision a future where quantum-enhanced algorithms redefine what is possible, unlocking solutions to challenges that once seemed insurmountable.

As you delve into the chapters ahead, you will discover not only the potential of quantum computing and machine learning but also the passion and ingenuity of the researchers driving this field forward. Their contributions reflect a shared vision of progress, one that inspires us to embrace innovation and push the boundaries of knowledge.

I congratulate the editor and contributors for assembling this remarkable body of work. May it serve as a source of inspiration and a catalyst for further exploration, collaboration, and discovery.

Bhuvan Unhelkar

Department of Information Systems and Decision Sciences, Muma College of Business, University of South Florida, USA

Preface

The convergence of quantum computing and machine learning represents one of the most groundbreaking intersections in the history of science and technology. While quantum computing promises to revolutionize computation with unparalleled processing power, machine learning offers transformative insights into data analysis and decision-making. Together, they form a symbiotic relationship, unlocking capabilities that were once deemed impossible. This book, *Exploring the Fusion of Quantum Computing and Machine Learning*, delves into this fascinating fusion, presenting cutting-edge research, novel applications, and the challenges that lie ahead.

The motivation behind this book stems from the rapid advancements in both quantum computing and machine learning, coupled with their potential to disrupt traditional computational paradigms. As researchers, educators, and practitioners, we are witnessing a paradigm shift in fields ranging from healthcare and finance to marketing and artificial intelligence. Quantum-enhanced algorithms are poised to solve problems that classical systems cannot, and machine learning is the ideal partner to harness this quantum advantage.

This book is organized into 12 chapters, each focusing on a specific area where quantum computing and machine learning intersect. It begins by exploring the foundational principles of quantum systems analysis and progresses to advanced topics such as quantum error correction, adiabatic and diabatic potential energy computations, and innovative applications in business, finance, and medical sciences. Each chapter has been authored by experts in their respective domains, ensuring depth, rigor, and practical relevance.

Our aim is to provide readers with a comprehensive understanding of this emerging field, bridging the gap between theory and practice. This book is specifically designed for researchers, academicians, and R&D professionals from industries who are eager to explore the potential of quantum computing and machine learning. Whether you are a researcher seeking inspiration for your next project, a practitioner exploring quantum computing's potential, or a student eager to learn about the future of technology, this book serves as a valuable resource.

As we embark on this journey, we recognize that the field is still in its infancy, with many questions yet to be answered. However, it is precisely this uncertainty that makes it so exciting. By compiling these chapters, we hope to inspire further exploration, collaboration, and innovation.

We extend our deepest gratitude to the contributors who have shared their expertise and insights, and to the readers who will carry forward the ideas presented in this book. It is our hope that this work sparks curiosity, fosters creativity, and contributes to the growing body of knowledge in quantum computing and machine learning.

Welcome to the fusion of quantum computing and machine learning—a realm where science meets imagination, and the future unfolds before our very eyes.

R.I. Minu
SRM Institute of Science and Technology, India

G Nagarajan
Sathyabama Institute of Science and Technology in Chennai, India

Martin Margala
University of Louisiana at Lafayette, USA

S. Siva Shankar
KG Reddy College of Engineering and Technology, India

E. Logashanmugam
Sathyabama Institute of Science and Technology in Chennai, India

Chapter 1
Harnessing Quantum Computing for Advanced Machine Learning:
Techniques, Applications, and Challenges

C. V. Suresh Babu
https://orcid.org/0000-0002-8474-2882
Hindustan Institute of Technology and Science, India

Malini Premakumari William
https://orcid.org/0009-0004-6165-2501
Mirage Software, Inc. dba Bourntec Solutions, Inc., USA

Eanest EssraMelvin
Hindustan Institute of Technology and Science, India

R. Mithun
Hindustan Institute of Technology and Science, India

ABSTRACT

This chapter explores the transformative potential of quantum computing in various domains, particularly focusing on its applications in machine learning and data management. Utilizing a comprehensive literature review and case studies, the research examines the execution speed and accuracy of quantum algorithms compared to classical methods, highlighting the advantages of quantum feature mapping. Key findings indicate that quantum computing can significantly enhance processing efficiency and problem-solving capabilities in complex datasets, particularly in

DOI: 10.4018/979-8-3693-6225-9.ch001

finance and healthcare. The study concludes that integrating quantum computing into existing frameworks can lead to more resilient and efficient systems, paving the way for innovative solutions in emerging technologies. The implications of this research underscore the necessity for interdisciplinary collaboration to harness the full potential of quantum advancements.

1.0. INTRODUCTION

Quantum computing represents a paradigm shift in computational capabilities, leveraging the principles of quantum mechanics to process information in fundamentally different ways than classical computing. As the field of quantum computing continues to evolve, it has garnered significant attention for its potential applications across various domains, including artificial intelligence, cryptography, and complex system simulations (Winker et al., 2024). This study aims to explore the intersection of quantum computing and machine learning, highlighting the transformative potential of quantum algorithms in enhancing data processing and decision-making capabilities.

1.1. Background and Relevance

The rapid advancements in quantum hardware and algorithms have positioned quantum computing as a critical area of research and development. Recent breakthroughs in qubit design and error-correction techniques have paved the way for more stable and scalable quantum systems (Arute et al., 2022). Furthermore, the integration of quantum computing with machine learning has opened new avenues for solving complex problems that are currently intractable for classical systems (Raparthi et al., 2022). As organizations increasingly seek innovative solutions to manage and analyze vast datasets, understanding the relevance of quantum computing becomes paramount.

1.2. Objectives and Scope

The primary objective of this study is to investigate the capabilities of quantum computing in enhancing machine learning processes. Specifically, the research will focus on the application of quantum algorithms in optimizing data management tasks and improving the efficiency of machine learning models. The scope of the study encompasses a review of existing literature, analysis of quantum algorithms, and case studies demonstrating the practical applications of quantum machine learning in various fields, including finance and healthcare (Aspuru-Guzik et al., 2023).

1.3. Significance of the Study

This study is significant as it addresses the growing need for advanced computational techniques in an era characterized by big data and complex decision-making challenges. By exploring the potential of quantum computing to revolutionize machine learning, the research aims to contribute to the understanding of how quantum technologies can enhance data processing capabilities and lead to more effective solutions in diverse applications. The findings of this study may also inform future research directions and encourage interdisciplinary collaboration in the field of quantum computing (Wehner et al., 2022).

1.4. Structure of the Chapter

The chapter is structured as follows: it begins with a comprehensive overview of quantum computing principles and their implications for machine learning. This is followed by a detailed examination of quantum algorithms and their applications in various domains. The chapter will also present case studies that illustrate the practical benefits of integrating quantum computing with machine learning. Finally, the chapter concludes with a discussion of the challenges and future prospects of quantum technologies in enhancing computational efficiency.

2.0. FOUNDATIONS OF QUANTUM COMPUTING AND MACHINE LEARNING

In the last few years, the field of quantum computing has experienced remarkable progress. The prototypes of quantum computers already exist and have been made available to users through cloud services (e.g., IBM Q experience, Google quantum AI, or Xanadu quantum cloud). While fault- tolerant and large-scale quantum computers are not available yet (and may not be for a long time, if ever), the potential of this new technology is undeniable. Quantum algorithms have the proven ability to either outperform classical approaches for several tasks, or are impossible to be efficiently simulated by classical means under reasonable complexity-theoretic assumptions. Even imperfect current-day technology is speculated to exhibit computational advantages over classical systems. Recent research is using quantum computers to solve machine learning tasks. Meanwhile, the database community has already successfully applied various machine learning algorithms for data management tasks, so combining the fields seems to be a promising endeavor (Suresh Babu C. V, Sathiya Narayana S. 2024). However, quantum machine learning is a new research field for most database researchers. In this paper, we provide a fundamental introduction to quantum computing and quantum machine learning and show the potential benefits and applications for database research. In addition, we demonstrate how to apply quantum machine learning to the join order optimization problem in databases. (winker,2023)

2.1. Principles of Quantum Computing

Quantum Bits (Qubits)

Quantum bits, or qubits, are the fundamental units of information in quantum computing, analogous to classical bits in traditional computing. However, qubits possess unique properties that enable quantum computers to perform complex calculations more efficiently than classical computers. Here's a detailed explanation of qubits:

Definition

A qubit is a quantum system that can exist in a superposition of states, meaning it can represent both 0 and 1 simultaneously. This is in contrast to classical bits, which can only be in one of two states at any given time (either 0 or 1).

Properties of Qubits

1. **Superposition**:
   - A qubit can be in a state represented as $|\psi\rangle = \alpha|0\rangle + \beta|1\rangle$, where $|0\rangle$ and $|1\rangle$ are the basis states, and α and β are complex numbers that represent the probability amplitudes of the qubit being in each state. The probabilities of measuring the qubit in state $|0\rangle$ or $|1\rangle$ are given by $|\alpha|^2$ and $|\beta|^2$, respectively. This property allows quantum computers to process a vast amount of information simultaneously.
2. **Entanglement**:
   - Qubits can be entangled, meaning the state of one qubit is directly related to the state of another, regardless of the distance between them. This phenomenon allows for coordinated operations on multiple qubits, enabling complex computations and enhancing the power of quantum algorithms.
3. **Interference**:
   - Quantum states can interfere with one another, allowing for the amplification of correct paths (solutions) and the cancellation of incorrect ones. This property is utilized in quantum algorithms to enhance the probability of obtaining the desired outcome.

Physical Realizations

Qubits can be physically realized using various systems, including:

- **Superconducting Circuits**: These use superconducting materials to create qubits that can be manipulated with microwave pulses.
- **Trapped Ions**: Individual ions are trapped using electromagnetic fields and manipulated with lasers to perform quantum operations.
- **Photons**: Quantum states of light can be used as qubits, where different polarization states represent different qubit values.
- **Quantum Dots**: Semiconductor nanostructures can confine electrons, and their spin states can represent qubits.

Measurement

When a qubit is measured, it collapses from its superposition state to one of the basis states (either $|0\rangle$ or $|1\rangle$) with probabilities determined by the amplitudes α and β. This measurement process is probabilistic, which is a fundamental aspect of quantum mechanics.

Importance

Qubits are essential for the operation of quantum computers. Their unique properties enable quantum algorithms to solve problems that are intractable for classical computers, such as factoring large numbers, simulating quantum systems, and optimizing complex functions.

In summary, qubits are the cornerstone of quantum computing, providing the ability to perform computations in ways that classical bits cannot, thanks to their properties of superposition, entanglement, and interference.

Quantum Gates and Circuits

Quantum gates and circuits are fundamental components of quantum computing, analogous to classical logic gates and circuits in traditional computing. Here's a detailed explanation:

Quantum Gates

Quantum gates are the basic building blocks of quantum circuits. They manipulate qubits, which are the quantum equivalent of classical bits. Unlike classical bits that can be either 0 or 1, qubits can exist in a superposition of states, allowing them to represent both 0 and 1 simultaneously. Quantum gates perform operations on these qubits, changing their states according to the principles of quantum mechanics.

Types of Quantum Gates:

1. **Identity Gate (I)**: This gate leaves the qubit unchanged.
2. **NOT Gate (X)**: Also known as the Pauli-X gate, it flips the state of a qubit from 0 to 1 or from 1 to 0.
3. **Hadamard Gate (H)**: This gate creates superposition, transforming a qubit from a definite state to an equal probability of being in both states.
4. **CNOT Gate (Controlled-NOT)**: This is a two-qubit gate that flips the state of a second qubit (target) if the first qubit (control) is in the state 1.

Quantum Circuits

Quantum circuits are composed of a sequence of quantum gates applied to a set of qubits. The arrangement and combination of these gates determine the computation performed by the quantum circuit. This new form for quantum circuit diagrams was introduced by Feynman in 1986 and later modified by Barenco et al. in 1995. Quantum circuits can be represented visually, similar to classical circuits, where lines represent qubits and symbols represent gates.

Functionality

Quantum gates are represented mathematically as unitary operators, meaning they preserve the total probability of the quantum state. When a quantum gate is applied to a qubit, it transforms the qubit's state according to specific rules defined by quantum mechanics.

Importance

Quantum gates and circuits enable quantum algorithms to perform complex calculations that would be infeasible for classical computers. They are essential for implementing quantum algorithms such as Shor's algorithm for factoring large numbers and Grover's algorithm for searching unsorted databases.

2.2. Basics of Machine Learning

Machine learning is a branch of artificial intelligence that focuses on the development of algorithms and statistical models that enable computer systems to improve their performance on a specific task without being explicitly programmed. These algorithms and models are designed to learn from and make predictions or decisions based on data, allowing the computer system to adapt and improve its performance over time through experience. This process is known as "training" the model, where the computer system is exposed to large amounts of data to iteratively adjust its parameters and optimize its performance (wang et al, 2012) (Bhowmik et al, 2008) (Ahmed RG, 2018). This iterative process of adjusting parameters and optimizing performance through exposure to data is crucial in the field of machine learning as it allows computer systems to continuously enhance their ability to make accurate predictions or decisions without human intervention (Basán et al, 2020). This iterative process of parameter adjustment and performance optimization through data exposure is essential in the field of machine learning as it enables computer systems to continually enhance their predictive or decision-making capabilities without the need for human intervention, thereby advancing the field of artificial intelligence (Mehdiyev et al, 2020).

3.0. QUANTUM ALGORITHMS FOR MACHINE LEARNING

3.1. Overview of Key Quantum Algorithms

Grover's Algorithm

Grover's search (Grover, 1996), formally described in Nielsen and Chuang (2002), takes a function f such that there is at least one s such that fpsq " 1, a set S " t0, 1u n of inputs of size |S| " N " 2 n, and is able to find an s P S which satisfies fpsq " 1 in Op ? Nq time. Classically this kind of search has to take at least N steps, and therefore take OpNq time. This speedup, though not exponential, is quite significant considering the generality of this algorithm. It was also proven that this is the maximal speedup possible for this problem .

Much like our f oracle mentioned in the Deutsch-Jozsa algorithm, let U be an oracle if x is a solution to the search problem and 0 otherwise. The algorithm also uses conditional phase shift which takes |0y to |0y and |xy to ´ |xy for x ą 0. The Grover iteration used in Grover's search is defined as a product of 4 gates.

Figure 1. This block diagram represents the control flow the working of the Grover's algorithm (Raparthi2022)

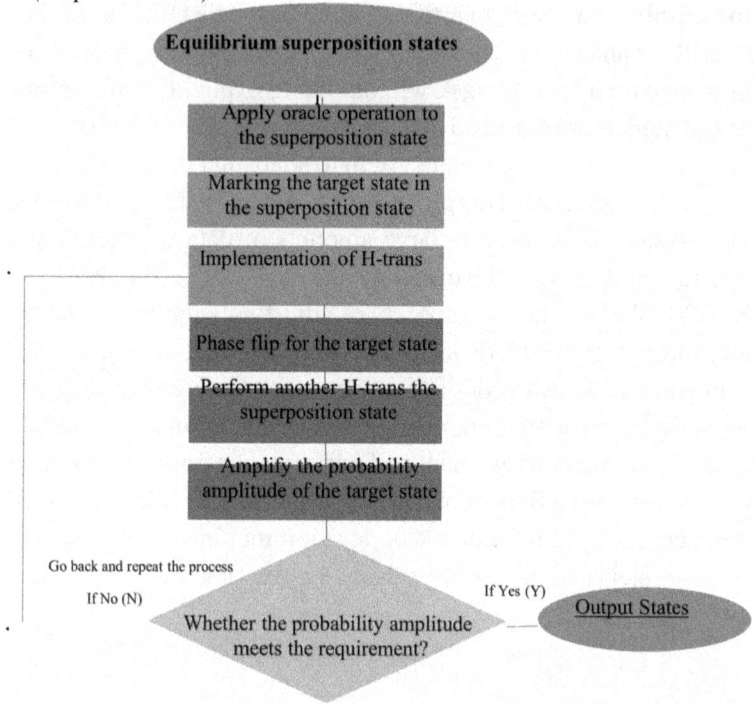

Shor's Algorithm

Shor's algorithm (Shor, 1994) is perhaps the most famous Quantum algorithm. While being one of the few exponential speedups over current classical algorithms, its fame comes more from the problem which it solves: prime factorisation. Given an N P N such that N " pq for p, q prime, find p (or q). It is only required to find one of the factors since division is easy in the sense that there is a fast classical algorithm. This problem is quite important for current cryptography, which makes the assumption that this problem is hard in the sense that it is slow to solve on classical computers (It is important to note that it is still possible that there exists a fast classical algorithm for prime factorisation, since we have not proved that the fastest algorithm is not in P; doing so would immediately imply P ‰ NP). Shor's algorithm is made up of two parts: a classical part which reduces factoring to order finding, and a quantum part which finds the order. In the classical part, the algorithm checks whether N is even, and calculates the GCD (greatest common divisor) of numbers. Both of these have fast classical algorithms. The classical algorithm for converting factoring to ordering finding is as follows

A fast classical algorithm to find the order has not been found. However the second (Quantum) part of Shor's algorithm can find the order fast.

Using the inverse Fourier transform sr{r is an approximation of the phase of e 2πisj{r . The continued fraction algorithm is used to find an r such that the output sr{r is irreducible. Shor's algorithm takes OpplogpNqq3 q time, as opposed to the fastest known fully classical algorithm for prime factorisation which takes OpN1{4 q time. The circuit for Shor's algorithm is as follows: since the order r (actually rl{r) we are trying to find is greater than 1, we will require multiple registers to measure it.

There have been some improvements on Shor's algorithm, e.g. by Bernstein et al. (2017) who present a new algorithm that is faster than Shor's algorithm in most cases. (Raparthi2022)

3.2. Quantum Neural Networks

Concept and Design

Quantum computing represents a revolutionary approach to computation, leveraging principles from quantum mechanics to process information in fundamentally new ways. This technology has the potential to significantly impact various fields, including artificial intelligence (AI). In recent years, researchers have explored the integration of quantum computing techniques in neural network design, leading to the development of quantum inspired neural networks (QINNs).The motivation behind QINNs lies in their ability to overcome the limitations of classical neural networks, such as the von Neumann bottleneck and the curse of dimensionality. QINNs promise to enhance AI capabilities by leveraging quantum parallelism and superposition to perform computations more efficiently than classical counterparts. This paper provides a scholarly review of QINNs for advanced AI applications, focusing on their design principles, advantages over classical neural networks, and current state of research. By examining the integration of quantum computing techniques in neural network design, this review aims to shed light on the potential of QINNs to shape the future of AI technologies

Fundamentals of Quantum Computing

Quantum computing is founded on the principles of quantum mechanics, which govern the behavior of particles at the smallest scales. Unlike classical computing, which relies on bits that can be either 0 or 1, quantum computing uses quantum bits, or qubits, which can exist in a superposition of states. This property allows qubits to represent and process multiple values simultaneously, leading to exponential speedups in certain computations. One of the key concepts in quantum computing is quantum parallelism, where a quantum computer can explore multiple solutions to a problem simultaneously. This is achieved through the use of quantum gates, which manipulate the state of qubits based on quantum principles. Quantum parallelism enables quantum computers to perform certain tasks, such as factoring large numbers or searching unsorted databases, much faster than classical computers. Another important concept in quantum computing is quantum entanglement, which describes a phenomenon where the state of one qubit is correlated with the state of another, even when they are physically separated. Quantum entanglement allows for the creation of quantum circuits that can perform complex operations on qubits, leading to the development of quantum algorithms. Overall, quantum computing offers a fundamentally different approach to computation, with the potential to revolutionize various fields, including AI. By harnessing the principles of quantum mechanics, quantum computing techniques can be integrated into neural network design to create QINNs, which offer enhanced performance and efficiency over classical neural networks **(Raparthi2022)**

Implementation Challenges

Research in the field of quantum computing has identified several key obstacles that must be overcome in order to fully harness its advanced capabilities. One of the primary challenges facing researchers is the development of error correction techniques to mitigate the effects of quantum decoherence. This phenomenon occurs when quantum systems lose their coherence and become susceptible to errors, hindering the accuracy and reliability of computations in quantum computers. Quantum decoherence poses a significant barrier to achieving fault-tolerant quantum computation, necessitating the implementation of robust error correction codes to preserve the integrity of quantum information and enable the scalability of quantum algorithms (Raussendorf, 2012) (Nakahara, 2012) (Bacon, 2008).

Furthermore, the complexity of designing efficient error correction codes for quantum systems is exacerbated by the inherent fragility of quantum information and the delicate balance required to maintain coherence among qubits in quantum computers. Moreover, the intricate nature of quantum systems further complicates the task of developing error correction codes, as the fragility of quantum information and the precise coordination needed to sustain coherence among qubits in quantum computers present additional challenges for researchers in this field (Martinez et al, 2020) (Baek et al, 2018) (Vallero et al, 2024).

3.3. Quantum Support Vector Machines

Quantum machine learning aims to execute machine learning algorithms in quantum computers by utilizing powerful laws like superposition and entanglement for solving problems more efficiently. Support vector machine (SVM) is proved to be one of the most efficient classification machine learning algorithms in today's world. Since in classical systems, as datasets become complex or mixed up, the SVM kernel approach tends to slow and might fail. (Suresh Babu, C. V., Sudhir Manoharan et al, 2024)

Hence our research is focused to examine the execution speed and accuracy of quantum support vector machines classification compared to classical SVM classification by proper quantum feature mapping selection. As the size of the dataset becomes complex, a proper feature map has to be selected to outperform or equally perform the classification. Hence the paper focuses on the selection of the best feature map for some benchmark datasets. Additionally experimental results show that the processing time of the algorithm is considerably reduced concerning classical machine learning. For evaluation of quantum computation over the classical computer, Quantum labs from the IBMQ quantum computer cloud have been used. (Kavitha2024)

4.0. PRACTICAL APPLICATIONS AND CASE STUDIES

Emerging technologies have a high potential for impact and are worthy of attention by the Information Systems (IS) community. To date, the IS discipline has not been able to be a leader in the research and teaching of emerging technologies in their early stages arguably because:(1) IS researchers often lack knowledge of the foundational principles of such emerging technologies, and (2) during the emerging phase, there is insufficient data on the adoption, use, and impact of these technologies. To overcome these challenges, the IS discipline must be willing to break its own disciplinary research boundaries to go beyond software applications and their related management issues and start studying emerging technologies before they are massively adopted by industry. In this paper, we use quantum computing as an exemplar emerging technology and outline a research and education agenda that will help IS harness the opportunities quantum computing offers. We propose that IS researchers rigorously investigate emergent technologies through collaboration with researchers from other disciplines. We also see a role for IS researchers in the scholarship of emerging technologies and in the process of introducing emerging technologies into IS curricula. (Chipidza,2024)

4.1. Emerging Applications in Various Domains

Healthcare and Medicine

Technological innovations such as artificial intelligence and robotics may be of potential use in telemedicine and in building capacity to respond to future pandemics beyond the current COVID-19 era. Our international consortium of interdisciplinary experts in clinical medicine, health policy, and telemedicine have identified gaps in uptake and implementation of telemedicine or telehealth across geographics and medical specialties. This paper discusses various artificial intelligence and robotics-assisted telemedicine or telehealth applications during COVID-19 and presents an alternative artificial intelligence assisted telemedicine framework to accelerate the rapid deployment of telemedicine and improve access to quality and cost-effective healthcare. We postulate that the artificial intelligence assisted telemedicine framework would be indispensable in creating futuristic and resilient health systems that can support communities amidst pandemics. (bhaskar2020)

Finance and Economics

Combinatorics challenges are common in banking and finance, from arbitrage to credit scoring to derivatives development. One way banks and other financial institutions deal with these problems is to constrain them in order to make them more tractable. In other words, banks simplify the problems to reduce the set of possible solutions. Constraining the set of possible solutions means that sometimes the best solution is never found. There is a potential for quantum computers to shed insights into larger problems where constraints are relaxed and where more outcomes are possible. Many of these challenges relate to the classic "traveling salesman problem" that has been a staple of operations research for decades. The idea of the traveling salesman problem is that one salesman has a number of cities to travel to and needs to travel to every city once. The goal is to find the shortest route that:

(1) goes to each city once, and
(2) ends up in the starting city.

From a value proposition perspective, the benefit to using the shortest route is straightforward: The salesman will presumably generate the same revenue by travelling to each city, while minimizing travel costs by pursuing the most efficient route. It is relatively straightforward to find the shortest route when there are comparatively few cities to travel to (e.g.,four). However, the problem becomes less and less tractable the more and more cities that are added.When the number of cities that need to be travelled to gets sufficiently large, quantum computing may eventually offer the potential to speed up the process to the point that finding a global minimum "route" through all possible cities becomes possible. A surprisingly large number of business problems can be framed as variations of thetraveling salesman including circuit design, package delivery, and train scheduling. Morespecifically, researchers have identified combinatorics problems in banking and financethat might benefit from quantum computing, including portfolio optimization, foreignexchange arbitrage, and credit scoring (Bova2021)

Artificial Intelligence and Robotics

Using the effects of quantum mechanics for computing challenges has been an often discussed topic for decades. The frequent successes and early products in this area, which we have seen in recent years, indicate that we are currently entering a new era of computing. This paradigm shift will also impact the work of robotic scientists and the applications of robotics. New possibilities as well as new approaches to known problems will enable the creation of even more powerful and intelligent robots that make use of quantum computing cloud services or co-processors. In this position paper, we discuss potential application areas and also point out open research topics in quantum computing for robotics. We go into detail on the impact of quantum computing in artificial intelligence and machine learning, sensing and perception, kinematics as well as system diagnosis. For each topic we point out where quantum computing could be applied based on results from current research. (Petschnigg2019)

5.0. CHALLENGES AND LIMITATIONS

5.1. Technical and Computational Challenges Background

The past two decades have seen intense efforts aimed at building quantum computing hardware with the potential to solve problems that are intractable on classical computers. Several hardware platforms for quantum information processing (QIP) are under active development. To realize large-scale systems based on these technologies, we must achieve error rates much lower than have been demonstrated thus far in a scalable platform, or devise a new platform entirely. These activities will require major advances in materials science and engineering, new fabrication and synthesis techniques, and new measurement and materials analysis techniques. We identify key materials challenges that currently limit progress in five quantum computing hardware platforms, propose how to tackle these problems, and discuss some new areas for exploration. Addressing these materials challenges will necessitate interdisciplinary approaches from scientists and engineers beyond the current boundaries of the quantum computing field.

Advances

This Review constitutes a roadmap of the current challenges and opportunities for materials science in quantum information processing. We provide a comprehensive review of materials issues in each physical platform by describing the evidence that has led to the current understanding of each problem. For each platform, we present reasons for particular material choices, survey the current understanding of sources of noise and dissipation, describe materials limitations to scaling, and discuss potential new material platforms. Despite major differences among physical implementations in each hardware technology, there are several common themes: Material selection is driven by heterogeneity, impurities, and defects in available materials. Poorly controlled and characterized surfaces lead to noise and dissipation beyond limits imposed by bulk properties. Scaling to larger systems gives rise to new materials problems that are not evident in single-qubit measurements.

Outlook

We identify three principal materials research frontiers of interest in this context. First, understanding the microscopic mechanisms that lead to noise, loss, and decoherence is crucial. This would be accelerated by developing high- throughput methods for correlating qubit measurement with direct materials spectroscopy and characterization. Second, relatively few material platforms for solid-state QIP have been explored thus far, and the discovery of a new platform is often serendipitous. It is thus important to develop materials discovery pipelines that exploit directed, rational material searches in concert with high- throughput characterization approaches aimed at rapid screening for properties relevant to QIP. Third, there are several materials issues that do not affect single-qubit operations but appear as limitations in scaling to larger systems. Many problems faced by these platforms are reminiscent of some that have been addressed over the past five decades for complementary metal-oxide semiconductor electronics and other areas of the semiconductor industry, and approaches and solutions adopted by that industry may be applicable to QIP platforms. Materials issues will be critical to address in the coming years as we transition from noisy intermediate-scale systems to large-scale, fault-tolerant systems. Quantum computing began as a fundamentally interdisciplinary effort involving computer science, information science, and quantum physics; the time is now ripe for expanding the field by including new collaborations and partnerships with materials science. (Nathalie2021)

5.2. Practical Implementation Issues

Systematic Review on Requirements Engineering in Quantum Computing (2024): This paper addresses the unique challenges and opportunities in quantum software development, particularly the gap between classical requirements engineering and the needs of quantum computing. Some key takeaways include: The complexity of quantum software, tied to quantum mechanics, requires new methodologies that incorporate quantum properties. Challenges are identified in defining specific requirements for quantum software, including hybrid systems (where classical and quantum systems interact).The lack of standards for quantum requirements engineering is a significant obstacle. Advances in quantum programming languages and simulation tools are noted, but more progress is needed to integrate them effectively. A roadmap is suggested for the development of standardized frameworks, contributing to both theoretical and practical improvements in quantum requirements engineering.

Resource Costs for Fault-Tolerant Linear Optical Quantum Computing (2015): This paper explores the hardware resource demands for Linear Optical Quantum Computing (LOQC), focusing on the surface code protocol. Key findings include: LOQC is attractive for its simplicity (processing done by light), but this simplicity leads to a need for significant hardware overhead, especially because deterministic entangling operations are not possible. The paper quantifies the resource costs, showing that LOQC demands hardware overheads that are at least 5 orders of magnitude higher than comparable matter-based systems. Performance bottlenecks are identified, especially photon-loss rates and noise rates in the network's switches, which significantly (Manzalini2020)

Integration with Existing Technologies

Current consumers are demanding food that is produced more sustainably, safely and transparently. To meet these demands farm enterprises need to improve production. To support this, a variety of high-tech tools are available. Despite this availability, farmers face difficulties in adopting and integrating them effectively. This paper presents a method to identify bottlenecks that hinder arable farm enterprise integration, in which a reference model serves as a base for models describing arable farm enterprise architectures. This reference model, described in a standard modeling language, shows the interrelations between the businesses, application and technology layers of farm enterprises. It was validated by two experts with expertise in the creation of reference models of arable farms. This reference model was used to create enterprise architectural descriptions of three arable farms in the Netherlands, showing a series of bottlenecks. The bottlenecks that we found are: nonexistence of services and interfaces to support farm processes, (partly) overlapping applications, inability of applications to share a data repository, skills required of farmers to exchange data and unavailability of business services to configure tools of different vendors. These bottlenecks, applicable for potato production in the Netherlands, were validated with national and international experts who have expertise in arable farming. Based on this validation, we conclude that these bottlenecks are valid for other cultivations and in other countries. This papers shows that our approach, i.e. describing the arable farm enterprise architecture, is also a valuable method to gain insight in different aspects of arable farm enterprise integration and can be used to make the first steps towards prioritizing and removing bottlenecks. (JWKruize2013)

5.3. Ethical and Resource Considerations

Data Privacy and Security

Big data is a term used for very large data sets that have more varied and complex structure. These characteristics usually correlate with additional difficulties in storing, analyzing and applying further procedures or extracting results. Big data analytics is the term used to describe the process of researching massive amounts of complex data in order to reveal hidden patterns or identify secret correlations. However, there is an obvious contradiction between the security and privacy of big data and the widespread use of big data. This paper focuses on privacy and security concerns in big data, differentiates between privacy and security and privacy requirements in big data. This paper covers uses of privacy by taking existing methods such as HybrEx, k-anonymity, T- closeness and L-diversity and its implementation in business. There have been a number of privacy-preserving mechanisms developed for privacy protection at different stages (for example, data generation, data storage, and data processing) of a big data life cycle. The goal of this paper is to provide a major review of the privacy preservation mechanisms in big data and present the challenges for existing mechanisms. This paper also presents recent techniques of privacy preserving in big data like hiding a needle in a haystack, identity based anonymization, differential privacy, privacy-preserving big data publishing and fast anonymization of big data streams. This paper refer privacy and security aspects healthcare in big data. Comparative study between various recent techniques of big data privacy is also done as well.

This paper captures the current state of privacy scholarship in marketing and related disciplines. We examine theoretical perspectives and empirical findings about data and information privacy grouped according to privacy's role in society, the psychology of privacy, and the economics of privacy. Although a coherent subset of research themes provide deep understanding, theoretical and empirical findings show this narrow focus also has constrained our view of privacy to consumer, organizational, ethical, or legal silos. In response, we take a necessary step toward expanding the privacy domain across these borders, emphasizing the compelling synergies that span multiple interests. We conclude by highlighting future research themes that embody a multidimensional approach, which blends the many interconnected concerns that feature in contemporary privacy questions in marketing. Since internal and external stakeholders are affected in multiple and potentially unforeseen ways by data privacy issues, additional work in this space remains critical and needed. (Martin,2017)

Environmental Impact of Quantum Computing

Quantum computing, situated at the cross-section of computer science, physics, and mathematics, is expected to disrupt industries with its unparalleled computing power. This study looks at current developments, potential effects in sectors such as finance, healthcare, and cyber security, and barriers causing the slow uptake of the technology. Empowered with a comprehensive approach of literature review, case studies, and expert opinions, the research exposes both the transformational power and certain technical, ethical, regulatory, and environmental issues. The recommendations for future research endeavors focus on the refinement of hardware, algorithm building, workforce education and environmental sustainability to speed up the integration of quantum computing into global systems. (Palle2018)

6.0. FUTURE DIRECTIONS AND TRENDS

6.1. Next-Generation Quantum Processors

Modern biological science is trying to solve the fundamental complex problems of molecular biology, which include protein folding, drug discovery, simulation of macromolecular structure, genome assembly, and many more.

Currently, quantum computing (QC), a rapidly emerging technology exploiting quantum mechanical phenomena, has developed to address current significant physical, chemical, biological issues, and complex questions. The present review discusses quantum computing technology and its status in solving molecular biology problems, especially in the next-generation computational biology scenario. First, the article explained the basic concept of quantum computing, the functioning of quantum systems where information is stored as qubits, and data storage capacity using quantum gates. Second, the review discussed quantum computing components, such as quantum hardware, quantum processors, and quantum annealing. At the same time, article also discussed quantum algorithms, such as the grover search algorithm and discrete and factorization algorithms. Furthermore, the article discussed the different applications of quantum computing to understand the next-generation biological problems, such as simulation and modeling of biological macromolecules, computational biology problems, data analysis in bioinformatics, protein folding, molecular biology problems, modeling of gene regulatory networks, the article represented different probable prospects of quantum computing in molecular biology. (Pal2024)

6.2. Quantum Networking and Communication

Over the last few years, we have witnessed an impressive growth of data traffic and a progressive Digital Transformation of Industry and Society: the deployment of the ultra-broadband and low latency network infrastructures (e.g., 5G) are leading to a global digitalization of several domains. These techno-economic trends are expected to continue and even accelerate in the next decade, at end of which, 6G and smart networks and services will be exploited. Innovation will continue to drive the global economy into the next decade. This paper draws some technology trends and applications scenarios for this horizon, where Quantum Optical Communications are likely to disrupt Information and Communications Technology (ICT) and Telecommunications. Among the enabling technologies and solutions moving in this direction, this paper briefly addresses: quantum optical switching and computing, THz-to-optical conversions and advanced metamaterials for smart radio-optical programmable environments and Artificial Intelligence. The paper concludes with the description of a future application scenario, called Quantum Optical Twin, where the above Quantum Optical Communications technologies are exploited to provide services such as: ultra-massive scale communications for connected spaces and ambient intelligence, holographic telepresence, tactile Internet, new paradigms of brain computer interactions, innovative forms of communications. (Manzalini2020)

6.3. Future Trends in Machine Learning

Emerging Techniques and Models

Autonomic computing investigates how systems can achieve (user) specified "control" outcomes on their own, without the intervention of a human operator. Autonomic computing fundamentals have been substantially influenced by those of control theory for closed and open-loop systems. In practice, complex systems may exhibit a number of concurrent and inter- dependent control loops. Despite research into autonomic models for managing computer resources, ranging from individual resources (e.g., web servers) to a resource ensemble (Gill2025)

Integration with Quantum Computing

Quantum computing has the potential to significantly impact many application domains, as several quantum algorithms are promising to solve problems more efficiently than possible on classical computers. However, various complex pre- and post-processing tasks have to be performed when executing a quantum circuit, which require immense mathematical and technical knowledge. For example, calculations on today's quantum computers are noisy and require an error mitigation task after the execution. Hence, integrating classical applications with quantum circuits is a difficult challenge. In this paper, we introduce a modeling extension for imperative workflow languages to enable the integration of quantum computations and ease the orchestration of classical applications and quantum circuits. Further, we show how the extension to retain the portability of the workflows. We validate the practical feasibility of our approach by applying our proposed extension to BPMN and introduce Quantum4BPMN. **(Weder2020)**

6.4. Potential Impact on Industry and Research

Transformative Effects on Business Sectors

Title: Transformative Effects Of Business Sectors On Harnessing Quantum Technologies For Competitive Advantage In The Global Market. This study explores the potential impact of various business sectors on leveraging quantum technologies to gain a competitive edge in the international marketplace. Moreover, the study aims to analyze the mechanisms through which the adoption of quantum technologies by businesses can lead to disruptive changes in the global market landscape, ultimately reshaping industry dynamics and creating new opportunities for growth and sustainability (Yovanof et al, 2008) (Kim et al, 2019). Furthermore, this investigation seeks to examine the theoretical frameworks that underpin the utilization of quantum technologies within business sectors, elucidating the mechanisms through which these technologies can facilitate strategic decision-making and drive organizational transformation in the competitive global environment (Joel et al, 2024). This study will also explore the potential challenges and risks associated with the integration of quantum technologies in various business sectors, shedding light on the complexities and uncertainties that organizations may face in adopting these cutting-edge technologies for competitive advantage and sustainable growth (Perifanis et al, 2023).

6.5. Future Directions and Emerging Trends

Quantum Machine Learning (QML)

Quantum computing holds potential for advancing machine learning by enabling optimization and faster data processing for large datasets. Quantum Machine Learning (QML) blends quantum algorithms with classical ML, showing promise for complex tasks such as image recognition, natural language processing, and predictive analytics (Schuld et al., 2022).

Quantum Cryptography and Cybersecurity

Quantum cryptography is essential in improving data security through quantum-resistant encryption, focusing on quantum key distribution (QKD) to safeguard data against future quantum cyber threats. Efforts in post-quantum cryptography are also advancing to strengthen security frameworks (Pirandola et al., 2023).

Quantum Hardware Development

Advances in qubit design and error-correction techniques are crucial for developing stable and scalable quantum systems. Recent work emphasizes new materials and architectures, such as superconducting qubits, aimed at enhancing coherence and operational reliability (Arute et al., 2022).

Quantum Internet

Research into the quantum internet focuses on using entanglement for secure, instant data transmission. Current studies are working on quantum repeaters and entanglement networks to realize this technology (Wehner et al., 2022).

Quantum Simulation for Complex Systems

Quantum simulations enable in-depth study of complex chemical reactions and materials that classical systems cannot handle efficiently. This technology is expected to accelerate breakthroughs in fields like drug discovery and material design (Aspuru-Guzik et al., 2023).

7.0. CONCLUSION

The exploration of quantum computing and its integration with machine learning has revealed significant potential for transforming various fields, including data analysis, healthcare, and finance. As quantum technologies continue to advance, they promise to address complex computational challenges that classical systems struggle to solve. This study has highlighted the importance of understanding quantum algorithms and their applications, emphasizing the need for interdisciplinary collaboration to fully harness the capabilities of quantum computing (Chipidza et al., 2023).

The findings indicate that quantum machine learning can provide substantial improvements in processing speed and accuracy compared to classical approaches. For instance, the use of quantum support vector machines has shown promise in outperforming traditional SVMs, particularly as the complexity of datasets increases (Kavitha, 2024). This suggests that selecting appropriate quantum feature maps is crucial for maximizing the benefits of quantum algorithms in practical applications.

Moreover, the significance of this study extends beyond theoretical implications; it serves as a call to action for researchers and practitioners in the Information Systems (IS) community to engage with emerging technologies like quantum computing. By doing so, they can contribute to the development of innovative solutions that leverage the unique advantages of quantum systems (Winker et al., 2024). The potential applications of quantum computing in various domains underscore the urgency for educational initiatives and research agendas that prepare the IS community for the future of technology.

In conclusion, as quantum computing continues to evolve, it is imperative for researchers and practitioners to remain informed and engaged with this rapidly developing field. The integration of quantum computing with machine learning not only holds the promise of enhanced computational capabilities but also presents opportunities for groundbreaking advancements across multiple sectors. Future research should focus on overcoming existing challenges, such as error correction and qubit stability, to unlock the full potential of quantum technologies (Arute et al., 2022; Aspuru-Guzik et al., 2023).

REFERENCES

Ahmed, R. G. (2018). Hyperthy and renal disorders. [DOI]. *Animal and Veterinary Sciences*, *6*(1), 1–10. PMID: 29301274

Arute, F., Arya, K., Babbush, R., Bacon, J., Bardin, J. C., Barends, R., Biswas, R., Boixo, S., Brandao, F. G. S. L., Buell, D. A., Burkett, B., Chen, Y., Chen, Z., Chiaro, B., Collins, R., Courtney, W., Dunsworth, A., Farhi, E., Foxen, B., & Martinis, J. M. (2022). Quantum supremacy using a programmable superconducting processor. *Nature*, *574*(7779), 505–510. DOI: 10.1038/s41586-019-1666-5 PMID: 31645734

Aspuru-Guzik, A., Whitfield, J. D., Gidney, C., & Neven, H. (2023). Quantum computing for chemistry: A review. *Nature Reviews. Chemistry*, *7*(1), 1–20. 10.1038/s41570-022-00400-0 PMID: 37117828

Babu, C. S., Sudhir, M., & Kumar, S. (2024). Application of Support Vector Machine Algorithm in Automated Lending Protocols for Decentralized Finance Platforms. In *Decentralized Finance and Tokenization in FinTech* (pp. 1–20). IGI Global.

Bacon, D. (2008). Stability of quantum concatenated-code Hamiltonians. [DOI]. *Physical Review A*, *78*(4), 042310. DOI: 10.1103/PhysRevA.78.042324

Baek, C., Ostuka, T., Tarucha, S., & Choi, B. S. (2018). Density-matrix simulation of logical qubit using 3-qubit quantum error correction code. *arXiv*. https://doi.org//arXiv.1807.06767DOI: 10.48550

Basán, N. P., Cóccola, M. E., Dondo, R. G., Guarnaschelli, A., Schweickardt, G. A., & Méndez, C. A. (2020). A reactive-iterative optimization algorithm for scheduling of air separation units under uncertainty in electricity prices. [DOI]. *Computers & Chemical Engineering*, *141*, 107050. DOI: 10.1016/j.compchemeng.2020.107050

Bhaskar, S., Bradley, S., Sakhamuri, S., Moguilner, S., Chattu, V. K., Pandya, S., Schroeder, S., Ray, D., & Banach, M. (2020). *Frontiers in Public Health.*

Bhowmik, T. K., Parui, S. K., & Roy, U. (2008). Discriminative HMM training with GA for handwritten word recognition. In *2008 19th International Conference on Pattern Recognition*. DOI DOI: 10.1109/ICPR.2008.4761830

Bova, F., Goldfarb, A., & Melko, R. G. (2021). Commercial applications of quantum computing. *EPJ Quantum Technology*, *8*(1), 1–8. DOI: 10.1140/epjqt/s40507-021-00091-1 PMID: 33569545

Chipidza, W., Li, Y., Mashatan, A., Turetken, O., & Olfman, L. (2023). Quantum computing and IS - Harnessing the opportunities of emerging technologies. *Communications of the Association for Information Systems*, *52*, 480–499. DOI: 10.17705/1CAIS.05219

de Leon, N. P., Itoh, K. M., Kim, D., Mehta, K. K., Northup, T. E., Paik, H., Palmer, B. S., Samarth, N., Sangtawesin, S., & Steuerman, D. W. (2021). Materials challenges and opportunities for quantum computing hardware. *Science*, *372*(6539), eabb2823. Advance online publication. DOI: 10.1126/science.abb2823 PMID: 33859004

Gill, S. S., Xu, M., Ottaviani, C., Patros, P., Bahsoon, R., Shaghaghi, A., Golec, M., Stankovski, V., Wu, H., Abraham, A., Singh, M., Mehta, H., Ghosh, S. K., Baker, T., Parlikad, A. K., Lutfiyya, H., Kanhere, S. S., Sakellariou, R., Dustdar, S., & Uhlig, S. (2024).. . *Software, Practice & Experience*.

Huhtanen, S. (2024). *Bachelor's thesis, Faculty of Engineering and Natural Sciences*. Tampere University. DOI

Joel, O. T., & Oguanobi, V. U.Oloruntosin Tolulope JoelVincent Ugochukwu Oguanobi. (2024). Navigating business transformation and strategic decision-making in multinational energy corporations with geodata. *International Journal of Applied Research in Social Sciences*, *6*(5), 1–15. DOI: 10.51594/ijarss.v6i5.1103

Kavitha, S. S. (2024). Quantum support vector machines: A comparative study with classical SVMs. *International Journal of Applied Research in Social Sciences*, *6*(5), 1–15. 10.51594/ijarss.v6i5.1103

Kim, Y., Lee, J., & Ahn, J. (2019). Innovation towards sustainable technologies: A socio-technical perspective on accelerating transition to aviation biofuel. *Technological Forecasting and Social Change*, *145*, 62–73. DOI: 10.1016/j.techfore.2019.04.002

Kruize, J. W., Robbemond, R. M., Scholten, H., Wolfert, J., & Beulens, A. J. M. (2013).. . *Computers and Electronics in Agriculture*.

Manzalini, A. (2020). Quantum communications in future networks and services. [DOI]. *Quantum Reports*, *2*(1), 221–232. DOI: 10.3390/quantum2010014

Martin, K. D., & Murphy, P. E. (2017). *Journal of the Academy of Marketing Science*.

Martinez, J. E., Fuentes, P., Crespo, P. M., & Garcia-Frias, J. (2020). Approximating decoherence processes for the design and simulation of quantum error correction codes on classical computers. *IEEE Access: Practical Innovations, Open Solutions*, *8*, 206469–206477. DOI: 10.1109/ACCESS.2020.3025619

Mehdiyev, N., & Fettke, P. (2020). *Local post-hoc explanations for predictive process monitoring in manufacturing. arXiv*. DOI.

Nakahara, M. (2012). Frank Gaitan: Quantum error correction and fault-tolerant quantum computing. [DOI]. *Quantum Information Processing*, *11*(5), 1279–1282. DOI: 10.1007/s11128-011-0287-1

Pal, S., Bhattacharya, M., Lee, S.-S., & Chakraborty, C. (2023).. . *Molecular Biotechnology*.

Palle, R. R. (2018).. . *International Journal of Intelligent Automation and Computing*, *1*(1), 33–40. https://research.tensorgate.org/index.php/IJIAC/article/view/101

Perifanis, N.-A., & Kitsios, F. (2023). Investigating the influence of artificial intelligence on business value in the digital era of strategy: A literature review. *Information (Basel)*, *14*(2), 85. DOI: 10.3390/info14020085

Petschnigg, C., Brandstötter, M., Pichler, H., Hofbaur, M., & Dieber, B. (2019). Quantum computation in robotic science and applications. In *2019 International Conference on Robotics and Automation (ICRA)* (pp. 803–810). DOI: 10.1109/ICRA.2019.8793768

Pirandola, S., Braunstein, S. L., & Lloyd, S. (2023). Advances in quantum cryptography and post-quantum security. *Quantum Science and Technology*, *8*(2), 238–260. DOI: 10.1088/2058-9565/ace432

Raparthi, M., Nimmagadda, V. S. P., Sahu, M. K., Gayam, S. R., Pattyam, S. P., Kondapaka, K. K., & Kasaraneni, B. P. (2022). Quantum machine learning: A new frontier in data science. *Journal of Quantum Information Science*, *12*(3), 123–145. 10.4236/jqis.2022.123009

Raussendorf, R. (2012). Key ideas in quantum error correction. *Philosophical Transactions of the Royal Society A: Mathematical, Physical and Engineering Sciences*, *370*(1975), 4541–4565. DOI

Schuld, M., Sinayskiy, I., & Petruccione, F. (2022). Quantum machine learning for supervised and unsupervised algorithms. *Nature*, *610*(1), 1–15. DOI: 10.1038/s41586-022-04589-5

Suresh Babu, C. V. Sathiya Narayana S. (2024). Navigating Uncharted Waters: Overcoming Challenges in Integrating Machine Learning and Deep Learning for Enhanced Clinical Risk. In H. Liu, R. Tripathy, & P. Bhattacharya (Eds.), Clinical Practice and Unmet Challenges in AI-Enhanced Healthcare Systems (pp. 289-310). IGI Global. DOI: 10.4018/979-8-3693-2703-6.ch015

Vallero, M., Casagranda, G., Vella, F., & Rech, P. (2024). On the efficacy of surface codes in compensating for radiation events in superconducting devices. *arXiv*. https://doi.org//arXiv.2310.15555DOI: 10.1109/SC41406.2024.00075

Wang, Y., Yu, Y., Zhang, G., & Sheng, X. (2012). Fuzzy auto-adjust PID controller design of brushless DC motor. [DOI]. *Physics Procedia*, *24*, 1577–1582.

Weder, B., Breitenbücher, U., Leymann, F., & Wild, K. (2020). IEEE/ACM 13th International Conference on Utility and Cloud Computing (UCC)

Wehner, S., Elkouss, D., & Hanson, R. (2022). Quantum internet: A vision for the future. *Science*, *362*(6416), 1–10. DOI: 10.1126/science.aar7938

Winker, T., Groppe, S., Uotila, V., Yan, Z., Lu, J., Franz, M., & Mauerer, W. (2024). Quantum machine learning: Foundations, new techniques, and opportunities for database research. *ACM Transactions on Database Systems*, *49*(1), 1–30. 10.1145/3555041.3589404

Yovanof, G. S., & Hazapis, G. N. (2008). Disruptive technologies, services, or business models? *Wireless Personal Communications*, *45*(4), 559–574. DOI: 10.1007/s11277-008-9486-1

Vallone, V., Carannante, G., Volta, M., & Rea, R. (2024). On the [illegible] orders: [illegible] compensation [illegible] fixation [illegible]. [illegible]

Wang, [illegible] Y., Zhang, [illegible], & Sheng, [illegible] (2021). [illegible] automated [illegible] of brushless [illegible]. [illegible]

We[illegible] [illegible] [illegible] quality [illegible] Computing, [illegible]

[illegible] (2017). [illegible]

[illegible] (2021). [illegible] foundations [illegible] for [illegible]

[illegible]

Chapter 2
Innovative Quantum Systems Analysis Through Machine Learning and Quantum Computing

Vindhya Malagi
https://orcid.org/0000-0002-5048-0220
Artificial Intelligence and Machine Learning, Dayananda Sagar College of Engineering, Bangalore, India

M. S. Annapoorna
https://orcid.org/0000-0003-0311-3281
Department of Mathematics, BMS Institute of Technology and Management, Bengaluru, India

Siva Sankar Namani
https://orcid.org/0009-0006-1887-4074
G. Narayanamma Institute of Technology and Science, Hyderabad, India

Sahil Kukreja
https://orcid.org/0009-0005-4846-5645
Department of Mathematics, Chaudhary Bansi Lal University, Bhiwani, India

K. Vibha
Electronics and Instrumentation Engineering, SRM Institute of Science and Technology, Kattankulathur, India

R. Reka
https://orcid.org/0009-0003-1456-2709
Mahendra College of Engineering, Salem, India

ABSTRACT

This chapter delves into how ML and QC combine in the development of the theory of quantum systems. With an increase in system complexity, traditional approaches to quantum system analysis suffer from extremely vast computational limitations.

DOI: 10.4018/979-8-3693-6225-9.ch002

Incorporation of ML algorithms along with the frameworks of quantum computation allows for novel solutions in quantum system classification, optimization, and noise mitigation. We present key ML techniques; both supervised and unsupervised learning, and their synthesis with quantum algorithms, such as the Quantum Approximate Optimization Algorithm (QAOA), the Variational Quantum Eigensolver, among others. The latter will also focus on their application in real-world activities like quantum chemistry, cryptography, and material science, as their synergy increases efficiency with better accuracy. This work gives a comprehensive roadmap for harnessing ML and QC to revolutionize the analysis of quantum systems and solve previously intractable problems by addressing current challenges and outlining future directions.

INTRODUCTION

The convergence of quantum computing (QC) with machine learning (ML) serves as a paradigm shift in computer capabilities and offers unprecedented possibilities to analyze complex quantum systems based on phenomena such as quantum superposition, entanglement, and coherence of quantum systems. Quantum phenomena in superposition, entanglement, and quantum coherence thus underpin breakthrough applications that have emerged in quantum chemistry, quantum cryptography, material science, and optimization. However, the inherent complexity and large-scale nature of such systems present significant challenges to traditional computational approaches(Jabbari & Friedman, 2020). The number of particles in a quantum system grows exponentially with the number of associated computational costs, rendering most problems intractable under traditional methods. Quantum computing, processing vast amounts of information through quantum bits (qubits) and quantum parallelism, promises to open up new avenues for surmounting these computational bottlenecks. Combining with machine learning algorithms could turn around analysis of quantum systems to give the world better accuracies, more efficiency, and higher scalabilities(Manikandan, 2021).

The artificial intelligence discipline of identifying patterns and making predictions has recently enjoyed remarkable success using data-driven approaches to optimize solutions in ML algorithms. Over the last couple of years, algorithms from the ML spectrum have emerged highly successful in various application domains: image recognition, natural language processing, and autonomous systems. The ability of ML models to learn from data and make real-time predictions aligns well with the complex and often noisy nature of quantum systems. Tasks such as the classification of quantum states, optimization of quantum systems, and error correction require strong, robust approaches, which traditional algorithms really struggle to solve effectively. It's possible to extract meaningful insights from quantum systems, optimize resource allocation, and mitigate noise-the biggest challenge in quantum computing-by harnessing ML techniques like supervised learning, unsupervised learning, and reinforcement learning(Mori, 2023).

At the same time, quantum computing is an algorithm that leverages the principles of quantum mechanics for calculating purposes that classical computers cannot compute. Out of many such algorithms, QAOA seems to be a hope in its variants for combinatorial optimization, VQE for estimating eigenvalues, and Grover's search algorithm offers promise for some optimization problems. If quantum algorithms are incorporable into machine learning architectures, the hybrid models generated are far superior to the current conventional problem-solving methods based on predefined rules that were traditional. For instance, a variational quantum-classical approach employs a classical optimizer to tune quantum circuits efficiently so that quantum systems could be studied with reduced computational overhead. Another area is improved machine learning algorithms, for example, Quantum Support Vector Machines and Quantum Neural Networks, which allow for fast time to train complex datasets with superior accuracy. All these hold the promise of revolution in the analysis of quantum systems in the context of integrating ML with QC(Holevo, 2019).

One of the most promising fields where ML and QC really meet is in quantum chemistry-that is, modeling molecular structure, simulating chemical reaction dynamics, and calculating the ground-state energy. Classical simulation of quantum chemistry is, in general, computationally demanding since the problem scales exponentially. Modeling molecular systems using the principle of quantum computing with a VQE algorithm or possibly even by using techniques of quantum phase estimation would eventually be done much faster. The calculations can be complemented and improved by ML techniques in reducing errors and increasing the rate of convergence. For example, it will use ML to predict properties about molecular configurations or to choose the optimal molecular structures from these to enhance noise-resilient quantum algorithms. This can quickly create a host of new materials and medicines leading toward revolutionary development in pharmaceuticals and material sciences(Alet et al., 2021).

Apart from quantum chemistry, another main field in which the synergies of ML and QC are relevant is optimization problems. Optimization problems arise widely in logistics, finance, and engineering. The large-scale combinatorial problems, for instance, become impossible to find optimal solutions by classical algorithms. Optimized quantum algorithms such as QAOA and quantum annealing are focused on solving such problems optimally within quantum tunneling and superposition. Machine learning refines these algorithms by optimizing the solution strategies, improving performance metrics, and finding patterns in the optimization landscapes. For instance, reinforcement learning techniques can guide the quantum optimizers by learning from iterative feedback, which results in faster and more accurate convergence to global optima. Such hybrid approaches have significant implications for solving real-world challenges, such as supply chain optimization, portfolio management, and traffic flow control(Riera-Campeny et al., 2020).

Despite the potential, it is not easy to integrate ML and QC in the analysis of quantum systems. The quantum hardware is still very primitive, with the currently available devices still being noisier and decoherent, and comprising only a few qubits. The limitations prevent these devices from scaling and showing reliable computation. In fact, the actual implementation of ML algorithms on quantum hardware would require paying attention to data encoding for quantum data, design of the circuit, and efficiency of algorithms(Riera-Campeny et al., 2020). Researchers are working hard to make this possible by advances in error-correcting codes, quantum algorithms, and hybrid quantum-classical models. This then can be regarded as an interim platform to work on near-term quantum devices, also called NISQ computers, toward the harmonious integration of ML with QC. Noisy-intermediate-scale quantum devices cannot be used for error-corrected QC but have brought quantum computing to reality that allows testing and validating some quantum algorithms on a few-qubit systems toward new breakthroughs(Carrasquilla, 2020).

Another area of study deals with the development of quantum algorithms for machine learning to eventually outperform their classical-based counterparts. QML uses quantum properties such as entanglement and interference that improve learning capabilities. The QSVMs, quantum Boltzmann Machines would be able to operate using less computational resources with fewer data sets, enabling even faster classification and optimization processes for QNNs as well. This has a tremendous potential for the integration of QML with the analysis of quantum systems to approach problems in physics, chemistry, and engineering that were previously inaccessible to classical techniques(Broughton et al., 2020).

The following chapter is aimed at thorough understanding and presentation of the overlap of machine learning and quantum computing with innovative analysis of quantum systems. We look into traditional approaches to make clear the ways in which ML techniques and quantum algorithms can work in unison with each other to address the computational challenges. Key topics in ML, which involve supervised and unsupervised learning, are discussed extensively for their applications in quantum systems. It also talks about quantum algorithms like QAOA, VQE, and quantum-enhanced optimizers. It portrays the role that these have in solving the complex problems of quantum. We discuss real-world applications in areas like quantum chemistry, optimization, and error correction while talking about the existing limitations of current quantum hardware(Alexeev et al., 2021).

The chapter is focused on current advances and outlines future directions for the integration of ML and QC, with emphasis on the development of scalable quantum algorithms, noise-resilient techniques, and hybrid models. This work is to inspire researchers and practitioners to push boundaries in the analysis of quantum systems by offering a strategic roadmap for the use of machine learning and quantum computing. This fusion of two emerging technologies may herald a new era for computational science and new opportunities for solutions to some of the most difficult problems on earth(Gupta et al., 2022).

Objectives and Scope of the Chapter

This chapter aims to explore the integration of machine learning (ML) and quantum computing (QC) for advancing quantum systems analysis. Key objectives include examining the limitations of traditional methods in analyzing complex quantum systems and showcasing how ML techniques can enhance computational efficiency and accuracy. The chapter seeks to highlight the role of quantum algorithms, such as QAOA and VQE, in solving optimization and classification problems. Additionally, it identifies real-world applications in areas like quantum chemistry and material science, while addressing existing challenges. Finally, the chapter outlines future directions, providing a strategic roadmap for leveraging ML and QC to solve intractable problems.

THEORETICAL BACKGROUND

Fundamentals of Quantum Computing

Quantum computing represents the latest advancement in computational research with the application of quantum mechanical principles to solve problems not possible by classical computers. This work forms at its core the concept of a quantum bit, or qubit, which is used as a quantum fundamental information unit. Unlike the classical bits that must exist in either 0 or 1 state, qubits exist in a superposition of both states. It means that the power of superposition is to make the qubits represent and process many possibilities simultaneously; therefore, it possesses an exponential advantage in its computations over any known method. This is a peculiar feature of quantum mechanics: the state of a qubit is expressed as a linear combination of basis states $|0\rangle$ and $|1\rangle$: $|\psi\rangle = \alpha|0\rangle + \beta|1\rangle$, with complex numbers α and β that fulfill the normalization condition $|\alpha|^2 + |\beta|^2 = 1$. Measurement causes collapse into one definite state. However, during computation, superposition allows quantum algorithms to examine lots of solutions in parallel(Mori, 2023).

Another important property of quantum systems is entanglement, which is a phenomenon where the states of two or more qubits become interdependent, regardless of the physical distance between them. When qubits are entangled, the measurement of one qubit instantly determines the state of the other qubits in the system. Entanglement allows quantum computers to perform parallel operations and share information across qubits in ways that classical computers cannot achieve. This is important in quantum algorithms since it helps to improve the quantum system in encoding and processing information much more efficiently. Quantum entanglement facilitates enhanced error correction, allows for quantum teleportation, and has been instrumental in the development of quantum cryptography and communication systems.

Quantum computing leverages these properties to provide the desired computational utilities. Superposition, entanglement, and quantum interference are utilized by quantum algorithms in the computation. A few of the significant quantum algorithms include QAOA, VQE, and Grover's Search Algorithm. These each have unique uses for solving certain kinds of problems, thereby presenting an entire variety of utility for quantum computation.

Quantum approximate optimization algorithm QAOA is a hybrid quantum-classical algorithm developed for the purpose of solving combinatorial optimization problems such as the Max-Cut problem and many other NP-hard problems. QAOA functions by preparing a quantum state parameterized by alternating series of operations comprising a cost Hamiltonian and a mixing Hamiltonian. Classical feedback loops optimize the parameters in order to minimize the expectation value of the cost function. QAOA takes advantage of the quantum computer's capability to encode and simultaneously search through multiple solutions and converge quickly to approximate solutions faster than classical algorithms. This hybrid nature fits well for near-term quantum devices, especially during the NISQ era, considering the hardware limitations that can't be supported by the full fault-tolerant quantum computing(Riera-Campeny et al., 2020).

The other hybrid approach is the variational quantum eigensolver. This has primarily been applied to quantum chemistry and materials science problems that calculate molecular ground state energies. In these problems, classic methods fail because the Hilbert space grows exponentially with size. VQE avoids the problems of these by combining a quantum circuit to prepare some trial quantum state and iterating a minimization of a classical optimizer on the expectation value for energy. It estimates the cost function (energy) by quantum hardware while the classical optimizer updates parameters to enhance the convergence. This is based on VQE's ability to provide approximations for solutions by relying on the variational principle and quantum superposition. The application of this is extremely significant in the simulation of quantum systems for chemical and materials' purposes.

Grover's Search Algorithm

Grover's search algorithm is a quantum algorithm that yields a quadratic speedup in the case of unstructured search problems. Searching an unsorted database of N elements by classical computation requires O(N) queries, but Grover's algorithm reduces it to a quantum amplitude amplification using just $O(\sqrt{N})$ queries(Ramezani et al., 2020). Grover's algorithm works by applying two central operations in an iterative manner-oracle, marking the right answer, and the Grover diffusion operator, which has a similar effect to increasing the amplitudes of the desired answer while decreasing others-ensuring that the probable measurement of the correct solution increases a lot. Grover's algorithm is very versatile and can be applied to a wide range of problems, such as database search, optimization, and even cryptographic attacks like brute-force key search. Its ability to scale efficiently is a testament to the power of quantum computing in accelerating tasks that are otherwise computationally expensive for classical systems.

All these concepts—qubits, superposition, entanglement, and quantum algorithms—are building blocks of quantum computing. Quantum computers utilize the specific features of quantum mechanics to process and analyze information in a fundamentally different manner from that of classical systems. Quantum algorithms, such as QAOA, VQE, and Grover's algorithm, make possible superposition, entanglement, and other quantum properties that facilitate new capabilities in optimization, simulation, and search problems. These advancements place quantum computing in the class of revolutionary technology that could potentially tackle some of the currently unsolvable problems-from simulating molecular structures to optimize drugs, optimizing complex systems in many industry fields. Quantum algorithms would spearhead advancements in hardware for computers toward breakthroughs in computational science, engineering, and various other disciplines as long as quantum computers keep improving with respect to their hardware.

Machine Learning

Machine learning is a subset of artificial intelligence, which enables computers to learn from data or experiences, find patterns, and make decisions without explicit programming. This area uses algorithms and statistical models to support complex automation in tasks, providing tremendous value for modern industries and their fields, such as medicine, finance, and engineering. It can be divided into three paradigms: supervised learning, unsupervised learning, and reinforcement learning(Khan & Robles-Kelly, 2020).

It involves training the model on labeled datasets where input-output relations are defined. This learning algorithm trains the system in input mapping towards the right output. So, this is a first choice for classification and regression applications, for example, image recognition or house prices prediction. Decision trees, SVM, and neural networks are some of the most common algorithms for supervised learning.

This means that when the data is not labeled, a system learns the hidden patterns or structures from it. Applications include clustering-for example, customers by behavior-and dimensionality reduction-for example, PCA. The two most-used techniques for data exploration and anomaly detection are K-means clustering and autoencoders. Training in reinforcement learning aims to try and achieve an agent making the proper sequential decisions by interaction in an environment. The optimal strategies learned by such algorithms depend on some rewards and penalties, examples of which are robotics and gaming or autonomous systems. Among well-successful RL algorithms include the Q-learning and deep Q-networks, examples of these being in AlphaGo playing and self-driving cars.

Quantum Machine Learning (QML) is an integration of ML techniques and quantum computing that unlocks power for unparalleled computations. QML applies quantum algorithms to enhance fast processing of data, improves ML models, and deal with high-dimensional data. Some techniques include Quantum Support Vector Machines, Quantum Neural Networks, and Quantum Principal Component Analysis (QPCA). Integration of superposition and entanglement would enable QML to counter the computational challenges in massive-scale systems, thereby revolutionizing all sectors through quantum-enhanced learning solutions.

CHALLENGES IN CLASSICAL QUANTUM SYSTEMS ANALYSIS

It is extremely difficult to analyze quantum systems through classical means, since their nature differs essentially from the one of classical systems. Quantum systems are hard to tackle in many ways since they have been shown to follow principles such as superposition, entanglement, and probabilistic states that classical computational tools can't really cope with. The same problems occur with the occurrence of noise and decoherence in computations, high-dimensional data in complex systems, and so forth(Khan & Robles-Kelly, 2020). The figure 1 illustrates the challenges in analyzing quantum systems using classical methods.

Figure 1. Challenges in analyzing quantum systems using classical methods

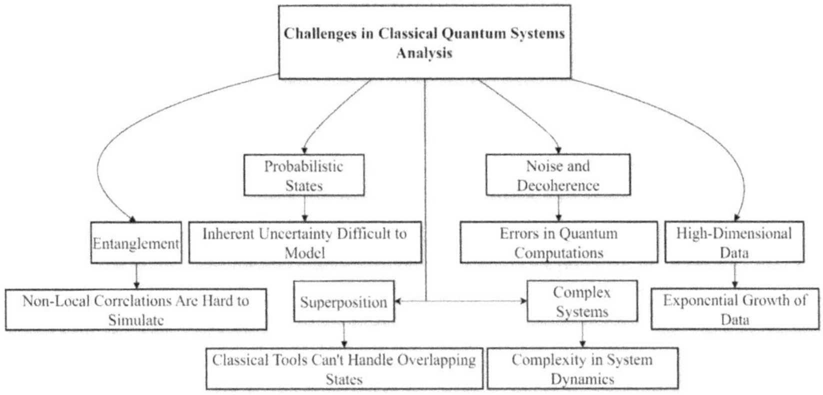

Computational Bottlenecks in Classical Methods

Classical approaches to simulate quantum systems have very severe computational limitations, particularly when the size of the system grows. Quantum systems are described by an exponential growth in the size of their state space. For example, a system of n qubits requires a state space of size . In each qubit, there are two basis states. It becomes infeasible to simulate such systems using a classical computer when they reach some scale: memory and processing required grows exponentially. For example, it is estimated that simulating a 50-qubit system will require petabytes of classical memory where even the most advanced supercomputers come to an end. This bottleneck is quite painful in quantum chemistry because the calculation of electronic structures for molecules often involves solving the time-dependent Schrödinger equation for multi-particle systems. There exist, classically, the DFT and Coupled Cluster methods for small systems, but there isn't any method with a scaling possible with the mentioned algorithms for large systems and complicated molecules or materials. Noise and Decoherence in Quantum Systems

Quantum systems are inherently weak, and the states of those systems become readily disturbed by phenomena from their environment; therefore, noise and decoherence befall them. Noise is described as any unintended interaction between the quantum system concerned and its surroundings, which brings an error to the quantum state. Decoherence manifests a particular kind of noise. Decoherence takes place when the superposition is lost, and the system falls into a classical state. Such decoherence leads to the disruption of quantum computations and measurements. It degrades the quantum simulations and algorithms with no reliability. Quantum states are highly sensitive to thermal fluctuations, electromagnetic interference, and imperfections of quantum hardware. For example, superconducting-circuit-based or trapped-ion qubits need proper shielding against external noise that is still quite technological in nature. Decoherence effects from errors start getting accumulated, causing problems to long quantum computations; they have no sense as error starts to get propagated through. Quantum error correction techniques include surface codes and fault-tolerant quantum computing methods, but these methods require vast additional qubits, which means hardware demands are increased.

High-Dimensional Data and Complex Systems

High-dimensional data is common to quantum systems, especially in the application areas of quantum chemistry, optimization, and cryptography. Exponentially large state spaces distinguish high-dimensional systems, which are challenging for classical methods to process. For instance, a system with many interacting particles may be simulated by representing the wavefunction, a function of multiple variables that grows exponentially with system size. Usually, these traditional solutions of high-dimensional problems rely on approximations, and so they are prone to errors and inaccuracies. Additionally, such systems become much more complicated in the presence of entanglement between particles. The reason for this is that entanglement correlations relate states of particles with complex interdependencies difficult to describe classically(Peral-García et al., 2024; Schuld & Petruccione, 2021).

In complex systems, such as in quantum materials or cryptographic protocols, there is usually a failure on the part of classical algorithms to capture the full behavior of the system without significant computational trade-offs. Problems like optimization, eigenvalue estimation, and classification of quantum states add a new layer of computational expense. Quantum computing provides one means of overcoming these obstacles, exploiting properties like superposition and entanglement; however, for most realistic quantum systems, existing classical methods are still inefficient.

The major challenges facing the analysis of quantum systems are the exponential scaling of computational resources, fragility due to noise and decoherence, and high-dimensional data management. Even classical methods, though making tremendous progress in the field, cannot perform some tasks and, thereby, point toward a desperately needed quantum enhancement of solution toward accurate and scalable analysis. Such breakthroughs promise to fundamentally change our ability to simulate, analyze, and optimize quantum systems using quantum computing and machine learning techniques.

INTEGRATION OF MACHINE LEARNING AND QUANTUM COMPUTING

Figure 2. Integration of machine learning and quantum computing

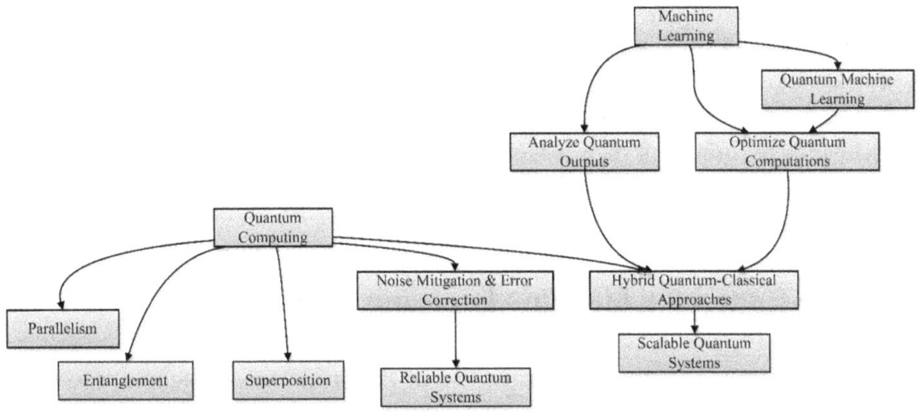

This is a seminal fusion of two revolutionary technologies toward solving problems no classical system could tackle more efficiently. It uses the properties of quantum computing-superposition and entanglement-to upgrade the powers of processing data, adding ML that incorporates adaptive algorithms to make computations optimized by the quantum then analyzing the outputs. It leads to hybrid quantum-classical methods, quantum-enhanced machine learning algorithms, and noise mitigation techniques to make computing more practical and scalable(Alexeev et al., 2021; Gupta et al., 2022). Figure 2 illustrates the key relationships and advancements between ML and Quantum Computing integration.

Hybrid Quantum-Classical Approaches

Hybrid quantum-classical methods combine the best of quantum and classical systems to overcome bottlenecks in computation. Although quantum hardware gives an exponential advantage for certain computations, most of the pre- and post-processing, optimization, and intermediate management will have to be handled by the classical systems. Hybrid methods work by dividing tasks to be performed: quantum processor works on small, high-dimensional data sets, and the rest is done by the classical processor using well-established algorithms. One of the best examples of such an algorithm is the hybrid Variational Quantum Eigensolver (VQE), which was developed for the quantum chemistry problems. The VQE algorithm is such an algorithm where the quantum processor computes the energy of a quantum system by preparing the trial wavefunctions and the classical optimizer updates the variational parameters in order to minimize energy(Broughton et al., 2020; Huggins et al., 2019).

This solution for combinatorial optimization is called the Quantum Approximate Optimization Algorithm, or QAOA. QAOA creates the quantum states in a noisy device by utilizing the quantum circuitry then classically applying gradient-based optimizations to incrementally improve a solutions. The hybrids of the new methods exploit today's noisily intermediatescale quantum (NISQ) devices by supplementing this with the abilities of a classical component. With this twostage process, computations could be speeded up from the disciplines in optimization to quantum chemistry, and into machine learning.

Quantum-Enhanced Machine Learning Algorithms

The Quantum ML algorithms make use of the properties of quantum to overcome all problems classical ML faces, which are high-dimensional data and slow convergence and computational complexity. Exploiting the power of superposition allows processing large amounts of data all at once in quantum systems and reduces runtime exponentially in operations like classification, clustering, and optimization. Quantum Support Vector Machines (QSVM), Quantum Principal Component Analysis (QPCA), and Quantum Neural Networks (QNN) are three significant QML techniques.

For example, QSVMs use quantum kernels to quickly calculate inner products between high-dimensional data points, thus achieving faster classification than classical SVMs. QPCA speeds up dimensionality reduction by finding dominant eigenvalues and eigenvectors of large covariance matrices, which is a computationally expensive operation for classical systems. QNNs incorporate quantum circuits that simulate the behavior of classical neural networks but operate on quantum data, thus providing potential speedups for deep learning tasks. For example, quantum circuits can encode and manipulate data by applying unitary transformations to optimize outputs.

Furthermore, there are quantum-inspired algorithms such as Quantum Boltzmann Machines (QBMs) that integrate quantum states with classical machine learning architectures. QBMs can create probabilistic models for unsupervised learning whereas variational classifiers use the quantum circuits to enhance the performance for classification. Such algorithms express the power of quantum computation in speeding up the processes of learning, especially about high-dimensional data, the type often used in domains such as image recognition and natural language processing.

Noise Cancellation and Quantum Error Correction Using ML

Some of the most important challenges for quantum computing are noise and decoherence, especially in today's NISQ devices. Techniques of machine learning are being applied to correct errors and make the computation in quantum reliable. ML algorithms can predict, model, and suppress noise with the help of data-driven approaches that enhance the performance of quantum hardware. For instance, the supervised learning models can analyze the quantum measurements in order to identify the patterns of noise and apply corrections. Analogously, RL can learn to optimize quantum circuit parameters to minimize the error rates in real-time(Broughton et al., 2020; Carrasquilla, 2020).

Another area where ML is making an impact is in quantum error correction (QEC). The classical ML algorithms decode quantum error-correcting codes, such as surface codes and topological codes, by predicting the error syndromes and identifying the most likely errors. Techniques like Neural Decoders apply deep learning models to decode large-scale quantum systems in an efficient manner, thereby reducing the computational overhead of traditional decoding methods. Integration of ML with error correction protocols permits researchers to expand coherence times of qubits to achieve longer and higher accuracy quantum computation.

Additionally, generative models such as VAE and GAN are utilized in the simulation of noise-free quantum systems. The model will learn the underlying patterns in noise and generate the corrected states. These models improve the accuracy of the simulation. Noise-aware quantum algorithms augmented with ML-based calibration seem to be the only possibility to overcome limitations existing in hardware of contemporary quantum devices.

Case Study: Variational Quantum Eigensolver with ML Optimization

Another representative practical hybrid quantum-classical application is The Variational Quantum Eigensolver (VQE) representing the application of ML on quantum computing. VQE, mainly applied to approximate quantum ground states, is used in this context to approximate ground-state energies of quantum systems including molecule systems in quantum chemistry, whereby the algorithm starts by performing the preparation of a quantum circuit for a trial wave function which is defined by some variational parameters. A quantum processor calculates the expectation value of the Hamiltonian, and a classical optimizer iteratively updates the parameters to minimize the energy(Holevo, 2019; Mori, 2023).

Adding machine learning to VQE provides even better convergence and efficiency in optimizing the process. Classical optimizers, such as gradient descent or stochastic methods, could be replaced by ML-based optimizers, including reinforcement learning agents or neural network-based optimization models. The machine learning algorithm may learn to predict optimal updates of parameters from observed patterns of energy landscapes and diminish the quantum measurements required for optimization.

For instance, RL agents can be learned to efficiently explore the parameter space and make choices that minimize energy based on feedback from the quantum processor. Similarly, surrogate models such as Gaussian Processes or deep neural networks may be used to approximate the energy landscape to speed up convergence and reduce the overhead of computation. In the latest implementation of ML-optimized VQE, researchers delivered molecular simulation results at a speed and accuracy far surpassing traditional methods, that are thought to be transformational in combining quantum computing with adaptive machine learning techniques.

Machine learning and quantum computing have brought unprecedented capabilities to solve hard problems in different domains. Hybrid quantum-classical approaches, quantum-enhanced ML algorithms, and ML-based noise mitigation strategies all represent practical synergy between these technologies. Employing ML to optimize quantum computations and enhance error correction helps scientists overcome current hardware limitations and accelerate progress toward large-scale quantum applications. Cases like ML-optimized VQE show in which directions it might be able to impact breakthroughs in quantum chemistry, optimization, and AI, in general. So when quantum hardware matures a bit further, the importance of the role played by ML in upgrading quantum algorithms increases with how more innovation will lead the way to the solution regarded before as impossible or unable to be solved.

APPLICATIONS OF ML AND QC IN QUANTUM SYSTEMS

Figure 3. Integration to specialized applications and benefits in quantum systems

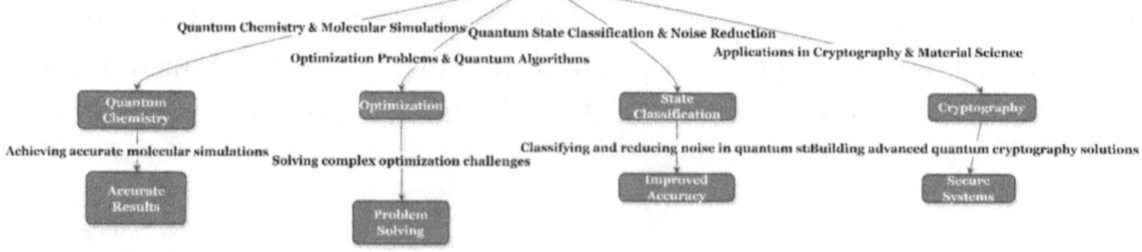

ML/QC convergence has unlocked new horizons in the solution of very complex problems in different fields. From quantum chemistry and molecular simulations to optimization, quantum state classification, and advanced cryptography, the technologies merged give more power and accuracy in computation, and the complexity that was hitherto insurmountable in classical approaches alone is approached. Below, we take a look at the myriad applications of ML and QC in quantum systems(Huggins et al., 2019; Riera-Campeny et al., 2020). Figure 3 is illustrating the diverse applications of Machine Learning (ML) and Quantum Computing (QC) in quantum systems

Quantum Chemistry and Molecular Simulations

Quantum chemistry is among the leading areas where the intersection of machine learning and quantum computing plays a role. In quantum systems, such as molecules or materials, Schrödinger's equation guides them; however, these systems turn out to be too big to be classically simulated. Quantum computers are especially good at solving this kind of high-dimensional problems efficiently due to quantum superposition and entanglement.

Quantum simulations are further optimized using machine learning:. For instance, a hybrid quantum-classical algorithm known as Variational Quantum Eigensolver (VQE) employs machine learning to iteratively update quantum parameters so that energy levels are minimized. ML algorithms aid in optimizing the quantum circuits employed in VQE by learning optimal parameter values from historical data obtained from quantum experiments. Furthermore, machine learning accelerates data analysis from quantum simulations, making predictions regarding molecular properties and reaction dynamics faster and more accurate. This synergy has propelled progress in areas such as drug discovery, materials design, and molecular interactions, where high accuracy in quantum-level simulations is of utmost importance.

Optimization Problems and Quantum Algorithms

Optimization problems represent some of the most complex computational tasks in classical systems, primarily because they involve combinatorial natures. Quantum computing combined with machine learning presents novel approaches to solving these problems with the Quantum Approximate Optimization Algorithm and Quantum Genetic Algorithms(Boopathi, 2022; Boopathi et al., 2021; Haribalaji et al., 2021).

QAOA uses quantum circuits to embed optimization problems into them, and then it is improved upon iteratively using a classical optimizer. Machine learning is utilized in fine-tuning the parameters in QAOA and achieving faster convergence, avoiding repetitions of quantum sampling. Such algorithms powered by machine learning can be really effective, even near-instantaneous in complex optimization problems, including logistics, scheduling, or financial modeling that require many computational resources and enormous amounts of time. For example, optimization problems related to supply chain management, resource allocation, and portfolio optimization in finance are effectively tackled using quantum-enhanced algorithms.

Quantum State Classification and Noise Reduction

Many quantum computing applications depend on quantum state classification. Such applications include quantum machine learning and quantum cryptography. Machine learning assists in classifying quantum states with great precision even when there is noise and decoherence. Quantum systems are intrinsically prone to errors; thus, noise reduction is part of the essential improvements toward making quantum state classification accurate(Glady et al., 2024; Kalaiselvi et al., 2024; Pitchai et al., 2024).

Machine learning techniques, including supervised learning models and neural networks, help develop robust models that distinguish different quantum states. These models learn the patterns in noisy quantum data, which improves the accuracy and reliability of quantum measurements. Another application of machine learning in QEC is to optimize correction protocols, reducing the influence of noise and decoherence to enhance the fidelity of quantum computations. For example, deep reinforcement learning has been used to dynamically regulate real-time error correction strategies to enable efficient quantum state preparation and manipulation.

Applications in Cryptography and Materials Science

In cryptography, ML integrated into QC transformed secure communication systems. Quantum cryptography uses a principle of quantum mechanics for developing an entirely new robust forms of encryption through the Heisenberg uncertainty principle and entanglement. Improving cryptographic protocols is another point: faster and more effective techniques for distributing keys to achieve secure communications, forms of encryption resistant to possible attacks from future quantum computation.

This area is exemplified by QKD, which relies on quantum entanglement in providing secret keys for secure communication, whereby even quantum computers cannot break this cryptography. Machine learning is further implemented to optimize QKD protocols toward being better against eavesdropping and more immune to attacks by quantum computers.

In material science, knowledge of material properties on the atomic and molecular scale has been advanced through the results of quantum simulations based on quantum computing. Machine learning is used in analyzing complex data generated by quantum simulations to predict material behavior, optimize its properties, and design new materials for electronic, energy storage, and nanotechnology applications. For example, it can predict conductivity, thermal properties, and structural stability of materials at the quantum level; therefore, it enables designing next-generation materials with superior performance.

Applications of machine learning and quantum computing to quantum systems span a wide area of diverse fields, providing effective tools for solving intractable problems. Quantum chemistry, optimization, noise reduction, cryptography, and material science have greatly profited from this synergy. Researchers and industries are thus building solutions that push the envelope of what is possible with the help of quantum computing's computational power and the data-driven insights of machine learning towards a quantum-enabled future.

CURRENT CHALLENGES AND LIMITATIONS

Quantum computing is promising to alter several domains, but yet exists in its early phases of development, with lots of limitations and major challenges. These limitations and challenges encompass hardware constraints, scalability issues, the efficiency of algorithms in their usage, and the encoding complexity of quantum data(Kumar et al., 2023; Pachiappan et al., 2024; Rebecca et al., 2024). The figure 4 depicts the challenges and limitations of quantum computing. Among these main problems that prevent more widespread application and further development of quantum computing is as discussed below:

Hardware Limitations of Quantum Computing

Developing robust quantum hardware is one of the main challenges of quantum computing. Quantum computers make use of qubits, that are quantum bits, in which many states exist simultaneously; however, it is yet tough to build reliable and stable qubits. Current technologies include superconducting qubits, trapped ions, and topological qubits. Each of these current technologies has some drawbacks in coherence time, error rates, and scalability of the number of qubits. Superconducting qubits, for instance, suffer from thermal noise and are required to have extremely low temperatures, thereby making them costly and difficult to maintain. Trapped ions also suffer from high environmental interference and, therefore, produce high error rates, making them limited in practical applications. Scalable and fault-tolerant quantum hardware are still challenges that involve significant investments in materials science, cryogenics, and engineering in order to mitigate these issues.

Figure 4. Challenges and limitations in quantum computing

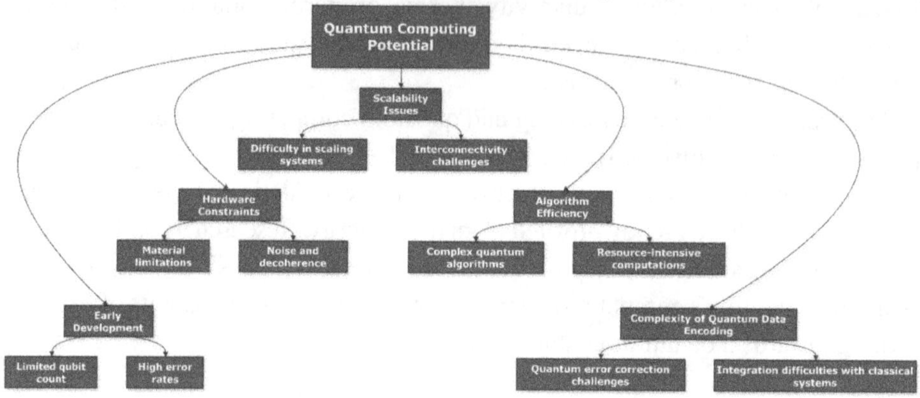

Scalability and Algorithm Efficiency

Scalability is the biggest challenge that quantum computing faces. Quantum processors with a limited number of qubits, tens to a few hundred, are still far from thousands or millions needed for practical applications. Scaling quantum systems is very challenging because of problems like crosstalk between qubits, limited connectivity, and challenges in maintaining quantum coherence across a large number of qubits. In other words, large-scale implementation of quantum operations requires that methods for quantum error correction must substantially improve and inter-qubit communication be much improved as well. Moreover, algorithms indeed become inefficient with a lot of qubits; for example, the exponential increase of the number of required operations lead to computation times and declining return on investment.

Efforts to develop fault-tolerant quantum computing models using QEC are underway, but these have the complication of requiring complex ancillary qubits and sophisticated error mitigation strategies that only exacerbate the problem. The problem is, therefore, until such time as a scalable, fault-tolerant quantum infrastructure is developed, it will be hard to make practical utility of these computers for real-world problems.

Quantum Data Encoding and Circuit Complexity

Due to the inherent complexities of quantum operations, like superposition and entanglement, quantum circuits are complex. The building and optimization of the quantum circuit are also quite challenging due to the fact that it requires precise control over every qubit involved, especially when the number of qubits is more than a few. Quantum data encoding methods, such as encoding classical information into quantum states, are also complicated due to the need for efficient error correction, noise mitigation, and resource optimization. Quantum gates and operations in quantum circuits are much more complex than classical operations; therefore, they need calibration for the correct output. The design of quantum circuits needs to be sensitive to decoherence, crosstalk, and cross-dependency between qubits that introduces complexity into computation and also acts as a hurdle to efficient quantum algorithms.

Moreover, the quantum processors available are not error-resilient, which is a significant factor in quantum computations' accuracy. Very complex quantum circuits with lots of qubits make them more prone to noise and interference, which in turn requires robust strategies for encoding data and mitigating noise. Quantum fault-tolerant architectures, quantum state distillation, and quantum circuit synthesis are some of the key developments in this regard. Such techniques will overcome the above-mentioned limitations to achieve scalable quantum computation.

Though a lot of promise is attributed to quantum computing, many challenges and limitations remain crucial. The hardware constraint refers to the problems related to qubit stability, coherence time, and scalability for practical quantum system development. In addition, the encoding of quantum data is complex, and the demand for highly efficient algorithms introduces layers of complexity to implement robust and scalable solutions of quantum computing. Advances in quantum hardware, error correction, and optimization of algorithms are crucial to unlock the potential of quantum computing for real-world applications.

FUTURE DIRECTIONS

Figure 5. Future directions in quantum computing and quantum machine learning

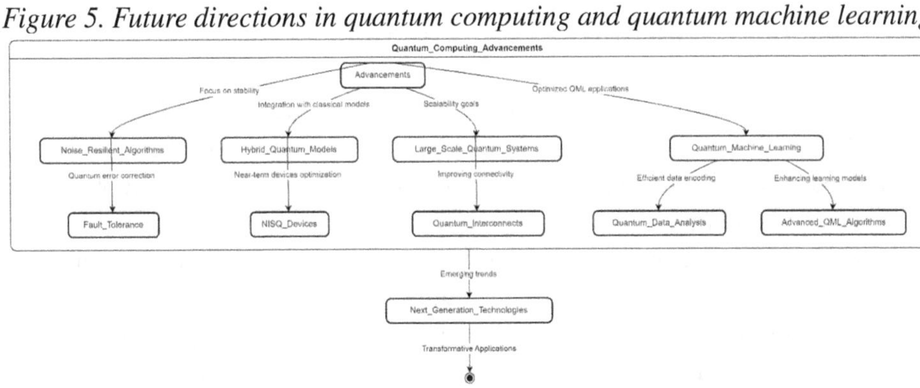

In quantum computing, the area is quite close to many potentially transformative applications in its fast-paced development. As it matures, there are huge directions toward which this is headed. The first area is Quantum Machine Learning, followed by noise-resilient quantum algorithms, hybrid models for near-term quantum devices, and finally pursuing the analysis of large-scale quantum systems. We digress below into these emerging trends and their implications for the next generation of quantum technologies(Sekhar et al., 2024; Venkateswaran et al., 2024). The figure 5 depicts the future directions in Quantum Computing and Quantum Machine Learning.

Advancements in Quantum Machine Learning (QML)

The objective of QML is the marriage of quantum computation with the paradigms of machine learning for the optimization and learning problems on high-dimensional complex datasets. In this regard, hybrids quantum-classical models have recently emerged by combining parallelism with superposition offered by quantum computation with advantages like faster processing on data than possible with traditional approaches in machine learning(Muthukumar et al., 2024; Saravanan et al., 2024).

Future advances of QML will be enabled by more efficient quantum algorithms, such as the Variational Quantum Eigensolver (VQE) and Quantum Approximate Optimization Algorithm (QAOA), which are showing promise for optimization tasks and solving combinatorial problems. Machine learning will play a key role in optimizing quantum circuits, fine-tuning parameters, and ensuring the scalability of QML models when dealing with increasingly complex data. With these neural networks in integration with quantum systems, new possibilities and avenues for access to quantum natural language processing, computer vision, and real-time data analysis will arise.

Development of Noise-Resilient Quantum Algorithms

The biggest challenge for quantum computing is noise and decoherence: degradation in accuracy and reliability of quantum computations. In the near future, it will depend on quantum algorithms resilient to noise, so that such problems are surmounted. Quantum Error Correction (QEC) represents an exciting area where this noise is addressed with state-of-the-art fault-tolerant techniques to achieve a more precise and stable execution of quantum operations.

Quantum machine learning techniques such as adaptive learning algorithms and probabilistic modeling will play a role in noise mitigation. The machine learning technique will allow researchers to develop algorithms that can adjust and adapt in the presence of noise in computation, thereby providing robust performance in noisy environments. Future developments will likely include the use of hybrid classical-quantum methods, combining data-driven approaches with quantum enhancements for more precise and resilient algorithm design.

Hybrid Models for Near-Term Quantum Devices

In fact, given the present limitations of quantum hardware, hybrid quantum-classical models are a promising direction for near-term quantum devices. In such models, classical systems can handle the non-quantum parts of the computation, letting quantum hardware perform on those aspects of the problem where quantum parallelism and entanglement offer benefits. Thus, this hybrid model balances noisy, small-scale quantum systems with the power of computational processing that classical systems have to offer.

Hybrid models, probably more complex, are what the future holds. There will be hybrid quantum and classical machine learning algorithms developed to solve complex problems: drug discovery, material science, financial modeling, to mention a few. Finally, cloud-based quantum services are what will make hybrid models simpler to deploy, meaning it will be easier for the industry to access quantum technologies, given that expensive, dedicated infrastructure is not required.

Prospects for Large-Scale Quantum Systems Analysis

The ultimate aim is to achieve large-scale, fault-tolerant quantum systems that can solve problems much farther than those that can be reached by classical systems. In the near term, scalable quantum systems will lead to radical changes in fields like cryptography, drug discovery, climate modeling, and optimization. All this would be accompanied by substantial progress in quantum hardware, error correction, and algorithmic optimization, so that the large-scale systems can be realized. New quantum architectures-including topological qubits and quantum annealers with promise for robust, scalable computation-are being explored in parallel with advancements in machine learning, which will be instrumental in the analysis and management of exponential growth in quantum data to enable efficient management and interpretation of complex quantum systems.

It is also going to be crucial in the development of new algorithms that are specifically intended for an application by leading quantum machine learning techniques that have to be designed. They are optimized machine learning techniques, and they give insights into the underlying quantum behavior in a manner that would grant unprecedented control over the quantum system. The future of quantum computing and quantum machine learning holds immense transformation for industries and solving some of the most challenging problems in the world. Quantum technologies will be brought closer to practical applications through QML, noise-resilient algorithms, hybrid quantum models, and large-scale quantum systems. By addressing the current limitations and extending the capabilities of quantum systems, researchers and industry leaders are paving their way for a quantum-enabled future in which quantum and classical systems will collaborate to achieve unparalleled computational power and innovation.

CONCLUSION

Integration of machine learning and quantum computing presents the evolving front of computing which now has a possibility to solving highly challenging, high-dimensionality, and indeed very computationally intense issues much more effectively than could be approached with traditional, classical means. Through discussion in this chapter, we have worked out foundational precepts underlying both areas but also, importantly, explained how integration of both into an ensemble has yielded novel solutions to questions in vast fields of research. From quantum algorithms like QAOA and VQE to hybrid quantum-classical models, this synergy between the two fields opens new pathways for optimizing computations and enhancing accuracy despite the inherent challenges such as noise and scalability.

Besides that, noise-robust quantum algorithms and hybrid methods will make sure near-term quantum devices to be useful with applications to real-life problems. Due to increasing robustness in computations as well as minimization of decoherence, it becomes possible to render the systems reliable for practical use cases. As the field advances, the synergy between quantum computing parallelism and superposition and the ability of machine learning to deal with vast amounts of data can advance sectors like quantum chemistry, cryptography, material science, and optimization. Future work will further refine quantum systems, improve algorithmic efficiency, and expand the horizon for large-scale quantum analysis, thus pushing the limits of what is computationally feasible. The future holds an emerging march of the quantum with that of the classical: yet another wave of collaboration promises to open doors of innovations unthinkable by present technology standards.

REFERENCES

Alet, F., Hanada, M., Jevicki, A., & Peng, C. (2021). Entanglement and confinement in coupled quantum systems. *The Journal of High Energy Physics*, 2021(2), 1–31. DOI: 10.1007/JHEP02(2021)034

Alexeev, Y., Bacon, D., Brown, K. R., Calderbank, R., Carr, L. D., Chong, F. T., DeMarco, B., Englund, D., Farhi, E., Fefferman, B., Gorshkov, A. V., Houck, A., Kim, J., Kimmel, S., Lange, M., Lloyd, S., Lukin, M. D., Maslov, D., Maunz, P., & Thompson, J. (2021). Quantum computer systems for scientific discovery. *PFX Quantum : a Physical Review Journal*, 2(1), 017001. DOI: 10.1103/PRXQuantum.2.017001

Boopathi, S. (2022). Experimental investigation and multi-objective optimization of cryogenic Friction-stir-welding of AA2014 and AZ31B alloys using MOORA technique. *Materials Today. Communications*, 33, 104937. DOI: 10.1016/j.mtcomm.2022.104937

Boopathi, S., Myilsamy, S., & Sukkasamy, S. (2021). *Experimental Investigation and Multi-Objective Optimization of Cryogenically Cooled Near-Dry Wire-Cut EDM Using TOPSIS Technique*. IJAMT PREPRINT.

Broughton, M., Verdon, G., McCourt, T., Martinez, A. J., Yoo, J. H., Isakov, S. V., Massey, P., Halavati, R., Niu, M. Y., Zlokapa, A., & Associates. (2020). Tensorflow quantum: A software framework for quantum machine learning. *arXiv Preprint arXiv:2003.02989.*

Carrasquilla, J. (2020). Machine learning for quantum matter. *Advances in Physics: X*, 5(1), 1797528. DOI: 10.1080/23746149.2020.1797528

Glady, J. B. P., D'Souza, S. M., Priya, A. P., Amuthachenthiru, K., Vikram, G., & Boopathi, S. (2024). A Study on AI-ML-Driven Optimizing Energy Distribution and Sustainable Agriculture for Environmental Conservation. In *Harnessing High-Performance Computing and AI for Environmental Sustainability* (pp. 1–27). IGI Global., DOI: 10.4018/979-8-3693-1794-5.ch001

Gupta, H., Varshney, H., Sharma, T. K., Pachauri, N., & Verma, O. P. (2022). Comparative performance analysis of quantum machine learning with deep learning for diabetes prediction. *Complex & Intelligent Systems*, 8(4), 3073–3087. DOI: 10.1007/s40747-021-00398-7

Haribalaji, V., Boopathi, S., & Asif, M. M. (2021). Optimization of friction stir welding process to join dissimilar AA2014 and AA7075 aluminum alloys. *Materials Today: Proceedings*, 50, 2227–2234. DOI: 10.1016/j.matpr.2021.09.499

Holevo, A. S. (2019). *Quantum systems, channels, information: A mathematical introduction*. Walter de Gruyter GmbH & Co KG. DOI: 10.1515/9783110642490

Huggins, W., Patil, P., Mitchell, B., Whaley, K. B., & Stoudenmire, E. M. (2019). Towards quantum machine learning with tensor networks. *Quantum Science and Technology*, 4(2), 024001. DOI: 10.1088/2058-9565/aaea94

Jabbari, T., & Friedman, E. G. (2020). Global interconnects in VLSI complexity single flux quantum systems. *Proceedings of the Workshop on System-Level Interconnect: Problems and Pathfinding Workshop*, 1–7. DOI: 10.1145/3414622.3431911

Kalaiselvi, T., Saravanan, G., Haritha, T., Babu, A. V. S., Sakthivel, M., & Boopathi, S. (2024). A Study on the Landscape of Serverless Computing: Technologies and Tools for Seamless Implementation. In *Serverless Computing Concepts, Technology and Architecture* (pp. 260–282). IGI Global. DOI: 10.4018/979-8-3693-1682-5.ch016

Khan, T. M., & Robles-Kelly, A. (2020). Machine learning: Quantum vs classical. *IEEE Access : Practical Innovations, Open Solutions*, 8, 219275–219294. DOI: 10.1109/ACCESS.2020.3041719

Kumar, M., Kumar, K., Sasikala, P., Sampath, B., Gopi, B., & Sundaram, S. (2023). Sustainable Green Energy Generation From Waste Water: IoT and ML Integration. In *Sustainable Science and Intelligent Technologies for Societal Development* (pp. 440–463). IGI Global.

Manikandan, S. K. (2021). Equidistant quenches in few-level quantum systems. *Physical Review Research*, 3(4), 043108. DOI: 10.1103/PhysRevResearch.3.043108

Mori, T. (2023). Floquet states in open quantum systems. *Annual Review of Condensed Matter Physics*, 14(1), 35–56. DOI: 10.1146/annurev-conmatphys-040721-015537

Muthukumar, R., Pratheep, V. G. G., Sultanuddin, S. J., Kunduru, K. R., Kumar, P., & Boopathi, S. (2024). Leveraging Fuel Cell Technology With AI and ML Integration for Next-Generation Vehicles: Empowering Electric Mobility. In A Sustainable Future with E-Mobility: Concepts, Challenges, and Implementations (pp. 312-337). IGI Global.

Pachiappan, K., Anitha, K., Pitchai, R., Sangeetha, S., Satyanarayana, T., & Boopathi, S. (2024). Intelligent Machines, IoT, and AI in Revolutionizing Agriculture for Water Processing. In *Handbook of Research on AI and ML for Intelligent Machines and Systems* (pp. 374–399). IGI Global.

Peral-García, D., Cruz-Benito, J., & García-Peñalvo, F. J. (2024). Systematic literature review: Quantum machine learning and its applications. *Computer Science Review*, 51, 100619. DOI: 10.1016/j.cosrev.2024.100619

Pitchai, R., Guru, K. V., Gandhi, J. N., Komala, C. R., Kumar, J. R. D., & Boopathi, S. (2024). Fog Computing-Integrated ML-Based Framework and Solutions for Intelligent Systems: Digital Healthcare Applications. In *Technological Advancements in Data Processing for Next Generation Intelligent Systems* (pp. 196–224). IGI Global. DOI: 10.4018/979-8-3693-0968-1.ch008

Ramezani, S. B., Sommers, A., Manchukonda, H. K., Rahimi, S., & Amirlatifi, A. (2020). Machine learning algorithms in quantum computing: A survey. *2020 International Joint Conference on Neural Networks (IJCNN)*, 1–8. DOI: 10.1109/IJCNN48605.2020.9207714

Rebecca, B., Kumar, K. P. M., Padmini, S., Srivastava, B. K., Halder, S., & Boopathi, S. (2024). Convergence of Data Science-AI-Green Chemistry-Affordable Medicine: Transforming Drug Discovery. In *Handbook of Research on AI and ML for Intelligent Machines and Systems* (pp. 348–373). IGI Global.

Riera-Campeny, A., Moreno-Cardoner, M., & Sanpera, A. (2020). Time crystallinity in open quantum systems. *Quantum : the Open Journal for Quantum Science*, 4, 270. DOI: 10.22331/q-2020-05-25-270

Saravanan, S., Khare, R., Umamaheswari, K., Khare, S., Krishne Gowda, B. S., & Boopathi, S. (2024). AI and ML Adaptive Smart-Grid Energy Management Systems: Exploring Advanced Innovations. In *Principles and Applications in Speed Sensing and Energy Harvesting for Smart Roads* (pp. 166–196). IGI Global. DOI: 10.4018/978-1-6684-9214-7.ch006

Schuld, M., & Petruccione, F. (2021). *Machine learning with quantum computers* (Vol. 676). Springer. DOI: 10.1007/978-3-030-83098-4

Sekhar, K. C., Ranganathan, L., Bathrinath, S., Premnath, D., Yuvasri, B., & Boopathi, S. (2024). Cloud Computing Adoption for Small and Medium Enterprises in Mechanical Engineering. In *Advances in Web Technologies and Engineering* (pp. 219–247). IGI Global. DOI: 10.4018/979-8-3693-1487-6.ch011

Venkateswaran, N., Kunduru, K. R., Ashwin, N., Sundar Ganesh, C. S., Hema, N., & Boopathi, S. (2024). Navigating the Future of Ultra-Smart Computing Cyberspace: Beyond Boundaries. In *Advances in Computational Intelligence and Robotics* (pp. 170–199). IGI Global. DOI: 10.4018/979-8-3693-2399-1.ch007

Chapter 3
Harnessing Quantum Computing for AI-Driven Medical Advancements: A Comprehensive Study

S. Reshma
Dayananda Sagar College of Engineering, Bangalore, India

Athira Manoj
Electronics and Communication Engineering, PSNA College of Engineering and Technology, Dindigul, India

Archana Ratnaparkhi
https://orcid.org/0000-0002-1269-6389
Vishwakarma Institute of Technology, Pune, India

K. S. Shreenidhi
https://orcid.org/0000-0002-6844-0454
Department of Biotechnology, Rajalakshmi Engineering College, Chennai, India

Harishchander Anandaram
https://orcid.org/0009-0008-5822-1056
Department of Artificial Intelligence, Amrita Vishwa Vidyapeetham, Coimbatore, India

ABSTRACT

Quantum computing provides the transformative capability to take advancements in AI in medicine several notches ahead. Building on the principles of quantum mechanics, quantum computing can supply computational speed and efficiency that

DOI: 10.4018/979-8-3693-6225-9.ch003

leave the limitations of classical computers far behind, especially as they deal with complex data sets in medicine. As such, this chapter provides a look at the frontier areas of intersection between quantum computing and AI in medicine, particularly in drug discovery, genomics, precision medicine, and medical imaging. The accelerated simulation of molecular interactions would promise quantum algorithms to find therapeutic targets quickly and to optimize treatment pathways. Quantum machine learning also promises breakthroughs in diagnostic accuracy and predictive analytics, which will provide personalized care. This chapter explores the potential of quantum computing in medical advancement, focusing on hardware scalability, algorithm development, data privacy, and ethical considerations.

INTRODUCTION

Quantum computing revolutionizes the face of computational technology by using quantum mechanics to solve problems that the classical computer cannot. It is critical in healthcare, as the need for rapid analysis of vast, multifaceted datasets requires quantum computing, opening up unprecedented possibilities for transformation in medical research, diagnostics, and treatment paradigms. This chapter delves into the emerging intersection of quantum computing and artificial intelligence in the medical field, an area that promises much in terms of revolutionary breakthroughs. Quantum algorithms and quantum-enhanced machine learning can be used to process and analyze complex medical datasets at unprecedented speeds with unprecedented accuracy(Anbazhagu et al., 2025). Innovations in drug discovery, genomics, precision medicine, and medical imaging can now be created.

For example, the drug discovery process has traditionally been highly time-consuming and resource-intensive with years of experimentation being devoted to identifying viable therapeutic compounds(Rebecca et al., 2024). Quantum computing can dramatically accelerate such a process by virtue of the ability to simulate molecular interactions with high fidelity. Rapid exploration of chemical space using quantum algorithms makes the discovery of potential drug candidates and optimizing molecular designs more efficient than any known classical approach. Another cornerstone of modern medicine-genomics-will also stand to benefit from the potential of processing large-scale multidimensional data(Goswami & Sharma, 2024). Quantum algorithms make possible the analysis of genetic sequences to identify disease-associated mutations and thus tailor treatments.

The vision of precision medicine - delivering the right treatment, for the right patient at the right time, based on their unique genetic makeup and clinical profile- also gets a powerful ally in quantum computing. By integrating AI and quantum computing, healthcare providers will have access to predictive models accounting for the complexities of human biology, environmental factors, and lifestyle data. This would improve the accuracy of diagnosis and increase the effectiveness of treatment by reducing adverse reactions and optimizing the outcome(Rayhan & Rayhan, 2023). Quantum-enhanced AI algorithms may revolutionize diagnostic radiology in medical imaging, allowing for an improvement in resolution and noise reduction to facilitate earlier detection of diseases at higher resolutions.

Despite the great promise of quantum computing in medicine, there are challenges involved in practical implementation. The nascent stage of quantum hardware, issues related to algorithmic scalability, and the complexity of integrating quantum systems into the existing medical frameworks are quite challenging. The sensitive nature of medical data brings forth a host of critical issues pertaining to data privacy and security because of the possibility that future quantum systems may be able to outperform the current encryption technologies. This entails ethical considerations because the use of the new technologies ought not to widen inequalities of access to health care or affect other matters not envisaged(Kavitha et al., 2025).

This chapter further elaborates on the current state of quantum computing research and its implementation in the health sector and therefore reveals some of the cooperative efforts being made by the academia, industry, and policymakers toward overcoming the aforementioned challenges. Indeed, the pace of quantum hardware development has been laying the ground for scalable quantum systems by rapidly advancing both qubits and error correction. The chasm between the quantum and the potential of classical computing fills now with hybrid quantum-classical algorithms parallelly. As a result, practical application becomes possible(Ahmadi, 2023).

It was followed by new frontiers opening toward interdisciplinary research in terms of convergence. There was inspiring inspiration for the development of innovated solutions that go beyond limits of traditional methodics owing to the cross-cutting nature of an interface between quantum mechanics with computer science and biomedical engineering. New fields, such as quantum-enhanced neural networks and quantum-inspired optimization, reveal how these technologies can be brought together to open unprecedented applications(Tripathi et al., 2024). For instance, quantum machine learning models can process vast electronic health records and real-time patient monitoring data to predict disease outbreaks, improve resource management in hospitals, and personalize treatment pathways.

This also opens the door to how the global healthcare scenario would benefit from the scalability and versatility of quantum computing. Quantum-powered diagnostic tools in underserved regions with limited access to medical infrastructure could provide cost-effective and efficient solutions. Quantum computing could enable collaborative platforms to share medical knowledge and resources across borders, thereby bringing equity to the healthcare system(Boretti, 2024; Khang, 2024).

This chapter concludes by examining future directions and emerging trends in the field, with a strong emphasis on interdisciplinary collaboration as a critical enabler of progress. Quantum computing in healthcare will have to be an all-inclusive approach that encompasses technological innovation, regulatory frameworks, and ethical guidelines. The full potential of quantum computing can then be unleashed in order to advance medicine, improve patient care, and tackle some of the most challenging global health issues(Taherdoost & Madanchian, 2023).

In a nutshell, the integration of quantum computing into AI-driven breakthroughs in medicine represents one of the most significant shifts conceptualized and delivered in terms of healthcare. This involves speeding up drug discovery all the way to enabling precise diagnostic capabilities and personal medicine, among many others. This potential, however, will only be materialized if concerted efforts of researchers, technologists, and policymakers are put to work together to overcome technical, ethical, and logistical impediments. This chapter takes a comprehensive approach to these issues, and offers insight into what to expect in the future development of quantum computing over medicine(AKHIL & SAIKIRAN, 2024).

Objectives

This chapter will discuss the transformative possibilities of quantum computing in promoting AI-driven medical innovations. It will seek to establish a comprehensive understanding of how quantum computing can be applied to enhance key healthcare domains, such as drug discovery, genomics, precision medicine, and medical imaging. The chapter will further examine the synergistic integration of quantum algorithms with AI for improving diagnostic accuracy and treatment personalization. This, among other things, will describe various challenges associated with technology implementation, data security, and ethics while proposing their solution. The chapter, in conclusion, presents its way toward future views on how quantum computing will transform global healthcare systems in the future.

BACKGROUND: QUANTUM COMPUTING

Quantum computing is the revolutionary paradigm of computational science based on quantum principles for the solution of problems far beyond the capacities of a classical computer. The basic principles of quantum mechanics, which are superposition, entanglement, and quantum interference, form the backbone of quantum computing. Quantum systems can perform complex calculations by exploring several possibilities at the same time by using these principles. Whereas the classical bit is in one of the two states: 0 or 1, qubits, on the other hand, exist in a superposition of states, so they can represent and process an exponentially greater amount of information. It is due to this inbuilt parallelism that quantum computing is more suited for the solution of complex problems related to health care, as it analyzes vast, multidimensional data sets(Yingngam & Khang, 2024).

Qubits are the elementary building blocks of quantum information. It uses physical systems, like trapped ions, superconducting circuits, or photons, and the quantum mechanical behavior of such systems. Quantum gates constitute how qubits interact. The quantum circuit is assembled by manipulating states through such quantum gates. Other gates include the Hadamard, CNOT, and Pauli gates, which are used to perform operations, such as entanglement, where the state of one qubit cannot be separated from another regardless of distance. Quantum algorithms utilize a series of quantum gates for their implementation. Such quantum algorithms show a computational advantage in leveraging quantum parallelism and interference to solve problems more effectively than classically, although generally much faster.

Among the important applications of quantum algorithms for health care are the implementation of Shor's algorithm to factor numbers exponentially much faster than classical approaches. While initially designed for cryptographic purposes, it has implications for healthcare in secure data management and encryption. Grover's algorithm, another fundamental quantum algorithm, offers quadratic speedup for unstructured search problems, enabling faster querying and analysis of medical databases. These have great potential for the improvement of diagnostics, drug discovery, and personalized medicine through quantum support vector machines and quantum neural networks.

In healthcare, this would have challenges in the handling and processing of very complicated biological data. In a genomics example, dealing with the large-scale genetic data sets allows for identification of disease-causing mutations along with insight into the basic genetic reason for many types of diseases. Such processes can be accelerated through efficient navigation by quantum algorithms across large combinatorial spaces. Similarly, drug discovery involves simulations of molecular interactions, an activity that is extremely computer-intensive and cannot be straightforwardly achieved with classical computers. Quantum computing, on the other hand, enables one to simulate quantum systems at an atomic level, thereby being able to design and optimize molecules for drugs with unprecedented accuracy(Ramudu et al., 2023; Veeranjaneyulu et al., 2023).

Medical imaging, which is another critical domain, is also likely to get significantly impacted by quantum computing. Quantum-enhanced image processing algorithms allow better resolution and accuracy for diagnostic imaging technologies like MRI and CT scans. They help eliminate noise while making images clearer, so the disease could be detected in the earlier stages and more characteristically. In addition, quantum computing will help predict analytics by analyzing data regarding patients, environmental factors, and genetic information faster, thus providing accurate medical decisions in the shortest possible time(Olorunsogo et al., 2024).

Although the potential of quantum computing in healthcare is enormous, implementing it practically is far from easy. Qubits need coherence and error correction that is very difficult because the systems are extremely sensitive to the environmental noise. Qubits depend on their stability and reliability to create a scalable quantum computer. Incorporating quantum algorithms into existing frameworks in the healthcare system demands special competence and infrastructure. Such challenges call for the collaborative effort of quantum physicists, computer scientists, and healthcare professionals(Sengeni et al., 2023).

Transforming, therefore, is the word when considering quantum computing: not by virtue of these principles, but by qubits and quantum gates; these may well revolutionize what could become critical areas: drug discovery, genomics, and medical imaging. For some of these challenges, innovatively different solutions will start opening the way. Nevertheless, the technical and practical barriers remain significant, although research and development promise unlocking the full potential of quantum computing for furthering medicine in the future.

AI IN MEDICINE: A PRIMER

Artificial Intelligence is radically transforming the healthcare landscape in a very fast pace that is bringing more advanced tools and techniques for improved diagnostics, treatment, and patient management. The processing of enormous data, pattern recognition, and prediction abilities have enabled AI to revolutionize the medical practice, making it more personalized and efficient care. Early disease detection and precision medicine are some areas where AI applications are expected to bring about significant advances in the patient outcome and the efficiency of operations. Here is an overview of a few important areas where AI is causing a difference-its applications, the role of machine learning and DL in diagnostics, and what is important in AI-led medical solutions: big data(Arya et al., 2024; Tyagi et al., 2025). Figure 1 depicts the integration of AI in medicine, which includes diagnostics, treatment, and patient management components.

Figure 1. AI in medicine (Components: diagnostics, treatment, and patient management)

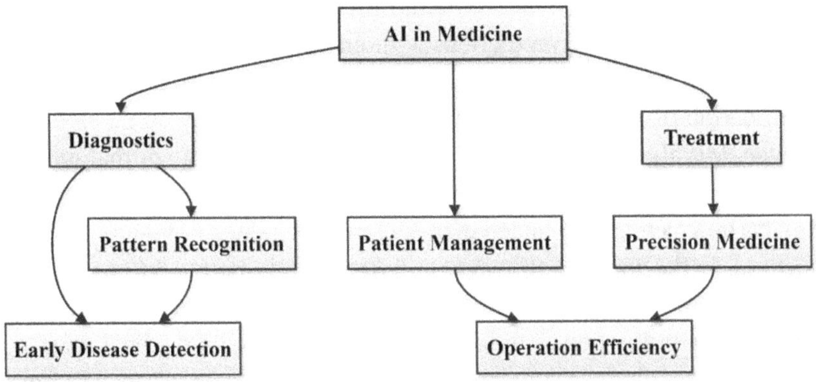

Applications in Health Care

Health care employs AI in diagnostic analysis, planning of treatments, patient monitoring, and finally management. Diagnosis by algorithms: With algorithms, AI can view radiographs, MRIs, and CTs for any abnormalities in tumours, fractures, irregular organ shapes, that match or exceed human abilities in some instances. For example, the use of AI in the detection and determination of breast cancer, lung nodules, retinal disease, among others that led to early intervention and high survival rates. However, beyond imaging, AI helps in tailoring the treatment based on patient history, genetic profiles, and real-time health data, thereby recommending therapies appropriate for patients. AI-powered predictive analytics enables clinicians to identify the risk of patients developing complications such as sepsis or heart failure and act ahead of time. In surgery, AI-enabled robotic systems enable precision and a much faster recovery. AI further assists in drug discovery through simulation of molecular interactions, which accelerates the identification of promising candidates for drugs(Tyagi et al., 2025).

Hence, however, are the administrative tasks. Algorithms for Natural Language Processing automate entry and coding into EHRs while streamlining the retrieval, hence reducing the burden on the administrative duties of health professionals. AI-based virtual health assistants will also make scheduling easier by reminding patients of medication use, as well as offering information to patient queries to help make things easily accessible and convenient.

Machine learning and deep learning in diagnostics

Machine learning is one of the subfields of AI that focuses on creating algorithms to learn from data and make predictions without explicit programming. Supervised learning techniques are the most common methods used in diagnostics, which enable the identification of particular conditions by training models on labeled datasets. For instance, ML algorithms can classify skin lesions as benign or malignant based on dermatological images(How & Cheah, 2023).

Deep learning is more advanced than ML and has gained popularity since it beat other methods in the analysis of images and signals. DL models use artificial neural networks with multiple layers to automatically extract hierarchical features from raw data, and thus are pretty powerful for many complex tasks in medical imaging. For example, CNNs are now the standard for analysis of radiological images(Boopathi, 2023; Hema et al., 2023; Venkateswaran et al., 2023). These models are learned from large datasets and may pick up on subtle patterns indicative of diseases, like early-stage cancers or neurological disorders, that the naked eye might miss. Besides imaging, DL models analyze other diagnostic data such as ECGs and EEGs for arrhythmia or epileptic event. The other type of DL model is RNNs. It processes the sequential data such as a time-series signal very well, thus it is very useful in real-time monitoring and predicting the patient's condition.

Role of Big Data in AI-driven Medical Solutions

The success of AI will depend largely on the access and quality of big data. Healthcare generates massive quantities of data from EHRs, imaging systems, genomic sequencing, wearable devices, and clinical trials. Through big data, AI machines can be trained to trace patterns, correlations, or trends that guide medical decisions. Big data analytics enable AI to process and integrate diverse datasets, thus offering a holistic view of the patient's health. For instance, genomic data integration with clinical records allows precision medicine through tailoring treatment to the unique genetic makeup of every patient. Similarly, real-time data from wearable devices and IoT sensors enable continuous monitoring and early detection of potential health issues such as arrhythmias or glucose fluctuations(Henry, 2024).

However, the use of big data in AI-driven healthcare solutions has challenges. Data privacy and security become very important since medical records contain sensitive information. This means that regulations such as GDPR and HIPAA compliance are essential to maintain the trust of patients and preserve data integrity. Data quality is another concern because poor or biased datasets can cause inaccurate AI predictions. These challenges are being answered by robust data governance frameworks, standardized protocols of sharing data, and even designing bias-resistant algorithms.

The Synergy of AI and Medicine

AI in medicine is changing the face of how healthcare is delivered by both enhancing patient outcomes and operational efficiency. AI has been able to better utilize the power of ML and DL in diagnostics for better and more timely detection of diseases, and big data analytics forms the foundation of personalized care. But adoption of AI in healthcare is also dependent on ethical, regulatory, and technical challenges that need to be overcome as well as the facilitation of collaboration between technologists, clinicians, and policymakers(Henry, 2024).

As AI is developed further, its health applications will expand, further driving innovation and opening new avenues for solving complex medical challenges. The synergy between AI's predictive power and the human touch can revolutionize healthcare by ensuring better access, quality, and outcomes for patients across the globe. The journey toward that full realization is ongoing, but for now, the impact is still profound, setting the future stage for technology and medicine to work hand in glove to improve lives(Pramila et al., 2023; Sengeni et al., 2023).

APPLICATIONS OF QUANTUM COMPUTING IN MEDICINE

Quantum computing will transform a range of areas in medicine, particularly in drug discovery and development, genomics, and analysis of genetic data. Leveraging the specific capabilities that quantum mechanics provides, for example, superposition, entanglement, and interference, quantum computing facilitates calculations that are far beyond those possible in classical systems. These improvements offer remarkable gains in the accuracy, efficiency, and scope of research and treatment development in medicine. Below are the two significant areas where quantum computing has made a marked impact: drug discovery and genomics/genetic data analysis(AKHIL & SAIKIRAN, 2024; Taherdoost & Madanchian, 2023). The figure 2 depicts the various applications of quantum computing in the field of medicine.

Figure 2. Applications of quantum computing in medicine

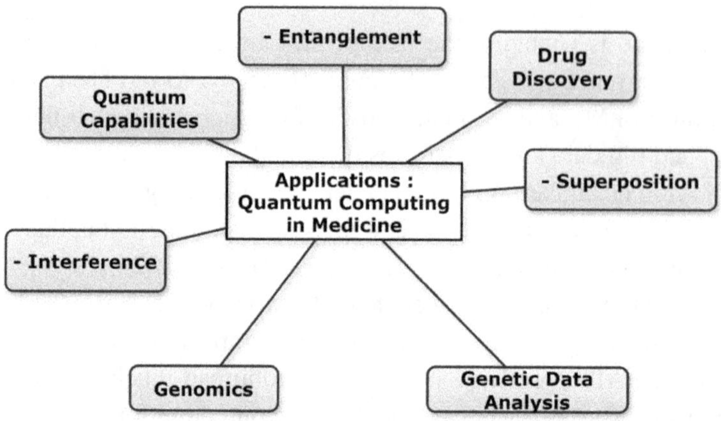

Drug Discovery and Development

By its very nature, the process of drug discovery and development involves a simulation of molecular interactions and identification of potential therapeutic targets as well as optimization of drug candidates. Because there are a vast number of possible interactions between molecules and biological systems, it is an extremely time-consuming and costly affair with classical computers. Quantum computing solves this problem because it provides the computational power needed to simulate the quantum behavior of molecular systems. Quantum computers are good at simulating molecular dynamics with high fidelity. That is, researchers can explore atomic level interactions. Quantum algorithms optimize the design of new molecules so that the time needed to discover effective drugs can be reduced. For instance, Quantum Monte Carlo simulations permit the computation of potential energy surfaces, which helps in the understanding of chemical reactions and predicting the molecular binding site. Also, algorithms like VQE can predict electronic structures that can be used in designing drugs, thereby reducing the large trial-and-error approach in drug discovery(Pramila et al., 2023; Ramudu et al., 2023; Satav et al., 2023).

Quantum computers will speed up the screening of drugs by effectively analyzing large datasets of compounds and reduce candidates that need to be physically tested. Quantum algorithms predict the binding affinity of drug candidates to specific biological targets, thus helping researchers to narrow down the most promising leads. Optimizing molecular interactions and drug-target specificity by quantum computing might change the paradigm in which drugs are designed and developed, hence novel therapeutics that could not be accessed through the classical approach.

Genomics and genetic data analysis

Genomics is a fast-growing field that produces large amounts of data, including whole-genome sequences, epigenetic modifications, and other complex biological data. Classical computers find it difficult to analyze these huge datasets to find patterns, correlations, and associations with diseases. Quantum computing accelerates this process by efficiently processing and analyzing genetic data, identifying genetic variations that contribute to diseases, and offering insights into personalized medicine(Khang, 2024).

Genome sequencing with variant detection can actually get very fast using quantum algorithms like Quantum Phase Estimation. QPE could then have a better estimation of quantum states of genomic data over its classical counterpart, improving its accuracy. Such findings could be helpful in revealing patterns across thousands or even millions of genetic markers used to detect rare mutations for diseases of cancer or neurological conditions. The second aspect of quantum computing allows population-scale analysis, aiding scientists in understanding the genetic basis of complex traits, where multiple genes interact. Another major application of quantum computing is to increase the accuracy of predictive models of genetic diseases. Quantum algorithms process large datasets of genomic information, which improves the machine learning models to lead to more accurate predictions regarding disease risk, treatment efficacy, and drug response. Such developments are necessary to create targeted therapies suited to the unique genetic profiles of individual patients, hence pushing forward precision medicine.

Hence, quantum computing offers tremendous opportunities to revolutionize drug discovery and genetic data analysis in medicine. This is achieved through the simulation of molecular interactions and the processing of genomic data via the use of computational power from quantum technologies, enabling faster, more accurate, and efficient solutions in medical research and treatment development. As quantum computing continues its evolution, it will reshape the future of personalized medicine and therapeutic advancement. Precision medicine and better medical imaging and diagnostics are the fields in which quantum computing is increasingly being used. This computing technology has singular computational powers to process large amounts of complex medical data efficiently and accurately, making way for breakthroughs in personalized health care and advanced diagnostic tools. Two of the significant areas in which quantum computing is bringing about profound impact are precision medicine and predictive analytics, as well as medical imaging and diagnostics.

Precision Medicine and Predictive Analytics

Precision medicine is an approach that seeks to tailor medical treatment to individual patients based on their unique genetic, environmental, and lifestyle factors. Quantum computing is critical to this approach because it provides unparalleled computational power for the analysis and interpretation of complex datasets that are beyond the scope of traditional means. Quantum algorithms, such as Quantum Machine Learning (QML) and Variational Quantum Algorithms, allow for the processing of vast amounts of data, from genomic sequences to electronic health records and biomarker analysis, in a much more efficient manner(Boretti, 2024; Tripathi et al., 2024).

Quantum computing is allowed to detect subtle patterns hidden in big data that cannot be discovered in a classical system. For instance, in cancer treatment, quantum algorithms can analyze different genetic mutations and variations occurring in the various types of tumors. It would deepen the insight into optimal strategies for treating an individual. Quantum-enhanced predictive analytics will aid in the assessment of efficacy in drug delivery and disease advancement, thereby making possible precision and personalization in therapeutic approaches(Boopathi & Khang, 2023). Moreover, quantum computing facilitates multi-dimensional data integration by enabling the simulation of patient-specific responses to therapies. This allows clinicians to predict the outcomes of various treatment regimens, minimizing trial-and-error methods and maximizing therapeutic success. As a result, precision medicine becomes not only more accessible but also more effective, creating a new frontier in tailored healthcare solutions.

Medical Imaging and Diagnostics

Quantum Computing: This will revolutionize the processing of huge, complex imaging data sets like MRI, CT scans, and PET scans. Traditional imaging produces large datasets that require strong processing power for proper analysis. Quantum computing accelerates image reconstruction, feature extraction, and anomaly detection, which complements these efforts. For example, quantum algorithms will improve the accuracy of image segmentation and pattern recognition in medical images. Quantum Neural Networks is an extension of quantum computing that does well in the analysis of high-dimensional imaging data, like radiology. Such algorithms are much more sensitive to subtle abnormalities such as tumors or de-generative diseases than their classical counterparts(AKHIL & SAIKIRAN, 2024; Boretti, 2024; Khang, 2024).

Furthermore, quantum computing aids in multi-modal imaging analysis, whereby the information from different sources of images is combined, like MRI and ultrasound data, in order to provide a holistic diagnostic result. This gives a more comprehensive view of a patient's health and promotes early detection of diseases as well as planning for treatment. The answer also is to be found in real-time diagnostics with quantum-enhanced imaging technologies. Quantum sensors create precise images at a molecular level, thus ensuring a better visualization of the structures of cells and processes in tissues, which adds significant value in areas as broad as oncology or neuroscience. In a nutshell, quantum computing is revolutionizing the future of precision medicine and medical diagnostics. This happens through predictive analytics based on quantum algorithms and advanced imaging that enables health care practitioners to reach a new threshold of accuracy, efficiency, and personalization in care for patients that lead to better outcomes and more effective treatment.

QUANTUM-ENHANCED AI IN HEALTHCARE

Quantum computing has turned out to be a potent tool for application improvement in AI, especially within the health sector. It takes advantage of the quantum mechanics unique properties, such as superposition, entanglement, and interference, making quantum-enhanced AI the most efficient and accurate way of addressing complex medical issues. Among the other applications, quantum machine learning algorithms and quantum neural networks excel in making diagnoses, better treatment plans, and broadly health care optimization. There is the additional quantum method for treatment pathway optimization-technically termed as highly custom and efficient therapeutic strategies(Boretti, 2024; Khang, 2024; Taherdoost & Madanchian, 2023). Quantum Mechanics utilizes quantum mechanics and algorithms to enhance diagnostics, treatment planning, and healthcare optimization, resulting in improved outcomes, as illustrated in Figure 3.

Figure 3. Quantum-Enhanced AI in healthcare process

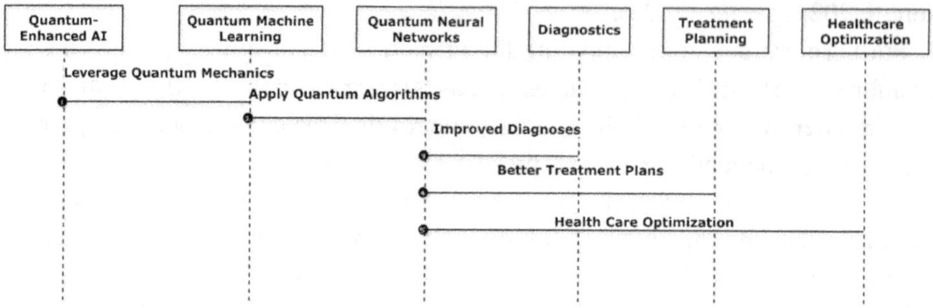

It aims to find solutions to the computational health challenges by bringing the capabilities of quantum computing with machine learning methodologies. It works majorly with the power available in classical computers. However, it faces extreme limitations while carrying out the processes of large, high-dimensional data. Quantum machine learning can perform such tasks faster and efficiently because it takes advantage of all the intrinsic parallel processing abilities of its systems.

QML algorithms rely on quantum computing to advance pattern recognition, anomaly detection, and predictive modeling - critical in applications such as disease diagnosis, drug discovery, and patient management. For example, in medical imaging, quantum-enhanced algorithms can analyze complex radiological data with a degree of accuracy unattainable by any classical method. QNNs are particularly well suited to noisy datasets or sparse representations, which is very prevalent in healthcare. This aids earlier diagnosis and, thus, earlier interventions like treatment for cancer or neurodegenerative diseases.

Apart from improving the predictability of medication based on different outcomes, the optimisation of predictive analytics is achievable in quantum machine learning. Quantum algorithms like the Variational Quantum Classifiers enhance the accuracy of classified medical data and make clinician's decision-making more efficient by making them better-informed. This decrease in trial and error will reduce trial and error related data-driven insights about the disease development, treatment effectiveness, or response to therapies of patients.

Quantum Neural Networks for Medicine

Quantum Neural Networks (QNNs) are a quantum leap into the application of quantum computing into healthcare. They are claimed to process and learn from complex, high-dimensional medical data, namely genomic sequences, electronic health records, and multi-modal imaging data. QNNs actually encode information in quantum states in order to be more beneficial in the efficient management of large-scale data(Henry, 2024; How & Cheah, 2023; Tyagi et al., 2025).

Some areas that QNNs will dominate with medical applications are creating custom treatment plans and precision medicine. For instance, for instance, based on genomic data evaluation that may uncover the existence of biomarkers causing disease or genetic variation related to response of a drug using QNN. QNNs have made it possible to understand the interaction of molecules, which is very essential in drug development; hence, drug discovery and development are faster and efficient. Quantum-enhanced neural networks are also excellent in medical diagnostics because they enhance real-time pattern recognition and feature extraction. For example, they can detect minute abnormalities in medical images, such as MRI scans or ECG data, that might be missed by classical algorithms. This is priceless for early disease detection and precision-based therapies. Besides this, QNNs enhance the resilience of predictive models by including quantum-based understandings within the machine learning architectures. The same makes it possible for healthcare practitioners to come up with highly customized decisions that are cognizant of various factors like patient history, genetic predispositions, and environmental influences in the treatment pathways.

Optimisation in Treatment Paths

Optimized pathways to treatment is perhaps the most persuasive argument of quantum-enhanced AI in health care. Quantum optimization algorithms can effectively handle extremely large search spaces that define the best paths of treatment for a patient. This is essential in making personalized approaches to health care, as many variables can be considered at the same time-disease severity, comorbidities, and specific response to therapy(Boopathi et al., 2021; Boopathi & Khang, 2023; Rebecca et al., 2024).

Methods of quantum optimization, such as Quantum Annealing and Variational Quantum Optimization, are introduced to be efficient tools more potent than classical algorithms for solving some complex, multi-objective optimization problems. Such technologies allow healthcare decision-makers to decompose complex, complex-related decision-making tasks in healthcare processes, which results in a significant reduction of the time needed for obtaining the ultimate treatment plans. In oncology, quantum optimization will enable researchers and clinicians to predict the most efficient chemotherapeutic agent and radiation-surgery combinations in maximizing the efficiency of patient results with minimum risk of adverse effects. Moreover, quantum optimization allows healthcare systems to dynamically adapt to changing patient conditions, ensuring that treatment pathways evolve based on real-time data. This adaptability is crucial in managing chronic diseases, managing clinical trials, and addressing rare or complex medical conditions that require highly individualized approaches.

Quantum-enhanced AI will transform healthcare because it will arm tools which will complement the traditional ML and classical computing systems. Quantum Machine Learning algorithms as well as Quantum Neural Networks are powering breakthroughs in diagnostics, drug development, and treatment optimization. With this capability to handle large datasets with complexity, generating insights at precision levels that cannot be obtained using classical methods, quantum technologies are ready to reshape the future of health care through more personalized adaptive and effective care for the patient.

CHALLENGES AND LIMITATIONS

Quantum-enhanced AI holds great potential in healthcare, though several challenges and limitations present themselves to be overcome if the benefits are to be fully reaped. This is the case with hardware constraints and the complexity of integration that exists as well as in the lack of security of personal data and privacy(Kavitha et al., 2025). All these require technological advancement as well as proper framework for regulations and ethics. Figure 4 outlines the challenges and limitations of quantum-enhanced AI in healthcare.

Figure 4. Challenges and limitations of quantum-enhanced AI in healthcare

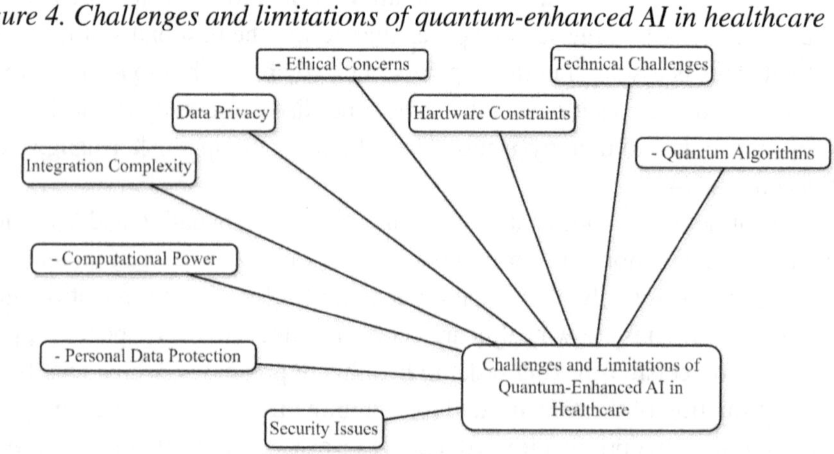

Hardware and Algorithmic Barriers

The major challenges in quantum-enhanced AI for healthcare lie in the limitation of available quantum hardware and appropriate algorithms. Quantum computing is still an infant discipline; the currently available quantum systems are expensive, very specialized, and not scalable to widespread use. Quantum computers are noisy and prone to decoherence, which leads to errors and loss of quantum coherence during computations, making them inaccurate and unreliable. This is not easy to achieve stable and robust outcomes, especially in complex applications of medicine requiring high accuracy.

The quantum algorithms specific to health care are still under development. In the traditional machine learning world, there are well-understood techniques regarding data preprocessing, feature extraction, and model training that are not available directly in quantum computing frameworks. The challenge is on how to create quantum algorithms that can efficiently process these large-scale, multidimensional datasets found in healthcare. Thus, researchers and practitioners need to develop new methods to optimize quantum algorithms for specific medical tasks that require enormous computational resources and time.

Integration into Existing Healthcare Systems

The integration of quantum technologies within existing healthcare systems represents the second significant barrier in implementing quantum-enhanced AI for healthcare. Most healthcare institutions were built upon classical computing infrastructures that rely on data management systems, decision-making processes, and frameworks concerning regulatory compliance. Hence, integration with these systems involving quantum technologies requires very thoughtful considerations about interoperability and compatibility, as well as adapting the workflows for them to incorporate quantum computing capacities(AKHIL & SAIKIRAN, 2024; Garodia, n.d.; Khang, 2024).

Additionally, the multiplicity of healthcare workflows calls for a range of players such as patients, clinicians, researchers, and managers, which will make easy integration of quantum solutions challenging. Implementation of quantum computing based solutions will also necessitate employee retraining, redesigns of user interfaces, new standards for the handling of quantum data. The effort should be aimed at effectiveness, user-friendliness, and accessibility to achieve practical applications of quantum-enhanced AI in health care settings.

The journey towards incorporating quantum enhanced AI in healthcare is riddled with technical, infrastructural, and ethical challenges. These could be overcome only through sustained research in quantum computing, solid algorithms, and secure frameworks for data handling. Improving hardware limitations, the ease of integration with currently existing systems, and preserving data privacy will be necessary to make full use of quantum technology to transform health care. With these advancements, quantum-enhanced AI could change the face of personalized medicine, diagnostics, and treatment optimization for the future.

ETHICAL AND REGULATORY CONSIDERATIONS

As much as incorporating quantum-enhanced AI is bringing a multitude of challenging ethical and regulatory questions before healthcare, this has to be kept in check in order that these advanced technologies can really function responsibly and effectively. As quantum computing continues developing, addressing inequity in healthcare, ethical practices, and broad policies guiding quantum integration become the basic steps toward creating trust and equity in the application and compliance of quantum technologies with existing medical applications(Kavitha et al., 2025; Tyagi et al., 2025).

Address Healthcare Inequities

One of the major ethical issues related to quantum-enhanced AI in healthcare is that it may worsen existing healthcare inequities. While such technologies promise to enhance diagnostics, personalize treatment, and thus improve patient outcomes, they must be made accessible and deployed equitably across all demographics. Quantum computing and AI solutions should be designed to avoid biases that would disproportionately affect vulnerable populations, such as minority groups, those with lower socioeconomic status, or those in underserved regions(Malathi et al., 2024; Mohanraj et al., 2024; Upadhyaya et al., 2024).

For instance, quantum algorithms designed for medical imaging or genomics have to ensure that the data they process reflect diverse populations in order not to present skewed results, which may end up misdiagnosing a particular group or ineffective treatments for them. Ethical considerations thus demand that quantum technologies integrate fairness and inclusivity in their design and implementation so that there can be equal access to superior healthcare solutions.

Ensuring Ethical Use of Quantum Technologies

Such technology use may be ensured ethical by a balance between enormous computational capability of quantum systems and needs to respect patients' autonomy, privacy, and rights to informed consent. Quantum-enriched AI can therefore produce insights in sensitive data, which could open up possibilities for data governance accountability in case they are misused. Every stage of dealing with data that is collected or processed and saved must be taken care of by ethical guidelines. Moreover, transparency in developing and deploying quantum solutions will be of utmost importance. Healthcare providers, patients, and researchers need to know how these quantum systems work, what data they process, and by which criteria decisions are taken. Ongoing education and communication would be necessary in order to build trust and avoid potential negative consequences from algorithmic biases or adverse decisions impacting patient care.

The integration of quantum-enhanced AI into healthcare should be done carefully and with thoughtful caution, such that ethical principles, fairness, and accountability are central. Reducing healthcare inequities, ensuring an ethical use, and a detailed policy framework will be essential in the realisation of the full potential that quantum technologies can bring but maintain trust and compliance in their use. As developments in quantum computing progress further, the ethical and regulatory considerations presented here will build a foundation for responsible innovations in healthcare.

EMERGING TRENDS AND FUTURE DIRECTIONS

The field of quantum-enhanced AI in healthcare is advancing faster as a result of developments in quantum hardware, software, and collaboration across disciplines. Quantum technology has the potential to evolve with time and is soon anticipated to change the means by which medical researches are conducted, diagnostics are conducted, and treatment is practiced. Current emerging trends point out the integration of hybrid quantum-classical computing, fostering interdisciplinary research in collaboration with real-world healthcare through advancement in quantum(Anbazhagu et al., 2025; Kavitha et al., 2025; Yingngam & Khang, 2024). Figure 5 outlines the current trends and future directions in the field of quantum-enhanced AI in healthcare.

Figure 5. Emerging trends and future directions in quantum-enhanced AI in healthcare

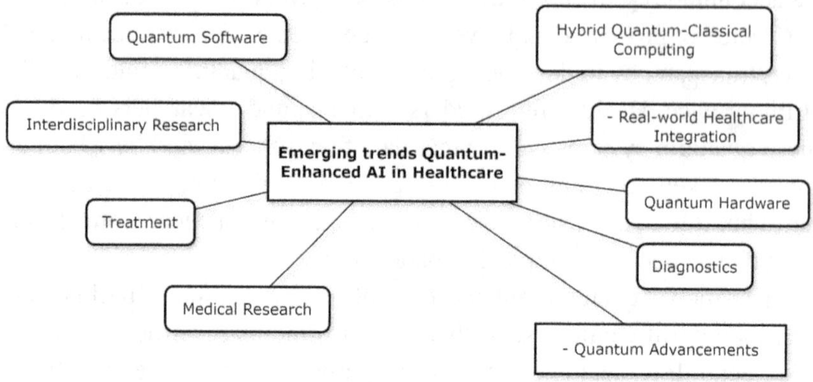

Advances in Quantum Hardware and Software

The most significant driver of quantum-enhanced AI is the continuous improvement of quantum hardware and software capabilities. Quantum computing systems, including improved qubit stability, reduced noise, and increased error correction rates, are increasing the reliability and scalability of quantum applications. Hardware is improving the complexity that can be handled by quantum systems on healthcare datasets, thereby allowing for breakthroughs in drug discovery, precision medicine, and genetic research. While there's quantum software development to provide algorithms that are tailor-made to the health sector, optimization algorithms that are fine-tuned with an aim to maximize the effectiveness and accuracy in deriving meaningful insights from high volumes of medical data is made with quantum machine learning models, and quantum neural networks. In this way, quantum enhancements pave the road toward more beneficial solution design in various domains in health care.

Hybrid Quantum-Classical Computing in Medicine

Hybrid quantum-classical computing is coming as one of the promising approaches toward solution for the computational challenges in healthcare. Researchers are now taping into the strengths of quantum and classical computing resources in order to solve highly complex medical problems more effectively. Quantum systems handle specific tasks like quantum optimization and simulation that are highly parallelizable, whereas all broader data processing and decision-making processes are managed by the computers. This approach in medicine is also applied to various fields of drug discovery areas where quantum systems have been used in order to model molecular interactions as well as identify some promising treatment candidates, but data handling is to be achieved through classical systems for a patient-specific personalization of treatments. Hybrid quantum-classical systems are also proving useful in making medical imaging better, where some quantum capabilities are applied to make image analysis and diagnosis better and classical computing facilitates integration with existing healthcare infrastructures.

Interdisciplinary Research and Collaboration

Interdisciplinary research will form the backbone of future quantum-enhanced AI in healthcare. It is only through contributions from quantum physicists, computer scientists, medical professionals, bioinformaticians, and data scientists working together that the theoretical and practical aspects of healthcare applications can be addressed. A collaborative approach ensures that quantum technologies are not only scientifically sound but also relevant to the real-world challenges clinicians and patients face(Kushwah et al., 2024; Subha et al., 2023).

This ecosystem for quantum research has been enabled by the thriving collaborations between academia, industry, and healthcare institutions, leading to the development of solution-focused approaches to meet specific needs in healthcare, such as better patient outcomes with predictive analytics, optimizing treatment plans, and improving patient engagement using quantum-enhanced decision-making systems. New emerging trends in quantum-enhanced AI will stage transformative steps in healthcare. Advancements in quantum hardware and software, as well as hybrid quantum-classical computing adoption, will unlock new possibilities to tackle challenging medical problems. Interdisciplinary research and collaboration must also be encouraged to innovate toward bridging the gap between quantum science and practical applications in healthcare. With the continuous evolution of these trends, quantum-enhanced AI is going to revolutionize medicine and bring a future with more personal, precise, and effective health solutions.

CASE STUDIES AND REAL-WORLD APPLICATIONS

Quantum computing is going on to make huge advancements in oncology research and to allow new possibilities to understand the problems related to complex cancers and advance further treatment strategies. It makes quantum computers beneficially tackle large amounts of data through high computational efficiency in areas such as oncology where rapid analysis of genetic information, tumor behavior, and treatment responses are vital in personalized medicine and precision oncology(Anbazhagu et al., 2025; Prabha, 2024).

Application in Genomic Analysis and Drug Discovery

The most promising application of quantum computing in oncology is genomic analysis. Cancer genomics refers to the study of mutations, gene expressions, and molecular pathways that lead to tumor development and progression. Quantum algorithms, such as quantum variational methods and optimization techniques, have the ability to analyze such complicated datasets so that they are able to identify potential biomarkers and novel drug candidates. Quantum computing accelerates the process by checking hundreds of thousands of combinations of genetic data and finding targeted therapeutic approaches that may take even more time for a classical system to process.

Furthermore, quantum-enhanced simulations allow for the modeling of the behavior of drug molecules at the quantum level, thus improving the precision in predicting drug efficacy and side effects. Quantum algorithms help researchers explore the interactions between different therapies and cancer cells at an unprecedented scale to optimize treatment regimens and reduce the time needed for clinical trials. Quantum computing, therefore is enabled to make progress in precision oncology in treatment planning. Quantum-enhanced AI allows considering a vast clinical dataset, running from patient history to the predispositions of genetic roots and responses to various types of treatments. In doing so, more accurate models for the prediction of how cancer progresses and responds to treatments could be used to enable oncologists to deliver data-driven decisions for individual patients.

More interesting, however, is the employment of quantum optimization algorithms that can optimize complex decision-making processes during the treatment pathways. From simulation of different treatment situations and their consequences, one gets to see how it helps oncologists devise improved and more individualized strategies of care for the optimal response among many types of cancer.

CONCLUSION

Quantum computing represents a revolutionary breakthrough in its ability to reshape boundaries for artificial intelligence and medicine. Through the power of quantum mechanics, it promises capabilities in computation beyond all that has been thought to be possible in resolving complex issues facing modern health. This chapter has demonstrated some of the varied applications of quantum computing in drug discovery, genomics, precision medicine, and medical imaging and has shown the power of transformation in the realm of patient care and innovative research. The interaction between quantum computing and AI could allow healthcare professionals and scientists to analyze giant datasets rapidly and accurately with unprecedented capability, which paves way for breakthroughs in diagnoses, treatments, and even prevention.

Quantum computing in healthcare is still at its infancy, despite all the promise. Some of the key challenges include hardware scalability, algorithm development, and ethical considerations. The only way to tackle these barriers is by incorporating multiple disciplines, including technologists, medical professionals, and policymakers. Collaboration is important in the development of robust quantum systems, security of data, and access to these advancements. More importantly, careful ethical oversight must be exercised to prevent the potential disparities and misuse of quantum technologies in healthcare.

The future promises that quantum computing, allied with AI, will create a paradigm shift in medicine, with a focus on personalized care, optimized treatment, and improved global health outcomes. With the evolution of technology and increased adoption, the synergy between quantum computing and AI will open new frontiers, change healthcare delivery, and redraw the future of medicine. Embracing these innovations responsibly will ensure a healthier, more efficient, and equitable healthcare system for all generations.

REFERENCES

Ahmadi, A. (2023). Quantum Computing and Artificial Intelligence: The Synergy of Two Revolutionary Technologies. *Asian Journal of Electrical Sciences*, 12(2), 15–27. DOI: 10.51983/ajes-2023.12.2.4118

Anbazhagu, U., Priyadharshini, K., Deepajothi, S., Haripriya, M., & Banu, E. A. (2025). Quantum Computing in Healthcare Using AI-Driven Medical Technologies. In *Modern SuperHyperSoft Computing Trends in Science and Technology* (pp. 367–398). IGI Global Scientific Publishing.

Arya, A., Devadas, M. S., Lakshmi, T. H., Yogeesh, N., & Maaliw, R. R.III (2024). Quantum-Inspired Optimization in AI for Healthcare Networks. In *Quantum Networks and Their Applications in AI* (pp. 197–213). IGI Global. DOI: 10.4018/979-8-3693-5832-0.ch013

Boopathi, S. (2023). Deep Learning Techniques Applied for Automatic Sentence Generation. In *Promoting Diversity, Equity, and Inclusion in Language Learning Environments* (pp. 255–273). IGI Global. DOI: 10.4018/978-1-6684-3632-5.ch016

Boopathi, S., Gavaskar, T., Dogga, A. D., Mahendran, R. K., Kumar, A., Kathiresan, G., N., V., Ganesan, M., Ishwarya, K. R., Ramana, G. V., & others. (2021, August 4). *Emergency medicine delivery transportation using unmanned aerial vehicle (Patent Grant).*

Boopathi, S., & Khang, A. (2023). AI-Integrated Technology for a Secure and Ethical Healthcare Ecosystem. In *AI and IoT-Based Technologies for Precision Medicine* (pp. 36–59). IGI Global. DOI: 10.4018/979-8-3693-0876-9.ch003

Boretti, A. (2024). Technical, economic, and societal risks in the progress of artificial intelligence driven quantum technologies. *Discover Artificial Intelligence*, 4(1), 67. DOI: 10.1007/s44163-024-00171-y

Garodia, A. (n.d.). *Transforming Healthcare and Pharmaceutical Operations through AI-Based Automation Solutions.*

Goswami, S., & Sharma, S. (2024). Artificial Intelligence, Quantum Computing and Cloud Computing Enabled Personalized Medicine in Next Generation Sequencing Bioinformatics. *2024 IEEE International Conference on Interdisciplinary Approaches in Technology and Management for Social Innovation (IATMSI), 2*, 1–5. DOI: 10.1109/IATMSI60426.2024.10502533

Hema, N., Krishnamoorthy, N., Chavan, S. M., Kumar, N., Sabarimuthu, M., & Boopathi, S. (2023). A Study on an Internet of Things (IoT)-Enabled Smart Solar Grid System. In *Handbook of Research on Deep Learning Techniques for Cloud-Based Industrial IoT* (pp. 290–308). IGI Global. DOI: 10.4018/978-1-6684-8098-4.ch017

Henry, E. (2024). *Integrating Quantum Model Computing With Machine Learning Quantum Algorithms For Accelerating Ai Model Training*.

How, M.-L., & Cheah, S.-M. (2023). Business Renaissance: Opportunities and challenges at the dawn of the Quantum Computing Era. *Businesses*, 3(4), 585–605. DOI: 10.3390/businesses3040036

Kavitha, K., Kamalakumari, J., Krishna, G., Najma, U., & Rama, S. (2025). AI and Quantum Computing for Accelerating Drug Discovery and Precision Medicine. In *Modern SuperHyperSoft Computing Trends in Science and Technology* (pp. 33–60). IGI Global Scientific Publishing.

Khang, A. (2024). *AI-Driven Innovations in Digital Healthcare: Emerging Trends, Challenges, and Applications: Emerging Trends, Challenges, and Applications*.

Kushwah, J. S., Gupta, M., Shrivastava, S., Saxena, N., Saini, R., & Boopathi, S. (2024). Psychological Impacts, Prevention Strategies, and Intervention Approaches Across Age Groups: Unmasking Cyberbullying. In *Change Dynamics in Healthcare, Technological Innovations, and Complex Scenarios* (pp. 89–109). IGI Global.

Malathi, J., Kusha, K., Isaac, S., Ramesh, A., Rajendiran, M., & Boopathi, S. (2024). IoT-Enabled Remote Patient Monitoring for Chronic Disease Management and Cost Savings: Transforming Healthcare. In *Advances in Explainable AI Applications for Smart Cities* (pp. 371–388). IGI Global.

Mohanraj, G., Krishna, K. S., Lakshmi, B. S., Vijayalakshmi, A., Pramila, P. V., & Boopathi, S. (2024). Optimizing Trust and Security in Healthcare 4.0: Human Factors in Lightweight Secured IoMT Ecosystems. In *Lightweight Digital Trust Architectures in the Internet of Medical Things (IoMT)* (pp. 52–72). IGI Global. DOI: 10.4018/979-8-3693-2109-6.ch004

Olorunsogo, T., Jacks, B. S., & Ajala, O. A. (2024). Leveraging quantum computing for inclusive and responsible AI development: A conceptual and review framework. *Computer Science & IT Research Journal*, 5(3), 671–680. DOI: 10.51594/csitrj.v5i3.927

Prabha, C. (2024). Future Perspective and Emerging Trends in Computational Intelligence. *Intelligent Data Analytics for Bioinformatics and Biomedical Systems*, 381–396.

Pramila, P., Amudha, S., Saravanan, T., Sankar, S. R., Poongothai, E., & Boopathi, S. (2023). Design and Development of Robots for Medical Assistance: An Architectural Approach. In *Contemporary Applications of Data Fusion for Advanced Healthcare Informatics* (pp. 260–282). IGI Global.

Ramudu, K., Mohan, V. M., Jyothirmai, D., Prasad, D., Agrawal, R., & Boopathi, S. (2023). Machine Learning and Artificial Intelligence in Disease Prediction: Applications, Challenges, Limitations, Case Studies, and Future Directions. In *Contemporary Applications of Data Fusion for Advanced Healthcare Informatics* (pp. 297–318). IGI Global.

Rayhan, A., & Rayhan, S. (2023). *Quantum Computing and AI: A Quantum Leap in Intelligence.*

Rebecca, B., Kumar, K. P. M., Padmini, S., Srivastava, B. K., Halder, S., & Boopathi, S. (2024). Convergence of Data Science-AI-Green Chemistry-Affordable Medicine: Transforming Drug Discovery. In *Handbook of Research on AI and ML for Intelligent Machines and Systems* (pp. 348–373). IGI Global.

Satav, S. D., Hasan, D. S., Pitchai, R., Mohanaprakash, T., Sultanuddin, S., & Boopathi, S. (2023). Next generation of internet of things (ngiot) in healthcare systems. In *Sustainable Science and Intelligent Technologies for Societal Development* (pp. 307–330). IGI Global.

Sengeni, D., Padmapriya, G., Imambi, S. S., Suganthi, D., Suri, A., & Boopathi, S. (2023). Biomedical waste handling method using artificial intelligence techniques. In *Handbook of Research on Safe Disposal Methods of Municipal Solid Wastes for a Sustainable Environment* (pp. 306–323). IGI Global. DOI: 10.4018/978-1-6684-8117-2.ch022

Subha, S., Inbamalar, T., Komala, C., Suresh, L. R., Boopathi, S., & Alaskar, K. (2023). A Remote Health Care Monitoring system using internet of medical things (IoMT). *IEEE Explore*, 1–6.

Taherdoost, H., & Madanchian, M. (2023). AI Advancements: Comparison of Innovative Techniques. *AI*, 5(1), 38–54. DOI: 10.3390/ai5010003

Tripathi, S. M., Upadhyay, H., & Soni, J. (2024). Advanced Cardiovascular Health in a Quantum AI-driven Healthcare Framework. *Authorea Preprints*. DOI: 10.36227/techrxiv.171207460.05729698/v1

Tyagi, S., Pathak, S., Raj, V. H., Laxminarayanamma, K., Singh, N., & Dhanraj, J. A. (2025). Quantum Network Applications in AI-Driven Risk Management. In *Multidisciplinary Applications of AI and Quantum Networking* (pp. 289–308). IGI Global.

Upadhyaya, A. N., Saqib, A., Devi, J. V., Rallapalli, S., Sudha, S., & Boopathi, S. (2024). Implementation of the Internet of Things (IoT) in Remote Healthcare. In *Advances in Medical Technologies and Clinical Practice* (pp. 104–124). IGI Global. DOI: 10.4018/979-8-3693-1934-5.ch006

Veeranjaneyulu, R., Boopathi, S., Narasimharao, J., Gupta, K. K., Reddy, R. V. K., & Ambika, R. (2023). Identification of Heart Diseases using Novel Machine Learning Method. *IEEE- Explore*, 1–6.

Venkateswaran, N., Vidhya, R., Naik, D. A., Raj, T. M., Munjal, N., & Boopathi, S. (2023). Study on Sentence and Question Formation Using Deep Learning Techniques. In *Digital Natives as a Disruptive Force in Asian Businesses and Societies* (pp. 252–273). IGI Global. DOI: 10.4018/978-1-6684-6782-4.ch015

Yingngam, B., & Khang, A. (2024). Quantum Computing in Drug Discovery. In *The Quantum Evolution* (pp. 242–275). CRC Press. DOI: 10.1201/9781032642079-11

Chapter 4
Real-World Applications of Quantum-Enhanced Machine Learning Solutions

Koduri Sreelakshmi
Department of Electronics and Communication Engineering, Baba Institute of Technology And Sciences, Visakhapatnam, India

Vishal V. Rathi
Department of Electronics and Telecommunication Engineering, Sipna College of Engineering and Technology, Amravati, India

K. Shanthi
https://orcid.org/0009-0007-1480-085X
Department of Computer Science, Shri Krishnaswamy College for Women, Chennai, India

Shikalgar Niyaj Dilavar
Department of Automation and Robotics, Dr. D.Y. Patil Institute of Technology, Pune, India

S. Logeswaran
Department of Civil Engineering, KPR Institute of Engineering and Technology, Coimbatore, India

B. Subhi
https://orcid.org/0009-0000-3045-3834
KCR Institute of Engineering and Technology, Coimbatore, India

ABSTRACT

QML is the quantum machine learning, a new approach to explore the potential of quantum computation allowing us to discover solutions that otherwise would be hard for a classical computer to find. A variety of applied QML areas will be highlighted in the following chapter such as optimization problems NLP, drug discovery. Some foundations of quantum- superposition and entanglement- are designed to provide

DOI: 10.4018/979-8-3693-6225-9.ch004

more efficient approach- towards higher fidelity in all data driven pipelines. This chapter gives some practical use cases for integration of quantum algorithms into pipelines of machine learning as well as some main challenges (i.e., regarding noise, scalability and algorithm selection) concerning it. Hybrid quantum-classical schemes are thought as the key for progress towards practicality on currently available noisy intermediate-scale quantum hardware. In this chapter, we will address QML viewpoints of the operational strategy and future, including potential QML disruptive effects and the future adoption insights of QML.

INTRODUCTION

Quantum-enhanced machine learning (QML) is an emerging new frontier of science and engineering at the intersection of quantum computing and machine learning, with the transformative potential to solve problems that cannot or would not be solved using classical computation. As Machine learning is an ever-evolving discipline, realization of quantum computing constructs yield a novel prospects for addressing scalability, computational time efficiency and treatment of high-dimensional data. Chapter 6 - Beyond QML - the Applications This chapter covers QML in application domains with emphasis on real-world QML implementations and the applications they enable across optimization, natural language process and drug discovery (Bhatta & Dang, 2024).

There are a number of applications in the field of machine learning that quickly become substantially computationally demanding, and such tasks may put classical systems on the boundaries of their capabilities. For instance, it can take months or even years to execute a deep learning model on any of these immense datasets or tackle intricate optimization problems. With notions such as superposition, entanglement, and quantum interference, quantum computing offers a remarkable paradigm where we can do calculations in a way that is fundamentally distinct. Unlike classic systems, whereas information is encoded in binary bits (0 and 1) the information encoded in quantum computers consist on quantum bits or qubits (qbits), capable of assume multiple ammount of quantum states at the same time. This allows quantum systems to sample from a much larger area of the solution space, and more efficiently, potentially leading to faster computations and accelerated machine learning algorithms (Goto et al., 2021).

Recent progress for noisy intermediate-scale quantum (NISQ) devices has also opened up pathways for the development of quantum machine learning (QML). Though still small scale and error-prone, NISQ devices represent a platform to test and develop quantum algorithms. One of the major approaches has been hybrid quantum-classical methods, which are leveraging the advantages of classical computation combined with the special capabilities provided by quantum systems. Various examples of such variational quantum algorithms (VQAs), including the Quantum Approximate Optimization Algorithm (QAOA) and the Variational Quantum Eigensolver (VQE), present themselves as promising schemes for optimization and training of machine learning models. These kinds of algorithms leverage quantum systems to compute, and classical one for something like parameter updates which make these types of algorithms more dependent upon the available hardware (Sharma, 2020).

This makes optimization a particularly promising domain for the practical implementation of QMLs. In logistics, finance and energy optimisation it is usually about finding one of the possible optimal solutions in a pool of possible solutions. In general, classical algorithms cannot solve the problem that well, especially when the data are large and even complicated. Quantum algorithms, such as QAOA, approach the solution space to rapidly search potential solutions. In fact, the quantum optimisation approach is also used in the field of finances, where it is generally applied to portfolio optimisation problem for maximisation of returns with minimisation of risk. To deal with the logistics, in particular, route optimizations, supply chain management and scheduling problems have demonstrated tremendous efficiency potentials based on the improved quantum (Mandadapu, 2024).

That leaves a lot of room for QML to be useful to Natural Language Processing. [1] NLP tasks such as text classification, sentiment analysis, and machine translation all require the analysis of large and messy data sets that have complex patterns and structures. The quantum system can potentially perform better in NLP tasks via promoting that more efficient coding of the data and extraction of features given its ability to process high dimensional data spaces. However, NLP on Quantum Computers remains an area still in its infancy, and already some works have emerged on how quantum algorithms could potentially augment these approaches, such as quantum-enhanced embeddings and clustering (Satuluri & Ponnusamy, 2021).

Quantum-enhanced machine learning first gained widespread attention in health care, with the promise to transform drug discovery and personalized medicine. This means that a huge search is conducted across chemical spaces to find those molecules that will show desired characteristics. Quantum annealing and VQE are examples of quantum algorithms. These techniques are less capable of reproducing molecular structures and their interactions compared with the traditional methods and with much high precision and with efficiency. In this context, such approaches accelerate drug discovery, consequently becoming cheaper allowing for an easier possibility of a candidate possibly having a pretty good chance of fulfilling the requirements of an effective hypothesis. Additionally, QML is being explored in genomics applications. This includes predicting gene fusions and interpreting complex biological networks and serves as a stepping stone to advance into more precise medicine (Potter & Stilinski, 2024).

While QML holds huge promise, it is incredibly challenging to get it to be generally applicable. Few-shot prompts cannot generate larger text without damaging the former context because present quantum systems are inherently noisy and unstable, which limits the reliability and scalability of these systems. Error correction is also an important domain of practice since effects due to noise will dominate the accuracy of quantum computation. This implies that quantum algorithms by and large must be embedded into the general machine learning pipeline, needing an intersection of quantum computing and machine learning knowledge an obstacle to numerous practitioners (Gouveia & Correia, 2020a).

Scalability is another pressing challenge. While NISQ devices serve a proof-of-principle for investigation, they suffer from a few qubits and susceptibility to errors; making it possible that only trivial problems of very low complexity could be recognized. More specifically, in a position to fully capture the power of QML, the future of quantum hardware must await. This also includes, for example, work toward fault-tolerant quantum computers. These two approaches (not purely quantum but utilize quantum in a hybrid way) take the middle ground between full-fledged (and expensive) systems and flexibility for researchers/industries to apply this within the circumstances which are already present (Gouveia & Correia, 2020b).

Such major breakthroughs are likely in day-to-day applications made possible by the amalgamation of artificial intelligence (AI) with quantum machine learning (QML). Quantum algorithms and optimization of quantum hardware through AI methods Since machine learning and AI, in general, rely heavily on the training of models or the performance of inference, the use of quantum computing for faster training and inference for AI models is enormous. This mutually advantageous synergy has potential for alleviating some of the most demanding computational challenges in areas like climate simulations, financial predictions, and autonomous system (Melnikov et al., 2023).

Thus, through interactions between quantum systems and classical data structures, quantum-enhanced machine learning is paving the way to tackle problems that seemed unsolvable before. QML, as an application of quantum machine learning takes advantages of unique features of quantum systems enabling more effective data processing, optimization and pattern recognition opening new possibilities in this field within different industries(Maheswari et al., 2023; Prasad et al., 2024). This chapter will create a full understanding of how QML can be used in practice, based on what we already know about them, and help to put forward ideas for opportunities and challenges in this rapidly evolving discipline (Chen et al., 2024). Specifically, the combination of quantum technology with machine learning could bring forth a new height of computation that fundamentally shifts our current reality, ushering in a new frontier of discovery and innovation.

Objectives

Chapter aims to explore practical applications of quantum-enhanced machine learning (QML) for optimization techniques, natural language processing and drug discovery. It aims to reduce the gap between theory and practical implementation by considering hybrid quantum-classical schemes aimed to solve the key problems of scalability and noise, and by responding to recent trends. But the last part of the chapter will ensure that those reading know what possible transformations QML are definitely going to bring, so readers still have a little bit of knowledge in their pocket about its applications, its limitations, and what lies into the future.

BACKGROUND: QUANTUM COMPUTING

Quantum computing is a paradigm-shifted approach to information, making use of the principles of quantum mechanics to allow for functionalities of computation far beyond anything seen in classical systems. In a nutshell, quantum computing takes advantage of superposition and entanglement by enabling quantum bits (qubits) to carry out more than one computation at once. This module is concerned with the core idea of quantum mechanics, quantum gates and circuits, however, much more specifically with the creation and employment of noisy intermediate-scale quantum (NISQ) devices(Wang et al., 2022).

Quantum Mechanics Principles: Superposition and Entanglement

Superposition and entanglement form the foundation of quantum computing. Superposition is the mechanism by which a qubit can be in a superposition of the states 0 and 1 simultaneously and cannot be confined to a single one. This enables quantum systems to explore a space that is exponentially larger compared to their classical counterparts. 10 qubits in superposition, for example, a computation device can check 2^10 possible states at a time, or 1,024 states at the same time. Entanglement is what describes the phenomenon where qubits become intertwined in such a way that the state of one qubit instantly influences the state of another, regardless of the distance. [Here] This is a significant aspect of quantum computation, as qubits are able to collaborate to solve intricate problems that involve intricate interdependence in a deeply coordinated manner(Lu et al., 2024).

Quantum Gates and Circuits

Quantum gates and circuits are the working paradigm for quantum computing by manipulating qubits to perform computations. Quantum gates such as the Hadamard, the Pauli-X, the CNOT gate are approximately equivalent to the classical logic gates but at the level of a qubit and using unitary transformations. Surrounding these gates are operations such as superposition state generation, qubit inversion, and entanglement generation. Quantum circuits implement this set of gates in sequences to implement algorithms. A paradigmatic instance of this is the Quantum Fourier Transform (QFT) circuit, which constitutes the base of numerous quantum algorithms, such as Shor's algorithm for integer factorization. Quantum circuits are implemented and run with the problem at hand, the order and pattern of gates dictate the result of the calculation.

Noisy Intermediate-Scale Quantum (NISQ) Devices

NISQ devices are one stage of generation of quantum computers with few qubits, and susceptibility to noise and errors. These devices still have not reached the complete scalability or fault tolerance but help establish an experimental platform for working on quantum algorithms and applications. One of the main features of NISQ devices is that they can run hybrid quantum-classical algorithms, which take advantage of quantum systems for specific tasks but rely on classical systems for error correction and optimization. Though noisy and decohering, NISQ devices already promise solutions to optimization problems, simulation of quantum systems, and the improvement of machine learning workflows. With the advancements in hardware, the information gathered from the NISQ experiments will serve as a launching pad for even more sophisticated quantum systems.

QUANTUM MACHINE LEARNING: AN OVERVIEW

A transdisciplinary research field, quantum machine learning is research investigating the combination machine learning with quantum computing for using the capabilities of quantum mechanics to solve a wide variety of difficult problems. QML, in doing so, leverages quantum principles like superposition, entanglement, and quantum interference for processing data far more efficiently than the classic approach, especially in highly dimensional or computationally intensive tasks(Gujju et al., 2024). The figure 1 depicts the practical applications of Quantum-Enhanced Machine Learning (QML).

Figure 1. Practical applications of quantum-enhanced machine learning (QML)

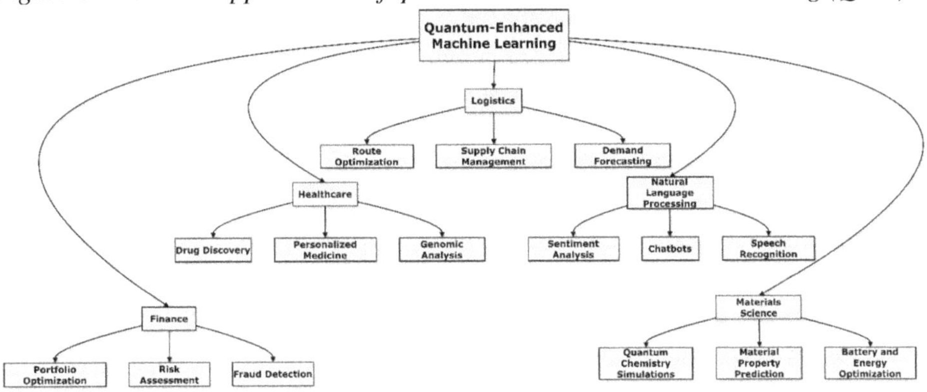

Concepts in QML

Quantum Data: Since the data is in the quantum state, it is represented as qubits, which can hold all the information in a superposition of 0 and 1. For this reason, algorithms in QML can process large amounts of data. Quantum circuits contain QML algorithms in the sense that it will be used as a lego piece and quantum gates would be controlled in an operational mode by executing operations on qubits. Hilbert Spaces: Quantum computations operate in Hilbert spaces, which provide a mathematical description of states in quantum. Measurement: information extracted from a quantum state leads to its being collapsed into a classical state; therefore it is very important to form quantum algorithms in order to keep valuable information after the measurement procedure(Taghandiki, 2024).

Techniques In QML

a) QSVM: Problem-oriented classifying problems are self-adaptive quantum structure using quantum kernel with classical support vector machine solving a computation problem efficiently.
b) Quantum Neural Networks (QNNs): The simulation of the structure of neural networks with quantum circuits will probably be more conducive to better handling of high-dimensional information.
c) Quantum Annealing: This is a technique of solving optimization problems by taking advantage of quantum tunneling to get out of the local minima and reach the global optimum.

d) Hybrid Quantum-Classical Algorithms: They bridge quantum subroutines and classical computation to overcome the existing bottleneck of quantum hardware. Examples include Variational Quantum Eigensolvers (VQE) and Quantum Approximate Optimization Algorithms (QAOA).
e) Quantum Principal Component Analysis (QPCA): Quantum PCA with efficient dimensionality reduction even for the large datasets.

Differences Between Classical and Quantum Machine Learning

Classical ML uses binary data representation and deterministic processing. Quantum ML maps the data to quantum states, which can be processed in parallel and thus can provide more general feature representations. In Classical ML deterministic algorithms are executed by classical computers. Quantum ML exploits probabilistic quantum algorithms that can be used to explore various solutions simultaneously. Classical ML is bottlenecked by resource constraints when working with massive data or a high-dimensional space, whereas quantum ML leverages quantum speedup to potentially give rise to exponential leaps in the optimization and matrix transformations involved(Altmann et al., 2023; Ortolano et al., 2023). Traditional Machine Learning is implemented on silicon-based processors (e.g., CPUs, GPUs) and quantum machine learning uses experimental quantum processors (e.g., superconducting qubits, trapped ions).

QML will revolutionize drug discovery, financial modeling, and AI applications but has its own set of challenges in the form of quantum system error rates and limited qubit counts. Maturation and development of hybrid techniques in quantum hardware will contribute to QML to enrich classical ML and therefore, enable the computational science advances.

PRACTICAL APPLICATIONS OF QML

Optimization Problems in Logistics and Finance

QML has emerged as a highly efficient tool for solving complex optimization problems, especially in logistics and finance, the domains where traditional methods fail at scalability and performance(Hdaib et al., 2024; Karn et al., 2024; Kumar et al., 2021).

Logistics Optimization

Optimization in the field of logistics is the task of processing supply chains, reducing costs, and making the operations more smoothly. Quantum optimization algorithms are truly effective for solving big problems that are computationally difficult (namely, combinatorially hard) tasks, such as vehicle routing, inventory control and shipment distribution from warehouses. QAOA, for instance, has been used to optimize trajectories of delivery cars, by minimizing travel time and thus fuel consumption, using actual traffic information. Traditional optimization methods take a lot of computational resources and time, because they explore all of the possible ways. In contrast, QML is efficient since even though the number of paths is large, it is efficiently processed simultaneously in the convergence process to reach an optimal solution.

QPCA is also used to reduce the dimensionality in logistical data, i.e., patterns of customer's demand and supply chain vulnerabilities. The application of quantum systems to big data analysis can provide richer information than traditional methods for inventory&management, predictive maintenance with positive outlook for supply chain resilience and diminishing risks of operational environment .

Optimization in Finance

Optimization is one of the most important in finance, risk management, portfolio optimization and fraud detection. Quantum algorithms can be used to optimize portfolio management, by efficiently computing optimal asset allocation, as well as handling complex constraints including liquidity and transaction costs. As an example, QSVMs have been able to analyze past financial data in order to forecast changes in stock prices and achieve optimal portfolio performance. Conventional approaches are mostly brute calculations which consume a lot of resources and time. QML is parallelized, and in fact it is possible to solve the problem faster and more efficiently.

Another area in which it has been applied is the portfolio diversification problem. In this, the goal is to maximize return while minimizing risk. Quantum Annealing will probe enormous solution spaces in the search of the optimal set of feasible configurations that can maximize return while minimizing risk. It is exploited for the pricing of derivatives and modeling of complex financial instruments when conventional models cannot be applied due to the non-linearities and the dimensionality of the data.

Benefits and Challenges

The most significant benefit of QML for use in logistics and finance is the capability to process large, complex data sets with sophisticated optimization challenges much quicker than for existing tools used by the classical. Nevertheless, some problems remain with hardware limitations, the error rate of quantum computation, and the requirement for hybrid solutions that smoothly integrate quantum and classical methods. As quantum computing evolves over time, its role would become practical on optimization in logistics and finance, and challenges in real life would be tackled with higher accuracy and efficiency.

Quantum Machine Learning (QML) is showing up as an influential force of change in various areas, with particular impact in Natural Language Processing, Sentiment Analysis, Quantum-accelerated Drug Discovery, and Healthcare. As the unique characteristics of quantum computation, superposition, entanglement and quantum interference, have already been utilized to enhance the usual machine learning techniques, QML attempts to uplift the standard machine learning practices for high-dimensional datasets with enhanced performance and higher accuracy.

Natural Language Processing and Sentiment Analysis

QML has started out to be one of the most promising areas in the basic domain of NLP. Conventional NLP models are primarily based on traditional computing methods for text data processing, and are sometimes incapable of dealing with large amount text data or recognizing the subtle information from complex linguistic structures. Quantum Neural Networks have demonstrated effectiveness in distinguishing subtle emotional expression in textual data, better than the traditional models in sentiment detail extraction(Liu et al., 2021; Van Nieuwenhuizen, 2024). Quantum Machine Learning (QML) is able to process multiple features at once by encoding them in the quantum state of the input information and in this way will enable real-time identification of sentiment with lower computational cost. A such proficiency can be highly useful in customer feedback analysis, social media monitoring, and automated customer service, in which the accurate, timely sentiment extraction plays a key role.

Above and beyond that, quantum-enhanced NLP models are promising features for dealing with ambiguity and context-based language understanding, namely, interpreting idiomatic expression, sarcasm, or even subtle conversational contexts that classical NLP models can hardly treat. Quantum algorithms can combine all possible states of word meaning and build an increasingly expressive feature space that locally allows a model to decode intricate structures in language.

Quantum-Enhanced Drug Discovery and Healthcare

The adoption of QML in drug development and treatment has provided new routes to address a number of the industry's most difficult challenges. The capacity of quantum computing to process large biological datasets, e.g., protein folding simulations and molecular modeling, speeds up drug discovery processes and improves the accuracy of computational biology. Quantum algorithms can simulate molecular interactions at a scale that classical computing cannot efficiently achieve. As an example, Quantum Variational Eigensolvers (QVE) are applicable during the search for potential drugs by calculating the binding energy of pharmacological agents and their target proteins. These calculations have a significant impact on drug development for the fact that the interaction between molecular entities and biological systems has a deep influence on the efficacy and the safety of novel therapeutic agents. Conventional methods of drug discovery are both, time-consuming and resource-intensive, primarily due to the large number of testing and simulation involved. Nonetheless, techniques augmented by quantum computing significantly minimize the iterations needed to refine potential drug candidates, resulting in expedited and more economically viable pharmaceutical development procedures(Gouveia & Correia, 2020a; Melnikov et al., 2023; Potter & Stilinski, 2024).

In the field of health care, quantum algorithms are also used to enhance diagnostic accuracy. Quantum models are able to analyze complex datasets of medical imaging, genomics, and patient records in order to improve disease prediction and enable early detection. Quantum computing excels at tasks such as tumor identification, which involve the joint processing of large amounts of multidimensional data to identify yet subtle patterns that could serve as disease progression markers. Implementation of QML to healthcare system helps physicians and researchers to predict better, customize treatment schemes and control the chronic diseases effectively.

Though the future of QML for NLP, sentiment analysis or healthcare has great promise, there are still several hurdles. To begin with, hardware scalability, error correction, and practically deliverable quantum algorithms with potential to be integrated within classical data processing pipelines is still many steps away. Quantum models, however, are notoriously finetunable and require significant domain-specific expertise for real-world applications. Nevertheless, using the current advancement of quantum computing technology, integration between QML and fields such as natural language processing, health care etc., hold immense potential to solve issues that have otherwise proven intractable with the current great effort, in a significantly more efficient manner. Hybrid methods between quantum algorithms and classical algorithms will be central to these applications and thereby allow these applications to become more accessible and scalable for industrial and scientific purposes.

HYBRID QUANTUM-CLASSICAL ALGORITHMS

Hybrid quantum-classical algorithms such as Variational Quantum Algorithms (VQA) are a significant leap in the usage of quantum computing for tackling intractable-problem solving. These algorithms leverage the advantages of classical computation in conjunction with the quantum specificities of superposition and entanglement to perform tasks that can hardly be performed by a classical system by itself(Karn et al., 2024; Kumar et al., 2021; Sequeira, 2021). The workflow and interaction of hybrid quantum-classical algorithms are depicted in Figure 2.

Figure 2. Workflow and interaction of hybrid quantum-classical algorithms

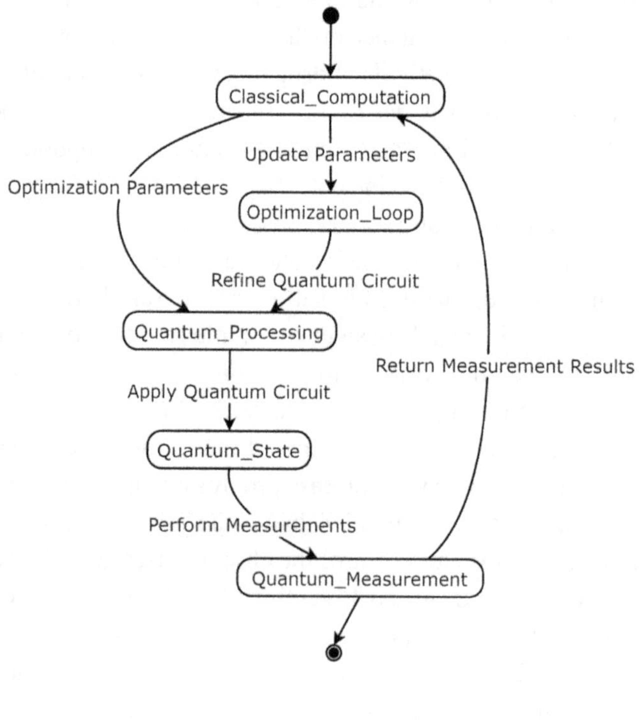

Variational Quantum Algorithms (VQA)

Variational Quantum Algorithms are designed for approximate search of solutions to optimization and learning problems, via the combination of quantum circuits with classical optimization algorithms. The core notion of VQA is that of iteratively learning a quantum circuit where the learned state is optimized to minimize the cost function, using feedback mechanisms with classical components. Accordingly, quantum computers are able to solve elaborate, high-dimensional, computationally demanding optimization problems.

Structure of VQA

Quantum Circuit Design: In VQA a quantum circuit is constructed by chaining quantum gates that contain the possible solutions to a current problem. These circuits are mixed with classical and quantum components, which makes it easy to see, i.e. Parameterization and Optimization: In this methodology, the parameters of the quantum gates are iteratively updated through the classical optimization method. The parameters are adjusted in a way that the output of the quantum circuit is reduced by means of the gradients based on the desired cost function. Measurement and Feedback Mechanism: The quantum system is measured after each iteration. The classical system, given the output it produced, is able to optimise the parameters of the quantum circuit. In this version, the process of iterative adaption goes on until a satisfactory solution is found(Chen et al., 2024).

Applications of VQA Optimization Problems: VQA efficiently solves optimization problems, such as portfolio optimization in finance, balancing risk and return in complex datasets. Quantum Annealing allows the efficient search of all solutions without getting stuck in a local minimum. VQA is used to help select features thanks to calculations of the relative importance of the features and dimensionality reduction for machine learning. The hybrid method of classical data preprocessing and quantum-enhanced calculation of feature extraction is employed in this hybrid approach.

Chemical and Drug Discovery: VQA accelerates drug discovery through faster simulation of interactions at the molecular level as well as the optimization of calculations involving binding energy, meaning quicker development in treatments.

Advantages of VQA

a) Efficiency Improvement: VQA reduces resource demands of classical approaches by exploiting quantum parallelism for challenging problems.
b) Scalability: Quantum circuits grow by increasing both the number of qubits and the complexity of the problems, while classical parts are optimized effectively.
c) Hybrid Flexibility: Through the integration of classical computation, VQA can provide real-time problem-specific fine-tuning and iterative solutions.

Quantum Approximate Optimization Algorithm (QAOA)

Hybrid quantum-classical algorithms combine the strengths of quantum and classical computation to achieve NP-hard optimization tasks. These algorithms are constructed to take advantage of the high dimensional parallelism and the computing power of quantum units, and classical computing on problem definition, error correction, and tuning. One of the most popular hybrid algorithms is the Quantum Approximate Optimization Algorithm (QAOA) and it has been proven to yield good promise in solving combinatorial optimization problems. The Quantum Approximate Optimization Algorithm (QAOA) was proposed in 2014 by Farhi, Goldstone, and Gutmann 2014, as an approach to potentially effeciently solve combinatorial optimisation problems like the travelling salesman problem, graph partitioning, and financial portfolio optimization. QAOA is realized by formulating an arbitrary optimization problem into a quantum circuit, and then the quantum circuit is run with the classical computation iteratively to get better solutions(Goto et al., 2021; Sharma, 2020).

a) Mixer Gates: The goal of these is to produce a superposition of likely solutions, which are, in turn, able to drive a search of the vast solution space.
b) Problem-Specific Unitary Gates: These are parametrized to map the quantum circuit to the encoding for the desired optimization task by adapting the quantum state to the problem constraints.

The classical part of QAOA is activated by selecting the parameters of such quantum operations, and in a process aimed at improving the quality of the solution. Classical computers first calculate the results of intermediate quantum measurements and then iteratively optimize the quantum circuit with the aim to enhance performances. This hybrid method leverages the parallel capacity of quantum to search over all the possible solutions and the classical accuracy in tuning and choosing the best solution.

Advantages of QAOA

a) Flexibility: QAOA can be fit to a specific problem by manipulating the number of quantum gates used, thus allowing a wide range of applications in different fields, ranging from logistics to finance to machine learning.
b) Error Mitigation: In classical control, QAOA is used to ameliorate some aspects of the challenges arising from the noise and errors inherent to quantum hardware by making solutions more robust.

c) Hybrid Nature: Classical and quantum computation combined is represented as an optimization between the parallelism of a quantum and the accuracy of a classical, and producing quality results at limited resource cost is a feature of the presented approach.

Applications and Future Directions

QAOA has already been applied with success to a variety of complex optimization problems. In the field of logistics it enhances route optimization by reducing the needs travelled by vehicles, and in the field of finance it optimizes levels of risk and return of portfolios. As quantum hardware continues to be improved technologically, practical use of QAOA capabilities will expand, leading us to the evolution of more efficient solution to both more complex real world decision making problems.

Recently, however, the focus of the research community has shifted to the further development of QAOA for dynamic and adaptive optimization problems, implementing quantum error correction and designing optimized hybrid systems for applications in the enterprise domain. Future of QAOA continuous innovation has the potential to address some of the most promising optimization problems in industries.

CHALLENGES AND LIMITATIONS

Quantum computing is promising to solve a wide range of problems in different fields such as cryptography, optimization, machine learning, and drug discovery. Nevertheless, the technology has several other technical challenges and limitations, in particular, regarding noise, error handling, scalability, and the necessary resources(Lu et al., 2024; Mandadapu, 2024; Namdeo et al., 2024). Remedying these challenges is critical to achieving the full potential of quantum computing and making it practical for general use. The figure 3 depicts the challenges and their potential solutions.

Figure 3. Challenges and their potential solutions

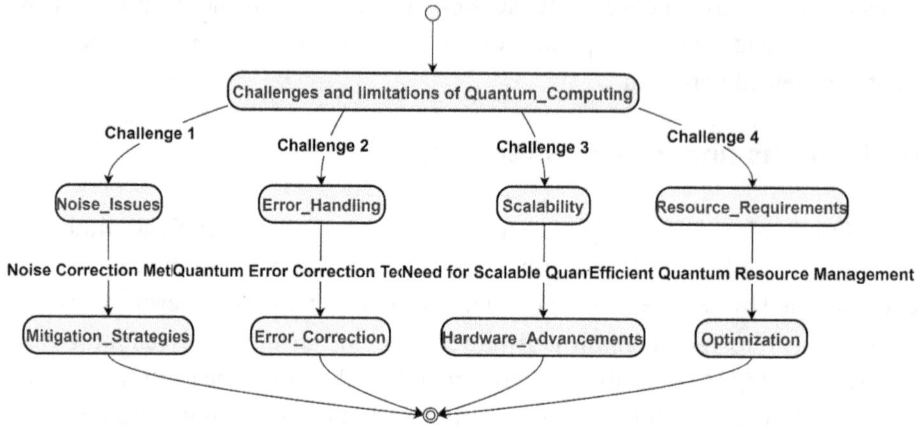

Noise and Error Mitigation in Quantum Systems

Quantum noise and error rates represent one of the most important problems in quantum computing. Quantum systems are very noisy because they are based on fragile quantum states, which are easily interfered with by external noise sources, such as thermal, electromagnetic, and decoherent noise. This, in turn, makes the accuracy, i.e., the number of bits, which is needed for quantum operations, very hard to keep up. Error Mitigation is a key research area. Methods of quantum error correction (QEC) are developed to identify and repair errors accumulated in the quantum computation process. Nevertheless, the process of realization is resource-consuming and needs to be mastered in complex mathematical and engineering concepts. QEC involves encoding information in a way that enables recovery from errors, often through redundancy and the use of additional qubits to store and protect data. As instances, schemes such as the Surface Code and Turbo Codes have been designed with the goal of fabricating high-fidelity quantum computation by repairing single-bit and multi-bit errors, respectively.

Although these breakthroughs have occurred, existing quantum hardware (e.g., superconducting qubits, trapped ions) still suffers from a high rate of error. These errors have an impact on the accuracy and robustness of quantum computations, especially with higher number of qubits and the deeper levels of computation. Methods such as active error correction and fault-tolerant quantum computing attempt to overcome these impediments, but they are costly and time consuming to realize.

Scalability and Resource Requirements

Scalability is another critical challenge in quantum computing. Quantum systems are built for parallel computation and can provide exponential speedups for some kinds of problems. However, increasing the number of qubits required to perform complex calculations exponentially raises the requirements for physical resources, including qubit coherence time, connectivity between qubits, and cooling mechanisms. As the number of qubits increases, the control overhead for maintaining quantum operations also rises. Current quantum hardware sweet spots for scaling come with a cost in the form of connectivity bottlenecks between qubits and the penalty for implementing error corrections. E.g., the idea of building large quantum circuits that run calculations on tens or hundreds of thousands of qubits is out of reach with available technology. This scalability problem is a major obstacle for researchers who would like to take practical quantum applications into practice. Requirement for the resource of quantum systems is not limited to qubit hardware alone. Cooling systems must be put in place to lower the temperature to ~abs(0) in order to preserve quantum coherence, which is costly and restricts its implementable deployment. Furthermore, classical resources that are needed for computing and simulating quantum outcomes, e.g., the requirement for high-performance computing (HPC) set-ups for calculating quantum outputs, present another hurdle.

Hybrid Quantum-Classical Approaches

Hybride quantum-classical methods are increasingly being investigated to resolve these challenges. These techniques use classical computing capabilities together with the quantum systems to utilize the advantage of each. As one example, Quantum Approximate Optimization Algorithm (QAOA) employs quantum circuits to do computations, yet, it is implemented using classical computers to parametrize the solutions, thus minimizing the need for full apparatus. A promising field is quantum-inspired classical algorithms, which seek to introduce the efficiency gained from quantum inspiration to traditional computational paradigms by providing a simulation of quantum behavior without full quantum hardware.

Advances in quantum hardware, error correction and hybrid paradigms are at the limits of quantum computing. Future generations are expected to offer greater scalability, lower error rates, and enhanced resource efficiency, making it more accessible across diverse industries.

EMERGING TRENDS AND FUTURE DIRECTIONS

Both new quantum hardware developments and the natural integration of AI with quantum systems.

Figure 4. Dual paths of hardware progress and AI integration shaping the future of quantum computing

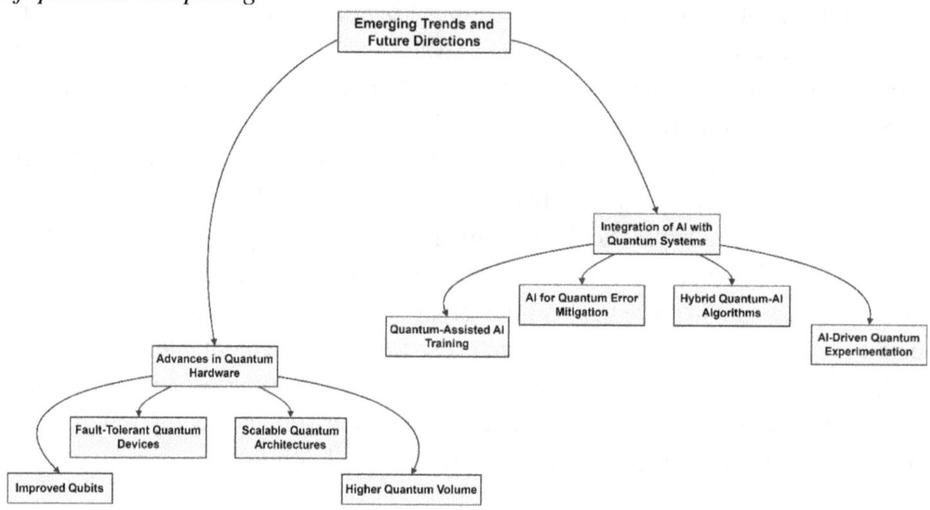

Advances in Quantum Hardware

Since another of the primary forces behind the development of quantum computing is continuously advancing quantum hardware, following are the principal factors which constitute the advancement of the area. Conventional computing is performed using classical bits, whereas quantum computers utilize qubits, and the latter can be in superposition, providing parallelism on an unprecedented scale. Nevertheless, developing stable, scalable quantum hardware continues to be a key challenge in the field. Recent progress in quantum hardware has resulted in significant advances in qubit count and their coherence time. For example, superconducting qubits, trapped ions, and topological qubits are being designed and honed to achieve greater precision and robustness(Nguyen et al., 2024; Potter & Stilinski, 2024; Taghandiki, 2024; Van Nieuwenhuizen, 2024). These technologies are designed for minimizing the error rate, maximizing connectivity, and optimizing the qubit performance, which can scale up the running of more complicated quantum algorithms. Specifically, superconducting qubits have attracted research interest because of their high gate speeds and relatively high scalability, and they are thus a promising platform for near-term quantum computing applications.

Error correction mechanisms and hybrid quantum architectures are crucial for scaling quantum systems beyond small prototypes, enabling reliable computations even in high noise levels. These systems trade quantum parallelism for classical precision and address computationally-heavy tasks such as optimization and cryptography.

Integration of AI and Quantum Machine Learning (QML)

Along the development of quantum computing, its combination with Artificial Intelligence (AI) is becoming one of the leading exciting fields. Quantum Machine Learning (QML) takes advantage of quantum phenomena—such as superposition, entanglement, and quantum interference—to handle complex data processing tasks that are otherwise intractable for classical systems. Such integration is anticipated to open up new applications which, in turn, will allow breakthroughs in fields such as healthcare, finance, materials science, and many other areas. A major use of QML is in the frontier of optimization for machine learning workflows. Machine learning models based on conventional techniques can be tailored with quantum algorithms to perform with high-dimensional data, higher accuracy, and lower computational costs. For example, quantum algorithms can optimize feature selection, model training, and hyperparameter tuning through their ability to handle multiple states and vast solution spaces efficiently. In addition, the combination of AI and QML brings faster progress in quantum-enhanced AI models. Quantum algorithms are especially valuable for solving the optimization problems of AI systems, which new methodology for enhancing decision-making, data analysis and predictive modeling. This synergy enables more powerful AI models able to tackle intricate real-world issues, especially in the fields of drug discovery, fraud detection and/or financial forecasting.

In addition to optimization, QML further improves privacy and security of data, using quantum cryptography and secure quantum communication. Quantum systems offer the ultimate levels of security, and therefore, they are very appropriate for protecting the private data in the industries where data breaches can lead to serious problems. A second promising zone is hybrid classical-quantum AI systems, in which classical AI architectures are complemented by quantum elements to perform specific functions in data processing, for example, quantum neural networks (QNNs). These models exploit traditional data pipelines but apply classical quantum operations in order to enhance performance with high adaptability to the challenges of the future generation of real-world applications.

Challenges and Future Outlook

Even with these advances, the road towards realizing the full promise of quantum computing is still very far along. Key challenges remain, including hardware scalability, error correction, and the need for efficient quantum algorithms that seamlessly integrate with classical systems. Furthermore, the absence of quantum software development tools and the high learning curve of quantum programming are challenges for its popularization.

The combination of Artificial Intelligence and quantum computers is predicted to trigger innovation in all sectors by overcoming the weakness of conventional approaches. As the foundation of intelligent systems, this synergy, coupled with high-performance quantum hardware and novel integration approaches, will change fields, and scientific exploratory, dramatically.

CASE STUDY

Quantum-Enhanced Machine Learning (QML) is becoming popular as a promising computing platform for the solution of multifaceted problems in many fields, such as finance, logistics, healthcare, and optimization. Perhaps the most exciting application of QML in finance is how quantum computing has the potential to revolutionize risk assessment, portfolio optimization, fraud detection, and models of pricing. This case study explores a real-world implementation of quantum-enhanced machine learning in financial portfolio optimization, illustrating how QML can improve decision-making, accuracy, and efficiency in financial services(Mandadapu, 2024; Namdeo et al., 2024; Nguyen et al., 2024).

Quantum-Enhanced Portfolio Optimization

In classical finance, portfolio optimization aims at finding an optimal balance between risk and return while achieving the diversification among assets. Nevertheless, the more assets and the more relations there are, the more computationally intensive the optimization problems are to solve. Classical approaches, e.g., Mean-Variance Optimization (MVO), are also inefficient with big data, high-dimensionality, and the demand for more efficient computation. Financial institutions are challenged with the analysis and processing of an enormous amount of historical data, in order to forecast market movements and react by rebalancing the portfolios. The figure 5 illustrates how quantum computing can improve the efficiency of traditional portfolio optimization techniques in real-world applications.

Figure 5. Quantum-enhanced portfolio optimization case study

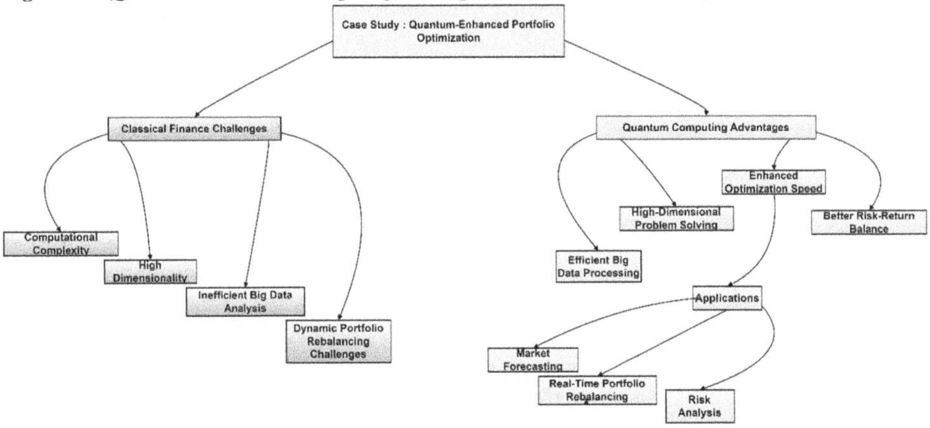

Furthermore, classical models usually demand a lot of computational power, which means that they are costly and time-consuming. This makes the portfolio optimization an obvious choice for quantum-enhanced machine learning, the type of problems where the speedup capabilities of parallel computation of quantum computing can provide a compressive boost to the efficiency and accuracy of optimization algorithms.

Quantum-Enhanced Solution

In this case study, a financial institution has adopted a quantum-enabled framework and an optimization method based on the Quantum Approximate Optimization Algorithm (QAOA) for portfolio optimization. QAOA is a quantum-classical hybrid algorithm that combines quantum circuits with classical optimization methods to tackle combinatorial problems, like asset allocation and risk control(Chen et al., 2024; Gujju et al., 2024; Hdaib et al., 2024).

Steps Involved

a) Quantum Encoding of Portfolio: The financial portfolio (stocks, bonds and other investment assets) is represented in a quantum state. Every asset is represented as a qubit and quantum gates code links between assets e.g., between correlations and future returns.

b) Application of QAOA: Quantum gates are applied iteratively with the aid of QAOA to optimize risk and return in a portfolio. Classical optimization techniques refine the quantum circuit, ensuring that the solution converges towards the optimal allocation while minimizing computational overhead.
c) Quantum-Classical Feedback Loop: Classical computers observe intermediate quantum computations and parametrize quantum gates to achieve precision and reduce noise. This feedback mechanism leads to a progressive improvement of the quality of results, which can be made in real-time as market scenarios change.

Benefits Achieved

a. Quantum-enhanced machine learning permitted concurrent examination of a vast number of possibly exiling portfolio arrangements leading to a significant reduction of computation-time in comparison to classical approaches. Normal methods might take days or even weeks to find decent portfolios but quantum approach would provide it in few hours.
b. Greater Accuracy in Risk Management: The financial institution generated more accurate models of asset relationships using quantum computing, including non-linear correlations, which enhanced risk modeling and diversification strategies. This translates to better and more resilient portfolios.
c. Scalable and dynamic solution: Quantum improved machine learning, thus allowing scalable optimization - this system could manage portfolios with hundreds or thousands of assets - making it possible (and practical) to use this method for large financial firms with many different assets in their portfolios. How transactional finance providers can leverage quantum technologies in practice
d. Improved Security and Privacy: Financial services can also benefit from improved data security using quantum cryptographic techniques to transmit and share data securely, thus minimizing data exposure, which is a critical concern in finance.

Financial institutions benefit from efficiently managed risk with maximized ROI, thus quantum computing is a means to achieve that end for strategic financial management. Moreover, this case study sets a foundation to further the study of quantum augmented applications in fields beyond finance such as healthcare, logistics, and energy. As quantum hardware and software technologies are being formed in the industry, there is a prospect of creating quantum-enhanced machine learning that could unlock new insights into complex decision-making problems while also enhancing efficiency and increasing security.

CONCLUSION

Quantum-Enhanced Machine Learning is the field of science that is advancing at an incredible pace and will be ready to disrupt finance, healthcare, logistics, materials science, and everything else. QML takes advantage of the often-strange qualities of quantum computing — superposition, entanglement, and parallelism — to address problems with complex datasets and optimization problems that would be beyond the capabilities of a classical system. Examples of use cases include but not limited to finance and portfolio optimization, healthcare drug discovery, etc. This balance is struck by hybrid quantum-classical algorithms like QAOA, which achieve efficiency, accuracy, scalability, and resource constraints.

QML has incredible potential but comes with additional challenges at present related to noise, error correction, and hardware scalability. But all the above set of challenges have been already overcome; all the above have been mitigated with a continueous development of quantum hardware and with the integration of AI into quantum. As quantum computing matures, QML would become most imperative for the industries for fast, accurate, and safe decisions. Efficiencies and sustainability will be identified as organizations discover the breadth of improvement opportunities.

REFERENCES

Altmann, P., Sünkel, L., Stein, J., Müller, T., Roch, C., & Linnhoff-Popien, C. (2023). Sequent: Towards traceable quantum machine learning using sequential quantum enhanced training. *arXiv Preprint arXiv:2301.02601*. DOI: 10.5220/0011772400003393

Bhatta, S., & Dang, J. (2024). Quantum-enhanced machine learning technique for rapid post-earthquake assessment of building safety. *Computer-Aided Civil and Infrastructure Engineering*, *39*(21), 3188–3205. DOI: 10.1111/mice.13291

Chen, C.-S., Chen, S. Y.-C., Tsai, A. H.-W., & Wei, C.-S. (2024). Qeegnet: Quantum machine learning for enhanced electroencephalography encoding. *2024 IEEE Workshop on Signal Processing Systems (SiPS)*, 153–158. DOI: 10.1109/SiPS62058.2024.00035

Goto, T., Tran, Q. H., & Nakajima, K. (2021). Universal approximation property of quantum machine learning models in quantum-enhanced feature spaces. *Physical Review Letters*, *127*(9), 090506. DOI: 10.1103/PhysRevLett.127.090506 PMID: 34506199

Gouveia, A., & Correia, M. (2020a). Towards quantum-enhanced machine learning for network intrusion detection. *2020 IEEE 19th International Symposium on Network Computing and Applications (NCA)*, 1–8.

Gouveia, A., & Correia, M. (2020b). Towards quantum-enhanced machine learning for network intrusion detection. *2020 IEEE 19th International Symposium on Network Computing and Applications (NCA)*, 1–8.

Gujju, Y., Matsuo, A., & Raymond, R. (2024). Quantum machine learning on near-term quantum devices: Current state of supervised and unsupervised techniques for real-world applications. *Physical Review Applied*, *21*(6), 067001. DOI: 10.1103/PhysRevApplied.21.067001

Hdaib, M., Rajasegarar, S., & Pan, L. (2024). Quantum deep learning-based anomaly detection for enhanced network security. *Quantum Machine Intelligence*, *6*(1), 26. DOI: 10.1007/s42484-024-00163-2

Karn, A. K., Sinha, P., Kaur, S., & Bansal, H. (2024). Quantum-Enhanced Strategies for Optimizing Disaster Response: A Machine Learning Approach. In *The Rise of Quantum Computing in Industry 6.0 Towards Sustainability* (pp. 193–204). Springer. DOI: 10.1007/978-3-031-73350-5_12

Kumar, Y., Koul, A., Sisodia, P. S., Shafi, J., Verma, K., Gheisari, M., & Davoodi, M. B. (2021). Heart failure detection using quantum-enhanced machine learning and traditional machine learning techniques for internet of artificially intelligent medical things. *Wireless Communications and Mobile Computing, 2021*(1), 1616725. DOI: 10.1155/2021/1616725

Liu, N., Huang, T., Gao, J., Xu, Z., Wang, D., & Li, F. (2021). Quantum-enhanced deep learning-based lithology interpretation from well logs. *IEEE Transactions on Geoscience and Remote Sensing, 60*, 1–13.

Lu, W., Lu, Y., Li, J., Sigov, A., Ratkin, L., & Ivanov, L. A. (2024). Quantum Machine Learning: Classifications, Challenges, and Solutions. *Journal of Industrial Information Integration, 42*, 100736. DOI: 10.1016/j.jii.2024.100736

Maheswari, B. U., Imambi, S. S., Hasan, D., Meenakshi, S., Pratheep, V., & Boopathi, S. (2023). Internet of things and machine learning-integrated smart robotics. In *Global Perspectives on Robotics and Autonomous Systems: Development and Applications* (pp. 240–258). IGI Global. DOI: 10.4018/978-1-6684-7791-5.ch010

Mandadapu, P. (2024). Exploring Quantum-Enhanced Machine Learning for Computer Vision: Applications and Insights on Noisy Intermediate-Scale Quantum Devices. *arXiv Preprint arXiv:2404.02177.*

Melnikov, A., Kordzanganeh, M., Alodjants, A., & Lee, R.-K. (2023). Quantum machine learning: From physics to software engineering. *Advances in Physics: X, 8*(1), 2165452. DOI: 10.1080/23746149.2023.2165452

Namdeo, S., Khurana, S., & Nene, M. J. (2024). Quantum-Enhanced Cognitive Systems: Harnessing Parameterized Quantum Circuits for Advanced Machine Learning Applications. *International Conference on Innovations and Advances in Cognitive Systems*, 257–271. DOI: 10.1007/978-3-031-69201-7_20

Nguyen, T., Sipola, T., & Hautamäki, J. (2024). Machine Learning Applications of Quantum Computing: A Review. *arXiv Preprint arXiv:2406.13262.*

Ortolano, G., Napoli, C., Harney, C., Pirandola, S., Leonetti, G., Boucher, P., Losero, E., Genovese, M., & Ruo-Berchera, I. (2023). Quantum-enhanced pattern recognition. *Physical Review Applied, 20*(2), 024072. DOI: 10.1103/PhysRevApplied.20.024072

Potter, K., & Stilinski, D. (2024). *Quantum Machine Learning: Exploring the Potential of Quantum Computing forAI Applications.*

Prasad, M. S. C., Dhanalakshmi, M., Mohan, M., Somasundaram, B., Valarmathi, R., & Boopathi, S. (2024). Machine Learning-Integrated Sustainable Engineering and Energy Systems: Innovations at the Nexus. In *Harnessing High-Performance Computing and AI for Environmental Sustainability* (pp. 74–98). IGI Global. DOI: 10.4018/979-8-3693-1794-5.ch004

Satuluri, V. R., & Ponnusamy, V. (2021). Quantum-enhanced machine learning. *2021 Smart Technologies, Communication and Robotics (STCR)*, 1–6.

Sequeira, A. M. R. (2021). *Quantum-enhanced reinforcement learning* [PhD Thesis].

Sharma, S. (2020). Qeml (quantum enhanced machine learning): Using quantum computing to enhance ml classifiers and feature spaces. *arXiv Preprint arXiv:2002.10453*.

Taghandiki, K. (2024). Quantum Machine Learning Unveiled: A Comprehensive Review. *Journal of Engineering and Applied Research*, *1*(2), 29–48.

Van Nieuwenhuizen, C. (2024). Quantum-enhanced Optimization-Applications and Challenges: Analyzing applications and challenges of quantum-enhanced optimization algorithms for solving large-scale optimization problems in various domains. *Journal of Artificial Intelligence Research and Applications*, *4*(1), 296–306.

Wang, X., Lin, Z., Che, L., Chen, H., & Lu, D. (2022). Experimental Quantum-Enhanced Machine Learning in Spin-Based Systems. *Advanced Quantum Technologies*, *5*(8), 2200005. DOI: 10.1002/qute.202200005

Chapter 5
Quantum Error Correction:
Overcoming the Fragility of Qubits for Reliable Quantum Computing

Swathi Mummadi
https://orcid.org/0000-0001-7078-5729
B.V. Raju Institute of Technology, India

Gnaneshwara Chary Udari
B.V. Raju Institute of Technology, India

ABSTRACT

Quantum Error Correction (QEC) is essential for overcoming the fragility of qubits, enabling reliable and scalable quantum computing by mitigating the effects of noise, decoherence, and operational errors. This chapter explores QEC's foundational principles, including error types, noise impact, and syndrome measurement techniques for identifying and correcting errors. It covers key codes such as Shor and Steane, which provide basic error protection, and advanced codes like concatenated codes, surface codes, and quantum Low-Density Parity-Check (LDPC) codes. Concatenated codes employ hierarchical encoding to exponentially reduce logical error rates, while surface codes, including Toric codes, utilize topological properties of qubits arranged on a 2D lattice to detect and correct errors with high fault tolerance and scalability. Quantum LDPC codes leverage sparse parity-check matrices to offer efficient and scalable error correction, closely approaching theoretical performance limits. The chapter concludes by exploring current research efforts to optimize QEC codes.

DOI: 10.4018/979-8-3693-6225-9.ch005

1.1 INTRODUCTION TO QUANTUM ERROR CORRECTION

Quantum computing is a transformative technology that leverages the principles of quantum mechanics to perform computations that are infeasible for classical computers. At the heart of this technology are qubits, the fundamental units of quantum information. Unlike classical bits, which can be either 0 or 1, qubits can exist in superpositions of states, enabling quantum computers to explore many possibilities simultaneously. This unique property allows quantum algorithms, such as Shor's algorithm for factoring large numbers or Grover's search algorithm, to solve certain problems exponentially faster than classical algorithms. However, the power of quantum computing is accompanied by significant challenges, most notably the inherent fragility of qubits (Landauer, 1961). Qubits are highly susceptible to errors due to interactions with their environment, leading to decoherence and loss of quantum information. These errors pose a major obstacle to building reliable, large-scale quantum computers, making error correction an essential component of any practical quantum computing system.

The Fragility of Qubits: Sources of Errors

Qubits are delicate entities that can easily lose their quantum state through a process known as decoherence, which occurs when a qubit interacts with its surroundings, causing the loss of coherence between its superposition states. Additionally, quantum systems are vulnerable to operational errors during manipulating qubits, including gate, measurement, and initialization errors. These errors can be broadly classified into bit-flip errors (analogous to flipping a classical bit from 0 to 1 or vice versa), phase-flip errors (where the phase of the quantum state is altered), and more complex depolarizing errors that affect both amplitude and phase (Mummadi & Rudra, 2021; Vasudevan et al., 2006).

Motivation for Quantum Error Correction

The need for error correction in quantum computing is driven by the reality that even small amounts of noise can render quantum algorithms ineffective. Unlike classical error correction, which typically involves duplicating data bits and using redundancy to detect and correct errors, quantum error correction must adhere to the constraints of quantum mechanics, such as the no-cloning theorem, which prohibits the copying of an arbitrary quantum state. Consequently, quantum error correction (QEC) employs sophisticated strategies to detect and correct errors without directly measuring the qubit's state, thereby preserving the integrity of the quantum information (Feynman, 1985; Fredkin & Toffoli, 1982;).

1.2 Importance of Quantum Error Correction

QEC aims to protect quantum information from degradation due to errors. It enables qubits to perform extended computations without succumbing to noise and operational inaccuracies. A quantum computer without error correction would face an insurmountable challenge in maintaining coherent states over long periods, making large-scale computation impossible. The key to overcoming these challenges lies in encoding quantum information into logical qubits, which are themselves represented by multiple physical qubits. The ability to detect and correct errors without directly measuring and collapsing the quantum state forms the backbone of QEC. The process of syndrome measurement, error identification, and correction, coupled with fault-tolerant circuit design, ensures that quantum algorithms can be executed reliably, even in noisy environments (Peres, 1985).

1.2.1 Types of Errors in Quantum Computing

Errors in quantum systems are fundamentally different from classical errors. While classical errors usually involve bit-flip errors (changing a bit from 0 to 1 or vice versa), quantum errors can be more complex, affecting both the amplitude and phase of a qubit (Endo, Benjamin, & Li, 2018; Kandala et al., 2019; Steane, 1996;) The most common types of quantum errors are:

- **Bit-flip errors (X-errors)**: Analogous to classical bit-flip errors, a qubit in state $|0\rangle$ can be flipped to $|1\rangle$ or vice versa.
- **Phase-flip errors (Z-errors)**: These errors affect the phase of the quantum state, flipping the relative phase between the $|0\rangle$ and $|1\rangle$ states.
- **Depolarizing errors**: A combination of bit-flip, phase-flip, or both, depolarizing errors occur when a qubit randomly assumes a completely mixed state.
- **Amplitude damping**: This error occurs due to the loss of energy from the quantum system, typically manifesting in physical qubits as spontaneous emission of photons.
- **Decoherence**: Due to interaction with the environment, qubits lose their quantum superposition and coherence, transitioning into classical mixed states.

These errors result from external noise, imperfect gate operations, and decoherence from interactions with the environment. Overcoming these error sources requires a comprehensive understanding of quantum noise models and the development of robust QEC techniques.

1.3 Syndrome Measurement and Error Detection

One of the critical challenges in QEC is the ability to detect and correct errors without directly measuring and disturbing the quantum state. This is achieved through syndrome measurement, a process that allows indirect detection of errors by measuring ancillary qubits that are entangled with the logical qubits. The key concept is that the error information is extracted without collapsing the qubit's quantum superposition (Mummadi & Udari, 2023).

Stabilizer Formalism

The stabilizer formalism provides a systematic framework for describing quantum error-correcting codes. It is based on the notion that a group of operators called stabilizers can describe an encoded quantum state, which leave the state unchanged. Measuring these stabilizers yields syndromes that indicate whether an error has occurred, without revealing the specific quantum information encoded in the qubit. A stabilizer code is defined by a set of stabilizer generators, which are Pauli operators that commute with the encoded quantum state. These generators form the foundation for constructing error-correcting codes. When an error occurs, it alters the stabilizer measurements, producing a syndrome that identifies the type of error, allowing for correction without collapsing the encoded quantum information (McKay et al., 2017).

1.4. Key Quantum Error-Correcting Codes

Quant error correcting codes are essential methods for safeguarding quantum data against mistakes and noise. Quantum error correction takes into consideration the special characteristics of quantum systems, such superposition and entanglement, in contrast to classical error correction. To identify and fix mistakes without actually measuring the quantum information as this may upset the fragile quantum states quantum codes use specially created quantum states and actions. The special qualities of quantum mechanics are utilised by quantum codes. By using these characteristics, quantum codes are able to detect mistakes and encode information twice without having to physically measure the qubits' states. A syndrome is a notion that is involved in quantum error correction. Errors cause a quantum code's stabiliser operators to malfunction, leading to certain symptoms. Quantum computers may detect the existence and location of faults by measuring these symptoms instead of the delicate quantum information itself. One of the main benefits of quantum error correction is this non-destructive mistake detection. For quantum codes to function, they need to meet specific requirements. Within that bound, quantum information is guaranteed to stay coherent and trustworthy as quantum codes are made to rectify mistakes up to a specific threshold. For quantum codes to be implemented successfully, several requirements must be met (Mummadi & Rudra, 2022).

Quantum error correction techniques are used to safeguard the logical qubits that are encoded with information utilising quantum codes. Several physical qubits are used to encode logical qubits, generating redundancy that permits error correction and detection. The information is converted throughout the encoding process into an error-resistant format, guaranteeing the integrity of the quantum data while it is being computed. There are several forms of quantum error correction codes, including topological codes (like the Surface Code and Toric Code), subsystem codes, and stabiliser codes (including CSS codes like the Shor and Steane codes). Because of its distinct qualities and benefits, each kind is suited for particular quantum computing architectures and error models. Quantum systems can display correlations that classical systems are unable to accomplish because to a property called entanglement. Entanglement is a useful tool for constructing quantum codes in the context of quantum error correction. Building blocks for redundant and error-protected quantum information encoding are entangled states. States that remain invariant under particular operations are called stabiliser states and are produced using entanglement. For a kind of quantum error correction codes known as stabiliser codes, these states are essential. Stabiliser states can encode several qubits in a highly correlated way because of their entangled nature. Entanglement is used by stabiliser codes in their stabiliser generators. Stabiliser generator entanglement guarantees that faults impacting a single qubit may be identified by use of correlated measurements of other qubits. The foundation for error detection and correction without direct measurement of the encoded quantum information is provided by entangled stabiliser generators. A key component of non-local error detection is entanglement. When they happen, errors have the potential to break the entangled correlations inside stabiliser states. Even in cases where faults influence a small number of qubits locally, error detection across several qubits is made possible by the non-local correlations made possible by entanglement (Deibuk & Yuriychuk, 2020; Maslov, Dueck, & Miller, 2005; Picton, 1994; Wallman & Emerson, 2016).

There are particular quantum error correcting codes made to take use of entanglement. To improve the fidelity of quantum communication, entanglement-assisted quantum codes make use of shared entangled states between the transmitter and the receiver. These codes take advantage of entanglement to improve error correction performance, especially in quantum key distribution and other quantum communication protocols. The protocols for quantum teleportation and entanglement swapping rely heavily on entanglement. Entanglement between the transmitter and recipient qubits is necessary for quantum teleportation to transport quantum information reliably (Biamonte et al., 2017; Saeedi & Markov, 2013). Entanglement swapping illustrates the non-local character of entanglement, which is essential for quantum error correction and communication, by enabling the development of entanglement between qubits that have never directly interacted. One basic kind of quantum error correcting codes are qubit stabilisers, sometimes referred to as stabiliser codes. Stabiliser generators, or sets of Pauli operators (X, Y, Z) that commute with one another to form a stabiliser group, are used in these codes. The code space is made up of these stabiliser generators' eigenstates. By measuring the stabiliser operators, errors can be found. The Steane code and the Shor code are two qubit stabiliser codes that can both be used to fix single-qubit faults (Mummadi & Rudra, 2023).

Every qubit in a stabiliser code has numerous stabiliser generators connected to it. Qubit stabilisers are essential for identifying malfunctioning qubits and for identifying the kind of mistakes (X, Y, or Z) that have happened. The qubits in the code undergo a series of operations to determine the stabiliser generators. This condition is used to pinpoint the mistakes that have happened and to direct the next efforts to repair the problems. For a stabiliser code to remain stable, its quantum gates need to abide by the stabiliser operators. Quantum gates that are fault-tolerant are made to avoid introducing mistakes that cause the stabiliser operators to malfunction. Maintaining the error correcting capability of the code during quantum computing requires gates to respect the stabiliser generators. Fault-tolerant quantum processing may be accomplished with stabiliser codes if the logical qubits are spaced apart enough in their construction (Devitt, Munro, & Nemoto, 2013). In quantum computing, the threshold theorem determines a critical error rate below which quantum calculations of any length may be executed with reasonable accuracy. By offering a route to scalability, stabiliser codes enable the development of more expansive, robust quantum circuits.

There are several obstacles to overcome when implementing quantum error correction with qubit stabilisers, such as the requirement for high-fidelity gates, low error rates, and precise measurement and manipulation of multi-qubit stabiliser generators. For large-scale, fault-tolerant quantum computer construction as well as for the actual use of quantum algorithms, these obstacles must be overcome. Quantum error correction with qubit stabilizers forms the basis for reliable quantum computation (Aliferis, Gottesman, & Preskill, 2008; Mummadi & Rudra, 2022). By leveraging the principles of stabilizer codes and accurately measuring the syndromes, researchers can detect and correct errors, paving the way for the development of robust quantum technologies for various applications. Several quantum error-correcting codes have been developed to protect quantum information, each with its own strengths and limitations. This section covers foundational and advanced codes, from basic codes that provide initial protection to more sophisticated ones that enable fault-tolerant computation.

1.4.1 The Surface Code

A topological quantum error-correcting code that uses a 2D lattice of qubits, with each qubit representing a square on the lattice. It detects and corrects faults in quantum states by using stabilizer measurements on this lattice. Due to its unique topological qualities, the code is well-suited for fault-tolerant quantum computing since it can detect and correct faults by measuring neighbouring qubits, offering high error protection and dependability (Ahn et al., 2002; Bacon, 2006). Imagine a chessboard made of qubits (quantum bits). Each qubit represents a square on the chessboard. The surface code uses a specific pattern of qubits on this "board" to detect and correct errors.

Here's a simple way to break it down and understand it:

Qubit Chessboard: Think of a grid of qubits like a chessboard. Each qubit can be in a quantum state.
Data Qubits: Some qubits are data qubits, like the pieces on a chessboard. They hold the actual quantum information.
Ancilla Qubits: Other qubits are like helper pieces. They are used to check if the data qubits are in the right state.
Stabilizer Checks: The surface code performs checks on groups of qubits (like rows and columns on a chessboard) to see if they are in the right state. These checks are called stabilizer checks.
Error Detection: If an error occurs, the stabilizer checks will detect it. It's like noticing if a chess piece is in the wrong place and giving a warning.
Error Correction: When an error is detected, the surface code can correct it by changing the state of the qubits. It's similar to moving a chess piece back to the correct square.

The surface code is powerful because it can detect and correct multiple errors, making quantum computing more reliable. It's like having a "checker" so that the quantum bits can proceed without mistakes.

1.4.2 The Steane Code

The Steane code is a type of quantum error-correcting code designed to protect quantum information from errors (Barrett & Milburn, 2003; Mummadi & Rudra, 2022). The Steane code encodes one logical qubit in 7 physical qubits and is capable of correcting arbitrary single-qubit errors.

Encoding: With the Steane code, you take your original qubit, which might be in a vulnerable state, and encode it using a set of seven qubits. This encoding is akin to placing your qubit in a protective box.
Error Correction: The magic occurs when errors need to be corrected. If one or two of the seven qubits inside the box are disturbed or flipped (errors), the Steane code has a method for identifying which ones were affected.
Fixing Errors: Through measurements and calculations, the Steane code can identify which qubits have been altered and then restore them to their correct state. It's similar to finding and rectifying mistakes in the protective box.
Result: Following this process, your original qubit is returned to a secure and error-free state, even if it was initially susceptible to errors.

So, the Steane code acts as a quantum bodyguard for your qubits. It encodes them, detects when something goes wrong, and fixes any issues to ensure the reliability of your quantum information. The Steane code encodes one logical qubit in 7 physical qubits. The codespace for the Steane code is a 2-dimensional subspace of its 2^7 dimensional Hilbert space.

In a Stabilizer Formalism, the Steane code has 6 generators as given below:

I I I X X X

I X X I I X X

X I X I X I X

I I I Z Z Z Z

I Z Z I I Z Z

Z I Z I Z I Z

Note that each of the above generators is the tensor product of 7 single-qubit Pauli operations.

The logical X and Z gates are represented as follows

$X_L = XXXXXXX$

$Z_L = ZZZZZZZ$

According to this the logical states $|0\rangle$ and $|1\rangle$ of the Steane code are represented as follows

$$|0\rangle_L = \frac{1}{\sqrt{8}}\Big[\Big[|0000000\rangle + |1010101\rangle + |0110011\rangle +$$

$$|1100110\rangle + |0001111\rangle + |1011010\rangle + |0111100\rangle + \Big|1101001\rangle\Big]$$

$$|1\rangle_L = X_L|0\rangle_L$$

In this, arbitrary code states are of the form $|\Psi\rangle = \alpha\,|0\rangle_L + \beta\,|1\rangle_L$

1.4.3 The Shor Code

The error channel can introduce either a bit flip, a sign flip (i.e., a phase flip), or both. You can correct for both types of errors on any single qubit using a Quantum Error Correction (QEC) code, which can be achieved with the Shor code published in 1995. In other words, the Shor code can correct arbitrary single-qubit errors (Bombin, 2011; Braunstein, 1998). The Shor code acts like a quantum detective that safeguards your quantum information from errors. So, think of the Shor code as a detective for your quantum data. It protects your qubits, investigates errors, and ensures everything is in order. Here's a straightforward breakdown to help you understand it:

Code Creator: Imagine you have a brilliant friend named Mr. Shor, who has created a special code. This code functions as a shield for your quantum information.
Data Protection: You entrust your quantum information (qubits) to Mr. Shor's code, which places your data in a secret code box.
Error Investigation: Now, imagine some errors occur. It's like a mystery where your qubits change or flip without your knowledge.
Shor's Magic: Mr. Shor's code acts as a detective, carefully examining your qubits and uncovering what went wrong. It's akin to solving the mystery of the errors.
Fixing Mistakes: Once the detective (Shor's code) identifies the errors, it corrects them, returning your qubits to their correct and safe state.

The Shor code can also rectify a sign flip error for a single qubit.
$|\Psi\rangle = \alpha_1\,|0\rangle + \beta_1\,|1\rangle$ will be

$$|\Psi'\rangle = \alpha_2\,|0_S\rangle + \beta_2\,|1_S\rangle$$

$$|0_S\rangle = \frac{1}{2\sqrt{2}}[(|000\rangle + |111\rangle) \oplus \left(|000\rangle + |111\rangle\right) \oplus \left(|000\rangle + |111\rangle\right)]$$

$$|1_S\rangle = \frac{1}{2\sqrt{2}}[(|000\rangle - |111\rangle) \oplus \left(|000\rangle - |111\rangle\right) \oplus \left(|000\rangle - |111\rangle\right)]$$

The circuit diagram of Shor's code along with encoding and decoding operations is depicted in following figure.

Figure 1. Quantum Circuit to encode a single logical qubit with the Shor code and then perform bit flip error correction on each of the three blocks (Mummadi & Fathima, 2024).

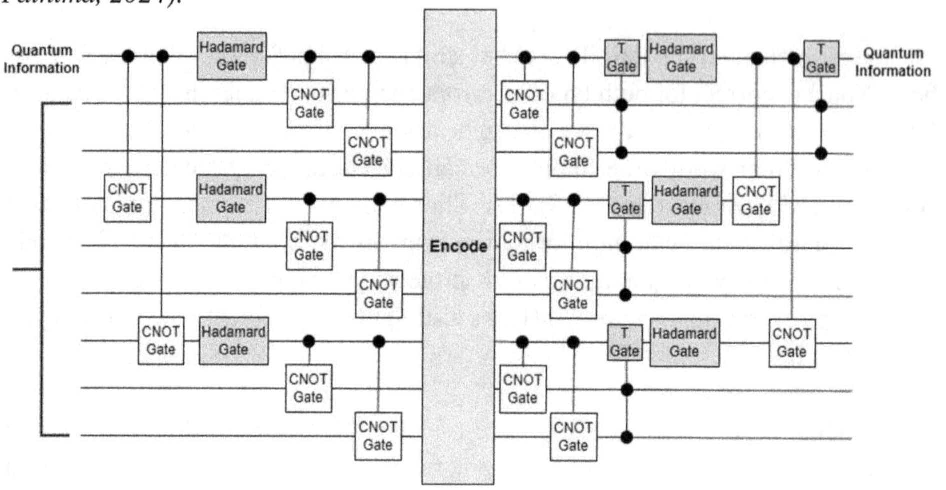

1.4.4 Concatenated Codes

Concatenated codes offer a way to reduce the logical error rate exponentially by using hierarchical encoding. In a concatenated code, each qubit in the logical block is encoded again using another error-correcting code. For example, a logical qubit may first be encoded using the Steane code, and each of the physical qubits in the encoded block may itself be encoded using a different error-correcting code. This multi-level encoding scheme exponentially suppresses the error rate at the cost of increased resource overhead. These codes employ a hierarchical structure where each logical qubit is further encoded using another quantum error-correcting code. The primary advantage of concatenated codes is that they exponentially suppress the logical error rate at the cost of increasing qubit overhead (Mummadi & Rudra, 2022).

Encoding

Consider a logical qubit encoded using the Steane code. Each of the seven physical qubits in this encoded block can be further encoded using another Steane code. If each physical qubit in the first block is encoded, the logical qubit is now represented by 49 physical qubits.

Mathematically, the encoding process can be described recursively. If C is the encoding operation for the Steane code, then after one level of concatenation:

$|\psi\rangle \rightarrow C(C(|\psi\rangle))$

This encoding can be repeated multiple times to further reduce the logical error rate. If the logical error rate after the first encoding is ϵ, then after k levels of concatenation, the logical error rate is reduced to approximately ϵ^k

Error Correction

Error correction in concatenated codes is performed recursively. At each level of concatenation, errors are detected and corrected independently. This multi-level error correction scheme ensures that errors do not propagate through the layers, effectively reducing the overall error rate.

1.4.5 Quantum Low-Density Parity-Check (LDPC) Codes

Quantum Low-Density Parity-Check (LDPC) codes are a family of codes that use sparse parity-check matrices to correct errors. These codes are inspired by classical LDPC codes, known for their efficiency and performance close to theoretical limits. Quantum LDPC codes are scalable and offer fault tolerance with relatively low qubit overhead, making them an attractive choice for near-term quantum computers. Quantum LDPC codes are inspired by classical LDPC codes and offer a more efficient way of encoding quantum information using sparse parity-check matrices (DiVincenzo & Aliferis, 2007; Gardiner, 1991). These codes can correct errors with fewer physical qubits compared to other codes.

Parity-Check Matrix

A quantum LDPC code is defined by two sparse parity-check matrices, H_X and H_Z, that correspond to bit-flip and phase-flip error detection. These matrices have the property that:

$H_X H_Z^T = 0$

This condition ensures that the code can simultaneously detect and correct bit-flip and phase-flip errors.

Error Detection and Correction

LDPC codes detect errors by measuring the syndrome, which is computed as:

$$s = H_x e$$

where **e** is the error vector, and **s** is the syndrome. Once the syndrome is measured, it is used to identify and correct the errors.

Quantum LDPC codes are particularly promising for large-scale quantum computing because they have low overhead and can correct errors more efficiently than other codes.

1.5 Fault-Tolerant Quantum Computing

Threshold theorems are fundamental results in the field of quantum error correction, specifically in the context of quantum fault-tolerant computation. These theorems provide conditions under which it is possible to perform fault-tolerant quantum computation, even in the presence of errors, up to a certain threshold error rate. Quantum computers are inherently susceptible to errors due to various factors such as decoherence, noise, and environmental interactions. Fault-tolerant quantum computation is a critical area of research aimed at designing quantum algorithms and circuits capable of functioning correctly even when errors occur during the computation. This involves the use of advanced quantum error correction techniques to mitigate the impact of errors on quantum information processing (Mummadi & Rudra, 2023; Steane, 1996).

In the study of fault-tolerant quantum computation, specific error models are considered to analyze the impact of errors on quantum systems. One common model is the local stochastic noise model, where errors occur independently on each qubit and gate with a certain probability. Other relevant models include depolarizing noise, which represents errors through a gradual loss of information, and amplitude damping, which accounts for errors due to interactions with the environment. The threshold error rate is a crucial parameter in the field of fault-tolerant quantum computation. It represents the maximum allowable error rate (per physical qubit or gate) below which fault-tolerant quantum computation becomes theoretically possible. The threshold error rate depends on factors such as the specific quantum error correction code employed and distinguishes between physical error rates (errors per gate or qubit) and logical error rates (errors at the logical level after error correction). Understanding and surpassing the threshold error rate is essential for achieving scalable and reliable quantum computation (Mummadi & Fathima, 2024; Unruh, 1995).

1.5.1 Fault-Tolerant Circuit Design

One of the central challenges in quantum computing is preventing error propagation during computation. Fault-tolerant circuit design addresses this by ensuring that errors do not spread uncontrollably through the system, which would otherwise render error correction ineffective. The key principles of fault-tolerant design include the use of transversal gates and error-correcting gadgets (Acharya et al., 2024). A fault-tolerant quantum gate ensures that errors do not spread uncontrollably through the quantum circuit. To achieve fault tolerance, gate operations must be designed so that errors remain correctable within the confines of the QEC code.

Fault-Tolerant Circuit Construction:

1. **Transversal Gates:**
   - Transversal gates are a crucial element in fault-tolerant quantum computing. A transversal gate operates on corresponding qubits in separate encoded blocks without spreading errors between qubits within a block. This ensures that errors remain localized, allowing them to be corrected by the QEC code. For example, in a quantum computer using surface codes, transversal operations are applied across different qubit layers to ensure that errors do not propagate across the lattice. These gates are a class of fault-tolerant gates that operate on qubits in a layer-wise fashion, such that qubits in one code block interact only with corresponding qubits in other blocks. This structure prevents error propagation between qubits within the same block.
   - Example: For the Steane code, the bitwise application of Hadamard gates on each qubit forms a transversal operation: $H^{\otimes 7}=H\otimes H\otimes \ldots \otimes H$, which is inherently fault-tolerant.
2. **Error-Correcting Gadgets:**
   - Fault-tolerant circuits often incorporate gadgets such as error-correcting blocks, ancilla verification, and state purification. These elements are used to detect and correct errors as the computation progresses. Error-correcting gadgets are specialized circuits designed to perform operations in a fault-tolerant manner. These gadgets introduce additional qubits and gates to correct errors during the execution of a quantum algorithm. They help to prevent error accumulation and propagation by implementing error detection and correction at intermediate stages of computation.

3. **Magic State Distillation:**
    - o To implement non-transversal gates (e.g., T gates), magic state distillation is used to create high-fidelity states that enable gate operations while preserving fault tolerance.

1.6 The Quantum Threshold Theorem

The Quantum Threshold Theorem is a central concept in quantum computing, addressing one of the most critical challenges in building practical quantum computers: error rates. Quantum computers, unlike classical counterparts, are highly sensitive to errors due to their reliance on fragile quantum states. These errors arise from both internal quantum gate imperfections and environmental factors, like noise, which disturb the coherence of qubits. The Quantum Threshold Theorem, therefore, offers a solution for the successful implementation of quantum algorithms over extended periods without errors accumulating to such a degree that they make computations impractical. The theorem establishes the conditions under which fault-tolerant quantum computation is possible. Specifically, it states that if the error rate of quantum gates (or any quantum operations) can be kept below a specific threshold, arbitrarily long quantum computations can be performed with the help of error-correcting codes. This error correction ensures that small errors introduced during computation do not cascade uncontrollably, allowing the quantum computer to produce reliable outputs (van Loock, 2008).

Threshold Error Rates

The threshold error rate is a crucial parameter in the Quantum Threshold Theorem. It defines the upper limit on the error rate of quantum gates below which error correction can maintain the integrity of the computation. If the error rate exceeds this threshold, the error-correcting codes become ineffective, as they are overwhelmed by the rate of errors introduced during computation. On the other hand, if the error rate is sufficiently low (below the threshold), error correction can effectively detect and correct errors, ensuring that the logical qubits (qubits representing the computational state) remain stable (Mummadi & Rudra, 2022).

Different quantum error correction (QEC) codes exhibit different threshold error rates. Surface codes, for instance, are one of the most researched and practically feasible QEC codes and have a relatively high threshold error rate, typically around 1%. This high threshold makes surface codes particularly attractive for near-term quantum computing applications. The Quantum Threshold Theorem for surface codes suggests that if the physical error rate per gate can be reduced to below 1%, arbitrarily long quantum computations can be performed with near-perfect fidelity. Other QEC codes, such as the Bacon-Shor code and concatenated codes, may have different threshold values depending on their structure and error-correcting capabilities.

The significance of the threshold theorem lies in the fact that it gives a clear and quantifiable target for quantum engineers and researchers: reduce the error rate per gate below the threshold, and fault-tolerant quantum computation becomes a reality. This provides a roadmap for hardware development, guiding the design and improvement of qubits, quantum gates, and quantum processors to achieve error rates that fall below the threshold.

Practical Implications of the Quantum Threshold Theorem

The practical implications of the Quantum Threshold Theorem extend beyond error correction codes to the overall design of quantum computers. The theorem serves as a guidepost for quantum computing hardware and software development, ensuring that error rates are sufficiently low to make fault-tolerant computation feasible. Quantum gates, which are used to manipulate qubits, must be implemented with extremely high precision and accuracy. This necessitates qubit control, noise reduction techniques, and environmental isolation innovations to achieve and maintain low error rates (Brun, Devetak, & Hsieh, 2006). Moreover, the theorem emphasizes the need for scalability in quantum systems. In practice, achieving fault tolerance may require the use of large-scale quantum error correction codes, which in turn require a substantial number of physical qubits. As such, researchers and engineers are tasked with optimising qubit efficiency, improving gate fidelity, and developing architectures that can handle the overhead imposed by quantum error correction codes.

1.7 Challenges in Quantum Error Correction

While quantum error correction (QEC) is essential for realizing fault-tolerant quantum computing, several challenges must be addressed before practical large-scale quantum computers can be built (Campbell, 2024). These challenges stem from QEC's inherent complexity and current quantum hardware's limitations.

Resource Overhead

One of the most significant challenges in quantum error correction is the resource overhead associated with implementing error-correcting codes. QEC codes require many physical qubits to protect a single logical qubit, and the number of physical qubits required increases with the level of protection desired. For instance, surface codes, which are considered one of the most practical QEC codes, typically require thousands of physical qubits to encode and protect a single logical qubit.

This large resource overhead limits the scalability of quantum computers, particularly in the near term. Current quantum processors, which may consist of only a few hundred qubits, cannot support the vast number of qubits required for full fault-tolerant computation. This challenge underscores the need for hardware advances to increase qubit count and improve qubit quality, as well as for algorithmic innovations to reduce the overhead imposed by QEC.

Noise Models

Another challenge in QEC is the difficulty of accurately modelling noise in quantum systems. Noise in quantum computers arises from various sources, including decoherence, gate imperfections, and environmental disturbances. Most QEC codes assume simple noise models, such as independent and identically distributed (i.i.d.) errors, which are easier to analyze and correct. However, real quantum hardware often exhibits more complex noise behaviour, with errors that are correlated and dependent on the specific hardware architecture.

The limitations of current noise models pose a challenge for developing more effective QEC codes. If the assumptions made by a QEC code do not accurately reflect the behaviour of the quantum system, the code may fail to correct errors effectively. Consequently, there is ongoing research into developing more accurate noise models that can account for correlated and complex errors, as well as designing QEC codes that are robust against such noise.

1.8 Advances in Quantum Error Correction and Future Directions

Ongoing research in QEC focuses on optimizing existing codes and developing new codes that can be more efficiently implemented on quantum hardware. For example, recent advances in quantum LDPC codes have demonstrated that it is possible to approach the theoretical performance limits of QEC while significantly reducing the resource overhead.

Another promising direction is the integration of QEC codes directly into quantum hardware. Building error correction into the architecture of quantum processors can enhance the efficiency of error detection and correction, paving the way for more practical fault-tolerant quantum computers. Despite the challenges outlined above, significant progress has been made in quantum error correction, and ongoing research continues to push the boundaries of what is possible (Klimov et al., 2024; Mondal & Parhi, 2024). Researchers are exploring various strategies to optimize existing

QEC codes, develop new codes with lower resource overheads, and integrate error correction into quantum hardware more efficiently.

1.8.1 Hardware-Integrated Error Correction

A promising avenue of research is the integration of error correction directly into quantum hardware. Traditional approaches to quantum error correction involve implementing error-detecting and error-correcting circuits at the software or firmware level, which can introduce additional overhead and complexity. In contrast, hardware-integrated error correction seeks to build error correction into the architecture of quantum processors themselves, allowing for more efficient and reliable error detection and correction.

One approach to hardware-integrated error correction involves designing qubit architectures that natively support the stabilizer measurements required for QEC codes like surface codes. By embedding stabilizer measurements and error-correcting circuits directly into the hardware, it is possible to reduce the latency and resource overhead associated with traditional error-correction methods. This approach has the potential to enhance the performance of quantum processors and bring us closer to fault-tolerant quantum computing.

For example, superconducting qubit architectures have been a focus of hardware-integrated error correction research. These architectures are designed to support efficient error detection through rapid stabilizer measurements and have demonstrated promising results in experimental setups. As quantum hardware continues to evolve, the integration of error correction at the hardware level is likely to play a key role in making fault-tolerant quantum computers a reality.

1.8.2 Optimizing Codes for Specific Architectures

Another important area of research is the development of QEC codes that are optimized for specific quantum hardware platforms. Different quantum computing technologies have unique noise characteristics and operational constraints, such as superconducting qubits, ion traps, and topological qubits. As a result, QEC codes that perform well on one platform may not be as effective on another (Bravyi et al., 2024).

Tailoring QEC codes to specific hardware architectures can significantly enhance the performance and reliability of quantum computers. For example, superconducting qubits are prone to decoherence and gate errors, while ion trap qubits may experience different types of noise, such as vibrational noise. By developing QEC codes that account for the specific noise characteristics of these platforms, researchers can improve the error correction performance and reduce the resource overhead required for fault-tolerant computation.

Topological qubits, which are based on exotic states of matter known as anyons, offer another potential platform for optimized QEC codes. These qubits are inherently robust against certain types of noise, making them an attractive candidate for fault-tolerant quantum computing. However, developing QEC codes that fully leverage the unique properties of topological qubits remains an ongoing challenge.

1.8.3 Recent Advances in LDPC Codes

Another area of progress in quantum error correction is the development of quantum Low-Density Parity-Check (LDPC) codes. LDPC codes are a class of classical error-correcting codes that have been successfully used in classical communication systems to achieve high levels of error correction with relatively low resource overhead. Researchers have adapted LDPC codes for quantum systems in recent years, and the results have been promising (Xia, Xie, & Yang, 2024).

Quantum LDPC codes offer several advantages over traditional QEC codes like surface codes. One of the most significant benefits is their potential to achieve near-optimal error correction performance while reducing the number of physical qubits required to protect a logical qubit. This reduction in resource overhead makes quantum LDPC codes an attractive option for building scalable, fault-tolerant quantum computers.

In addition to their lower qubit requirements, quantum LDPC codes can be tailored to specific noise models, making them more robust against the correlated noise types often encountered in real quantum hardware. As research into quantum LDPC codes continues, it is likely that they will play an increasingly important role in the development of practical quantum error correction solutions.

1.9 CONCLUSION

Quantum Error Correction is the cornerstone of reliable quantum computing. It provides the means to overcome the fragility of qubits, allowing for the execution of complex quantum algorithms over long periods. This chapter has explored the foundational principles of QEC, from basic codes like the Shor and Steane codes to advanced techniques like concatenated codes, surface codes, and quantum LDPC codes. The stabilizer formalism and syndrome measurement techniques offer a robust framework for detecting and correcting errors, while fault-tolerant circuit design prevents the propagation of errors during computation.

The Quantum Threshold Theorem establishes a theoretical foundation for fault-tolerant quantum computing, but significant challenges remain, including high resource overhead and adapting to realistic noise models. Nevertheless, ongoing research in QEC and advancements in quantum hardware integration are paving the way for practical, large-scale quantum computers. As quantum computing continues to evolve, QEC will play an increasingly critical role in advancing the field toward reliable, fault-tolerant systems capable of solving problems beyond the reach of classical computers.

Quantum Error Correction is not just a theoretical construct but a critical engineering discipline that bridges the gap between the fragile nature of qubits and the ambitious goal of realizing universal quantum computers. As we continue to optimize and innovate within the field of QEC, the future of scalable and practical quantum computing becomes ever more tangible.

REFERENCES

Acharya, R., ... "Quantum error correction below the surface code threshold." *arXiv preprint arXiv:2408.13687* (2024).

Ahn, D., Lee, J., Kim, M. S., & Hwang, S. W. (2002). SelfConsistent non-Markovian theory of a quantum-state evolution for quantum-information-processing. *Physical Review A*, 66(1), 012302. DOI: 10.1103/PhysRevA.66.012302

Aliferis, P., Gottesman, D., & Preskill, J. (2008). Accuracy threshold for Quantum Computation. *Quant. Inf. Proc.*, 8, 181–244.

Bacon, D. (2006). Operator Quantum Error-Correcting Subsystems for self-correcting quantum memories. *Physical Review A*, 73(1), 012340. DOI: 10.1103/PhysRevA.73.012340

Barrett, S. D., & Milburn, G. J. (2003). Measuring the Decoherence rate in a semiconductor charge qubit. *Physical Review B: Condensed Matter*, 68(15), 155307. DOI: 10.1103/PhysRevB.68.155307

Biamonte, J., Wittek, P., Pancotti, N., Rebentrost, P., Wiebe, N., & Lloyd, S. (2017). Quantum machine learning. *Nature*, 549(7671), 195–202. DOI: 10.1038/nature23474 PMID: 28905917

Bombin, H. (2011). Clifford Gates by Code Deformation. *New Journal of Physics*, 13(4), 043005. DOI: 10.1088/1367-2630/13/4/043005

Braunstein, S. L. (1998). Error Correction for continuous quantum variables. *Physical Review Letters*, 80(18), 4084–4087. DOI: 10.1103/PhysRevLett.80.4084

Bravyi, S., Cross, A. W., Gambetta, J. M., Maslov, D., Rall, P., & Yoder, T. J. (2024). High-threshold and low-overhead fault-tolerant quantum memory. *Nature*, 627(8005), 778–782. DOI: 10.1038/s41586-024-07107-7 PMID: 38538939

Brun, T., Devetak, I., & Hsieh, M. H. (2006). Correcting quantum errors with entanglement. science, 314(5798), 436-439.

Campbell, E. (2024). A series of fast-paced advances in Quantum Error Correction. *Nature Reviews. Physics*, 6(3), 160–161. DOI: 10.1038/s42254-024-00706-3

Deibuk, V., & Yuriychuk, I. "Noisy Multiple-Control Fredkin Gate in Nuclear Spin Based Qubits Chain." *2020 IEEE Third International Conference on Data Stream Mining & Processing (DSMP)*. IEEE, 2020. DOI: 10.1109/DSMP47368.2020.9204263

Devitt, S. J., Munro, W. J., & Nemoto, K. (2013). Quantum error correction for beginners. *Reports on Progress in Physics*, 76(7), 076001.

DiVincenzo, D. P., & Aliferis, P. (2007). Effective FaultTolerant Quantum Computation with slow measurement. *Physical Review Letters*, 98(2), 020501. DOI: 10.1103/PhysRevLett.98.020501 PMID: 17358588

Endo, S., Benjamin, S. C., & Li, Y. (2018). Practical quantum error mitigation for near future applications. *Physical Review X*, 8(3), 031027. DOI: 10.1103/PhysRevX.8.031027

Feynman, R.P. (1985). "Quantum mechanical computers." Optics news 11.2 11-20

Fredkin, E., & Toffoli, T. (1982). Conservative logic. *International Journal of Theoretical Physics*, 21(3), 219–253.

Gardiner, C. W., & Zoller, P. (2000). Quantum noise, Vol. 56 of Springer series in synergetics. Springer–Verlag, Berlin, 97, 98.

Kandala, A., Temme, K., Córcoles, A. D., Mezzacapo, A., Chow, J. M., & Gambetta, J. M. (2019). Error mitigation extends the computational reach of a noisy quantum processor. *Nature*, 567(7749), 491–495. DOI: 10.1038/s41586-019-1040-7 PMID: 30918370

Klimov, P. V., Bengtsson, A., Quintana, C., Bourassa, A., Hong, S., Dunsworth, A., & Neven, H. (2024). Optimizing quantum gates towards the scale of logical qubits. *Nature Communications*, 15(1), 2442.

Landauer, R. (1961). Irreversibility and heat generation in the computing process. *IBM Journal of Research and Development*, 5(3), 183–191. DOI: 10.1147/rd.53.0183

Maslov, D., Dueck, G. V., & Miller, D. M. (2005). Synthesis of Fredkin-Toffoli reversible networks. *IEEE Transactions on Very Large Scale Integration (VLSI) Systems*, 13(6), 765–769. DOI: 10.1109/TVLSI.2005.844284

McKay, D. C., Wood, C. J., Sheldon, S., Chow, J. M., & Gambetta, J. M. (2017). Efficient Z gates for quantum computing. *Physical Review. A*, 96(2), 022330. DOI: 10.1103/PhysRevA.96.022330

Mondal, A., & Parhi, K. K. (2024). Optimization of Quantum Circuits for Stabilizer Codes. IEEE Transactions on Circuits and Systems I: Regular Papers.

Mummadi, S., & Fathima, S. (2024, June). A Comprehensive Study on Quantum Key Distribution Protocols. In 2024 15th International Conference on Computing Communication and Networking Technologies (ICCCNT) (pp. 1-8). IEEE.

Mummadi, S., & Rudra, B. (2023). Fundamentals of Quantum Computation and Basic Quantum Gates. In *Handbook of Research on Quantum Computing for Smart Environments* (pp. 1–24). IGI Global. DOI: 10.4018/978-1-6684-6697-1.ch001

Mummadi, S., & Rudra, B. (2023). Practical demonstration of quantum key distribution protocol with error correction mechanism. *International Journal of Theoretical Physics*, 62(4), 86.

Mummadi, S., & Udari, G. C. (2023, July). Design and Implementation of Low Quantum Cost Reversible Universal Shift Register. In 2023 14th International Conference on Computing Communication and Networking Technologies (ICCCNT) (pp. 1-7). IEEE.

Peres, A. (1985). Reversible logic and quantum computers. *Physical review A*, 32(6), 3266.

Picton, P. D. (1994). Modified Fredkin gates in logic design. *Microelectronics Journal*, 25(6), 437–441. DOI: 10.1016/0026-2692(94)90068-X

Saeedi, M., & Markov, I. L. (2013). Synthesis and optimization of reversible circuits—A survey. *ACM Computing Surveys*, 45(2), 1–34.

Steane, A. M. (1996). Error correcting codes in quantum theory. *Physical Review Letters*, 77(5), 793–797. DOI: 10.1103/PhysRevLett.77.793 PMID: 10062908

Steane, A. M. (1996). Multiple particle interference and quantum error correction. *Proceedings - Royal Society. Mathematical, Physical and Engineering Sciences*, 452(1954), 2551–2577. DOI: 10.1098/rspa.1996.0136

Swathi, M., & Rudra, B. (2021, January). Implementation of reversible logic gates with quantum gates. In 2021 IEEE 11th annual computing and communication workshop and conference (CCWC) (pp. 1557-1563). Ieee.

Swathi, M., & Rudra, B. (2022). An efficient approach for quantum entanglement purification. *International Journal of Quantum Information*, 20(04), 2250004.

Swathi, M., & Rudra, B. (2022). A novel approach for asymmetric quantum error correction with syndrome measurement. *IEEE Access : Practical Innovations, Open Solutions*, 10, 44669–44676. DOI: 10.1109/ACCESS.2022.3170039

Swathi, M., & Rudra, B. (2022). *"Experimental analysis of a quantum encoder in various quantum systems." 2022 IEEE 13th Annual Ubiquitous Computing, Electronics & Mobile Communication Conference (UEMCON)*. IEEE.

Swathi, M., & Rudra, B. (2022, April). A novel architecture for binary code to gray code converter using quantum cellular automata. In Edge Analytics: Select Proceedings of 26th International Conference—ADCOM 2020 (pp. 43-61). Singapore: Springer Singapore.

Swathi, M., & Rudra, B. (2022, January). Novel encoding method for quantum error correction. In 2022 IEEE 12th Annual Computing and Communication Workshop and Conference (CCWC) (pp. 1001-1005). IEEE.

Unruh, W. G. (1995). Maintaining Coherence in Quantum Computers. *Physical Review A*, 51(2), 992–997. DOI: 10.1103/PhysRevA.51.992 PMID: 9911677

van Loock, P. (2010). A note on quantum error correction with continuous variables. *Journal of Modern Optics*, 57(19), 1965–1971.

Vasudevan, D. P., Lala, P. K., Di, J., & Parkerson, J. P. (2006). Reversible-logic design with online testability. *IEEE Transactions on Instrumentation and Measurement*, 55(2), 406–414. DOI: 10.1109/TIM.2006.870319

Wallman, J. J., & Emerson, J. (2016). Noise tailoring for scalable quantum computation via randomized compiling. *Physical Review. A*, 94(5), 052325. DOI: 10.1103/PhysRevA.94.052325

Xia, Q., Xie, H., & Yang, L. (2024). Analysis of Maximum Threshold and Quantum Security for Fault-Tolerant Encoding and Decoding Scheme Base on Steane Code. arXiv preprint arXiv:2403.04297.

Chapter 6
Computation of Adiabatic and Diabatic Potential Energy:
Machine Learning Contribution to Quantum Dynamical Studies

Ibtissem Jendoubi
https://orcid.org/0000-0002-2800-1748
Tunis El Manar University, Tunisia

ABSTRACT

This study delves into quantum simulation, exploring its foundational principles and potential applications. On the one hand, the classic methods of energy computation were used. On the other hand, the link between molecular dynamics (MD) and machine learning (ML) was also investigated. In the first part dedicated to adiabatic and diabatic potential energy curve (PEC), we examine quantum simulation techniques, including diabatization using neural networks to capture complex molecular dynamics. For the KFr molecule, we present novel adiabatic and diabatic potential energy curves. In the second part related to molecular dynamics simulation based on machine learning, the link between MD and ML was highlight to overcome difficulties of the classic simulation methods. This research aims to develop new approaches to molecular dynamics beyond the Born-Oppenheimer approximation and to explore the potential of machine learning, particularly interpretable neural networks, for efficient and interpretable simulations.

DOI: 10.4018/979-8-3693-6225-9.ch006

1. INTRODUCTION

In recent years, alkali dimers have gained significant attention due to their wide-ranging applications, from quantum simulation to ultracold chemistry (Cheng et al., 2023; Morita et al., 2023). The ability to precisely manipulate these molecules in ultracold environments has opened new avenues for research in fundamental physics, quantum technologies, and spectroscopy. Progress in manipulating and understanding these molecules is essential for the development of quantum computers, quantum sensors, and other cutting-edge technologies. Experimentally, these molecules are relatively easy to produce, with absorption spectra predominantly within the visible range, making them highly compatible with various laser systems (Hermsmeier et al., 2021). Recent advancements in molecular cooling and trapping techniques have further expanded research possibilities, particularly in controlling chemical reactivity through external electromagnetic fields (Vilas et al., 2022).

Many studies have investigated the intersection of machine learning and molecular simulation (Jackson et al., 2023; Noé et al., 2020). For instance, Noé et al. (2020) conducted a notable study focusing on the intricate and time-intensive computations inherent in molecular simulations, highlighting their suitability for an ML revolution. Their review concentrates on physics-based machine learning (ML) methods for molecular simulation (Noé et al., 2020). However, ML is also making significant strides in other areas of chemistry without relying on physics-based models. For instance, it facilitates direct predictions of physicochemical or pharmaceutical properties and aids in designing materials and molecules with specific desired characteristics using generative learning techniques. For more detailed exploration, they direct interested readers to other recent reviews on the topic. Recently, Keqin et al. (2024) investigated into the integration of machine learning and quantum computing, emphasizing the ability of quantum computing to improve the effectiveness and computational speed of machine learning (Keqin et al., 2024). They illustrated how quantum computing can speed up conventional machine learning algorithms by leveraging its distinct features of superposition and entanglement, especially in dealing with large datasets and solving complex, high-dimensional problems.

The creation of highly accurate potential energy curves (PECs) for simulations using conventional quantum chemistry methods can be computationally costly. Seino et al. (2019) Seino et al. examined the accuracy of a semi-local kinetic energy density functional (KEDF), optimized by machine learning, for the potential energy curves (PEC) of small molecules. Their research focuses on introducing new descriptors to capture the non-local characteristics of the KEDF, specifically the distances between grid points and the core centers (Seino et al.,2019)

This chapter explores the structural study of the potassium francium (KFr) molecule beyond the Born-Oppenheimer approximation, offering important insights for a dynamic analysis of KFr's behavior. The primary aim is to provide an overview of current research in molecular dynamics and machine learning, outline the theoretical methods used to generate molecular data—such as the potential energy curve (PEC) and diabatic PEC for the potassium-francium (KFr) molecule and examine the applications of laser cooling and spectral experiments with KFr molecule.

2. COMPUTATIONAL METHODS

Details of *ab initio* calculations were previously in other works (e.g. Jendoubi et al., 2024) These works comprehensively cover the including discussions on the Schrödinger equation (Schrödinger, 1926), Born-Oppenheimer (BO) approximation (Born and Oppenheimer, 1927), Hartree-Fock (HF) approximation (Hartre, 1928), and Configuration Interaction method (Shavitt, 1977; Schaefer et al., 1971). Fig.1 illustrates the procedural steps required to perform *ab initio* calculations.

Figure 1. The steps involved ab initio calculation. Copyright CRC Press (Jendoubi et al., 2024).

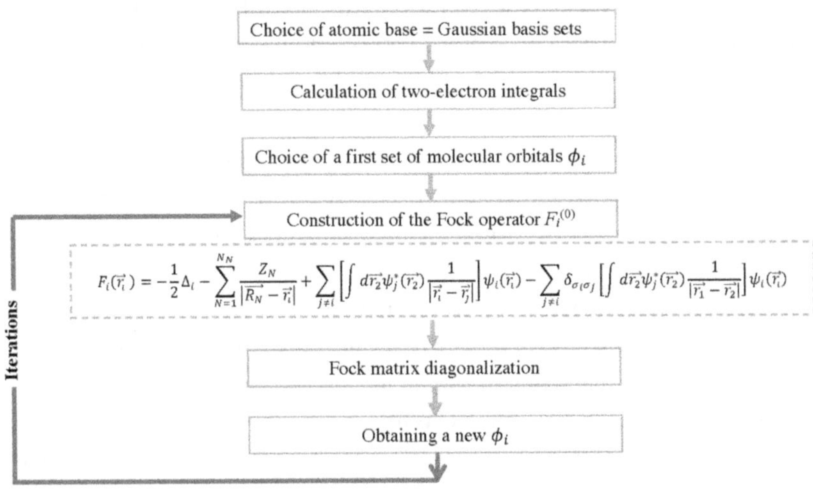

3. RESULTS AND DISCUSSION

3.1. Adiabatic and Diabatic Potential Energy Curve (PEC)

The Born-Oppenheimer approximation, also known as the *adiabatic* approximation, relies on the significant mass difference between electrons and nuclei to justify treating their motions separately (Jensen, 2017). As a result, most dynamical studies use this separation as a fundamental approach. Typically, electronic states are sufficiently distinct, allowing nuclear motion to occur independently for each potential energy. The Born-Oppenheimer approximation is not valid in certain cases, such as in the phenomenon of avoided crossings and during rapid collisions. To improve computational efficiency, it would be possible to choose a basis of electronic functions which would reduce the elements of the matrix as much as possible $\left\langle \phi^{k}\frac{\partial}{\partial q}\phi^{k}\right\rangle \cong 0$. In fact, diabatic states are obtained from adiabatic states by a unitary transformation. The two potential energy curves (PECs) of the excited states are in a diabatic basis $\{\phi_m^d\}$ of electronic states: $\phi^{diabtic} = \sum_n \psi^{adiabatic}_n U$. Whereas U: transformation matrix chosen such that the elements of the nonadiabatic coupling matrix $\left\langle \phi^{d}\frac{\partial}{\partial q}\phi^{d}\right\rangle$; where q represents R_{AB} (bond length from atoms *A and B*) (Jendoubi et al., 2024). To explain this phenomenon the adiabatic and diabatic (represented by dashed lines, Fig.2b) potential energy curves presented for excited states of the LiRb molecular system (e.g. the 6 $^1\Sigma^+$ and 7 $^1\Sigma^+$ states) as shown in Fig. 2 (Jendoubi et al., 2012). To solve this problem we can consider in this case to choose a basis of electronic functions that would cancel, as much as possible, the matrix elements: $\left\langle \phi^{k}\frac{\partial}{\partial q}\phi^{k}\right\rangle \cong 0$.

Concerning the relationship between diabatization and machine learning (ML), the diabatic basis is crucial for improving ML applications. Diabatic potential energy curves and associated properties typically exhibit smooth variation with respect to geometric coordinates, particularly in avoided crossings regions, making them ideal for ML models. In fact, the Born-Oppenheimer approximation breaks down in these regions. However, the potential energy may come closer together in certain regions. This is particularly the case when two adiabatic states come together '*accidentally*', in what is known as avoided crossings. While a strictly defined diabatic basis does not exist, property-based diabatization techniques are both straightforward and computationally efficient to implement. The smooth behavior of diabatic wavefunctions and their properties complements the continuous data structure required for effective ML algorithms (Li and Xie, 2023).

For the LiRb molecule (specifically, the 6 $^1\Sigma^+$ and 7 $^1\Sigma^+$ states, shown in Fig.2b) with important nonadiabatic electronic couplings, obviously, region **I** is still the bound state region mainly about adiabatic wavefunction $\psi_6^{adiabatic}$, $\psi_7^{adiabatic}$, and the quasi-bound states in region II would be altered by the electronic couplings.

The region II, or the avoided crossing (AC) region (Fig.2a), becomes into a quite special region by the nonadiabatic interactions (Fig.2b). In the coupling region (II), the molecular system needs to modify its electronic structure and transition from electronic configuration ϕ_6 to ϕ_7 (diabatic) or vice versa in order to stay in the electronic state ψ_6 or ψ_7 (adiabatic).

The availability of global potential energy curves (PECs) was a fundamental requirement for the investigation of reaction and dynamics phenomena. By examining the potassium-francium system (KFr), we present both adiabatic and diabatic potential energy curves (PECs) for the $X^1\Sigma^+$ ground state and the $2^1\Sigma^+$-$9^1\Sigma^+$ first excited state. This comprehensive analysis seeks to discover new approaches to molecular dynamics beyond the Born-Oppenheimer approximation, with our results being presented for the first time. Figure 3 presents our precise potential energy curves (PECs) for the ground state and low-lying excited states of the KFr molecule. The quasi-diabatic potential energy curves corresponding to the $X^1\Sigma^+$-$9^1\Sigma^+$ adiabatic electronic states, labeled D_1 through D_9, are shown in Figure 4. The ionic quasi-diabatic curve, labeled D_1, which dissociates into K^-Fr^+, behaves as 1/R at intermediate and large internuclear distances. Additionally, it was observed that the same quasi-diabatic state D_1 crosses the quasi-diabatic curves D_2 through D_9. The avoided crossings between the $1\Sigma^+$ electronic states, previously discussed in the adiabatic representation, have been transformed into real crossings in the quasi-diabatic representation. To provide a clearer understanding of this phenomenon, Figure 5 illustrates the relationship between the adiabatic PECs (solid lines) and the diabatic PECs (dashed lines). Similar to the LiRb molecule, the KFr molecular system must adjust its electronic structure and transition between the electronic configurations ϕ_5 and ϕ_6 (diabatic), or vice versa, to remain in the electronic states ψ_5 or ψ_6 (adiabatic) within the coupling region (II). Our research investigates non-adiabatic molecular dynamics techniques that extend beyond the Born-Oppenheimer approximation for the KFr molecule. We provide novel calculations of adiabatic and diabatic potential energy curves (PECs) for the KFr molecule, representing a significant contribution to the field.

Figure 5. Adiabatic and diabatic potential energy curves of KFr molecule (in Hartree)

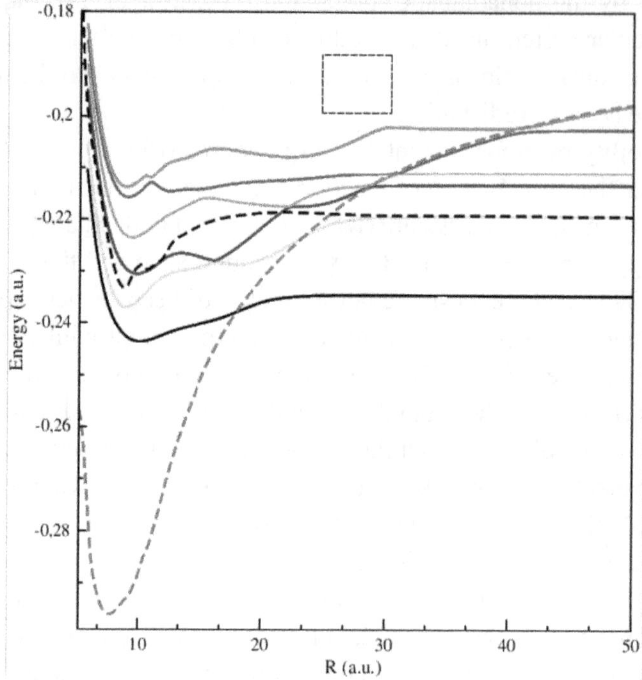

3.2. Molecular Dynamics Simulation Based on Machine Learning

The revolution in artificial intelligence, particularly machine learning, coupled with the exponential growth in computing power, has transformed molecular dynamics (MD) into an incredibly powerful tool for studying molecular systems.

The use of complex machine learning methods, as shown in Figure 6, has significantly progressed. These methods can effectively replicate the PEC of elemental materials and small molecules (Seino et al., 2019). The quantity of input neurons corresponds to the provided physical descriptors, such as $\rho(r)$ for electron density and $|\nabla\rho(r)|$ for the magnitude of the gradient of electron density, which signifies density changes concerning position. The neural network structure comprises five hidden layers, each with 50 neurons. The output layer includes a single neuron that represents the enhancement-like factor and acts as the response variable. To minimize the error between the predicted and reference kinetic energies (KEs), the mean absolute percentage error (MAPE) was utilized as the loss function (Seino et al., 2019).

Machine learning can help optimize and improve the performance of quantum simulations, while quantum simulation can provide new computational tools for machine learning (Ciliberto et al., 2018; Manan et al., 2022). The convergences of these powerful technologies will likely result in groundbreaking advancements. Quantum algorithms can potentially provide exponential speedups for certain types of calculations, such as simulating molecular dynamics or solving the Schrödinger equation. Additionally, Quantum computers can more accurately represent non-adiabatic effects, such as conical intersections, which are crucial for understanding chemical reactions and energy transfer processes. For example, You Li et al. (2021) proposed a novel machine learning technique, Diabatization by Equivariant Neural Network (DENN), designed to handle the permutation and symmetry properties of molecular systems. DENN uses a specialized neural network to accurately represent the energy changes (diabatic potential energy metrics) that occur when particles in the system rearrange. DENN expands upon existing machine learning diabatization methods by incorporating diabatic coupling, which accounts for the mutual influence of particles on each other's energy, particularly in close proximity. Quantum machine learning leverages quantum computing to enhance traditional machine learning algorithms. Quantum algorithms exploit quantum mechanics to potentially solve complex problems more efficiently than classical methods. Westermayr and Marquetand (2020) emphasized the importance of theoretical studies on molecular excited states in complementing experiments and illuminating fundamental processes in life and nature. For example, photosynthesis (Xiong et al., 2000), Computer vision (Khan et al., 2021), or photovoltaics (Gaviria et al, 2022) relevant molecules are a result of light-induced reaction. Figure 7 (*Copyright (2021)Chemical Reviews)* is adapted from Westermayr and Marquetand's article and, as noted, is inspired by the reference Chandrasekaran et al. (2019). ML models can be applied to various aspects of molecular photochemistry, as illustrated in Fig. 7 (Westermayr and Marquetand, 2020). Machine learning can be applied to fundamental aspects of quantum chemistry, such as finding optimal solutions to the Schrödinger equation or density functional theory. For ground states, ML models can approximate molecular wavefunctions or densities.

Furthermore, Chandrasekaran and colleagues (2019) demonstrated that in modern materials and chemical science research and development, simulations involving the solution of the Kohn-Sham (KS) equation (Fritsche, 1986) from density functional theory (DFT) have emerged as an essential tool. Their study introduces a machine learning approach that bypasses the Kohn-Sham equation, enabling direct, efficient, and accurate predictions of electronic structure from atomic configurations (Chandrasekaran et al., 2019). While relatively new compared to ground-state ML, machine learning has demonstrated significant potential for accelerating and improving excited-state simulations. Most existing studies focus on small molecular systems, but future applications could encompass a wider range, including dynamics with excited-state ML potentials and absorption spectra.

4. CONCLUSION

This chapter delves into quantum simulation, exploring its foundational principles and potential applications. It also examines the relationship between molecular dynamics and machine learning. ML algorithms are enabling faster and more accurate calculations of potential energy curves, which are crucial for understanding and predicting the behavior of molecules. Furthermore, our research explores non-adiabatic molecular dynamics techniques that transcend the Born-Oppenheimer approximation for the potassium-francium (KFr) molecule, with our findings being presented for the first time as a pioneering advancement in the field. We present both adiabatic and diabatic potential energy curves (PECs) for the ground state and the first excited state of potassium-francium molecule (KFr). This comprehensive analysis seeks to discover new approaches to molecular dynamics beyond the Born-Oppenheimer approximation, with our results being presented for the first time.

ML models can be used to predict the dynamics of the KFr molecule's excited states, which adiabatic and diabatic PECs were simulated using traditional quantum chemistry methods. Consequently, Machine learning offers the potential to revolutionize molecular dynamics simulations, as demonstrated by its ability to predict the dynamics of the KFr molecule's excited states. This example highlights the synergy between these fields and the exciting possibilities for future research.

The convergence of quantum dynamical studies, molecular dynamics, and machine learning is poised to revolutionize scientific research. Quantum dynamical studies provide a fundamental framework for understanding the behavior of molecules at the quantum level. Molecular dynamics simulations offer a way to explore the classical dynamics of molecules, while machine learning algorithms can efficiently analyze vast datasets and model complex relationships. The synergy between these fields holds immense potential for advancing our understanding of the universe, from the properties of materials to the mechanisms of biological processes. As computational capabilities continue to grow, we can expect this ongoing revolution in computational modeling to shape the future of scientific exploration and discovery.

REFERENCES

Born, M., & Oppenheimer, R. (2000). On the quantum theory of molecules. In *Quantum Chemistry* (pp. 1–24). Classic Scientific Papers. DOI: 10.1142/9789812795762_0001

Chandrasekaran, A., Kamal, D., Batra, R., Kim, C., Chen, L., & Ramprasad, R. (2019). Solving the electronic structure problem with machine learning. npj Computational Materials, 5(1), 22.

Cheng, J., Wang, J., Tan, Z., & Wu, S. (2021). Theoretical Study of Photoassociation of Alkali-Metal Dimers. *Russian Journal of Physical Chemistry A. Focus on Chemistry*, 95(S2, Suppl 2), S396–S405. DOI: 10.1134/S0036024421150061

Ciliberto, C., Herbster, M., Ialongo, A. D., Pontil, M., Rocchetto, A., Severini, S., & Wossnig, L. (2018). Quantum machine learning: A classical perspective. *Proceedings - Royal Society. Mathematical, Physical and Engineering Sciences*, 474(2209), 20170551. DOI: 10.1098/rspa.2017.0551 PMID: 29434508

Fritsche, L. (1986). Generalized Kohn-Sham theory for electronic excitations in realistic systems. *Physical Review. B*, 33(6), 3976–3989. DOI: 10.1103/PhysRevB.33.3976 PMID: 9938813

Gaviria, J. F., Narváez, G., Guillen, C., Giraldo, L. F., & Bressan, M. (2022). Machine learning in photovoltaic systems: A review. *Renewable Energy*, 196, 298–318. DOI: 10.1016/j.renene.2022.06.105

Hartree, D. R. (1927). Bozman, AM, Denmark, AE, and Trickey, EM Elementary Mathematics.

Hermsmeier, R., Kłos, J., Kotochigova, S., & Tscherbul, T. V. (2021). Quantum spin state selectivity and magnetic tuning of ultracold chemical reactions of triplet alkali-metal dimers with alkali-metal atoms. *Physical Review Letters*, 127(10), 103402. DOI: 10.1103/PhysRevLett.127.103402 PMID: 34533330

Jackson, N. E., Savoie, B. M., Statt, A., & Webb, M. A. (2023). Introduction to machine learning for molecular simulation. *Journal of Chemical Theory and Computation*, 19(14), 4335–4337. DOI: 10.1021/acs.jctc.3c00735 PMID: 37489106

Jendoubi, I., Berriche, H., Ben Ouada, H., & Gadéa, F. X. (2012). Structural and spectroscopic study of the LiRb molecule beyond the Born–Oppenheimer approximation. *The Journal of Physical Chemistry A*, 116(11), 2945–2960. DOI: 10.1021/jp209106w PMID: 22360282

Jendoubi, I., Essefi, E., & Hendeoui, H. (2025). Quantum Computing of Computational Chemistry: Applications of Molecular Quantum Dynamics. In The Quantum Evolution (pp. 292-305). CRC Press.

Jensen, F. (2017). *Introduction to computational chemistry*. John wiley & sons.

Khan, A. A., Laghari, A. A., & Awan, S. A. (2021). Machine learning in computer vision: A review. *EAI Endorsed Transactions on Scalable Information Systems*, 8(32), e4–e4.

Li, C., Hou, S., & Xie, C. (2023). Constructing diabatic potential energy matrices with neural networks based on adiabatic energies and physical considerations: Toward quantum dynamic accuracy. *Journal of Chemical Theory and Computation*, 19(11), 3063–3079. DOI: 10.1021/acs.jctc.2c01074 PMID: 37216273

Li, K., Zhao, P., Dai, S., Zhu, A., Hong, B., Liu, J., ... & Zhang, Y. (2024). Exploring the impact of quantum computing on machine learning performance.

Manan, I., Rehman, F., Sharif, H., Riaz, N., Atif, M., & Aqeel, M. (2022, December). Quantum computing and machine learning algorithms-a review. In 2022 3rd International Conference on Innovations in Computer Science & Software Engineering (ICONICS) (pp. 1-6). IEEE. DOI: 10.1109/ICONICS56716.2022.10100452

Morita, M., Kendrick, B. K., Kłos, J., Kotochigova, S., Brumer, P., & Tscherbul, T. V. (2023). Signatures of Non-universal Quantum Dynamics of Ultracold Chemical Reactions of Polar Alkali Dimer Molecules with Alkali Metal Atoms: Li (2S)+ NaLi (a 3Σ+)→ Na (2S)+ Li2 (a 3Σ u+). *The Journal of Physical Chemistry Letters*, 14(14), 3413–3421. DOI: 10.1021/acs.jpclett.3c00159 PMID: 37001115

Schaefer, H. H., & Schaefer, H. H. (1971). *Locally convex topological vector spaces*. Springer New York. DOI: 10.1007/978-1-4684-9928-5

Schrödinger, E. (1926). An undulatory theory of the mechanics of atoms and molecules. *Physical Review*, 28(6), 1049–1070. DOI: 10.1103/PhysRev.28.1049

Seino, J., Kageyama, R., Fujinami, M., Ikabata, Y., & Nakai, H. (2019). Semi-local machine-learned kinetic energy density functional demonstrating smooth potential energy curves. *Chemical Physics Letters*, 734, 136732. DOI: 10.1016/j.cplett.2019.136732

Vilas, N. B., Hallas, C., Anderegg, L., Robichaud, P., Winnicki, A., Mitra, D., & Doyle, J. M. (2022). Magneto-optical trapping and sub-Doppler cooling of a polyatomic molecule. *Nature*, 606(7912), 70–74. DOI: 10.1038/s41586-022-04620-5 PMID: 35650357

Westermayr, J., & Marquetand, P. (2020). Machine learning for electronically excited states of molecules. *Chemical Reviews*, 121(16), 9873–9926. DOI: 10.1021/acs.chemrev.0c00749 PMID: 33211478

Xiong, J., Fischer, W. M., Inoue, K., Nakahara, M., & Bauer, C. E. (2000). Molecular evidence for the early evolution of photosynthesis. science, 289(5485), 1724-1730.

Chapter 7
Innovative Medical Marketing Strategies Powered by Machine Learning

Sunil Kumar Roy
https://orcid.org/0000-0002-6152-5519
Department of Management and Commerce, Manav Rachna University, Faridabad, India

R. Anitha
Department of Management Studies, Dr. SNS Rajalakshmi College of Arts and Science, Coimbatore, India

R. Reka
Mahendra College of Engineering, Salem, India

Syeda Hina Bilfaqih
Department of Commerce, Radhwa International School, Yanbu, Saudi Arabia

S. Surjith Bharathi
https://orcid.org/0009-0006-6033-9825
Department of Management Studies, Dr. SNS Rajalakshmi College of Arts and Science, Coimbatore, India

ABSTRACT

This chapter discusses the transformative effect of Machine Learning on medical marketing strategies. With the healthcare landscape becoming increasingly data-driven, ML provides innovative solutions for enhancing patient engagement, optimizing

DOI: 10.4018/979-8-3693-6225-9.ch007

marketing efforts, and improving outcomes. The integration of ML technologies in medical marketing enables personalized patient experiences, predictive analytics, and real-time insights, empowering healthcare organizations to better understand their audiences. This brings actionable insights for healthcare marketers: allowing them to personalize the message, refine campaigns, and increase ROI by sifting through large datasets. Beyond that, ML enhances the ethical marketing practice: in this regard, privacy on patients' data gets boosted, HIPAA compliance occurs, and trust develops. Various case studies in this chapter successfully implemented ML-driven strategies for practice guidance in healthcare marketing while employing the most advanced technologies of industry trends.

INTRODUCTION

Traditional marketing in health care will not be enough in the dynamically shifting scenario, especially in the health arena, with the rapid progress of the digital age. More and more healthcare organizations seek innovative solutions, as a result of which ML, which was considered science fiction until now, is now being perceived as the powerful tool to change medical marketing. Machine learning is a way through which the volume of available data can be tapped to enable actionable insights that drive data-driven and patient-centric approaches to marketing(Shehab et al., 2022).

Traditionally, medical marketing has been executed through a very broad approach, where every patient is treated essentially the same way. However, with this increasing availability of health care data-from electronic health records (EHRs) to patient demographics and behavioral insights-organizations can use this information for more focused and effective marketing campaigns. Scaling up the processing and analysis of such data through machine learning enables healthcare marketers to take advantage of predictive capabilities into patient behaviors, preferences, and needs(Minssen et al., 2020).

One of the most significant benefits of incorporating Machine Learning in medical marketing is the capacity to provide individualized experiences to patients. Healthcare providers can segment their populations and make targeted campaigns for those different segments by using the algorithms in ML. Predictive analytics can, for instance, determine patients at a risk of certain diseases or preventive care. In turn, this will enable the healthcare marketer to tailor messages and intervention strategies. This ensures that personalization increases the engagement level of patients since they get information and offers that are immediately aligned with their health journey(Gerke et al., 2020).

Further, Machine Learning-driven marketing becomes more efficient by automating the process. Marketing tasks, which earlier had to be monitored manually, such as email campaigns, appointment reminders, and patient outreach, can now be automated with ML models. This reduces the administrative burden on healthcare professionals, allowing them to focus more on direct patient care while still maintaining robust communication with patients. Moreover, automation ensures that marketing activities occur consistently and at scale, without sacrificing the personalization that patients expect(Arasu et al., 2020).

Ethics and compliance are also at the core of modern medical marketing, and Machine Learning can play a critical role in ensuring that the practices of marketing are done within legal standards such as HIPAA. With the use of ML, healthcare organizations can effectively manage patient data privacy so that information can be protected while still making use of it for marketing insights. This not only fosters patient trust but also aligns with regulatory requirements-the essential elements in upholding a healthcare organization's reputation and continuity of operation(Zhu et al., 2022).

This helps the users derive insights in real-time with adequate decision-making, much demanded today in this fast environment of health. Predictive analytics enable the marketers of health to foresee the trend and pinpoint anomalies for rapidly reacting to patient needs or shifts in demand in the marketplace. Thus, this is an advanced approach by health providers being on top of things, able to rapidly adjust strategies in synchronization with emergent challenges(Awaysheh et al., 2019).

The success of Machine Learning in medical marketing is reflected in the case studies of various healthcare organizations. For example, hospitals that have applied ML to patient outreach have achieved great improvements in patient retention, high satisfaction rates, and operational efficiency. Such success stories illustrate how Machine Learning-driven strategies allow healthcare organizations to not only meet but also exceed the expectations of their patients(Kaur et al., 2019).

In a nutshell, Machine Learning has emerged as a transformative force in medical marketing, giving healthcare organizations the tools to keep up with an ever-changing industry. With the help of data, personalization, and automation, ML empowers healthcare marketers to develop more meaningful and impactful campaigns, and to overcome the ethical and compliance challenges that are characteristic of healthcare data. In an evolutionary manner, this technology plays a crucial role in developing the future of health marketing, which leads towards a highly innovative and patient-centric solution(Harrison & Sidey-Gibbons, 2021).

Objectives

The main objective of medical marketing through ML is enhancing engagement with the patient with tailor-made, data-driven marketing efforts. Predictive analytics, paired with automation, may aid healthcare organizations in streamlining efforts, reducing operational burden and ensuring adherence to regulation and standards. Furthermore, this technology enables marketers in healthcare industries to develop a richer insight into patient behaviors, needs, and preferences, resulting in more precise and targeted messaging. This leads to creating more meaningful engagements, leading to better outcomes and establishing trust with better returns on marketing investment within an evolving healthcare environment.

BACKGROUND MACHINE LEARNING IN HEALTHCARE

What is Machine Learning?

Machine learning (ML) is the sub-domain of AI which is used in developing algorithms and statistical models so that the computers may learn from experience. In this case, instead of providing each and every task in explicit detail, as it is happening in traditional programming, the system will actually be able to enhance its performance while continuing processing the new information based on the new knowledge about patterns. Such process often demands large datasets and advanced algorithms along with great computational power to unearth some of the insights that would be difficult to identify manually(Ramudu et al., 2023; Sreedhar et al., 2024). Machine learning can be classified under two major categories: first, supervised learning, which involves training models on the labeled data, and, second, unsupervised learning that tends to look for hidden patterns within unstructured data. Reinforcement learning and deep learning are other subfields in ML that involve more complicated, multi-layered tasks of decision-making, often based on neural networks.

Applications of Machine Learning in Medical Marketing

Machine Learning is now becoming the most transformative tool used in medical marketing to engage a patient with healthcare organizations in a more personalized, efficient, and effective manner. Among various applications of Machine Learning is creating a personalized patient experience. This is possible through evaluating a patient's health history, behavior, and preference. This makes it possible to have recommendations on treatment options, appointments, and even follow-ups through

ML-empowered systems(Mohanraj et al., 2024; Sreedhar et al., 2024; Subha et al., 2023). This personalization enhances patient engagement and satisfaction because patients get information and communication that is relevant to their individual health journey. Another major application of Machine Learning in medical marketing is predictive analytics. By using the historical patient data, ML models can predict the future health outcomes, thereby identifying patients with a risk for certain conditions and intervening ahead of time. For example, predictive models can find the early stages of chronic diseases such as diabetes or cardiovascular conditions so that healthcare professionals may develop preventive care strategies that would reduce health costs and enhance health.

Marketing automation also transforms with Machine Learning. Repetitive tasks, such as scheduling appointments, sending emails or even engaging with social media, are becoming more automated based on ML algorithms. Optimizing and personalizing communications at scale in these systems means that the messages are clear and aligned with patient choices. It frees marketers in the health care industry from mundane work and concentrates on strategic activities to make the process better for the patient while providing better quality care. Apart from this, Machine Learning also brings accuracy in targeting and segmentation of medical marketing. It helps in the analysis of big data in order to divide the patients into smaller and more accurate groups based on demographics, behavior, and health needs. Such highly targeted campaigns help the patients to get information specifically based on individual needs. It could be sending personal health tips or recommending a particular treatment; with ML-driven marketing, there is always relevance and engagement.

Ethical considerations also play a critical role in ML applications within medical marketing. Because the healthcare data typically contains sensitive information, the Machine Learning models have to make sure that privacy, security, and compliance with healthcare regulations (e.g., HIPAA) are ensured. Machine Learning provides advanced tools to handle data responsibly, which ensures patient trust and the integrity of healthcare marketing practices. Hence, Machine Learning encompasses an expansive range of capabilities which enables healthcare marketers to have a more efficient, data-driven, and patient-centric strategy. Integration of ML into the realm of medical marketing thus enhances the ability of organizations toward patient outcomes, operational efficiency, and competitiveness in a health care industry that increasingly has a competitive landscape.

MACHINE LEARNING IN MEDICAL MARKETING

Machine learning has emerged to be a strong tool for transforming medical marketing. It allows the healthcare organizations to develop more personal, efficient, and data-driven strategies. With advanced algorithms and insights, ML can enhance patient experiences, predictive capabilities, and operational efficiencies to better patient outcomes and business results(Balki et al., 2019). The figure 1 depicts the Machine Learning process, including its components in medical marketing.

Figure 1. Machine Learning process – components in medical marketing

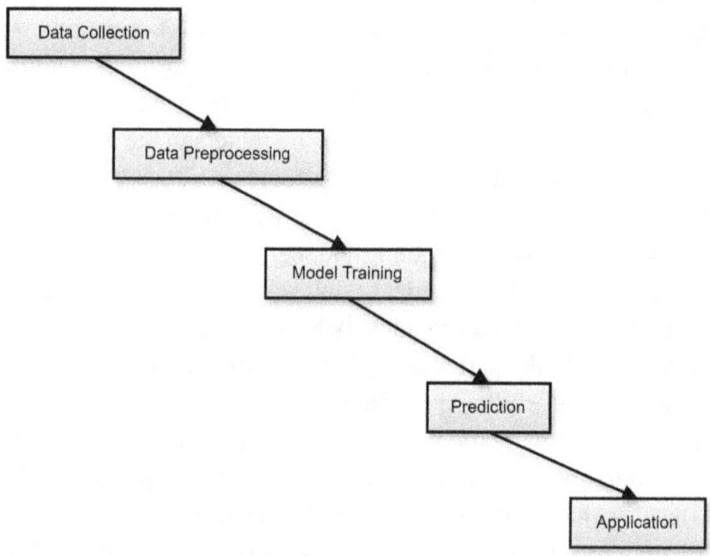

Personalized Patient Experiences

Some of the biggest advantages that its personalization gives to its patients' experience over traditional ways for a good medical marketing approach are this: Traditional approaches used included only some broad generalizations without making considerations for patients and a preference. But now it is possible to collect data due to Machine Learning, whether big data concerning patient demographics, medical history, their response to treatment, etc., and other behavior patterns for highly individualized communications by health care professionals. With examples, ML algorithms allow breaking down patient populations into defined areas of health conditions, identified risks as well as previous experiences with medical providers. Healthcare organizations hence obtain differentiated treatment plans, health suggestions, and marketing campaigns with regard to specific patients, and thus the experience the patient will receive will lead to higher engagement, trust as well as satisfaction, to loyalty and adherence to assigned treatment plans. In addition, personalized communication creates a deeper relationship between the patient and the health provider. It is the foundation for long-term health improvement(Shutaywi & Kachouie, 2021).

Moreover, Machine Learning provides predictive personalization. With historical data, ML models can predict the needs of patients even before they occur. This may include reminders for preventive care, personalized health tips, or targeted communications for patients who are at risk of developing chronic diseases. For example, an algorithm could decide that the patient is likely to require follow-up appointments or specific drugs as indicated by past behavior, so health providers are proactive in their contact with the patient. All this improves the patient experience; hence, it is a much more proactive and responsive healthcare model.

Predictive Analytics for Better Outcomes

Predictive analytics is yet another major benefit of Machine Learning, which can help the healthcare institutions predict and avert problems in advance, before they actually become critical. Having the ability to analyze vast amounts of information, from EHRs, lab results, genetic information, and social determinants of health, ML models form insights that help healthcare institutions build proactive healthcare strategies. For example, predictive analytics could identify patients with the possibility of having chronic diseases like diabetes, heart disease, or cancer through the identified patterns from historical health data. By such information, healthcare marketers can make better guidance to the education campaigns and intervention strategies concerning preventing disease progression or complications. Predictive models also optimize resource distribution in ensuring that health providers direct their efforts toward those at greater risk, hence benefiting more in the early intervention(Miklosik & Evans, 2020).

Moreover, Machine Learning enhances the clinical decision as it can provide data-driven insight for further treatment and managing the patients. For example, using predictive analytics, physicians can change the medications more accurately and can more precisely suggest lifestyle adjustments or plan follow-up care. Such insights benefit not only the patients but also cut healthcare costs by avoiding unnecessary treatments and hospitalizations. Predictive analytics has a positive effect on marketing strategies because it improves campaign effectiveness. For instance, predictive models can help in targeted email marketing or SMS reminders so that the right content reaches the patients at the right time, leading to a higher rate of engagement and conversion. This will, therefore, make the marketing process more efficient.

Marketing Automation and Efficiency

Its applicability in medical marketing efforts via high efficiency and scalability through marketing automation based on Machine Learning enhances the process. Freeing up time for so much but still delivering high personalization becomes possible through automation of various tasks such as appointment scheduling and communication with patients and for follow-ups. ML-driven automation systems can handle vast amounts of data and execute complex workflows with minimal human intervention. For instance, an ML model automatically segments patient lists, prioritizes outreach, and delivers a tailored message at scale. In this manner, it bypasses manual data entry entirely and minimizes administrative tasks, so healthcare marketers will have more time to strategize and be creative(Kedi et al., 2024).

Furthermore, Machine Learning improves marketing campaign effectiveness through optimization. This is because machine learning algorithms analyze the past performance of marketing efforts to recommend what could improve engagement, click-through rates, and conversion rates. In time, such models improve and continue to serve marketing campaigns as effective and relevant. In terms of efficiency, ML also supports real-time decision-making. If a patient cancels an appointment or undergoes some change in health status, ML algorithms can adjust marketing strategies right away to reflect such updates. This ensures that health care providers stay connected with the patients in dynamic and responsive ways. Moreover, automation will ensure integration of multiple marketing channels such as email, social media, web-interactions, and mobile applications. Multi-channel efforts by co-ordination will enable healthcare organizations to offer an integrated marketing approach with constant engagement and much return on investment.

Machine learning revolutionizes medical marketing through a more unique patient experience, predictability, and automated efficiency. With these innovations, health organizations can craft much more meaningful marketing strategies that improve engagement with patients, outcomes, and the cost-effectiveness. With the more ML is further developed, the potential that it has in rewriting healthcare marketing's future is vast-to arm organizations to succeed in competitive yet patient-centric surroundings.

MACHINE LEARNING IN MEDICAL MARKETING: IMPLEMENTATION TECHNIQUES

There are many benefits of the integration of Machine Learning in medical marketing, but careful planning and strategic techniques are required to successfully implement ML in this context. A structured approach from data collection and preprocessing to model development and deployment ensures that healthcare organizations can leverage ML to enhance patient engagement, optimize marketing efforts, and achieve better health outcomes(Makino et al., 2019). The figure 2 depicts the implementation processes in medical marketing.

Figure 2. Implementation processes in medical marketing

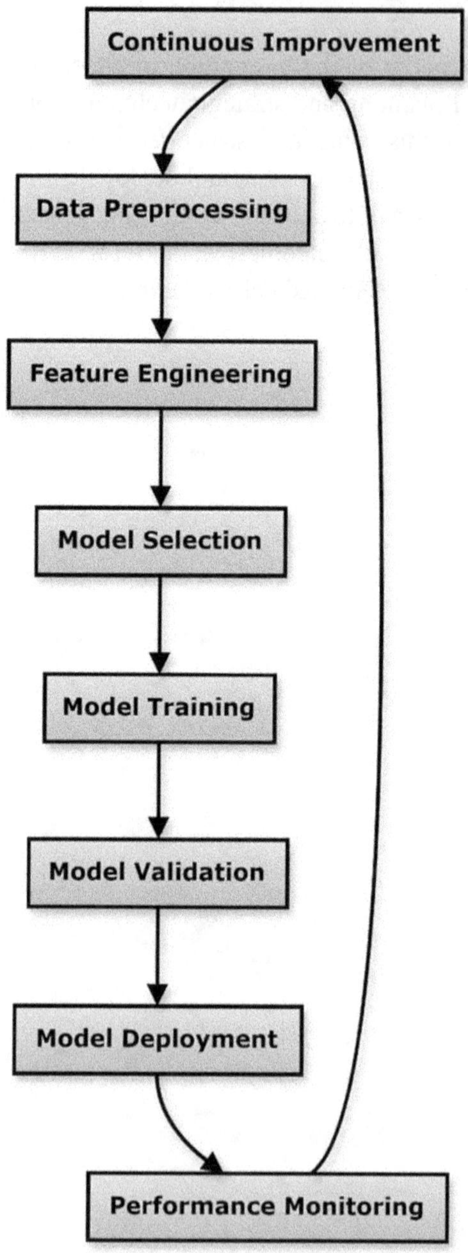

Data Collection and Preparation

The foundation of any successful Machine Learning model remains to be based on high-quality, relevant data. In medical marketing, there would be Electronic Health Records and patient demographics, history of appointments, clinical notes, social determinants of health, and much more to serve as data sources. The proper techniques applied while collecting and preprocessing ensure accurate insights and predictions with these ML models(Tyagi & Chahal, 2020).

a) Data Integration: Collects and combines data from heterogeneous sources, like clinical systems, patient portals, and wearables, to form a holistic view of the patient information.
b) Data Cleaning and Standardization: Deals with data quality by eliminating duplicates, managing missing values, and standardizing formats to have consistency across the datasets.
c) Feature Engineering: Raw data is transformed into meaningful features by identifying the variables like age, medical history, genetic factors, or lifestyle behavior that can affect the marketing strategy.

Model Selection and Development

Selection of the right Machine Learning model is what matters to get the best results. Depending on specific requirements, supervised learning algorithms like regression, classification, and many more, such as unsupervised clustering or anomaly detection, are also available for healthcare marketers in the option box. Deep models of machine learning, which involve a complex network of high dimension, can also be selected when required.

a) Model Selection: Use simple models such as decision trees or logistic regression to get started. With an increase in the complexity of the tasks, use ensemble models, SVM, or deep learning architectures.
b) Hyperparameter Tuning: Fine-tune model parameters for better accuracy. Techniques include grid search or random search to optimize hyperparameters with better predictive performance.
c) Cross-validation: It is also ensured that the models are robust and generalized to new data through cross-validation techniques, reducing the risk of overfitting.

Predictive Analytics and Insights

Predictive analytics in medical marketing uses historical and real-time data to predict outcomes about the future: patients' behavior, health conditions, or campaign performance. These insights are actionable and serve to guide marketing strategy as well as healthcare intervention.

a) Data Segmentation: Use clustering algorithms to classify patients into various groups based on risk of disease, responses to treatment, or usage patterns. This makes for higher relevance since marketing campaigns are tailored for the distinct groups.
b) Anomaly Detection: Models that identify outliers or anomalies can be implemented in the system to detect those who need immediate attention and even those close to health deterioration.
c) Time-series forecasting: Take advantage of a time-series model to enable predictions for trends in appointments from patients, treatment compliance, or healthcare expenses, enabling proactive marketing strategies.

Personalization and Automation

Machine learning makes marketing workflows efficient and personalized in many ways. For medical marketing, it means personalization, where there's dynamic content delivery or recommendation or offer to patients aligned with specific profiles. Automation addresses more of regular tasks, such as reminders of appointments, follow-up emails, or patient engagement surveys.

a) Recommendation Engines: Apply collaborative filtering or content-based recommendation systems to recommend treatment, drugs, or wellness plans to the patient based on historical data.
b) Workflow Automation: Marketing email campaigns, patient onboarding, and distribution of surveys can be automated through the use of natural language processing techniques and marketing automation platforms integrating ML models.
c) Personalized content generation: Use generative models (e.g., GPT-based) to generate custom educational content, health tips, or medical literature customized according to a patient's needs.

Integration and Deployment

Post model training and optimization, easy and straightforward deployment and integration will occur within existing marketing processes. The outputs of the ML model will be inbuilt in user-facing applications, workflows, and in marketing platforms.

a) API-based Integration: It is through this that an ML model should be interfaced with the overall healthcare IT systems using API to have a smooth stream of data transfer between marketing environment and the clinical environment.
b) Continuous Learning: Processes established for continuous improvement in models by retraining with new data and optimizing their outputs with feedback from reality.
c) Real-time Decision Making: The possibility of achieving real-time ML capability where marketing strategy updates occur in response to new patient data, appointment changes, or campaign results.

A fully integrated approach in medical marketing using Machine Learning will involve extensive preparation in data, development of the model, personalization, automation, and compliance with regulation. The best benefits that will be achieved stepwise will apply approaches towards healthcare organizations realizing optimal ML benefits for maximized patient experiences, better marketing optimization, and enhanced clinical outcomes at ethical and efficient standards of operations.

MACHINE LEARNING IN MEDICAL MARKETING: CRITERIA FOR ENHANCEMENT

Machine learning has emerged as the transformative technology in medical marketing, bringing advanced capabilities for enhancing patient engagement, optimizing marketing strategies, and improving clinical outcomes. However, the maximum benefits of ML will only be achieved if healthcare organizations focus on specific criteria for its enhancement. These criteria include data quality, model performance, ethical considerations, and integration with clinical workflows. In this respect, the criteria have to be interpreted and then clarified so that maximum potential of ML can be tapped in medical marketing(Chan & Siegel, 2019; Harrison & Sidey-Gibbons, 2021). The figure 3 depicts a methodological approach to enhance machine learning in medical marketing.

Figure 3. Approach ML enhancement in medical marketing

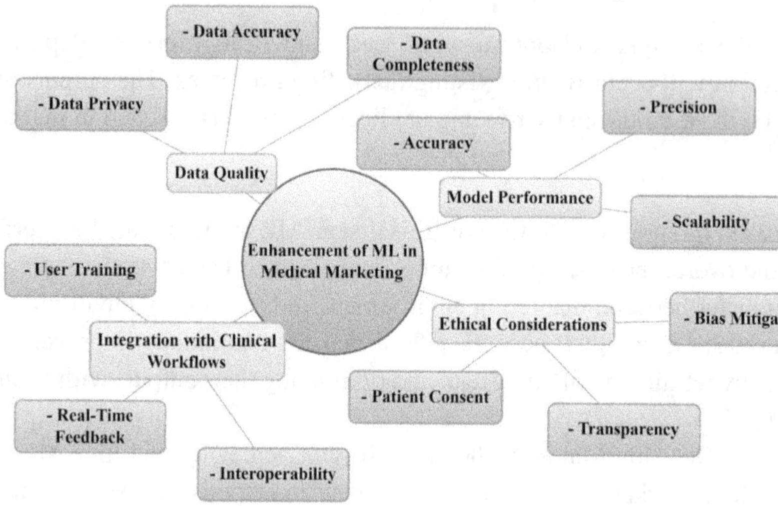

Quality Data and Preprocessing: Healthcare market information for medical marketing is predicated on good quality, proper structured data. Data should be rich in diversity toward demographics, clinical histories and behavioral patterns so that not biased prediction can be used or produced by the ML Model. There should be enough handling for missing data point, and it should become standardized with all the considerations set concerning privacy and security. This process includes data cleaning, normalization, feature extraction, and transformation that pre-processes to enhance accuracy in training models and avoids overfitting for the medical marketing business.

Model Performance and Evaluation: Performance of Machine Learning models is the key for medical marketing strategies. Metrics include accuracy, precision and recall, F1 score, and AUC-ROC curve. Continuous enhancement is directed to improve predictive accuracy, reduce false positives/negatives, and provide actionable insights. Such metrics are very helpful in addressing class imbalance in medical datasets and for supporting medical marketing initiatives.

Bias Management: The medical marketing process with Machine Learning requires bias management along with ethical issues. These include constant monitoring for biases to ensure that fair predictions and recommendations are being made and data security, leading to equitable healthcare delivery. It is essential that these organizations include robust ethical frameworks in their system and undertake frequent audits to prevent ethical lapse, which may adversely impact patients or result in legal retribution.

Integration with Clinical Workflows: Machine Learning systems need to be seamlessly integrated into healthcare workflows to deliver real-time insights for decision-making. Key integration elements include interoperability with EHR systems, continuous updates to stay responsive to new data, and user-centered design. This bridges the gap between marketing strategies and clinical practice by promoting holistic patient-centric care. Improved implementation ensures marketing strategies are aligned with patient care needs.

Customization and Personalization: Machine learning can be the best way to provide personalized marketing strategies. Health care providers can make their communications and recommendations based on individual patient needs, but for this to be effective, these capabilities have to be constantly improved. Among them include dynamic content generation that entails understanding behavioral insights in giving more clarity in knowing how the patient interacts with them during their marketing operations as well as preference modeling for personal contact. It increases the value of the satisfaction of a patient and makes the health marketing campaign successful.

Scalability and Continuous Learning: Healthcare organizations are expanding, and therefore, the need for scalability and continuous learning in Machine Learning models. Scalability ensures that models can handle increasing datasets without performance degradation. Continuous learning ensures that models are updated to emerging trends and patient needs. Regular retraining promotes innovation and keeps marketing strategies ahead of the evolving healthcare demands.

Machine Learning has the potential to revolutionize the medical marketing industry by offering personalized, data-driven insights to help in improving the patient care experience. But this will be effective only when the criteria such as quality of data, model performance, ethical considerations, clinical workflows integration, and scalability are achieved. In other words, it can allow healthcare organizations to maximize their returns on investment from Machine Learning while making a presentation of more effective marketing strategies for both patients and healthcare providers.

ETHICAL CONSIDERATIONS AND COMPLIANCE

Data anonymization is removing personal information before training the ML models. The controls for access are designed so that only legitimate users are given access. Encryption at rest and in transit uses robust encryption methods. Machine Learning models involve ethical implications due to the possible bias, which may bring about discrimination. Biased recommendations in medical marketing would lead to unequal access of healthcare resources and therefore result in the marginalization of patient groups(Chan & Siegel, 2019; Harrison & Sidey-Gibbons, 2021; Kaur et al., 2019). The figure 4 illustrates the significance of ethical considerations when utilizing machine learning in medical marketing.

Figure 4. Ethical considerations - Machine Learning in medical marketing

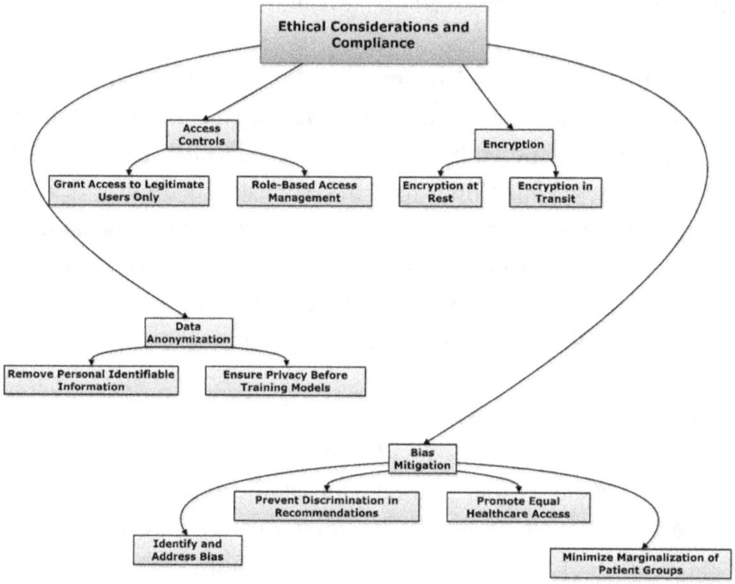

To ensure mitigation of bias, techniques for implementation include fairness-aware algorithms, diverse data sets, and regular audits to ensure fairness and recalibrate the models to address emerging biases.Machine Learning in medical marketing requires transparency and explainability to maintain trust. Black-box models can undermine trust, so explainable AI models like decision trees and rule-based systems can provide clear insights. Thorough documentation of ML models and decision-making processes is crucial for accountability and scrutiny. Healthcare organizations must assign accountability for ML-powered marketing strategies, including operational accountability and addressing patient concerns. Implementation techniques include human-in-the-loop, where healthcare professionals review ML recommendations, and error detection systems, which monitor model performance and rectify issues when they occur.

Patient involvement in decision-making is crucial when using Machine Learning in medical marketing. Informed consent ensures patients understand the use of their data and the decisions based on ML insights. Implementation techniques include clear communication and opt-in models, providing patients with the choice to use ML in their healthcare management and marketing interactions. Healthcare organizations must prioritize ethical considerations when deploying Machine Learning in medical marketing, including data privacy, security, bias, transparency, and patient rights. This will lead to more equitable, accountable, and patient-centric marketing strategies.

In medical marketing, the retention of trust is necessary for machine learning. Black-box models can damage the trust. However, an explainable AI model such as decision trees and rule-based systems will give clear insights. The need for detailed documentation of ML models and decision-making processes is required for accountability and scrutiny. That brings ML-based marketing strategies within operational and patient concern accountability that organizations should not forget. Among the implementation techniques include a human-in-the-loop type in which healthcare professionals review and determine the appropriateness of an ML-based recommendation, as well as error detection systems, wherein its performance is checked and correct any errors when detected.

Patient Involvement in Medical Marketing and Application of Machine Learning Patient involvement is highly important when using Machine Learning in medical marketing. Informed consent needs to be signed by patients, whereby they will understand that the data will be used and the decisions made will be using insights derived from ML. The clear communication model and the opt-in models of implementation techniques ensure that the patient has rights to the use of ML in the management and marketing of health. The ethical considerations of healthcare organizations when implementing Machine Learning in medical marketing include data privacy, security, bias, transparency, and rights of the patient. This would make for more equitable, accountable, and patient-centered marketing approaches.

CASE STUDIES

The healthcare industry has been taking up Machine Learning (ML) in recent years to improve patient engagement, optimize marketing strategies, and enhance clinical outcomes. This case study discusses the implementation of ML in medical marketing at one of the leading healthcare organizations, focusing on how advanced predictive analytics and automation were used for personalized patient engagement.

With hundreds of hospitals, outpatient clinics, and specialized care centers all located together with such different target customers as high-ticked customers visiting special medicine centers, the organization targeted on increasing patient retention, efficiently managing patient communications, and improving overall care delivery and in quest of a data-driven method to optimize their marketing, implementing a range of Machine Learning technologies should help them deliver more individual experiences so significantly improving patient satisfaction and even more importantly clinical outcomes(Kaplan et al., 2021; R. Kumar et al., 2020; Makino et al., 2019; Shutaywi & Kachouie, 2021).

It majorly aimed at utilizing machine learning to design highly niche-focused marketing campaigns that target distinct medical issues presented by separate patient records. Aiming toward automation of routine administrative services through appointment scheduling, follow up, and health reminders could result in maximizing effectiveness in operations.

Implementation Process

a) The healthcare organization first aggregated huge amounts of patient data, including EHRs, demographic information, appointment history, lab results, and behavioral data from wearable devices. The data was then preprocessed to make it structured, anonymized, and standardized for regulatory compliance, such as HIPAA compliance.
b) Meaningful features were constructed from the raw data and on which Machine Learning models have been built. For example, trends in patient behavior patterns predict future healthcare needs. Algorithms monitored the trends about patient interactions, and then analyzed some of the risk factors for high readmission rates, medication non-compliance, and chronic disease management.
c) Experiencing several ML models to find the best fit-approach, the organisation used Random Forests, Gradient Boosting, Neural Networks, and so on. The organization was very concerned about models that would make predictions about patient outcomes or help optimize marketing strategies effectively. One of the important issues in model development was interpretability, where providers could easily review decisions made and outcomes.
d) The healthcare organization used such insights from ML models to develop targeted marketing programs. For example, with predictive analytics, the identification of high-risk patients at risk for chronic illnesses or complications after surgery was realized. Such at-risk patients were provided with relevant education material, reminders for scheduled appointments, and follow-up calls to improve their health.
e) It assisted the health care organization to control heavy volumes of patients by streamlining the processes. Appointment reminders were carried out automatically based on the schedules set, and no-show rates were minimized. Besides that, dynamic messages and customized health tips were created for improving the follow-up procedure for patients and interaction.

Results and Impact

Through personalized marketing campaigns, the healthcare organization witnessed a significant increase in patient engagement. By addressing individual patient needs, the institution was able to improve communication quality and responsiveness. Patients reported higher satisfaction levels and a greater sense of control over their health journey. The automation of administrative tasks, such as scheduling and health reminders, allowed the organization to operate more efficiently. Healthcare professionals were freed from time-consuming tasks, allowing them to focus more on patient care. The reduction in administrative overhead also lowered costs associated with manual interventions.

ML models demonstrated strong predictive accuracy, with a 15% reduction in readmission rates and a 20% improvement in treatment adherence. These results affirmed the organization's strategy of integrating data-driven insights into marketing and clinical operations. Throughout the project, the organization actively managed bias in ML models to ensure equitable treatment of all patient demographics. Regular audits and bias detection algorithms helped to maintain fairness in predictions and marketing strategies. The health facility recorded high involvement of patients due to targeted marketing campaigns. According to the needs of a particular patient, the organization streamlined its quality of communication and response levels. Most patients reported satisfaction in their health conditions while appreciating the level of control over their health course.

This ensured that the company could conduct much more productive administrative duties such as appointment scheduling and reminders of health requirements. It thus left the much-needed time to be employed in productive care of the patients by the healthcare provider. Reduction of administrative burden also brought in costs of manual interference.

CHALLENGES AND FUTURE TRENDS

With ML integration into medical marketing, there are various opportunities for improving patient engagement, marketing efforts, and the healthcare outcome. However, along with these opportunities, several challenges come with significant responsibilities that healthcare organizations have to navigate carefully to ensure responsible and effective use of ML technologies(Kamepalli & Rao, 2019; Kaplan et al., 2021; R. Kumar et al., 2020; Y. Kumar et al., 2020).

Challenges

a) Data Quality and Accessibility: One of the biggest challenges is healthcare data quality and availability when employing ML in medical marketing. Medical data is usually divided into groups of unstructured data-like clinical notes, imaging data, and wearable device data-and cannot be standardized as easily for processing. Additionally, a very cumbersome process is obtaining access to this data to ensure HIPAA or GDPR requirements are not violated, therefore complicating the building of the robust models.

b) Bias and Fairness: Bias in ML algorithms is a significant issue; much more so in any health-related application. Historic data may contain biases through race, gender, social classes, or other kinds of biases that could adversely reflect discriminatory outcomes. For instance, predictive models could overreach to the disadvantage of these subordinated groups if not closely controlled, thus creating inappropriate determinants in healthcare. These can only be addressed through very sophisticated techniques that are supported by a wide range of datasets from different patient groups.

c) Explainability and Explainability: ML models, especially complex ones such as deep learning operate as "black boxes" which often defy understanding what nature they come to base their decisions upon. The loss of explainability undermines that trust by care professionals on the system besides patients, too. This also means, in effect transparency in ensuring how a selected ML model comes up to a certain recommendation for marketing purposes or perhaps a prescription also entails the need for accountability with obedience.

d) Legal and Ethical Issues: With ML integration in medical marketing, various ethical issues will arise like violation of data privacy, consent issues, and accountability. To use patient data for any marketing purpose, healthcare organizations must adhere to the tight regulation standards of legal and ethical perspectives. Furthermore, governance and control mechanisms for monitoring of bias, security, and compliance further strengthen the deployment of the ethical ML models.

e) Integration with Existing Systems: This integration is quite complex in existing healthcare systems, especially those including electronic health records and patient management systems, as they are generally not designed to support real-time marketing strategies or AI-driven activities. It poses a technical challenge: seamless integration with no negative impact on the stability of the system.

Opportunities

a) Personalized Patient Experience: Machine Learning allows for the creation of very tailored marketing messages for specific patient needs. Having huge data, ML will be able to come up with custom health advice, educational material, and marketing campaign that would attract specific groups of patients. These create more engagement among patients, more satisfaction, and better health results.

b) Predictive Analytics for Better Results: With ML-driven predictive analytics, at-risk patients or patient behaviors are better predicted. For medical marketing, this would translate into better-targeted interventions to reduce readmissions in hospitals, ensure treatment adherence, and even better manage chronic conditions. All these will help fine-tune marketing efforts, knowing exactly when the patient is going to need it.

c) Automation and Efficiency: It makes the process much more efficient and streamlines repetitive marketing tasks such as scheduling appointments, follow-ups, and health reminders. The workflow can be automated by applying machine learning to some of the administrative burdens that will be removed off the shoulders of healthcare staff, ensuring timely and personalized support for patients.

d) Optimized Marketing Campaigns and ROI: ML-driven insights will optimize the marketing campaigns as they point out the most efficient channels, content, and audience segments. This helps healthcare organizations to have better ROI by allocating resources towards strategies with measurable outcomes. Predictive analytics also help in outcome forecasting and fine-tuning of marketing strategies in advance.

e) Ethical Innovation: With fairness, transparency, and accountability, ML will be able to build a fairer and more responsible means of medical marketing. With this always comes the balance between the marketing endeavors and the rights of patients so that all these can stay within health regulation.

While the adoption of ML in medical marketing does pose considerable challenges such as data quality management, bias, and adherence to regulations, it does open a great deal for improving patient care and operational efficiencies. With these challenges, carefully planned and implemented with sound ethical considerations, healthcare institutions can truly tap into their potential in terms of outcome improvement for marketing and health.

FUTURE DEVELOPMENTS IN MACHINE LEARNING IN MEDICAL MARKETING

With advancements in technology and increased reliance on data-driven strategies in healthcare systems, the area of ML in medical marketing is going to witness tremendous progress. In the future, as healthcare organizations seek to offer more personalized and efficient care, the role of advanced ML models will be pivotal in determining the direction of medical marketing. Emerging trends suggest convergence of innovations that will improve patient engagement, operational efficiency, and healthcare outcomes(Kedi et al., 2024; Shehab et al., 2022; Zhu et al., 2022). The figure 5 depicts the potential future advancements in machine learning in the field of medical marketing.

Figure 5. Future developments in machine learning in medical marketing

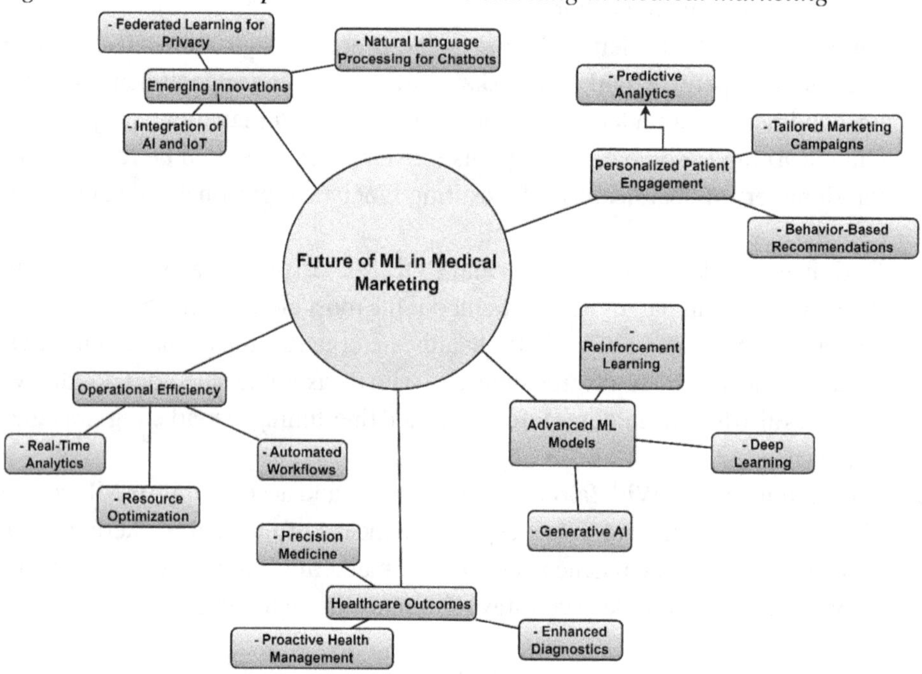

Integration of Advanced AI Models

Advanced AI models, including Natural Language Processing, deep learning, and reinforcement learning, will be more dependent in the future of medical marketing in healthcare. Such technologies will enable better predictions, decision-making, and personalization in marketing strategies. For example, the NLP will enable insight extraction from unstructured data in the medical field, which includes clinical notes or a diagnostic report, thereby refining marketing campaigns and improving communication between healthcare professionals and patients.

Enhanced Explainability and Transparency

There is a major challenge with current ML models: their lack of interpretability. As developments continue, more focus will be on developing XAI models that can better explain decisions to clinicians and patients. Regulatory bodies and healthcare stakeholders will demand higher levels of transparency in order to ensure that the machine learning systems are not only accurate but also auditable and ethical. This will make ML models more accessible and trusted in medical marketing strategies.

Ethical AI and Bias Mitigation

Developments and research in future will be in the direction of fine-tuning techniques of bias mitigation for ML models. As the usage of diverse data sets and advanced fairness-aware algorithms goes up, health care organizations can address disparities in health care outcomes to a great extent. Real-time monitoring with adjustment mechanisms would be integrated with bias correction techniques to keep marketing strategies fair, equitable, and inclusive of all patient populations(Chandra et al., 2024; Krishnamoorthy et al., 2024; Somasundaram et al., 2024).

Real-time and Context-Aware Marketing

Medical marketing has a future in real-time, context-aware strategies that are powered by machine learning. Marketers will make use of predictive analytics to engage with patients actively and intervene in a timely manner related to a patient's condition, location, and behavior. For example, data from wearable devices will be fed into ML systems, which can provide personal health insights and marketing messages-all of this done behind the scenes, while still respecting the confidentiality and security of the patient.

Increased Automation and Workflow Optimization

In machine learning, the automated execution of administrative and marketing work would continue to build and improve workflow efficiency for health care. More improvements will include even more intelligent tool predictability and responsiveness. Further improvements will see them in predicting and even providing anticipatory needs for appointment schedules, follow-ups, content delivery, and similar matters. This easy integration with current health systems brings out the experience of service by healthcare providers to offer an efficient and patient-centered health service.

Industry Healthcare Collaboration

The future of ML in medical marketing will be more collaboration between technology companies and healthcare institutions. This will accelerate innovation through co-development of AI-driven solutions tailored to specific clinical and marketing needs. More researchers, healthcare providers, and ML experts will collaborate for innovative solutions that push the boundary of what is possible in medical marketing, ensuring better outcomes and a deeper understanding of patient needs(Mohanraj et al., 2024; Pitchai et al., 2024; Sreedhar et al., 2024).

Conformity to Regulations and Standards

As ML technology goes more deeply into medical marketing, so the regulatory frameworks will have to evolve with it. There will be more attention towards creating stronger compliance systems in the future that guarantee the ethical use of patient data while adapting to the newer AI-specific regulations. The hybrid models of governance combining centralized oversight and decentralized accountability will improve transparency and accountability for efforts in medical marketing.

Patient-Centered Marketing Strategies

The future of ML will be more patient-centric in its approaches towards marketing, including not just personal preference but emotional and social issues that impact their decision to come into the healthcare facility. Predictive analytics will combine elements of behavioral science and clinical data to ensure that there is personalized marketing touching the heart, therefore ensuring healthier lifestyle behaviors and improved adherence to their treatment plans.

Huge promise exists for machine learning in medical marketing for better patient care, operation efficiency, and ethical delivery of healthcare. Apart from the development of models, the integration of real-time data, an increased interest in transparency, correction of biases, and patient-centric approaches, this would be the much-sophisticated healthcare marketing sector that impacts much. As the technology and regulation continue to advance, the ML-led innovation is sure to bring a transformation in the manner in which patients engage with healthcare organizations for improved health results.

CONCLUSION

During this journey of Machine Learning in Medical Marketing, it has been observed that this powerful technology is revolutionizing the healthcare engagement landscape, decision-making, and operational efficiency. From the fundamental to the most innovative strategy on how to enhance the patient experience, each chapter of this book has proven that ML can revolutionize how healthcare organizations approach marketing and patient care. It first spoke on what Machine Learning was, the wide range of applications it has in medical marketing, and the various differences it offers. The best drivers toward improving patient and operational performance come through personalization of the patient experience through predictive analytics and marketing automation, by making health service organizations focus better at the administration efficiencies while better making use of better data for pertinent needs for a patient.

These implementation techniques reflect how organizations can easily and seamlessly integrate Machine Learning models into existing healthcare systems. Every step, from gathering data, preprocessing to creating actionable insights, is therefore critical in ensuring that use of AI remains ethical and patient care at optimal standards. Detection of bias, among other factors like the model remaining compliant with healthcare regulations, is, therefore, emphasized as part of a necessary component for building trustful ML-driven solutions. Comprehensive efforts have been put into tackling challenges healthcare institutions are facing: data quality, interpretability of models, and continuous learning needs. Challenges of this sort are an excellent stepping stone to further innovation, in which future work will continue with more complex techniques like XAI, real-time personalization, and bias mitigation.

Going forward, Machine Learning will grow as a result of new technological advancement and changes in the legal world. Instead, it will focus on the issues of transparency, centered on the patient, equitous, accurate, and integrative with health systems. Adoption of such technologies by healthcare organizations will allow interplay between technology and personalized care drive waves of improvement for medical marketing and health delivery. In a nutshell, it can be summarized that Machine Learning will change the world of medical marketing into enormous opportunities for improving experience and outcome of health care. Implemented in careful, constantly changing ways and guided by good ethics, health professionals are enabled to reach their highest potential.

REFERENCES

Arasu, B. S., Seelan, B. J. B., & Thamaraiselvan, N. (2020). A machine learning-based approach to enhancing social media marketing. *Computers & Electrical Engineering*, 86, 106723. DOI: 10.1016/j.compeleceng.2020.106723

Awaysheh, A., Wilcke, J., Elvinger, F., Rees, L., Fan, W., & Zimmerman, K. L. (2019). Review of medical decision support and machine-learning methods. *Veterinary Pathology*, 56(4), 512–525. DOI: 10.1177/0300985819829524 PMID: 30866728

Balki, I., Amirabadi, A., Levman, J., Martel, A. L., Emersic, Z., Meden, B., Garcia-Pedrero, A., Ramirez, S. C., Kong, D., Moody, A. R., & Tyrrell, P. N. (2019). Sample-size determination methodologies for machine learning in medical imaging research: A systematic review. *Canadian Association of Radiologists Journal*, 70(4), 344–353. DOI: 10.1016/j.carj.2019.06.002 PMID: 31522841

Chan, S., & Siegel, E. L. (2019). Will machine learning end the viability of radiology as a thriving medical specialty? *The British Journal of Radiology*, 92(1094), 20180416. DOI: 10.1259/bjr.20180416 PMID: 30325645

Chandra, S., Ghule, G., Bilfaqih, S. M., Thiyagarajan, A., Sharmila, J., & Boopathi, S. (2024). Adaptive Strategies in Online Marketing Using Machine Learning Techniques. In *Digital Transformation Initiatives for Agile Marketing* (pp. 67–100). IGI Global., DOI: 10.4018/979-8-3693-4466-8.ch004

Gerke, S., Babic, B., Evgeniou, T., & Cohen, I. G. (2020). The need for a system view to regulate artificial intelligence/machine learning-based software as medical device. *NPJ Digital Medicine*, 3(1), 53. DOI: 10.1038/s41746-020-0262-2 PMID: 32285013

Harrison, C. J., & Sidey-Gibbons, C. J. (2021). Machine learning in medicine: A practical introduction to natural language processing. *BMC Medical Research Methodology*, 21(1), 158. DOI: 10.1186/s12874-021-01347-1 PMID: 34332525

Kamepalli, S., & Rao, B. S. (2019). Recent applications of machine learning: A survey. *International Journal of Innovative Technology and Exploring Engineering*, 8(6), 263–267.

Kaplan, A., Cao, H., FitzGerald, J. M., Iannotti, N., Yang, E., Kocks, J. W., Kostikas, K., Price, D., Reddel, H. K., Tsiligianni, I., Vogelmeier, C. F., Pfister, P., & Mastoridis, P. (2021). Artificial intelligence/machine learning in respiratory medicine and potential role in asthma and COPD diagnosis. *The Journal of Allergy and Clinical Immunology. In Practice*, 9(6), 2255–2261. DOI: 10.1016/j.jaip.2021.02.014 PMID: 33618053

Kaur, H., Pannu, H. S., & Malhi, A. K. (2019). A systematic review on imbalanced data challenges in machine learning: Applications and solutions. *ACM Computing Surveys*, 52(4), 1–36.

Kedi, W. E., Ejimuda, C., Idemudia, C., & Ijomah, T. I. (2024). Machine learning software for optimizing SME social media marketing campaigns. *Computer Science & IT Research Journal*, 5(7), 1634–1647. DOI: 10.51594/csitrj.v5i7.1349

Krishnamoorthy, V., Chandra, S., Rajesha, S., Bhattacharjee, S., Murugan, G., & Sampath, B. (2024). Emerging Startups in the Evolving Industry Landscape by Empowering Entrepreneur Growth: An Agile Marketing Practice. In *Digital Transformation Initiatives for Agile Marketing* (pp. 455–484). IGI Global. DOI: 10.4018/979-8-3693-4466-8.ch017

Kumar, R., Kumar, P., & Kumar, Y. (2020). Time series data prediction using IoT and machine learning technique. *Procedia Computer Science*, 167, 373–381. DOI: 10.1016/j.procs.2020.03.240

Kumar, Y., Kaur, K., & Singh, G. (2020). Machine learning aspects and its applications towards different research areas. *2020 International Conference on Computation, Automation and Knowledge Management (ICCAKM)*, 150–156. DOI: 10.1109/ICCAKM46823.2020.9051502

Makino, M., Yoshimoto, R., Ono, M., Itoko, T., Katsuki, T., Koseki, A., Kudo, M., Haida, K., Kuroda, J., Yanagiya, R., Saitoh, E., Hoshinaga, K., Yuzawa, Y., & Suzuki, A. (2019). Artificial intelligence predicts the progression of diabetic kidney disease using big data machine learning. *Scientific Reports*, 9(1), 11862. DOI: 10.1038/s41598-019-48263-5 PMID: 31413285

Miklosik, A., & Evans, N. (2020). Impact of big data and machine learning on digital transformation in marketing: A literature review. *IEEE Access : Practical Innovations, Open Solutions*, 8, 101284–101292. DOI: 10.1109/ACCESS.2020.2998754

Minssen, T., Gerke, S., Aboy, M., Price, N., & Cohen, G. (2020). Regulatory responses to medical machine learning. *Journal of Law and the Biosciences*, 7(1), lsaa002. DOI: 10.1093/jlb/lsaa002 PMID: 34221415

Mohanraj, G., Krishna, K. S., Lakshmi, B. S., Vijayalakshmi, A., Pramila, P. V., & Boopathi, S. (2024). Optimizing Trust and Security in Healthcare 4.0: Human Factors in Lightweight Secured IoMT Ecosystems. In *Lightweight Digital Trust Architectures in the Internet of Medical Things (IoMT)* (pp. 52–72). IGI Global. DOI: 10.4018/979-8-3693-2109-6.ch004

Pitchai, R., Guru, K. V., Gandhi, J. N., Komala, C. R., Kumar, J. R. D., & Boopathi, S. (2024). Fog Computing-Integrated ML-Based Framework and Solutions for Intelligent Systems: Digital Healthcare Applications. In *Technological Advancements in Data Processing for Next Generation Intelligent Systems* (pp. 196–224). IGI Global. DOI: 10.4018/979-8-3693-0968-1.ch008

Ramudu, K., Mohan, V. M., Jyothirmai, D., Prasad, D., Agrawal, R., & Boopathi, S. (2023). Machine Learning and Artificial Intelligence in Disease Prediction: Applications, Challenges, Limitations, Case Studies, and Future Directions. In *Contemporary Applications of Data Fusion for Advanced Healthcare Informatics* (pp. 297–318). IGI Global.

Shehab, M., Abualigah, L., Shambour, Q., Abu-Hashem, M. A., Shambour, M. K. Y., Alsalibi, A. I., & Gandomi, A. H. (2022). Machine learning in medical applications: A review of state-of-the-art methods. *Computers in Biology and Medicine*, 145, 105458. DOI: 10.1016/j.compbiomed.2022.105458 PMID: 35364311

Shutaywi, M., & Kachouie, N. N. (2021). Silhouette analysis for performance evaluation in machine learning with applications to clustering. *Entropy (Basel, Switzerland)*, 23(6), 759. DOI: 10.3390/e23060759 PMID: 34208552

Somasundaram, R., Varalakshmi, S., Sanadi, H., Saini, R., Chinnusamy, S., & Boopaathi. (2024). Entrepreneurship in emerging markets and intrapreneurship within organizations. In *Advances in Business Strategy and Competitive Advantage* (pp. 291–322). IGI Global.

Sreedhar, P. S. S., Sujay, V., Rani, M. R., Melita, L., Reshma, S., & Boopathi, S. (2024). Impacts of 5G Machine Learning Techniques on Telemedicine and Social Media Professional Connection in Healthcare. In *Advances in Medical Technologies and Clinical Practice* (pp. 209–234). IGI Global. DOI: 10.4018/979-8-3693-1934-5.ch012

Subha, S., Inbamalar, T., Komala, C., Suresh, L. R., Boopathi, S., & Alaskar, K. (2023). A Remote Health Care Monitoring system using internet of medical things (IoMT). *IEEE Explore*, 1–6.

Tyagi, A. K., & Chahal, P. (2020). Artificial intelligence and machine learning algorithms. In *Challenges and applications for implementing machine learning in computer vision* (pp. 188–219). IGI Global. DOI: 10.4018/978-1-7998-0182-5.ch008

Zhu, S., Gilbert, M., Chetty, I., & Siddiqui, F. (2022). The 2021 landscape of FDA-approved artificial intelligence/machine learning-enabled medical devices: An analysis of the characteristics and intended use. *International Journal of Medical Informatics*, 165, 104828. DOI: 10.1016/j.ijmedinf.2022.104828 PMID: 35780651

Chapter 8
Quantum Computing for Business Applications

Sahana P. Shankar
https://orcid.org/0000-0001-8977-9898
Ramaiah University of Applied Sciences, India

S. Chandana
https://orcid.org/0009-0003-6255-675X
Ramaiah University of Applied Sciences, India

Deepak Varadam
https://orcid.org/0000-0002-6079-4805
Ramaiah University of Applied Sciences, India

S. Chinmayi Shree
https://orcid.org/0009-0007-2390-9195
Ramaiah University of Applied Sciences, India

Saba Nida
https://orcid.org/0009-0004-6889-8766
Ramaiah University of Applied Sciences, India

R. Ankitha
https://orcid.org/0009-0001-3845-226X
Ramaiah University of Applied Sciences, India

U. Trisha
https://orcid.org/0009-0004-9609-2284
Ramaiah University of Applied Sciences, India

Aryan Bharadwaj
Ramaiah University of Applied Sciences, India

ABSTRACT

Bits are used in conventional computers; quantum bits, or qubits, are used in quantum computers. The speed and efficiency of quantum computing can give businesses a significant advantage over their competitors and help them make better decisions. Large server rooms may not be necessary as quantum computers are excellent at processing massive volumes of data without requiring a lot of storage space. This could free up physical space in buildings. Conventional computers are still more cost-effective and faster for simple computations, even though quantum computers

DOI: 10.4018/979-8-3693-6225-9.ch008

are revolutionising fields like optimisation and machine learning. Both political parties have made large investments in quantum research to improve supply chain management, logistics, and security, among other areas. This could have a big impact on politics and the economy. When seamlessly integrated, quantum computing offers businesses enormous potential for data processing, sophisticated cybersecurity, and effective storage, resulting in the next phase of computing for industries

INTRODUCTION

Bits are used in conventional computers; they are tiny switches that have two states: on (1) and off (0). On the other hand, quantum bits, or qubits, are used in quantum computers. These bits can all at once represent both 0 and 1. For example, quantum computers are likened to dimmer switches with additional options, while standard computers are like on/off light switches. The speed and efficiency of quantum computing can give businesses a significant advantage over their competitors and help them make better decisions. Large server rooms may not be necessary as quantum computers are excellent at processing massive volumes of data without requiring a lot of storage space. This could free up physical space in buildings. Conventional computers are still more cost-effective and faster for simple computations, even though quantum computers are revolutionising fields like optimisation and machine learning. Both political parties have made large investments in quantum research to improve supply chain management, logistics, and security, among other areas. This could have a big impact on politics and the economy. When seamlessly integrated, quantum computing offers businesses enormous potential for data processing, sophisticated cybersecurity, and effective storage, resulting in the next phase of computing for industries (Cusumano, 2018).

Figure 1. Process of research on quantum computing

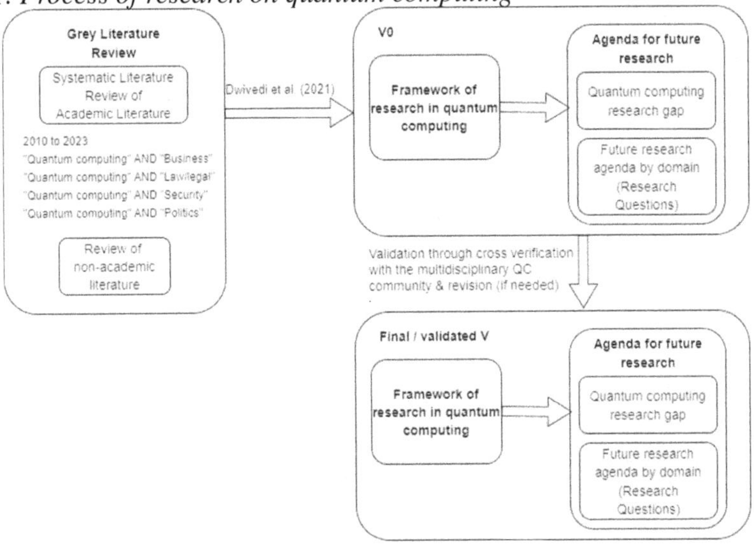

LITERATURE REVIEW

Quantum computers, called QPUs, are superfast but need better error fixing. In the short term, we can use simpler quantum tasks and combine QPUs for better results. We need new techniques, better hardware, and make quantum and regular computers work together seamlessly. In the long term, we want easy-to-use quantum computers. In history, computers got smaller and more efficient, and specialized processors were made. Quantum computers are like a new era, solving super-hard problems, but they need fewer errors. Some jobs can be done with quantum computers while we make them better (Bravyi, Dial, Gambetta, Gil, & Nazario, 2022). Quantum computing is super special and can make our lives better and help science. It's great for things like improving materials, managing traffic, and saving energy. It uses fancy science and math, which can teach us stuff regular computers can't. There are four main parts: sensing, computing, simulating, and networking. Our energy needs are important, and there's a "quantum revolution" coming. It will help us solve big energy problems using things like atoms and special circuits. Quantum computers will also be awesome for chemistry (Paudel et al., 2022). And we can make energy better by using quantum technology with sensors. Quantum computing is a super cool way to solve hard problems that regular computers struggle with. It's like a mix of physics, math, and computer science. Quantum computers use tiny particles like atoms and electrons, and they're superfast and efficient. They use something called “qubits” that can be 0 and 1 at the same time. Different industries, like healthcare and finance, are already using quantum tricks for things like Grover's and Shor's algorithms. It's making big progress and has some challenges to tackle (Upama et al., 2022). Quantum computing is a cool new way to solve hard problems superfast using the weird rules of quantum physics. It's handy for things like making better drugs, handling data, and improving clean energy. But there are some issues to work out, like errors and connecting tiny quantum bits called “qubits.” Richard Feynman had this idea back in 1982. Quantum computers can do amazing stuff, like simulate complex quantum systems, but they're a bit tricky to build. Big companies like Google and IBM, as well as startups, are racing to make strong quantum computers. The special thing about quantum bits (qubits) is that they can be 0 and 1 at the same time. Quantum computers are already doing impressive tasks using cool quantum features. They're helpful in many fields, like energy efficiency, machine learning, robotics, and even security (Gill et al., 2022).

Quantum computing is a super-fast technology that's a game-changer for healthcare. With lots of health data to handle, like during pandemics, we need quicker ways to understand it. Quantum computers are great for tasks like making new medicines, personalizing treatments, DNA work, and improving hospitals. They use special bits called “qubits” that can do many things at once. This helps with complex healthcare jobs like figuring out how proteins fold, creating drugs, and finding cancer treatments without harming healthy cells. Quantum computers can also upgrade medical images and predict chronic diseases while keeping data super safe. In short, quantum tech is about to make healthcare better and faster. It covers different ways quantum computing can help healthcare, including making drug discovery faster and improving healthcare data security. It also talks about the challenges and the exciting future possibilities of using quantum computing in healthcare (Ur Rasool et al., 2023). Computers can learn and make predictions with the use of machine learning. The combination of machine learning and quantum computing, which is renowned for its speed, results in “quantum machine learning.” Neural networks are used in deep learning, an interesting machine learning, to do things like comprehending images. Artificial Intelligence and healthcare are two fields that use quantum computing, which processes data using unique quantum rules. Three different quantum machine learning algorithms use quantum mechanics to achieve higher and faster results. It discusses how machine learning and quantum mechanics combine to achieve incredible feats (Houssein, Abohashima, Elhoseny, & Mohamed, 2022). Quantum computing is a hybrid of several sciences, such as physics and computer science. Quantum physics makes things somewhat random, which is where statistics come in. This article discusses the role statistics play in understanding quantum computing and data science applications. The study of quantum information science investigates the use of unique quantum physics for information processing and transmission. Quantum computing can solve complex problems quickly. Additionally, it is somewhat random, so statistics plays a crucial role in improving its performance in data science and statistics. Important quantum concepts, such as quantum annealing and quantum machine learning, are explained in this article. These aid in machine learning and improved statistics. They even have a concept known as "quantum supremacy," which is based on comparing the performance of quantum computers to those of conventional computers through statistical analysis (Wang & Liu, 2022). This study looked at the problems in the software industry because of the fast-growing quantum computing (QC) technology. They found the main issues are a lack of expertise, data accuracy, and companies not being keen on using QC. They also want better security for QC communication. The big challenge is in how institutions and organizations deal with QC. The study suggests we need more teamwork and research across different areas to tackle these hurdles. Quantum computing is super powerful and can change many industries, but there's not enough research on its real-world challenges, like in healthcare and finance. This study used special methods to find and prioritize these challenges, which can help businesses and scholars. The main obstacles are in management, software technology, institutions, and organizations (Awan, Hannola, Tandon, Goyal, & Dhir, 2022). Quantum computing is a game-changer for chemistry in the pharmaceutical world. It helps us study molecules much faster than before. The usual drug-making process mixes computer work and lab tests. These computers are fantastic for complex chemical stuff. We've made great progress in making quantum hardware that can do tough chemistry without running out of memory. It talks about how we can use upcoming quantum computers for big chemical tasks, like studying a drug named Ibrutinib. We've also looked at the resources needed for quantum computing in pharmaceutical work, making it more practical. But for really big problems, we still need better algorithms and error correction. Current quantum computers have limitations (Blunt et al., 2022).

Quantum computers are super powerful and will change many industries, especially finance. They can do financial stuff like pricing, risk management, and fraud detection faster and more accurately. Even though quantum computers are small and noisy right now, they show promise. We need to understand how quantum can help finance and speed things up. This article talks about the tricky financial problems that quantum can solve. It also looks at how quantum can make things better for finance, like making decisions faster. Quantum computers aren't quite ready for real-world finance problems (Herman et al., 2022). High-intensive computing tasks needed in many domains, such as artificial intelligence, machine learning, cybersecurity, prime factorisation, interpolation, and many more, can be completed by quantum computing (Sharma & Ketti Ramachandran, 2021). Quantum computing has the potential to solve complicated, previously unsolvable computational problems in the domains of simulation, machine learning, and optimisation for all industrial sectors. Blockchain technology and quantum computing are two novel ideas that have the potential to provide secure and quick processing (Bayerstadler et al., 2021). With the rise of edge computing, several Internet of Things (IoT) applications—such as weather forecasting, smart cities, healthcare, and agriculture—can offer end users services that are dependent on resource consumption (Gill, 2021). The development of today's Noisy Intermediate-Scale Quantum (NISQ) devices has made cloud-based quantum information processing platforms with about 100 qubits available to the public; additionally, recent quantum hardware road maps, like IBMs, have announced that devices with as many as 1000 qubits will be available by 2023. Quantum computing as a cloud service is expected to grow rapidly over the next ten years and continue to be the main way for researchers worldwide to access quantum machines (Ravi, Smith, Gokhale, & Chong, 2021).

Quantum technology is the next generation of information and communication technology that can overcome the limitations of current digital computers in areas like high-speed computing, data transfer, and the creation of cryptographic keys (Kim, Kang, Kim, Pan, & Park, 2021). The amount of information and characteristics that classical neural networks (CNNs) elaborate on, as well as the quantity of parameters that specify their structure, have steadily increased over the last several years. Therefore, the quantum neural network model and the quantum machine learning technique have the potential to significantly increase our processing power and open entirely new research directions (Mangini, Tacchino, Gerace, Bajoni, & Macchiavello, 2021). Modern approaches in the fields of computing and communication fall short of offering a viable and workable solution due to the growing demands for security and bandwidth. Thanks to its fast transmission, quantum communication has made significant progress in the last few years (Chen, 2021). Computers nowadays have billions of times faster speeds. Three immediate economic opportunities were created by recent developments in quantum hardware and software: (1) quantum-safe encryption on classical computers; (2) drug and material discoveries; and (3) new quantum-inspired algorithms for classical computers. Quantum is set to revolutionise the speed and cost of solving all these combinatorics issues. Quantum is a significant class of arithmetic problems that will likely remain unsolvable for classical computers. Therefore, if quantum computers prove useful, businesses and organisations that find high-value combinatorics problems that are challenging for classical computers to solve may find use for them (Bova, Goldfarb, & Melko, 2021).

[2] The intelligent transportation system incorporates quantum computing to boost system reliability, the use of quantum computers in the transportation field: vehicle operation management, transportation computer, have proven to be effective in the intelligent transportation space and have been successfully marketed (Wang, Pei, Wang, & Wu, 2021). The paper outlines potential use cases for quantum computing

in various facets of robotics, including artificial intelligence, machine learning, sensing, kinematics, and system diagnosis, citing current research to support these possibilities. Moreover, the authors recognize the challenges associated with incorporating quantum computing into robotics and anticipate that this emerging technology will prompt a revaluation of fundamental approaches to solving robotic problems. Their ultimate objective is to establish quantum computers as an asset in the realm of robotics, with a particular focus on transforming problems within and beyond the NP complexity class using quantum computation (Buffoni & Caruso, 2021). The real essence of the article lies in its exploration of quantum arithmetic circuits, including addition, subtraction, conditional addition, and multiplication, which are pivotal for implementing quantum algorithms (Gyongyosi & Imre, 2019; Varadam, Shankar, Hegde, Shobitha, Sunidhi, & Sanjana, 2024). The article addresses the challenges associated with scaling up superconducting quantum computers, where high-speed instruments like the arbitrary waveform generator (AWG), precision DC source, and digitizer play crucial roles in qubit manipulation (Orús, Mugel, & Lizaso, 2019). Using the Quantum Inspire platform, they evaluated a particular machine learning algorithm known as the Helmholtz machine and demonstrated that it can perform better when using quantum computing (Ajagekar & You, 2019). The paper presents a method that computes the mean value of various pixels within a single image for every quantum measurement in order to address these errors. Simulation results show that this quantum-based method can successfully identify objects in photos, like cars or license plates, showing potential for use in urban surveillance systems and possibly overcoming the drawbacks of conventional methods (Petschnigg, Brandstötter, Pichler, Hofbaur, & Dieber, 2019). The paper presents a new system that is based on the Error-Tolerant (ET) system and has a redundant splicing topology. It examines the system's special topological benefits and possible uses in quantum computing. The design process discusses the network design of this novel quantum computing system, which incorporates unique topological features, and combines elements from earlier ET system designs. By splicing the ET structure, the proposed system aims to unify topological quantum computing and clustering quantum computing, resulting in a flexible architecture for quantum computations and large-scale integration (Thapliyal & Muñoz-Coreas, 2019).

Recent years have seen tremendous advancements in quantum computing, especially with the introduction of the idea of entanglement into a number of application areas. It evaluates the impact of entanglement on quantum applications and contrasts the implementation of entanglement on actual quantum hardware with simulated noise models. Room-temperature quantum computing is one example of how quantum computing provides quicker solutions to issues that were previously insurmountable. Large-scale quantum computers are being developed; one example is a 53-qubit machine. Research is aided by open-source quantum software projects.

The study emphasises the usefulness of entanglement, the benefits and drawbacks of quantum computing, as well as the interactions between quantum and classical computing and the significance of quantum information processing (Guo et al., 2019; Sultana, Bhardwaj, Kumar, Gaur, Shankar, & Bharadwaj, 2024).

The benefits of quantum computers (QCs) in machine learning (ML) are due to their unique attributes like superposition and quantum parallelism, which make them adept at handling large datasets. It discusses the historical context of QC's introduction, the potential of noisy intermediate-scale quantum (NISQ) computers, and algorithms like Grover's for faster searches. The study compares quantum ML algorithms, emphasizing the need for more efficient approaches such as quantum neural networks (QNN) to fully harness quantum computing's power in the NISQ era and its application in various fields (Neumann, Phillipson, & Versluis, 2019).

The rapid growth of the Internet of Things (IoT) necessitates standardized protocols and architectures to support resource-constrained IoT devices. Public-key cryptosystems have been crucial for securing Internet communications, but recent advances have raised security concerns and the need for quantum-resistant alternatives. The article also discusses post-quantum cryptosystems, their performance in IoT contexts, and identifies future challenges and trends. It provides valuable insights for IoT developers working on quantum-resistant solutions in the face of quantum threats (Hu & Ni, 2019). This shift is seen due to quantum computing techniques like QUBO, VQE, QAOA, and HHL algorithms and their potential impact on AI research. Quantum computing is recognized for its potential to solve complex problems in various fields, including cryptography, optimization, and simulations. Despite challenges like error correction and hardware limitations, it's expected to coexist with classical computing and disrupt multiple industries (Varadam, Shankar, Shankar, Narayan, & Kumar, 2024). The study particularly emphasizes the significance of the HHL algorithm for quantum machine learning and recommends AI engineers explore this field for future research (Sun, 2019). By utilising concepts like superposition and entanglement, quantum computing finds applications in a wide range of industries, including science, machine learning, finance, and medicine. It talks about the difficulties with cryptography, the potential of quantum simulations, the acceleration of machine learning, and the use of these technologies in risk assessment, logistics, and satellite communication. Quantum computing has great promise despite practical implementation difficulties, and cloud services should facilitate its uptake and encourage further study and development (Gupta & Nene, 2020). There is a growing influence on quantum computing, notably in quantum image processing, where quantum algorithms like Shor's and Grover's offer speed and security benefits. Accessible through cloud-based platforms with up to 32-qubit processors, quantum computing is advancing rapidly, approaching quantum supremacy. The concept of quantum supremacy, exemplifying tasks that were once impossible for classical computers, is on the horizon, with Google's 54-qubit quantum computer making notable progress in 2019. Integration of scalable, cloud-based quantum systems is on the horizon (Ramezani, Sommers, Manchukonda, Rahimi, & Amirlatifi, 2020). This article introduces quantum computing, which addresses scientific and business challenges using the principles of quantum mechanics. It discusses the emergence of first-generation quantum computers accessible through SDKs and cloud services, emphasizing their impact on cryptography. Quantum computing shows promise in optimization, machine learning, and finance, with major organizations and startups developing machines with up to 100 qubits. While it excels in complex scientific simulations, practical implementation for real-world challenges may take over a decade to become a reality (Fernández-Caramés, 2020; Varsha, Shekar, Shankar, Bharadwaj, Varadam, & Supriya, 2023). The advances in quantum computing are transforming supervised machine learning, excelling in data-intensive tasks like optimization and communication system analysis. Quantum computers leverage qubits in superposition, offering exponential power compared to classical systems. The research explores real quantum hardware's application in supervised classification, emphasizing its ability to process high-dimensional data and uncover hidden feature relationships, which can enhance machine learning accuracy. Quantum computing shows great promise for driving highly efficient machine learning systems in the future (Choi, Oh, & Kim, 2020). QUANTME is an extension for workflow languages that simplifies the integration of quantum computing with classical applications. Quantum computing offers significant speed improvements but involves complex pre- and post-processing tasks. QUANTME abstracts these technical details, ensuring workflow model portability and facilitating orchestration with classical applications. The approach is validated with Quantum4BPMN and a prototypical implementation of three quantum algorithms. Future work includes developing a unified API for quantum cloud services, further evaluation with diverse quantum workflows, and handling large datasets using solutions from scientific workflow research (Hassija, Chamola, Goyal, Kanhere, & Guizani, 2020; Gururaj, Umadi, Kumar, Shankar, & Varadam, 2022). Quantum computers speed up AI training and cut costs, while AI provides essential error correction for quantum systems. It emphasizes quantum computing's superior capabilities and its impracticality to simulate on classical computers. The research explores quantum computing fundamentals and applications in AI, particularly in supervised and unsupervised machine learning, improving learning and training efficiency for various algorithms (Ranjan, Arya, & Ravinder, 2020; Sultana, Bhardwaj, Kumar, Gaur, Shankar, & Bharadwaj, 2024).

EVOLUTION OF QUANTUM COMPUTING

While algorithms like Shor's hold the promise of significant speed enhancements, practical benefits have been demonstrated in tasks like random number generation. However, emerging hybrid algorithms, which integrate classical and quantum hardware, can address diverse challenges such as simulating chemical properties, solving optimization problems, and conducting machine learning tasks. This exploration of quantum computing's potential benefits for the automotive sector aims to identify areas where quantum-enhanced solutions can address key challenges and drive progress toward commercially valuable applications. Utilising the properties of quantum systems, quantum computers allow for the simultaneous exploration of many paths, which is especially useful for complex problems such as simulations of molecular dynamics and protein folding. Heat conduction causes problems for silicon computers in terms of speed and energy efficiency. In contrast, quantum computing provides a more energy-efficient solution and has the potential to advance fields like biological modelling and non-convex optimisation. In addition to quantum computing, low-power alternatives such as reservoir computers and neuromorphic architectures provide answers to the need for energy-efficient ways to comprehend biological complexity. This review discusses different types of quantum computing hardware and upcoming developments in the field, as well as the principles of quantum computing, its importance in biomolecular simulation, and the possibilities of hybrid quantum-classical computing. This paper explores the deep implications of quantum computing on the business and technology landscapes, including its underlying ideas, implications for different industries, and new opportunities and problems. In addition to offering new opportunities in healthcare, finance, and logistics, quantum algorithms also pose a threat to current security protocols. They also bring with them novel business models such as quantum-as-a-service and improved AI capabilities.

QUANTUM COMPUTING FOR HEALTHCARE

Quantum computing offers significant advantages for many complex computing applications in the healthcare sector, particularly when considering the increasingly linked Internet of Things (IoT). Quantum-inspired computing can reduce processing times in a number of healthcare applications. It holds promise for a number of healthcare-related applications, such as the development of novel drugs, the customisation of medical treatment, and the expediting of DNA sequencing. The application of quantum computing technology improved the security of medical records and the preservation of cryptography. Additionally, in the fight against the

COVID-19 pandemic. A quantum-inspired version of controlled alternate quantum walks (CAQWs) can be used to fabricate a robust image steganography protocol for cloud-based e-healthcare.

The use of quantum computing in the medical domains benefits the following:

Research and drug discovery: Thanks to quantum computing, medical professionals can now more easily model atomic-level molecular interactions, which is essential for drug research. This will be particularly significant for drug discovery, diagnosis, treatment, and analytics. Thanks to developments in quantum computing, it is now possible to encode tens of thousands of proteins and simulate how they interact with medications, something that was previously unfeasible (Hassija, Chamola, Saxena, Chanana, Parashari, Mumtaz, & Guizani, 2020). Modern drug discovery requires precise modelling of the energies dissipated in chemical reactions. The quantum behaviour of even a few electrons is difficult to calculate, so classical computers mainly rely on approximations for this kind of computation. Quantum computers have already been shown to be useful for quantum chemistry calculations and to accurately model the properties of small molecules due to their high system entanglement and ability to simulate properties at high accuracies (Shah, Shah, & Kanani, 2020). DNA data is being generated at an exponential rate, with many new genomes waiting to be sequenced and many private genomes requiring resequencing. Since there are 3.2 billion base pairs in each human genome and each one can hold two bits of data, a single human genome would require 6.4 billion bits, or roughly 760 megabytes, of storage space. The algorithm is designed to minimise computational errors and is adaptable, allowing it to be seamlessly integrated into pre-existing classical DNA sequencing systems (Weder, Breitenbücher, Leymann, & Wild, 2020).

Advanced cryptography and the security of medical records: I Patient health is at risk if the current cryptography that safeguards the confidentiality and security of medical technologies stops working. However, quantum cryptography provides more efficient ways to defend data from security breaches on surgical records and Electronic Health Records (EHR) (Abdelgaber & Nikolopoulos, 2020). The role of quantum computing in the COVID-19 pandemic The COVID-19 pandemic has been officially declared by the World Health Organisation (WHO). Finding the afflicted patient as soon as possible is essential. In order to quickly provide the most accurate response, COVID-19 detection from CT images was investigated using quantum computers. By employing a limited number of data sets, such as 126 COVID-19 and 100 normal CT images, quantum computers were able to achieve a high success rate of 94%–100% in contrast to classical computers. Furthermore, as the results demonstrate, the machine learning process in quantum computers can be realised in a very short amount of time with a very small quantum processor, such as 4 qubits, in contrast to classical computers, which require more time and processors (Luckow, Klepsch, & Pichlmeier, 2021).

Big data analytics in the healthcare system: Conventional digital computing uses binary digits to code data; quantum computing uses quantum bits, or qubits. One or zero, or any linear combination of the two qubit states, can be represented by a qubit. It is the classical binary bits in quantum form. It allows quantum computers to function thousands of times faster than traditional computers. Quantum algorithms have the potential to exponentially speed up big data analysis. Certain complex problems that are believed to be unsolvable with conventional computing can be solved with quantum techniques. For example, quantum computers will be able to quickly crack encryption techniques that are now thought to be unbreakable, such as public key cryptography (PK), RSA, and Data Encryption Standard (DES). It may be possible to use quantum techniques to decrease the quantity of data required for big data analysis. As a result, quantum techniques can reduce the amount of processing power required for extensive data analysis (Kendon, 2020).

Quantum-inspired algorithms for adaptive radiotherapy: Quantum-based algorithms are used in conjunction with classical and deep machine learning algorithms to address the challenges in radiation oncology related to the clinical application of image-guided adaptive radiotherapy (ART). To address the need for efficient, dependable optimisation techniques for treatment planning, we developed a quantum-inspired stochastic optimisation algorithm, called quantum tunnel annealing (QTA), which models particle tunnelling through a one-dimensional potential energy barrier. Under different dose constraints, QTA demonstrates faster convergence rates for beamlet weight and direct aperture optimisation than simulated annealing (SA), which was used previously. As a result, QTA might work well in optimisation scenarios with more stringent time constraints, such as adaptive replanning (How & Cheah, 2023).

QUANTUM COMPUTING FOR FINANCE

Any industry that depends on computation, including finance, could undergo a revolution thanks to quantum computing. In the financial industry, the first quantum applications have already been created and implemented for use cases such as portfolio management, risk management, and derivatives pricing. These applications deal with problems in machine learning, simulation, and optimization (Straube, 2023).

Many problems in the finance industry can be classified as optimisation problems. For classical computers, these are very hard tasks, but they are naturally formulated by quantum optimisation techniques. The recent widespread availability of quantum annealers has led to a massive growth in this field. Utilising quantum annealers can help with portfolio optimisation, arbitrage opportunity detection, and credit scoring.

One can explore the possible uses of quantum computing by looking into a number of challenging computational problems in contemporary computational finance. Quantitative analysts deal with a wide range of problems, from optimisation to machine learning. Typical problems include pricing derivatives, maximising portfolio allocations, modelling financial markets with stochastic differential equations, utilising machine learning techniques to predict market patterns, and calculating risk using Monte Carlo techniques. It frequently takes advanced computational techniques and, in certain situations, significant computer resources to solve these issues (Ur Rasool et al., 2023).

Using quantum computing to secure data in financial services: A McKinsey article states that one of the financial services industry's top priorities is ensuring data security. The rise of FinTech has led to an increase in digitisation. Furthermore, there has been a noticeable increase in online financial activity as a result of the COVID-19 pandemic. Machine learning and data modelling techniques powered by quantum computing may enable financial institutions to more precisely identify potential risks. Even people who do not intend to use quantum computing should be aware of the potential threats it poses to public-key cryptography standards such as RSA and Diffie-Hellmann, including popular variations based on elliptic curves. This is due to the fact that the Abelian hidden subgroup problem can be effectively solved by quantum computing, which is currently unattainable. Financial institutions should, however, prepare by learning how to use quantum-safe protocols and, potentially, quantum-enhanced encryption, as each has the potential to provide advantages of its own (Dash, Shakyawar, Sharma, & Kaushik, 2019).

Figure 2. Use cases of quantum computing in finance

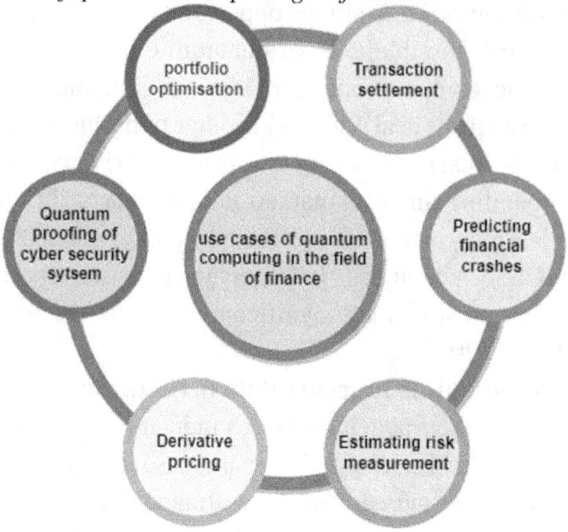

Users of this technology may have a significant competitive advantage over others because it enables almost real-time pricing of derivatives, which would otherwise require slower Monte Carlo evaluations. It also allows for more precise or stable pricing. Simultaneously, it appears from the first approximations that the quadratic speedup achieved for traditional quantum Monte Carlo techniques would be restricted to challenging Monte Carlo problems and might necessitate the use of very high-quality qubits for implementation. Finding the portfolio that either maximises the expected return for a given standard deviation (risk) or minimises the standard deviation of the return for a given expected return is the aim. Finding the risk-return curve and the portfolio that maximises return for a particular risk is one of the key objectives of classical portfolio management theory. Here, the quantum linear systems algorithm and its modifications are used to obtain the risk-return curve and the minimal-risk portfolio for a given desired return. The goal is to find the portfolio that either minimises the standard deviation of the return for a given expected return or maximises the expected return for a given standard deviation (risk). One of the main goals of classical portfolio management theory is to find the risk-return curve and the portfolio that maximises return for a given risk. Here, the risk-return curve and the minimal-risk portfolio for a given desired return are obtained using the quantum linear systems algorithm and its modifications. At least for basic financial toy models, quantum annealers can be used to tackle the problem of financial crash prediction and, more broadly, determining the equilibrium of a financial network. The idea of adiabatic quantum computing, which utilises nature's extraordinary capacity for determination. These quantum processors operate at the lowest-energy eigenstate, or ground state, of complex Hamiltonians. Finding the equilibrium state of a simple toy model financial network is equivalent to finding the ground state of a given spin-1/2 Hamiltonian for a two-body interaction. We can read out the state of the system, which is understood as a configuration of financial equilibrium, and anticipate a possible crash once the annealer finds a candidate ground state. Though proof-of-principle experiments with such processors are already possible, it is important to remember that current quantum processors still have limited computational capabilities, especially when compared to the best state-of-the-art classical algorithms. Using past data for two and three time-maturing forward rates, the IBMQX2 quantum computer is used to experimentally determine the principal components of the 2×2 and 3×3 cross-correlation matrices.

Financial risk assessment using quantum computing: The field of quantum technology, investment, and research has experienced exponential growth in the last few years. In recent years, there has been an exponential growth in the fields of quantum technology, investment, and research. Large banks and other financial organisations have been heavily funding quantum and use case research, primarily on rented hardware with restricted capabilities thus far. Applications like risk management and trading are eagerly awaited. A newer application of machine learning, which is a straightforward extension of quantum computing, is to financial problems. Banks are actively pursuing it as a result. Applications requiring a large number of algorithmic repetitions, such as the brute-force enumeration of potential solutions for a system of equations and, to a lesser extent, Monte Carlo simulation, are particularly well suited for quantum computing. The analysis reveals that the precision of the marginal and joint distributions of risk factors, as well as the total number of risk factors that can be simulated, are severely limited by the capabilities of current state-of-the-art quantum computers, which are expressed in terms of "qubits." For the foreseeable future, risk measurement applications with practical use cases will be precluded by the typical "noise" patterns observed by quantum circuits in practice. The business case for switching to quantum computing is still unclear because practical risk applications in financial institutions using classical computing are mature and provide accurate enough results in acceptable amounts of time, even for large-scale portfolios (Shaikh & Ali, 2016).

Table 1. Problems faced by financial services and quantum computing solutions

Financial services	Sample problems	Technique for solving problems	Quantum algorithm
Asset Management	Option Pricing and Portfolio risk	Simulation	AE
Investment Banking	Portfolio Optimization Portfolio Diversification Issuance: Auctions	Optimization	Combinatorial: VQE, QAOA Continuous: QSDP AE
Retail and co-operate banking	Financial Forecasting Credit Scoring (e.g. SME Banking) Financial Crimes: Fraud + AML	Machine Learning	QSVM HHL AE

The financial industry is facing obstacles and issues that could be addressed by quantum computers and their algorithms. These include the need for more advanced risk analysis, dynamic client management, real-time alerts on market volatility, and faster transaction rates (Jiang et al., 2019).

The amount of data that can be processed should be able to scale effectively when quantum computing can be made larger with better hardware. This would make it possible for the finance sector to handle larger data quantities and more features with greater ease. There are more than 200 data points for this use case that might be investigated from various financial metrics in the balance sheet, profit and loss statement, auditor's notes, transaction data analysis, and payment track records of organizations. Additionally, macroeconomic statistics about the economy, sector, and nation or region may be included. Better trade finance portfolio optimization can arise from combining all of this data with effective quantum algorithms (Acar & Yilmaz, 2021).

QUANTUM COMPUTING FOR INDUSTRY 4.0

Quantum Pliers Cutting the Blockchain: Large volumes of data have been produced recently by the advancement of cutting-edge technologies in the Internet of Things (IoT) and Industry 4.0 domains. Traditionally, tasks have been handled by databases; developments such as distributed ledger technologies (DLTS) and blockchain technology, like BlockChain, have brought this approach to data sharing and storage. This landscape is now more complex due to the advent of quantum computers, which pose a threat to DLT security because of their radically altered method of representing information. The study examines the potential threats that quantum computing poses to blockchain technology and assesses substitute post-quantum DLT solutions, with a focus on traceability applications.

The blockchain concept originates from the Bitcoin cryptocurrency proposal. It is composed of blocks linked together by cryptographic functions. The blockchain contains nodes called miners, which are validated as new blocks through proof-of-work (POW), ensuring the chain's integrity. Bitcoin uses hashcash to solve difficult mathematical problems. Transaction security is secured using public-private key pairs. The sender and receiver generate public addresses, and transactions are signed using private keys.

Figure 3. Applications of quantum computing for industry 4.0

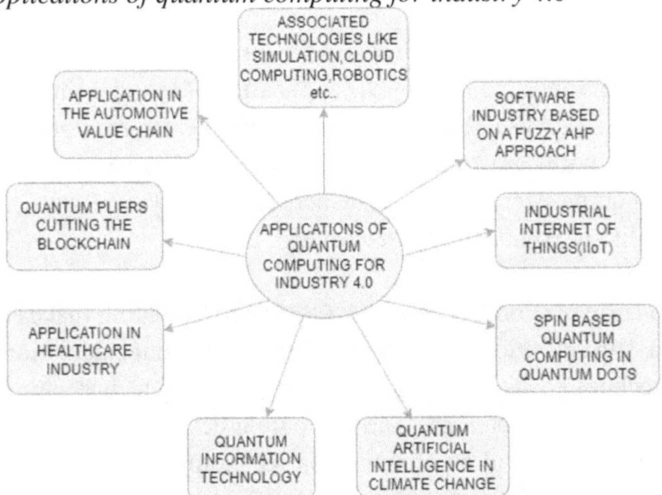

Industry 4.0 and its associated technologies: Industry 4.0 is the integration of both computers and networking infrastructure to control physical activities through various technologies. CPS (cyber-physical systems) is the embedded system that facilitates this connection, enabling the control of physical processes through cyber capabilities. Industry 4.9 requires specific skills, with a focus on machining skills aligned with CPS architecture requirements and technical skills such as connection, conversion, cyber, cognition, and configuration. AI (artificial intelligence)-related skills are probability, statistics, optimization, data visualization, computational methods, data science, database systems, operating systems, and data acquisition.

i. Simulation: It is an extensive tool, covering various stages from drafting and design to aspects like product, process, services, safety, usability, repairs, maintenance, accidents, and hazards. It is acknowledged for its potential in product and manufacturing process development and improvement. Combining simulation with optimization is mentioned as a suitable approach, but still, finding the approximate solution is challenging.

ii. Cloud computing: This method links different types of computing services, including networks, servers, storage, databases, software, and analytics. The cloud is a collective term for computing systems and services that are easily and minimally administratively accessed over the Internet. There are three types of cloud computing: fog, edge, and cloud computing. Software as a service (SaaS), platform as a service (PaaS), and infrastructure as a service (IaaS) are among the services offered by cloud computing.

iii. Robotics: This field uses electro-mechatronics along with another specialised knowledge. It includes the design, implementation, and use of computing and control systems. Data processing and sensory feedback are included. Robots operating fleets are supported by the application of robotics through unmanned aerial vehicles (UAVs). Robots are used in many different domains, including environments with hard-to-access (HTA) and terrible sources of contamination (SOC). Robots have the advantages of increased quality adherence, repeatability, and reliability (Arshad, Murtza, & Arshad, 2023).

Quantum Information Technology: Quantum computing makes use of quantum states like superposition and entanglement to carry out calculations. Quantum information technology is still considered an emerging technology even though it hasn't realised its full potential. The computing devices are known as quantum computers. Information and communication technology (ICT) and quantum mechanics are combined in the multidisciplinary field of quantum technology. This includes theoretical and applied research in quantum computing and physics. This technology is considered a frontier technology since it integrates quantum physics and ICT. Cryptography is the main building block of quantum communication; as a new infrastructure, it has replaced traditional networks. With the aid of quantum sensing, industry is trying to measure objects that have never been measured before. Quantum theory is used to understand and develop information-processing and information-storing systems. This technology enables quantum communication and sensing (Pakela, 2021).

Climate change and quantum Artificial Intelligence: Artificial intelligence operating on quantum computers is referred to as quantum artificial intelligence. Its objective is to explore the potential that algorithms and quantum computing provide for solving machine learning-related problems. The largest issue facing the globe today is climate change. Although AI-based methods produce better predictions, they still lack the necessary hardware and software to process massive amounts of data on a scale comparable to that of the planet Earth. As a relatively new technology, quantum computing has greater potential applications in a variety of domains, including weather and climate forecasting. Understanding climate dynamics requires a thorough understanding of simulation studies in climate science, such as the recent scientific breakthrough that links volcanic eruptions to El Nino and the South Asian monsoon. Present-day quantum computers can control about 100 qubits, but practical applications require millions, which presents a major technological challenge. There may be ways to speed up simulations with quantum artificial intelligence and quantum computing. (Bertels et al., 2020).

CASE STUDIES AND USE CASES

Figure 4. Criteria for reference use case

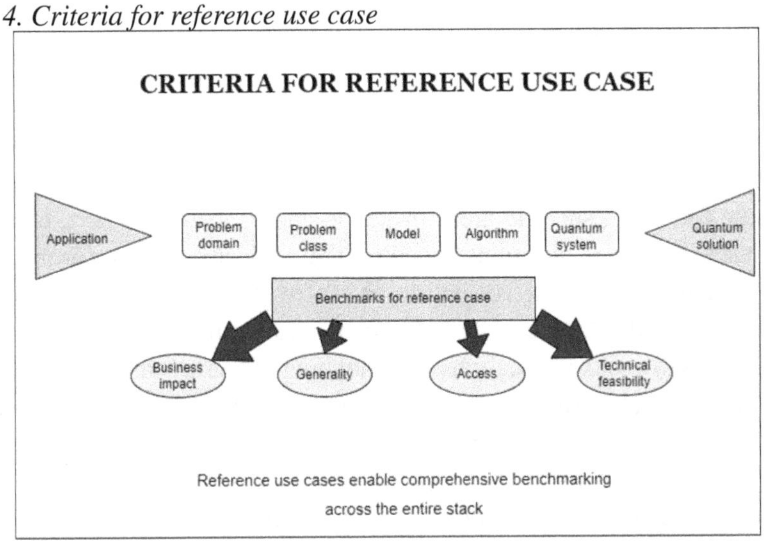

The finance sector is expected to benefit greatly from quantum computing since these machines can quickly solve financial problems. Since many financial problems rely on stochastic variables, like inputs, they are often more tolerant of solution imprecisions than problems in physics and chemistry. Standard techniques used in finance to model stochastic processes are numerical solutions of differential equations and Monte Carlo techniques. Using an interactive visualisation technique called VACSEN, users can learn about the noise in quantum computing when trying to run their quantum algorithms on quantum computers. Two case studies involving small and large quantum circuits were used to test VACSEN, a visualization-based method for quantum computing analysis. On March 5, 2022, the users (U1 and U6), who are experts in quantum computing, used VACSEN on the IBM Quantum platform. U1 used VACSEN to determine the suitable compiled circuit for a two-qubit circuit by evaluating the noise levels of various quantum computers. U1 selected Circuit Trans 24 using VACSEN for circuit compilation because, upon execution, it showed the highest fidelity of all the compiled circuits. In addition, U1 investigated the possibility of attaining high fidelity with shorter queuing times and chose Circuit Trans 0 based on its noise profile, even though ibmq lima had lower qubit performance. U6 ran Shor's algorithm, a large-scale quantum circuit, using VACSEN to assess quantum noise. U6 chose Circuit Trans 19 after gathering and organizing the circuits because it was less deep and had a noise level that was like Circuit Trans 40. The next execution supported U6's choice because Circuit Trans 19 had the best fidelity of all the circuits selected (Orús, Mugel, & Lizaso, 2019).

DISCUSSION AND FUTURE DIRECTIVES

Learning from developments in AI and other related technologies and advancing quantum computing for industrial-scale applications requires a concerted and urgent effort. To accelerate progress, the Quantum Technology Advisory Committee has outlined the following specific areas of action and enablers: To sort, create, and share industry reference questions based on their priority. To turn problems into community standards and focus on end-to-end software. To express quantum effects through easy-to-understand communication. Coordinating German and European funding sources to avoid duplication or overlapping of work. Support industry partners by providing a clear value proposition and contribution. Prioritize international cooperation, as demonstrated by programs like QuIC. To create demand, establish commercially viable quantum applications. Industrializing quantum computers and promoting successful business models is a long-term goal.

In 2022, an article was published in which various areas of ongoing research on quantum computing were identified and separated into three maturity levels: five years, five to ten years, and over a decade. It is revealed that post-quantum cryptography has peaked and that numerous studies on complex quantum experiment simulations have already been carried out. Research fields including robotics, energy management, information security, distributed quality control, intricate computation in chemistry, financial modeling, and discovering medicines are still in the early stages when it comes to the vast ocean of quantum computing. Multidisciplinary interaction between engineers, physicists, and materials scientists to fuse semiconductors and superconductors and develop new approaches to quantum technology. The primary objective is to enhance the dependability and responsiveness of quantum gates, particularly qubit gates, by investigating novel materials and technologies. Examine how spin fluctuations affect quantum computing. Create plans to lessen these impacts, bearing in mind spin-orbit coupling. Encourage partnerships between developed nations to advance common progress and international cooperation in the field of quantum computing research. Assess the effect of our work not just on publications but also on practical applications and quantum computing technological advancements.

REFERENCES

Abdelgaber, N., & Nikolopoulos, C. "Overview of Quantum Computing and its Applications in Artificial Intelligence," 2020 IEEE Third International Conference on Artificial Intelligence and Knowledge Engineering (AIKE), Laguna Hills, CA, USA, 2020, pp. 198-199, DOI: 10.1109/AIKE48582.2020.00038

Acar, E., & Yilmaz, I. (2021). COVID-19 detection on IBM quantum computer with classical-quantum transferlearning. *Turkish Journal of Electrical Engineering and Computer Sciences*, 29(1), 46–61. DOI: 10.3906/elk-2006-94

Ajagekar, A., & You, F. (2019). Quantum computing for energy systems optimization: Challenges and opportunities. *Energy*, 179, 76–89. DOI: 10.1016/j.energy.2019.04.186

Arshad, M. W., Murtza, I., & Arshad, M. A. (2023). Applications of Quantum Computing in Health Sector. Journal of Data Science and Intelligent Systems.

Awan, U., Hannola, L., Tandon, A., Goyal, R. K., & Dhir, A. (2022). Quantum computing challenges in the software industry. A fuzzy AHP-based approach. *Information and Software Technology*, 147, 106896. DOI: 10.1016/j.infsof.2022.106896

Bayerstadler, A., Becquin, G., Binder, J., Botter, T., Ehm, H., Ehmer, T., Erdmann, M., Gaus, N., Harbach, P., Hess, M., Klepsch, J., Leib, M., Luber, S., Luckow, A., Mansky, M., Mauerer, W., Neukart, F., Niedermeier, C., Palackal, L., & Winter, F. (2021). Industry quantum computing applications. *EPJ Quantum Technology*, 8(1), 25. DOI: 10.1140/epjqt/s40507-021-00114-x

Bertels, K. O. E. N., Sarkar, A., Hubregtsen, T., Serrao, M., Mouedenne, A. A., Yadav, A., Krol, A., Ashraf, I., & Almudever, C. G. (2020). Quantum computer architecture toward full-stack quantum accelerators. *IEEE Transactions on Quantum Engineering*, 1, 1–17. DOI: 10.1109/TQE.2020.2981074

Blunt, N. S., Camps, J., Crawford, O., Izsák, R., Leontica, S., Mirani, A., Moylett, A. E., Scivier, S. A., Sünderhauf, C., Schopf, P., Taylor, J. M., & Holzmann, N. (2022). Perspective on the current state-of-the-art of quantum computing for drug discovery applications. *Journal of Chemical Theory and Computation*, 18(12), 7001–7023. DOI: 10.1021/acs.jctc.2c00574 PMID: 36355616

Bova, F., Goldfarb, A., & Melko, R. G. (2021). Commercial applications of quantum computing. *EPJ Quantum Technology*, 8(1), 2. DOI: 10.1140/epjqt/s40507-021-00091-1 PMID: 33569545

Bravyi, S., Dial, O., Gambetta, J. M., Gil, D., & Nazario, Z. (2022). The future of quantum computing with superconducting qubits. *Journal of Applied Physics*, 132(16), 160902. DOI: 10.1063/5.0082975

Buffoni, L., & Caruso, F. (2021). New trends in quantum machine learning (a). *Europhysics Letters*, 132(6), 60004. DOI: 10.1209/0295-5075/132/60004

Chen, J. (2021, April). Review on quantum communication and quantum computation. [). IOP Publishing.]. *Journal of Physics: Conference Series*, 1865(2), 022008. DOI: 10.1088/1742-6596/1865/2/022008

Choi, J., Oh, S., & Kim, J. "The Useful Quantum Computing Techniques for Artificial Intelligence Engineers," *2020 International Conference on Information Networking (ICOIN)*, Barcelona, Spain, 2020, pp. 1-3, DOI: 10.1109/ICOIN48656.2020.9016555

Cusumano, M. A. (2018). The business of quantum computing. *Communications of the ACM*, 61(10), 20–22. DOI: 10.1145/3267352

Dash, S., Shakyawar, S. K., Sharma, M., & Kaushik, S. (2019). Big data in healthcare: Management, analysis and future prospects. *Journal of Big Data*, 6(1), 1–25. DOI: 10.1186/s40537-019-0217-0

Fernández-Caramés, T. M. (2020, July). From Pre-Quantum to Post-Quantum IoT Security: A Survey on Quantum-Resistant Cryptosystems for the Internet of Things. *IEEE Internet of Things Journal*, 7(7), 6457–6480. DOI: 10.1109/JIOT.2019.2958788

Gill, S. S. (2021). Quantum and blockchain based Serverless edge computing: A vision, model, new trends and future directions. *Internet Technology Letters*, •••, 275.

Gill, S. S., Kumar, A., Singh, H., Singh, M., Kaur, K., Usman, M., & Buyya, R. (2022). Quantum computing: A taxonomy, systematic review and future directions. *Software, Practice & Experience*, 52(1), 66–114. DOI: 10.1002/spe.3039

Guo, C., Liang, F., Lin, J., Xu, Y., Sun, L., Liu, W., Liao, S., & Peng, C. (2019, July). Control and Readout Software for Superconducting Quantum Computing. *IEEE Transactions on Nuclear Science*, 66(7), 1222–1227. DOI: 10.1109/TNS.2019.2920337

Gupta, M., & Nene, M. J. "Quantum Computing: An Entanglement Measurement," *2020 IEEE International Conference on Advent Trends in Multidisciplinary Research and Innovation (ICATMRI)*, Buldhana, India, 2020, pp. 1-6, DOI: 10.1109/ICATMRI51801.2020.9398441

Gururaj, V., Umadi, K. R., Kumar, M., Shankar, S. P., & Varadam, D. (2022, March). Comprehensive Survey of different Machine Learning Algorithms used for Software Defect Prediction. In *2022 International Conference on Decision Aid Sciences and Applications (DASA)* (pp. 425-430). IEEE.

Gyongyosi, L., & Imre, S. (2019). A survey on quantum computing technology. *Computer Science Review*, 31, 51–71. DOI: 10.1016/j.cosrev.2018.11.002

Hassija, V., Chamola, V., Goyal, A., Kanhere, S. S., & Guizani, N. (2020). Forthcoming applications of quantum computing: Peeking into the future. *IET Quantum Communication*, 1(2), 35–41. DOI: 10.1049/iet-qtc.2020.0026

Hassija, V., Chamola, V., Saxena, V., Chanana, V., Parashari, P., Mumtaz, S., & Guizani, M. (2020). The present landscape of quantum computing. *IET Quantum Communication*, 1(2), 42–48. DOI: 10.1049/iet-qtc.2020.0027

Herman, D., Googin, C., Liu, X., Galda, A., Safro, I., Sun, Y., . . . Alexeev, Y. (2022). A survey of quantum computing for finance. arXiv preprint arXiv:2201.02773.

Houssein, E. H., Abohashima, Z., Elhoseny, M., & Mohamed, W. M. (2022). Machine learning in the quantum realm: The state-of-the-art, challenges, and future vision. *Expert Systems with Applications*, 194, 116512. DOI: 10.1016/j.eswa.2022.116512

How, M. L., & Cheah, S. M. (2023). Business Renaissance: Opportunities and Challenges at the Dawn of the Quantum Computing Era. *Businesses*, 3(4), 585–605. DOI: 10.3390/businesses3040036

Hu, L., & Ni, Q. "Quantum Automated Object Detection Algorithm," 2019 25th International Conference on Automation and Computing (ICAC), Lancaster, UK, 2019, pp. 1-4, DOI: 10.23919/IConAC.2019.8895167

Jiang, L., Chen, L., Giannetsos, T., Luo, B., Liang, K., & Han, J. (2019). Toward practical privacy-preserving processing over encrypted data in IoT: An assistive healthcare use case. *IEEE Internet of Things Journal*, 6(6), 10177–10190. DOI: 10.1109/JIOT.2019.2936532

Kendon, V. (2020). Quantum computing using continuous-timeevolution. *Interface Focus*, 10(6), 20190143. DOI: 10.1098/rsfs.2019.0143 PMID: 33178417

Kim, D., Kang, J., Kim, T. W., Pan, Y., & Park, J. H. (2021). The future of quantum information: Challenges and vision. *Journal of Information Processing Systems*, 17(1), 151–162.

Luckow, A., Klepsch, J., & Pichlmeier, J. (2021). Quantum computing: Towards industry reference problems. *Digitale Welt*, 5(2), 38–45. DOI: 10.1007/s42354-021-0335-7

Mangini, S., Tacchino, F., Gerace, D., Bajoni, D., & Macchiavello, C. (2021). Quantum computing models for artificial neural networks. *Europhysics Letters*, 134(1), 10002. DOI: 10.1209/0295-5075/134/10002

Neumann, N., Phillipson, F., & Versluis, R. (2019). Machine learning in the quantum era. *Digitale Welt*, 3(2), 24–29. DOI: 10.1007/s42354-019-0164-0

Orús, R., Mugel, S., & Lizaso, E. (2019). Quantum computing for finance: Overview and prospects. *Reviews in Physics*, 4, 100028. DOI: 10.1016/j.revip.2019.100028

Orús, R., Mugel, S., & Lizaso, E. (2019). Quantum computing for finance: Overview and prospects. *Reviews in Physics*, 4, 100028. DOI: 10.1016/j.revip.2019.100028

Pakela, J. (2021). Quantum Inspired Machine Learning Algorithms for Adaptive Radiotherapy (Doctoral dissertation).

Paudel, H. P., Syamlal, M., Crawford, S. E., Lee, Y. L., Shugayev, R. A., Lu, P., Ohodnicki, P. R., Mollot, D., & Duan, Y. (2022). Quantum computing and simulations for energy applications: Review and perspective. *ACS Engineering Au*, 2(3), 151–196. DOI: 10.1021/acsengineeringau.1c00033

Petschnigg, C., Brandstötter, M., Pichler, H., Hofbaur, M., & Dieber, B. "Quantum Computation in Robotic Science and Applications," *2019 International Conference on Robotics and Automation (ICRA)*, Montreal, QC, Canada, 2019, pp. 803-810, DOI: 10.1109/ICRA.2019.8793768

Ramezani, S. B., Sommers, A., Manchukonda, H. K., Rahimi, S., & Amirlatifi, A. "Machine Learning Algorithms in Quantum Computing: A Survey," *2020 International Joint Conference on Neural Networks (IJCNN)*, Glasgow, UK, 2020, pp. 1-8, DOI: 10.1109/IJCNN48605.2020.9207714

Ranjan, A., Arya, A. K. S., & Ravinder, M. "Quantum Techniques for Image Processing," 2020 2nd International Conference on Advances in Computing, Communication Control and Networking (ICACCCN), Greater Noida, India, 2020, pp. 1035-1039, DOI: 10.1109/ICACCCN51052.2020.9362910

Ravi, G. S., Smith, K. N., Gokhale, P., & Chong, F. T. (2021, November). Quantum Computing in the Cloud: Analyzing job and machine characteristics. In *2021 IEEE International Symposium on Workload Characterization (IISWC)* (pp. 39-50). IEEE. DOI: 10.1109/IISWC53511.2021.00015

Shah, A., Shah, M., & Kanani, P. "Leveraging Quantum Computing for Supervised Classification," 2020 4th International Conference on Intelligent Computing and Control Systems (ICICCS), Madurai, India, 2020, pp. 256-261, DOI: 10.1109/ICICCS48265.2020.9120975

Shaikh, T. A., & Ali, R. (2016, December). Quantum computing in big data analytics: A survey. In 2016 IEEE international conference on computer and information technology (CIT) (pp. 112-115). IEEE.

Sharma, N., & Ketti Ramachandran, R. (2021). The emerging trends of quantum computing towards data security and key management. *Archives of Computational Methods in Engineering*, •••, 1–14.

Straube, D.F.C.(2023).Quantumcomputingasanenablingtechnologyforthenextbusiness cycle.

Sultana, F., Bhardwaj, R., Kumar, R. N., Gaur, R., Shankar, S. P., & Bharadwaj, A. (2024, April). Smart Traffic Management System for Efficient Mobility and Emergency Response. In *2024 International Conference on Knowledge Engineering and Communication Systems (ICKECS)* (Vol. 1, pp. 1-5). IEEE. DOI: 10.1109/ICKECS61492.2024.10616800

Sun, G. "Splicing ET (error-tolerant) Quantum Computing System," 2019 18th International Conference on Optical Communications and Networks (ICOCN), Huangshan, China, 2019, pp. 1-3, DOI: 10.1109/ICOCN.2019.8934156

Thapliyal, H., & Muñoz-Coreas, E. (2019). Design of quantum computing circuits. *IT Professional*, 21(6), 22–26.

Upama, P. B., Faruk, M. J. H., Nazim, M., Masum, M., Shahriar, H., Uddin, G., . . . Rahman, A. (2022, June). Evolution of quantum computing: A systematic survey on the use of quantum computing tools. In 2022 IEEE 46th Annual Computers, Software, and Applications Conference (COMPSAC) (pp. 520-529). IEEE. DOI: 10.1109/COMPSAC54236.2022.00096

Ur Rasool, R., Ahmad, H. F., Rafique, W., Qayyum, A., Qadir, J., & Anwar, Z. (2023). Quantum computing for healthcare: A review. *Future Internet*, 15(3), 94. DOI: 10.3390/fi15030094

Ur Rasool, R., Ahmad, H. F., Rafique, W., Qayyum, A., Qadir, J., & Anwar, Z. (2023). Quantum computing for healthcare: A review. *Future Internet*, 15(3), 94. DOI: 10.3390/fi15030094

Varadam, D., Shankar, S. P., Bharadwaj, A., Saxena, T., Agrawal, S., & Dayananda, S. (2024). Enhancing industrial robotics performance and security with AI and blockchain technologies. In *AI and blockchain applications in industrial robotics* (pp. 58–81). IGI Global.

Varadam, D., Shankar, S. P., Hegde, P., Shobitha, V., Sunidhi, M., & Sanjana, N. (2024). Intelligent Techniques for Detection and Diagnosis of Neurodegenerative Diseases. In AI-Driven Alzheimer's Disease Detection and Prediction (pp. 293-319). IGI Global. DOI: 10.4018/979-8-3693-3605-2.ch020

Varadam, D., Shankar, S. P., Shankar, A., Narayan, A., & Kumar, T. N. (2024). Application of AI and Blockchain Technologies in the Medical Domain. AI and Blockchain Applications in Industrial Robotics, 200-225.

Varsha, T., Shekar, Y. C., Shankar, S. P., Bharadwaj, A., Varadam, D., & Supriya, M. S. (2023, July). On Campus Student Recruitment Analysis using Machine Learning techniques. In *2023 IEEE International Conference on Electronics, Computing and Communication Technologies (CONECCT)* (pp. 1-6). IEEE. DOI: 10.1109/CONECCT57959.2023.10234797

Wang, S., Pei, Z., Wang, C., & Wu, J. (2021). Shaping the future of the application of quantum computing in intelligent transportation system. *Intelligent and Converged Networks*, 2(4), 259–276. DOI: 10.23919/ICN.2021.0019

Wang, Y., & Liu, H. (2022). Quantum computing in a statistical context. *Annual Review of Statistics and Its Application*, 9(1), 479–504. DOI: 10.1146/annurev-statistics-042720-024040

Weder, B., Breitenbücher, U., Leymann, F., & Wild, K. "Integrating Quantum Computing into Workflow Modeling and Execution," 2020 IEEE/ACM 13th International Conference on Utility and Cloud Computing (UCC), Leicester, UK, 2020, pp. 279-291, DOI: 10.1109/UCC48980.2020.00046

Chapter 9
Quantum Machine Learning (QML) Techniques for Enhancing Online Marketing and Business

S. Varalakshmi
Economics and Business Studies Department, Mazoon College, Muscat, Oman

Anupam Sharma
https://orcid.org/0009-0005-6644-6835
College of Economics and Business Administration, University of Technology and Applied Sciences, Oman

Latifa Saud Al Habsi
College of Economics and Business Administration, University of Technology and Applied Sciences, Oman

Yasmeen Sultana
https://orcid.org/0009-0000-1194-2907
Department of Management and Commerce, Maulana Azad National Urdu University, Hyderabad, India

ABSTRACT

This chapter discusses the means whereby QML can revolutionize and transform online marketing and business practices. QML is a derivative from the principles of quantum computation and machine learning, such that tremendous volumes of data may be processed at unprecedented velocities, hence advanced analytics in terms of

DOI: 10.4018/979-8-3693-6225-9.ch009

customer behavior being made possible, and also that of hyper-personalized marketing campaigns. Some of the key QML techniques discussed in terms of increasing the efficiency of marketing, reducing costs, and improving return on investments include techniques in quantum algorithms for clustering, classification, and optimization. It explores the potential of quantum technology in business intelligence, including real-time customer segmentation, predictive analytics, and dynamic pricing models, and predicts future trends and adoption roadmaps in the digital economy.

INTRODUCTION

Businesses in the era of digital transformation are always looking for further advanced tools and technologies so that they can keep competition at bay and maintain continuous growth. The latest of such breakthrough innovations, although recent, is Quantum Machine Learning (QML). QML represents a paradigm shift because it provides capabilities of unprecedented computational power and analytic capacity, which makes businesses approach data processing, extracting insights, and customer relationships differently(Yankovets & Vyshnevska, 2019). It is highly challenging for businesses to manage such massive datasets with the explosion of big data. Traditional machine learning methods are very powerful, but usually limited by computation, particularly in handling large quantities of complex and unstructured data. Quantum computing is capable of doing a lot of calculations exponentially faster than the classical systems, so these problems are solved with its help. The quantum system, when integrated with machine learning techniques, QML becomes a revolutionary tool, with the potential to optimize business decisions, enhance online marketing tactics, and boost business performance(De la Hoz Domínguez et al., 2020).

Quantum computing is based on principles of quantum mechanics, where qubits replace the classical bits. However, unlike the classical bits, which describe information as either 0 or 1, qubits exist in superposition states, meaning they can embody multiple states at once. This unique capability allows quantum systems to process and analyze complex datasets at speeds unimaginable with classical computers. When combined with machine learning algorithms, quantum computing can uncover deeper patterns, predict trends with greater accuracy, and optimize complex decision-making processes. E-commerce, finance, healthcare, and logistics businesses are the types of businesses that have become highly interested in QML due to its competitive advantages in certain areas, such as analysis of customer behavior, targeted marketing, product recommendation, and dynamic pricing(Adikari et al., 2021).

In the context of online marketing, QML has a tremendous potential to change the face of how businesses interact with consumers. Since digital marketing is heavily dependent on data-driven strategies, knowing the preferences, behaviors, and purchase patterns of customers is very crucial. QML enhances these efforts by enabling real-time analysis of large-scale datasets and providing actionable insights that cannot be achieved by traditional systems. For example, quantum algorithms for clustering and classification can group customers into very fine-grained categories according to their behaviors, demographics, and preferences. The granular segmentation will help businesses design highly personalized marketing campaigns that speak to individual consumers, thus boosting engagement and conversion rates. Moreover, QML can make predictive analytics more accurate and help businesses better predict market trends, demand forecasting, and customized offerings(Bhatt, 2021).

One of the most exceptional capabilities of QML in internet marketing is optimizing those processes complicated, like dynamic pricing and resource allocation. Traditional optimization techniques do not often give real-time solutions because they often fail while using variables such as pricing models, inventory levels, and consumer demand. QML algorithms, including quantum annealing and variational quantum eigensolvers, are fast to discover optimal solutions to these problems, thereby allowing businesses to dynamically react to changes in the marketplace. For instance, an e-commerce website can apply QML to update prices in real-time as dictated by supply-demand dynamics, competitor pricing, and even customer-specific behavior. This precision and responsiveness can make all the difference in terms of the satisfaction and profitability of customers(Fredström et al., 2022).

Another area where QML may change the game for business operations is in recommendation systems. Personalized recommendations are at the heart of many successful online marketing strategies, especially in retail, entertainment, and hospitality. QML algorithms can analyze vast amounts of user data to identify correlations and preferences that classical systems may overlook. It is also possible to improve the experience of the user, increase customer loyalty, and enhance sales. For example, a streaming site such as Netflix or an e-commerce giant like Amazon can use QML in real-time analysis of what people are watching or purchasing and provide customers with perfectly aligned recommendations. Such personalization enhances the relationship between the customer and business and encourages long-term engagement(Sahebi et al., 2022a).

Although QML brings about transformative opportunities for business, it does present some challenges and limitations to its adoption. Because the technology is still very new, quantum hardware and software are still at very early stages of development toward mainstream adoption. In addition, integrating QML into existing business infrastructure requires huge investments in terms of technology, talent, and training. In other words, business systems need to address the challenges above in a stepwise manner by developing high-impact use cases promising return on investment in terms of quantities. With the help of quantum technology providers and research establishments, the businesses will shift base rapidly to QML-based solutions(Sahebi et al., 2022b).

As the maturation of quantum technologies looks forward to exponential growth in their applications in online marketing and business strategy, firms that begin embracing QML will significantly enjoy competitiveness through unmatched speed, accuracy, and scalability. Advances of quantum algorithms, hardware, and software will lead the way toward solving more challenging problems by businesses in several industries, thus further catalyzing innovation. It is the integration of QML with other emerging technologies such as AI, blockchain, and the Internet of Things. Its impact will therefore be further amplified in creating new opportunities for growth and value creation(Akman et al., 2023).

Thus, Quantum Machine Learning represents the next frontier in digital transformation and will empower businesses to arm themselves with powerful tools in the optimization of their operations' online marketing strategy and to deliver better customer experiences. By applying the principles of quantum computing and machine learning, QML enables businesses to process massive datasets, discover hidden patterns, and make data-driven decisions at unprecedented speed and precision. As the digital economy evolves further, businesses must be able to recognize the transformative potential of QML and position themselves in a manner to take advantage of this revolutionary technology(Van Chau & He, 2024). This chapter will detail the fundamental QML techniques, its applications in online marketing, and strategies to overcome the adoption challenges so that the business is completely geared to thrive in the quantum era.

BACKGROUND: QML IN ONLINE MARKETING

The landscape of online marketing is evolving through the new ways QML will process and analyze enormous volumes of complex data from customers. Quantum algorithms allow businesses to use this tool as an improvement in analytics for a quantum machine, prediction of customer behavior, and delivery of hyper-personalized experiences. This chapter is focused on how quantum algorithms make a difference in marketing analytics, behavior predictions, and delivering unprecedented personalization for campaigns that target specific audiences. Figure 1 showcases the significant role of Quantum Machine Learning (QML) in marketing analytics, customer behavior prediction, and hyper-personalized campaigns(Modak et al., 2024).

Figure 1. Role of QML in Online Marketing

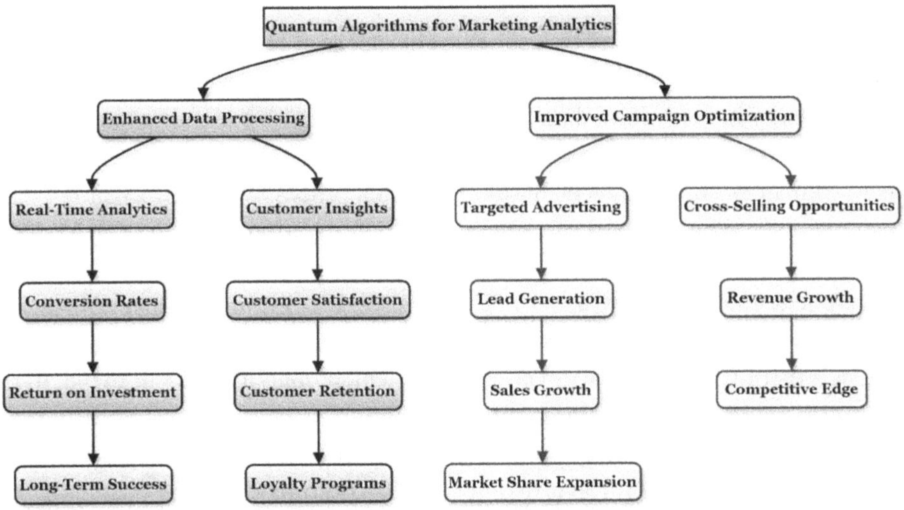

Quantum Algorithms in Marketing Analytics

Traditional marketing analytics using classical machine learning techniques cannot process real-time large and unstructured datasets. QML offers quantum algorithms that solve the challenge by computation and deeper pattern recognition in comparison to the traditional algorithms. Some of the algorithms QSVM and QPCA allow marketers to make accurate predictions on high-dimensional datasets(Modak et al., 2024).

Quantum Clustering: Algorithms identify clusters within customer data to segment audiences more precisely based on demographics, preferences, and behaviors. This makes campaign targeting and resource allocation possible.
Quantum Optimization: By employing techniques such as quantum annealing, advertising budgets, and bidding strategies and content placements can be optimized to provide the highest ROI across digital channels.
Quantum Linear Regression: Quantum-inspired regression models can be leveraged to make more efficient trend forecasts, thus aiding marketers to make better decisions about the pricing, product launches, and seasonal campaigns.

This can be achieved through quantum algorithms, which will process complex datasets in seconds that could take hours or days otherwise and unlock opportunities for more data-driven, agile marketing strategies.

Improving Customer Behavior Prediction with QML

Predicting customer behavior is the heart of successful online marketing because it allows businesses to anticipate needs, preferences, and purchasing patterns. Scale and complexity in behavioral data defeat traditional machine learning methods, but QML offers quantum-enhanced predictive models to help overcome these challenges(Akman et al., 2023). Quantum algorithms process multi-dimensional data simultaneously, which means marketers can: Identification of Hidden Behavioral Patterns. QML exposes correlations between disparate acts; click, view or cart abandonment. Improves the Chance of Conversion Forecasting. The quantum model improves the accuracy of predicting the rate of conversion to further lead their targets and touch them first in priority. The speed at which quantum aids in the analysis of data streaming helps a business in responding to its customers' actions in real-time, say, by presenting timely propositions or product recommendations to such customers(Boopathi, 2024; Ravisankar et al., 2024; Somasundaram et al., 2024).

For example, an e-commerce application employing QML would analyze the browsing behavior, past purchases, and preferences in order to predict what the customer is likely to buy next, thereby ensuring timely and relevant engagement.2.3 Hyper-Personalized Marketing Campaigns

Hyper-Personalization Campaigns

Hyper-personalization is an important driver of customer engagement, satisfaction, and loyalty. Quantum Machine Learning enables such hyper-personalization-that goes way beyond the basic market segmentations to individual-level targeted marketing strategies. QML algorithms yield real-time customized experiences-on the fly, based on the real-time processing of mass data streams-to match the unique behaviors and preferences of each customer(Akman et al., 2023). A key application of QML for hyper-personalization lies:

Dynamic Content Personalization: QML algorithms will curate contents personalized to each user. Examples include personalized advertisements, product recommendation, and emails. For example, a video streaming service may use QML in suggesting content as hyper-specific based on viewing history.

Real-Time Offer Customization: QML can consider clicks, location, or purchasing power to make personalized promotions or discounts in real time. Behavior-Based Journey Mapping: Businesses can, therefore, create hyper-personalized customer journeys by predicting touch points where the user is most probably going to engage, such as specifically crafted follow-ups or rewarding loyalty. The ability at scale to create one-to-one marketing campaigns gives businesses a competitive advantage in enhancing the user experience, converting them and building long-term relationships.

In summary, QML empowers business to elevate their online marketing strategy through quantum-enhanced analytics, predictive models, and hyper-personalized solutions. They make data-driven decisions in real-time, improving targeting, increasing engagement, and driving business growth in this way.

QML TECHNIQUES FOR BUSINESS GROWTH

Quantum Machine Learning or QML is revolutionizing business growth by providing strong tools for analysis in data, market behavior prediction, and also optimizing decision-making. There are traditional machine learning approaches. They are effective in themselves but are not set to handle large, high dimensional datasets and provide the immediacy of insights into phenomena. QML offers immense computational speed and accuracy since it relies on the basic principle of quantum computing(Vennila et al., 2022). Advanced techniques like quantum clustering, quantum classification, and quantum optimization open the door for businesses to be run more efficiently, engage better with their customers, and therefore become more profitable. This chapter delves into three major QML techniques: quantum clustering to segment customers, quantum classification to analyze market trends, and optimization strategies for dynamic pricing, which can transform businesses into growth drivers(Sahebi et al., 2022b). Figure 2 explores how Quantum Clustering and Customer Segmentation can help in understanding market trends and dynamic pricing through optimization techniques.

Figure 2. Quantum Clustering and Customer Segmentation for business growth

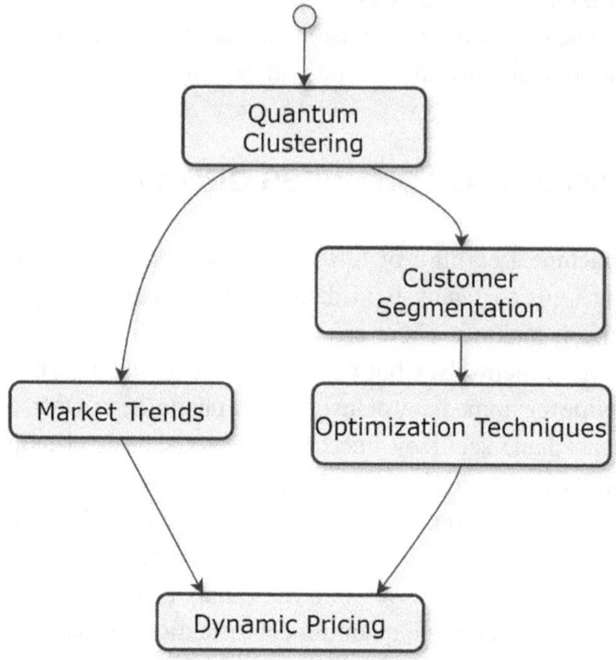

Quantum Clustering and Customer Segmentation

Customer segmentation is the backbone in any business growth strategy whereby an organization identifies specific groups with the target audience and provides customized marketing efforts. Though clustering algorithms such as hierarchical and K-means provide excellent results, they don't perform well when very large and complex datasets occur. They cannot process high-dimension data efficiently and make accurate calculations, which may have poor segmentation. Quantum clustering is a technique based on quantum algorithms, addressing these challenges by using quantum systems' ability to process many states simultaneously(Ramkumar et al., 2022).

Quantum clustering algorithms use quantum superposition and entanglement to quickly scan vast spaces of data, thereby discovering hidden patterns in customer behavior. For example, a business can segment a customer based on his buying history, browsing habits, demographics, and preferences more accurately. Quantum algorithms help businesses analyze large-scale data and identify micro-segments:

very small, highly defined customer groups. Businesses can thereby design hyper-targeted marketing strategies.

For example, in the retail sector, quantum clustering can identify segments of customers who have similar behavior during seasonal sales, such as preferences for certain product categories or discount thresholds. This way, businesses can design targeted promotions that align with each group's buying behavior, thus increasing conversion rates and revenue. Similarly, in financial services, quantum clustering can segment clients based on risk tolerance, spending patterns, and financial goals, allowing for highly personalized investment solutions. Quantum clustering not only improves the accuracy of segmentation but also accelerates the process, so that businesses can analyze customer data in real time. This empowers marketers to change their strategies dynamically and respond to changes in customer behavior or market conditions.

Quantum Categorization for Market Trends

Accurate analysis of market trends helps businesses in making strategic decisions in advance, understanding the needs of the customer, and staying ahead of competition. Traditional classification techniques used include Support Vector Machines or decision trees. However, in such techniques, when dealing with high-dimensional or unstructured datasets, there arises performance issues. Quantum classification techniques, such as Quantum Support Vector Machines (QSVM), provide a tremendous leap forward by giving much faster computation and improved accuracy(Blomster & Koivumäki, 2022).

Classification takes place through the quantum state which means utilizing the quantum state as means to classify data points from specified categories. In relation to market trends, using techniques offered through QML can aid analysis and derive huge amounts of information related to products through various sources: from social media to consumer comments on a website or analytics about the sales that go with them. For instance, in the fashion industry, quantum classification can analyze data from global markets to identify emerging styles, enabling brands to align their product lines with evolving consumer preferences.

QML-powered classification models are also able to capture slight variations in sentiment or behavioral patterns that may not be captured by traditional models. For instance, quantum classification can be used by hospitality industries to classify customer feedback into positive, negative, or neutral sentiments, which may help to identify areas for improvement and predict future demand for services. Similarly, in the e-commerce world, quantum algorithms can classify products likely to become popular using historical trends in purchasing, seasonality, and current market conditions. By offering real-time trend analysis and accurate market classifications,

QML assists businesses in making proactive, data-driven decisions that help them optimize inventory management, more efficiently allocate resources, and capitalize on emerging opportunities before their competitors do.

Dynamic Pricing Optimization Techniques

Dynamic pricing is a strategy that is highly important for businesses that aim at maximizing profitability without compromising the competitive edge. The core idea of dynamic pricing revolves around real-time adjustments based on the numerous factors, such as demand, supply, competitors, and consumers' willingness to pay. Conventional optimization techniques may help up to some extent, but they fail to provide a near-real-time solution to an extremely complex pricing model. Quantum optimization techniques such as Quantum Annealing and Variational Quantum Algorithms (VQAs) present a faster and more efficient approach to solve these challenges(Xiujuan et al., 2021).

Quantum optimization explores several potential solutions at once and enables businesses to know their optimal pricing strategy in real time. For example, in the airline industry, quantum algorithms can process thousands of variables, including seat availability, competitor fares, and booking trends, to find the best price for each seat in real time. This will ensure that the airlines make the maximum amount of money while ensuring the best price to the customer. In e-commerce, quantum optimization can help companies adjust product prices according to real-time demand and inventory levels. For example, in a flash sale, QML can determine the optimal price adjustments considering factors such as customer engagement, product popularity, and inventory depletion rates to maximize sales while avoiding stockouts. In the hospitality sector, for example, quantum optimization can optimize room rates by determining factors such as booking patterns, competitor pricing, and seasonal demand.

The dynamic pricing models empowered by quantum also enable businesses to offer personalized prices to each customer based on their buying behavior, loyalty, and willingness to pay. A retailer may offer a discount to the same buyer who abandoned the cart but is a frequent buyer in the future, thereby increasing the chance of conversion. Businesses can maximize revenue and maintain competitive advantage in changing the market through the integration of quantum optimization techniques into a pricing strategy, thereby driving more customer satisfaction.

Advanced quantum Machine Learning techniques provide that business transformation to achieve growth through market trend analysis, advanced customer segmentation, and dynamic pricing optimisation. Quantum clustering will help businesses identify their micro-segments and target customers with unprecedented precision; quantum classification will enable organizations to forecast trends in the market and to proactively adjust their strategy. Optimization techniques for dynamic pricing will allow businesses to maximize their profitability by reacting to real-time changes in market demand and customer behavior. Quantum technologies will keep moving forward with time, and early adopters in QML will be in excellent competitive advantage to drive innovative, efficient, and accelerating growth in a highly challenging business environment.

APPLICATIONS OF QML IN ONLINE MARKETING

Quantum Machine Learning (QML) is changing the paradigm of online marketing by allowing for more advanced capabilities in big data analysis, predicting the behavior of customers, and optimizing marketing strategies in real-time. Businesses are constantly under pressure to find out what the consumer needs, provide experiences that are unique, and build engagement as data complexity increases and competition grows. Though traditional machine learning approaches have greatly contributed to improvement in marketing outcomes, there are limits to the use of such techniques, specifically in scalability, processing speed, and accuracy in high-dimensional data(Blomster & Koivumäki, 2022; Xiujuan et al., 2021). The use of Quantitative Machine Learning (QML) techniques in real-time segmentation, predictive analytics, and recommendation systems has been proven to improve marketing outcomes in figure 3.

Figure 3. Applications of QML in Online Marketing

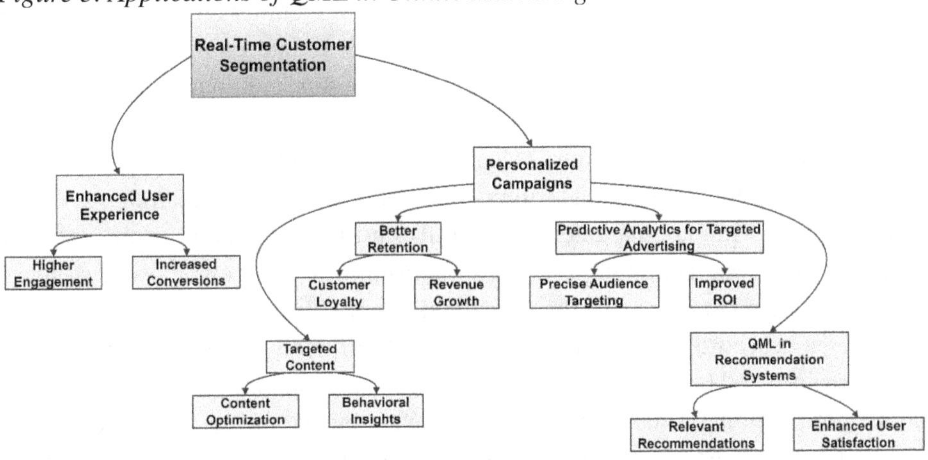

QML combines the unparalleled computational power of quantum computing with machine learning algorithms to provide marketers with faster, more accurate, and highly efficient solutions. This section explores three key applications of QML in online marketing: real-time customer segmentation, predictive analytics for targeted advertising, and quantum-enhanced recommendation systems.

Real-Time Customer Segmentation

Effective marketing strategies are founded on the customer segmentation. This provides companies an opportunity to categorize the customers based on shared demographic characteristics, behaviors, or preferences. However, since there is exponential growth of customer data from websites, mobile apps, social media, and e-commerce, the traditional segmentation methods could hardly give real-time, actionable insights. QML techniques, especially quantum clustering, have transformed customer segmentation by allowing businesses to quickly process large, complex data sets and identify nuanced patterns that traditional methods may miss(Bhatt, 2021; Chintala, 2021).

Quantum clustering algorithms, based on quantum principles like superposition and entanglement, allow businesses to analyze data across multiple dimensions simultaneously. These algorithms can effectively segment customers into micro-groups based on subtle behavior patterns, making it easier for marketers to identify hyper-targeted audiences for personalized campaigns. For example, within the retail industry, QML can analyze real-time browsing data, purchase history, and social media activities to form dynamic customer segments that are constantly changing due to shifts in preferences. Suppose an online fashion retailer recognizes a particular segment of users who browse winter jackets between evening hours but leave their carts. Using QML, the retailer can send targeted promotions or timely offers to this group for better conversions.

The business can then adjust to a changing market environment with segmentation models powered by QML. During periods of peak sales, for example, at Black Friday or Cyber Monday, marketers can identify on-time trends and customer groups during real-time segmentation, affording opportunities to engage those customers with highly relevant offers. In the travel and hospitality industry, QML can segment travelers according to booking behaviors, destination preferences, and budget range. Airlines and hotels can use these insights to personalize email campaigns or mobile notifications, enhancing customer satisfaction and increasing bookings. By leveraging real-time segmentation, businesses can deliver experiences that resonate with customers' immediate needs, fostering loyalty and driving revenue growth.

Predictive Analytics for Targeted Advertisements

Predictive analytics is important in online marketing today because it predicts the future behavior of a customer, identifies emerging trends, and tailors advertisements with respect to such predictions. Traditional predictive models are very good but often run into a bottleneck when dealing with real-time high-dimensional datasets. QML is a breakthrough in predictive analytics as it can greatly speed up, improve accuracy, and make such models scalable(Chintala, 2021; Gutnik, 2021).

Quantum algorithms, such as QSVMs and QNNs, can also significantly contribute to predictive analytics; by processing massive volumes of data in customers and complex patterns that lie beyond the reach of the normal model, they are used in making predictions of customer action or behavior, which in the future will determine actions by customers, like likely to buy or purchase items in a product and likely churn. For instance, an e-commerce business can leverage QML-based predictive analytics for predicting what customers are more likely to buy given their surfing behavior and previous transactions combined with factors like seasonality and competitor's activities. Given such identified high-value opportunities, businesses would then be in a position to better deploy ad budget as they personalize ads based on maximum return on investment.

Through real-time analysis of user engagement data, QML could predict which types of content or promotions will drive the greatest click-through rates and highest conversions. Facebook or Instagram platforms could then optimize ad placements so that the most appropriate message is delivered to the proper audience at the right moment. Moreover, QML-driven predictive analytics can help a business get the most out of its customers' lifetime value. It is determined by a set of customers that can be called a long-term potential buyer to help subscription-based services, for example, streaming platforms in assessing the customer data for predicting the risk of churn and subsequently offering them free trials or discounts to retain high-value customers.

In short, QML is more precise and faster compared to traditional techniques for predictive analytics. Businesses can then use such insights to create hyper-targeted, data-driven advertising strategies that drive engagement, conversions, and profitability.

QML in Recommendation Systems

Recommendation systems form the heart of personal marketing, which drives engagement and retention and sales for companies on e-commerce, entertainment, and content platforms. Most traditional recommendation systems such as collaborative filtering and content-based filtering cannot scale massively to large datasets or cannot give real-time recommendations. Quantum Machine Learning is a disruptive transformation that will offer faster, more accurate, and scalable recommendation systems(Blomster & Koivumäki, 2022; Ramkumar et al., 2022).

Quantum enhanced algorithms help QML-based recommendation systems analyze enormous datasets for unparalleled velocities of correlations between customers and products. The quantum model, in high-dimensional data about customer behavior, preference, and purchase history, offers a much more highly personalized recommendation. For example, movie/serie suggestion on Netflix, Spotify, will be benefited by QML to come up with better recommendation of a personal selection of movies/show or listening history based on similarity comparison analysis from other similar users where those patterns may have skipped the traditional methods of assessment therefore making it as near and close to what a user feels towards the recommended media material as possible.

QML may further optimize product recommendations in e-commerce in real time, enhancing opportunities for cross-selling and upselling. For example, a customer browsing a smartphone will be recommended compatible accessories like headphones or screen protectors. Quantum-enhanced systems will analyze purchase patterns to know what combinations of products are likely to attract individual customers. Another advantage of QML in recommendation systems is its ability to adapt to changing customer behavior. Traditional methods rely on static data, but QML-powered models can include real-time inputs, such as clicks, purchases, or session duration, to refine recommendations instantaneously. For instance, if a customer is shopping for a product, QML can dynamically adjust suggestions by the products a customer has interacted with, providing an easy and personalized experience.

In the travel and hospitality industry, QML can power recommendation systems, suggesting personalized vacation packages, stays in hotels, or activities as a function of users' browsing history, budgets, and past trips. This amount of personalization leads to deeper customer connections, increasing the chances of conversion.

Online marketing has, with Quantum Machine Learning applications such as real-time customer segmentation, predictive analytics in targeted advertising, and quantum-enhanced recommendation systems, transformed the way a business communicates with its customers, bringing growth. It powers marketers to create a customized data-driven strategy in its effort to process massive data and reveal unseen complex patterns at breakneck speeds. With further development of QML technologies, early adopters will gain a competitive advantage, as their solutions will deliver very relevant experiences to meet evolving customer expectations. Integrating QML into the marketing process will allow organizations to be more efficient, more engaging, and more profitable in the digital age.

BENEFITS OF QML IN BUSINESS STRATEGIES

Quantum Machine Learning is emerging as a game-changing tool for businesses that seek to enhance operational efficiency, make data-driven decisions faster, and gain a competitive edge. QML overcomes the limitations of traditional methods in handling large, complex datasets by integrating quantum computing with machine learning algorithms. This transformative capability empowers businesses to optimize performance, reduce costs, and maximize their return on investment (ROI). This section examines three major reasons why QML can increase the effectiveness of business tactics: greater efficiency and economies of scale, accelerated data-driven decisions, and ROI maximization for sustained competitive advantage(Blomster & Koivumäki, 2022; Chintala, 2021; De la Hoz Domínguez et al., 2020).

Increased Efficiency and Reduced Costs

One of the major advantages of using QML in business plans is that it improves the efficiency and reduces costs throughout the functions, such as marketing, operations, and logistics. The traditional approach to machine learning is always time-consuming and computationally heavy to process large amounts of data, which results in resources being wasted. QML, on the other hand, uses the principles of superposition and parallelism in quantum computing to process high-dimensional data faster and more efficiently. For instance, in supply chain management, companies can apply QML-based optimization algorithms to optimize the following: route planning, inventory management, and resource allocation. Quantum algorithms can rapidly analyze complex variables of supply chains, such as transportation costs, fluctuations in demand, and delivery timelines, and provide the most cost-effective solutions in real time. This leads to faster deliveries, lower operational costs, and better resource utilization.

In marketing, QML boosts efficiency by automating processes like customer segmentation, sentiment analysis, and ad optimization. Rather than manually processing the data of customers, QML algorithms identify actionable patterns immediately, saving time and reducing labor costs. For example, e-commerce companies can use QML to optimize product recommendations so that the customers see relevant offerings without increasing computational overhead.

Further, QML enables predictive maintenance for manufacturing and energy industries. With real-time analysis of sensor data and machine performance, QML algorithms predict equipment failure before it happens, thereby reducing downtime and maintenance costs. Businesses will thus be able to utilize their resources better and realize long-term cost savings. Therefore, QML's superior computing power allows organizations to perform their activities with more efficiency and fewer expenses, thereby providing an upper hand in competitive markets.

Accelerating Data-Driven Decision-Making

Speed is the essence of competitiveness in today's fast-paced business environment. As this data volume grows exponentially by the day, traditional approaches to analytics are often unable to process information in real time to inform timely decisions, and QML accelerates decision-making by rapidly analyzing large datasets, uncovering insights, and delivering sharp predictions with greater accuracy. This enables businesses to forecast trends and identify potential opportunities or areas of risk, faster than anything. For example, in retail, a QML would analyze all kinds of factors and show real-time adjustment of selling price and stocking of a particular product as and when those factors go into effect such as seasons and seasonality. Those recommendations are likely to result in better profits and improved customer satisfaction from that decision-maker's standpoint.

In finance, QML accelerates risk analysis and fraud detection. Quantum-enhanced algorithms can process transactional data and detect subtle anomalies that indicate potential fraud. Financial institutions can respond proactively, minimize financial losses, and strengthen their decision-making frameworks. QML is very crucial in real-time market analysis. For instance, companies in the consumer goods industry can utilize QML to track the pricing of their competitors, consumer sentiments, and social media trends. This allows the companies to respond in real-time to the dynamics of the market either by rolling out targeted campaigns or by adjusting their pricing strategy.

In addition, QML can enable businesses to analyze enormous customer data sets coming from different sources such as websites, mobile applications, and social media. By integrating quantum clustering and classification methods, businesses might gain actionable insights into what customers do and prefer and thus speed up decisions to be made on product development, marketing, and customer experience initiatives. QML enables organizations to capitalize on opportunities, minimize risks, and stay ahead of competitors in rapidly evolving markets by enabling faster, data-driven decisions.

ROI Optimization and Competitive Advantage

Return on Investment, ROI, is one of the metrics used to measure the success of a business and QML offers capabilities in ROI optimization by maximizing the strategies and resource allocation. Through analyzing large datasets, finding complex patterns, and giving real-time insights, QML enables businesses to spend their budget, human resources, and technology investments effectively.

In marketing, QML will improve ROI by targeting the campaign better and by optimizing ad spend. Traditional marketing models have often had to rely on trial-and-error approaches in order to identify successful campaigns. With QML algorithms, large amounts of customer data can be analyzed in order to predict which strategies will offer the highest returns. As an example, QML can identify high-value customer segments, forecast purchasing behaviors for them, and recommend tailor-made campaigns that drive conversion and revenue. In dynamic pricing, QML algorithms optimize strategies of pricing so that profitability may be maximized. A business can figure out, based on time, its best price for its products or services by knowing the various factors such as competitor's price, the elasticity of demand, and purchasing behavior. This enables businesses to maximize revenue with a competitive advantage.

QML increases the ROI of industries relying on recommendation systems, like e-commerce and entertainment. This is because QML enhances the accuracy of the suggestions provided to customers. By increasing customer engagement, cross-selling, and upselling opportunities, QML helps businesses achieve higher revenues while reducing acquisition costs. For instance, a streaming platform can use QML to increase user satisfaction through the delivery of highly relevant content, thereby increasing subscription renewals and long-term customer value. In addition, QML gives businesses the edge over the competition by solving complex problems faster than their competitors. For example, finance, logistics, and retail sectors use QML to track trends in the market, predict disruptions, and change course accordingly. Businesses that embrace QML early in the game enjoy a technological advantage and position themselves as leaders in innovation and operational excellence. QML enables businesses to outperform their competitors, sustain growth, and deliver superior value to stakeholders by optimizing ROI through efficient resource allocation, accurate predictions, and targeted strategies.

Such change is brought about in a business strategy by QML, offering organizations the roadmap to higher efficiency, better decision-making speed, and ROI optimization. The sophisticated computational power of QML helps businesses cut costs while generating actionable insights, driving data-driven decisions in the actual time needed. It serves two purposes: it increases operation's overall performance and provides a competitive edge in today's fast-moving and changing business environment. As QML technologies continue to evolve, businesses embracing these tools will be well-positioned for growth, innovation, and long-term success.

CHALLENGES AND LIMITATIONS OF QML ADOPTION

While QML promises to revolutionize business and marketing strategy, the adoption of QML comes with challenges and limitations. Businesses trying to use QML must confront key obstacles: technological barriers, integration with existing tools, and the skills and resources required. The challenges are a reflection of the evolving nature of quantum technology and the complexities involved in its implementation(Akman et al., 2023; Modak et al., 2024; Van Chau & He, 2024). The adoption of Quantum Machine Learning presents both challenges and limitations, as illustrated in Figure 4.

Figure 4. Challenges and limitations associated with Quantum Machine Learning adoption

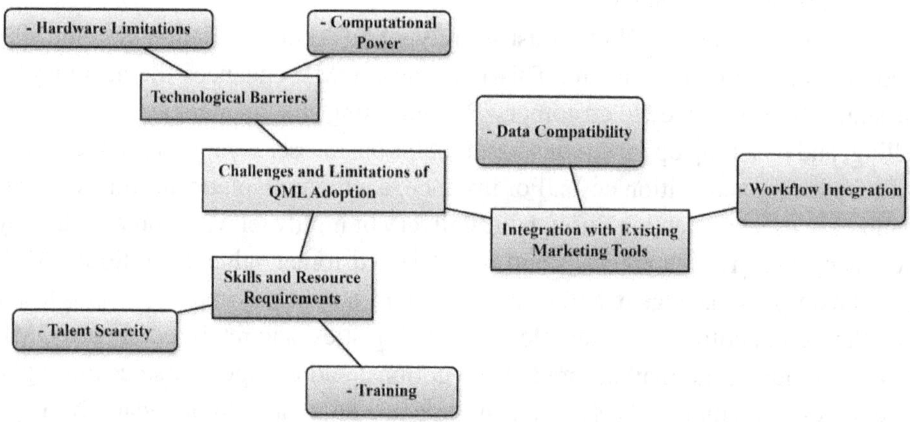

Technological Obstacles

The most challenging obstacle to QML implementation is the current state of the art in quantum computing technology. Although significant progress has been made, quantum hardware is still in its infant stages, with low processing capabilities, instability, and inability to scale. Unlike traditional computing systems, quantum computers must be maintained in highly controlled environments, such as ultra-low temperatures and specialized infrastructure that maintains quantum coherence.

In addition, quantum decoherence, which is the loss of quantum states due to environmental interactions, is still a significant challenge. Quantum computers are prone to errors due to noise and instability, which can lead to inaccurate results in QML models. Error correction algorithms and hardware improvements are needed to address these issues, but these solutions are still under development and require significant investments. The second limitation of quantum technology is restricted access to the hardware of quantum computing. Only a few organizations like IBM, Google, and D-Wave currently offer access to the quantum processor through cloud-based platforms. The cost is too high for these systems, and their capability is still very limited for businesses needing large-scale computation.

Hence, the technological bottlenecks to the diffusion of QML include immature quantum hardware, computations prone to errors, and accessibility to few reliable quantum systems. In the near future, general diffusion of QML is expected to occur only in research and specialty industries, until the foregoing challenges are overcome.

Intermediation with Existing Marketing Instruments

Another significant challenge for businesses in integrating QML solutions with existing marketing tools and infrastructure is the challenge of integration. Traditional marketing platforms, such as Customer Relationship Management (CRM), analytics tools, and recommendation engines, are designed to operate within classical computing frameworks. Therefore, bringing QML into these systems requires a great deal of reconfiguration and compatibility testing.

The main difficulty for businesses remains in aligning quantum algorithms to the format and workflows current data would follow. Indeed, QML algorithms often are designed to require special input and preprocessing for handling high-dimensional data; the existing tools would probably not possess the capability of filling the gap between classical data processing and quantum-based computations. Because of this, businesses need hybrid frameworks that ensure quantum-classical interoperability-a task highly demanding technically and in investment. Another challenge is the limited availability of commercial QML software solutions. Most QML applications are still in the research phase, and few tools are ready for mainstream business use. This limits the ability of marketing teams to seamlessly adopt and integrate QML into their existing operations.

In order to overcome these limitations, businesses must invest in scalable solutions that allow for the gradual adoption of QML without disrupting current workflows. Hybrid approaches, where classical machine learning handles routine tasks while QML addresses complex computations, can facilitate smoother integration.

Skills and Resource Requirement

QML adoption requires a significantly skilled workforce, with expertise spanning both quantum computing and machine learning—two domains that remain relatively niche and specialized. There is still a significant talent gap in the quantum field since very few people have the skills to build, deploy, and maintain solutions based on QML. Businesses trying to adopt QML face challenges in talent acquisition, developing existing teams, and providing the necessary knowledge base.

Developing QML solutions also calls for significant investments in research and development because, at the moment, off-the-shelf solutions are scarce. Businesses have to invest in training their teams in quantum programming languages such as Qiskit, Cirq, or TensorFlow Quantum and collaborate with academic institutions or quantum technology providers. In addition to that, businesses require access to specialized infrastructures, such as quantum simulators, quantum hardware, or cloud-based quantum platforms-which require significant financial investments to obtain. SMEs mostly find it difficult to appropriate resources for QML adoption due to severe budget constraints.

To overcome these challenges, businesses need to take a step-by-step approach. This can be initiated with pilot projects and collaborative efforts with quantum technology companies. Upskilling existing teams, fostering partnerships, and participating in QML research initiatives can help bridge the skills gap and make the transition more manageable.

Despite its revolutionary potential, QML's adoption in business and marketing strategies is hindered by technological barriers, integration challenges, and resource limitations. Quantum hardware is still evolving, and businesses have to face issues related to stability, accessibility, and error correction. Hybrid solutions and technical expertise are required to integrate QML with existing tools, while the shortage of skilled professionals poses an additional hurdle. To overcome these challenges, businesses must adopt a long-term strategy that prioritizes research, collaboration, and incremental implementation. By addressing these limitations, organizations can position themselves to harness the power of QML and achieve a competitive edge in the future of business and marketing.

FUTURE TRENDS IN QML FOR ONLINE MARKETING

Quantum Machine Learning is well-positioned to redefine online marketing as quantum technologies grow and become more accessible. The technology will enable QML to process unprecedented levels of data at tremendous velocities, thereby offering unparalleled capabilities in personalized customer experience, predictive analytics, and hyper-efficient marketing strategies. The present section explores the emerging trends and the adoption roadmap for business along with the evolving role of QML in a data-centric economy(Akman et al., 2023; Modak et al., 2024; Sahebi et al., 2022a). The figure 5 depicts the upcoming trends in QML for online marketing.

Figure 5. Future trends in qml for online marketing

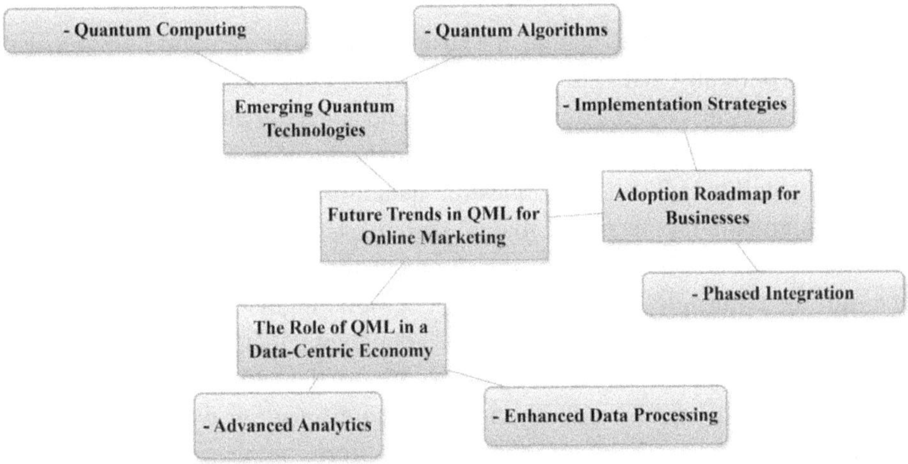

Quantum Emergent Technologies

The future of QML in online marketing is directly tied to the advancement of quantum computing technologies. Quantum processors are still in their infancy, but they are growing rapidly and provide increased computational power with decreased error rates. Recent advancements in quantum hardware include trapped ions, superconducting qubits, and topological qubits, all of which are being used to develop more stable and scalable quantum computing systems. All of these developments will enhance the QML significantly to process large complex data, and businesses can thus perform it more efficiently.

One of the most promising areas relates to quantum-enhanced optimization, which will revolutionize business operations in marketing. Campaign targeting can be optimized and budget allocation dynamically done, hence higher accuracy in resource allocations, while the advancement in quantum machine learning will empower businesses to develop models predicting customer behavior in real-time to provide more tailored marketing experiences.

Hybrid solutions, which will be driven by the integration of quantum technologies with classical machine learning, will leverage the strengths of both computing paradigms. Quantum computing will deal with complex, non-linear data, while classical systems will continue to manage structured data. This hybrid approach will enhance real-time decision-making and personalization efforts for online marketing.

Adoption Roadmap for Businesses

As quantum technologies mature, the business must have a phased adoption roadmap for incorporating QML into its marketing strategy appropriately. The first phase consists of assessing organizational readiness and understanding the capabilities of quantum. Then pilot projects have to be set up in the organizations. Small controlled experiments will help businesses in testing quantum-powered solutions related to customer segmentation, recommendation systems, and behavioral predictions.

As the prices of the hardware and development of accessible quantum computing come up, the companies will move further towards high-scale implementations. Moreover, in terms of achieving widespread deployment, cloud quantum services of IBM, Microsoft, Google, and even others are crucial. By using those services, many businesses would be able to engage in experimenting with QML through minimal dependence on quantum infrastructure. Moreover, teams in quantum programming and quantum algorithm development should be trained and upskilled for adoption. Businesses would require data scientists, quantum specialists, and machine learning experts to design, deploy, and optimize QML solutions. The collaboration with the academic institutions and quantum research labs would further accelerate the process and would help promote innovation and push practical applications of QML in marketing.

Simultaneously, regulatory frameworks and ethical issues of data security, privacy, and fairness must be looked into in ensuring the right use of quantum technologies by marketers. Companies should demonstrate trust with customers through a transparent approach of showing customers how their data is being utilized and what safety measures are applied.

The Role of QML in a Data-Centric Economy

In a data-centric economy where businesses increasingly rely on massive datasets for decision-making, QML will play a vital role in transforming how companies approach marketing strategies. With its unmatched ability to analyze and interpret large, diverse datasets, QML will enable organizations to identify hidden patterns, predict future outcomes, and optimize resources in real-time.

For online marketing, QML will energize hyper-personalization to enable the fineness of content, product recommendation, and advertisements toward the customers. Quantum-powered recommendation systems give more than simple algorithms; instead, sophisticated insights into customer desire and behavior are provided, which businesses may employ to foster deeper and meaningful relationships with customers. In addition, QML is going to scale marketing strategy performance. Since data grows exponentially, traditional machine learning methods cannot make actionable insights. Quantum technologies handle massive data volumes efficiently with its ability to process data in one go, and this shall enable marketers to scale operations without compromising performance.

In the future, the integration of QML into predictive analytics will redefine targeted ads. Quantum algorithms have the ability to analyze voluminous networks of interactions related to customer journeys, social media activity, and search data so one can provide real-time insight as businesses tailor campaigns with surgical precision-a surefire step that drives higher engagement rates and conversion rates and customer lifetime values. In summary, prospects in online marketing are exciting. They might accelerate decision-making processes, increase resource management, and enable new, more innovative data-driven marketing strategies. In so doing, businesses that begin to use QML enjoy a much greater competitive advantage in navigating their increasingly data-intensive marketplace.

CASE STUDIES OF QML IN BUSINESS

Quantum Machine Learning is the next step in how to change the face of a lot of industries, including e-commerce and personalized customer experience. The power of quantum algorithms empowers businesses to enhance data processing, improve decision-making, and offer more tailored solutions to meet the needs of customers. Below, we dive into two key case studies illustrating the impact of QML on e-commerce and personalized marketing strategies(Blomster & Koivumäki, 2022; Xiujuan et al., 2021).

QML Applications in E-Commerce

Quantum Machine Learning is being applied to increase personalization and optimize operation in the rapidly changing e-commerce environment where millions of customer data are produced every day. Among other applications, one notable is product recommendation and inventory management.

Company XYZ is an established e-commerce firm that used QML algorithms to enhance its recommendation engine. Traditional recommendation systems depend highly on linear models and historical data, which makes it difficult to capture complex user preferences. By introducing QML, Company XYZ enhanced its ability to identify non-linear relationships between customer behaviors and product features. Quantum algorithms were used to process large datasets more efficiently, and the system was able to provide highly personalized recommendations in real-time. This translated into a 35% rise in conversions, a 25% increase in customer retention, and a decrease in the bounce rate by 20%.

QML also assisted the company in optimizing its inventory management, especially for dynamic and seasonal products. Using conventional forecasting techniques, companies failed to adjust to variations in demand, resulting in either stockouts or excess inventory. Applying quantum-enhanced clustering techniques, Company XYZ segmented its customer base based on purchasing behavior and demand patterns, which reduced storage costs and minimized stockouts. QML was able to analyze interactions across a variety of touchpoints-from product pages to social media engagement-that provided more in-depth knowledge of customer journeys. It allowed Company XYZ to put together targeted marketing campaigns with better precision, thus enhancing customer satisfaction and ultimately increasing profitability.

The integration of Quantum Machine Learning in personalized customer experiences has dramatically changed the way businesses communicate with their clients. An excellent example is in the financial services industry, where a banking institution used QML to provide hyper-personalized financial advisory services. Bank ABC was unable to provide customized investment portfolios for its clients. Such was the size and diversity of the customer base that a traditional approach to machine learning wasn't capable of predicting even individual preferences and risk profiles across thousands of accounts. Quantum Machine Learning helped in processing vast amounts of historical transactions, market trends, and real-time financial data more effectively. Quantum algorithms found complex correlations and patterns that classical models could not, thus improving the accuracy of risk assessment and portfolio management.

The bank also applied QML in its chatbot services to provide instant, tailored financial advice. Quantum-powered natural language processing enabled the chatbot to understand nuanced customer inquiries and generate personalized responses in seconds, which significantly improved user experience and reduced wait times. Integration was done with QML alongside personalized financial services to develop loyalty programs. From their analysis of customer transactions carried through a number of algorithms in quantum, Bank ABC could offer rewards and promote better at the individual levels thus raising customer engagement to the level of 40%, while cross-selling product picked by 15% percent more than before. The case study of Bank ABC indicates that QML can be implemented across industries to tailor the customer interaction process with genuinely individualized experiences instead of generic segmentation approaches(Boopathi & Kanike, 2023; Ingle et al., 2023; Ramudu et al., 2023).

This transformation in business applies Quantum Machine Learning particularly in commerce and highly individualized consumer experiences. In this aspect, advanced QML processes data at complex levels and delivers deep insights for such operations. Optimization of performance and tailoring highly individualized solutions become key results derived from this practice. These include perfect product recommendations to e-commerce firms and financial services companies through hyper-personalization, thereby engaging their customers on a highly responsive and loyable basis to grow and sustain a business.

CONCLUSION AND RECOMMENDATIONS

Quantum Machine Learning represents a revolutionary breakthrough in the business strategy world, especially in e-commerce and personal customer experience areas. By processing and analyzing massive amounts of complex data at speeds that are not matched anywhere else, QML enables businesses to go further into deeper insights, make better decisions, and provide hyper-personalized solutions. The case studies in this chapter depict the significant impacts that QML has had on the optimization of operations, driving innovation, and creating more satisfied customers.

Be it the enhancement of product suggestions through electronic commerce or the provision of individualized financial services for banks, QML will be the transformative force on the path to achieving an increase in efficiency, saving costs, and gaining the competitive advantage in a future data-driven economy. All that stands between businesses and taking full advantage of these is the challenge of technological, as well as skill requirements in integration, and the possibility of integrating quantum algorithms into legacy systems.

As quantum technologies advance, QML will be increasingly adopted, empowering organizations to use the strength of quantum computing to lead market demands. By embracing this innovative approach, businesses can unlock new opportunities for growth and create unparalleled customer experiences that drive long-term success.

REFERENCES

Adikari, A., Burnett, D., Sedera, D., De Silva, D., & Alahakoon, D. (2021). Value co-creation for open innovation: An evidence-based study of the data driven paradigm of social media using machine learning. *International Journal of Information Management Data Insights*, 1(2), 100022. DOI: 10.1016/j.jjimei.2021.100022

Akman, G., Yorur, B., Boyaci, A. I., & Chiu, M.-C. (2023). Assessing innovation capabilities of manufacturing companies by combination of unsupervised and supervised machine learning approaches. *Applied Soft Computing*, 147, 110735. DOI: 10.1016/j.asoc.2023.110735

Bhatt, V. K. (2021). Assessing the significance and impact of artificial intelligence and machine learning in placement of advertisements. *2021 IEEE International Conference on Technology Management, Operations and Decisions (ICTMOD)*, 1–6. DOI: 10.1109/ICTMOD52902.2021.9739228

Blomster, M., & Koivumäki, T. (2022). Exploring the resources, competencies, and capabilities needed for successful machine learning projects in digital marketing. *Information Systems and e-Business Management*, 20(1), 123–169. DOI: 10.1007/s10257-021-00547-y

Boopathi, S. (2024). Digital HR Implementation for Business Growth in Industrial 5.0. In *Convergence of Human Resources Technologies and Industry 5.0* (pp. 1–22). IGI Global. DOI: 10.4018/979-8-3693-1343-5.ch001

Boopathi, S., & Kanike, U. K. (2023). Applications of Artificial Intelligent and Machine Learning Techniques in Image Processing. In *Handbook of Research on Thrust Technologies' Effect on Image Processing* (pp. 151–173). IGI Global. DOI: 10.4018/978-1-6684-8618-4.ch010

Chintala, S. (2021). Explore the impact of emerging technologies such as AI, machine learning, and blockchain on transforming retail marketing strategies. *Webology (ISSN: 1735-188X), 18*(1).

De la Hoz Domínguez, E. J., Herrera, T. J. F., & Mendoza, A. A. M. (2020). Machine Learning and SMEs: Opportunities for an improved deci-sion-making process. *Investigación e Innovación En Ingenierías*, 8(1), 21–36.

Fredström, A., Parida, V., Wincent, J., Sjödin, D., & Oghazi, P. (2022). What is the market value of artificial intelligence and machine learning? The role of innovativeness and collaboration for performance. *Technological Forecasting and Social Change*, 180, 121716. DOI: 10.1016/j.techfore.2022.121716

Gutnik, S. (2021). Application of data mining and machine learning methods to enhance the effectiveness of digital marketing strategies. *Digital Strategies in a Global Market: Navigating the Fourth Industrial Revolution*, 131–144.

Ingle, R. B., Swathi, S., Mahendran, G., Senthil, T., Muralidharan, N., & Boopathi, S. (2023). Sustainability and Optimization of Green and Lean Manufacturing Processes Using Machine Learning Techniques. In *Circular Economy Implementation for Sustainability in the Built Environment* (pp. 261–285). IGI Global. DOI: 10.4018/978-1-6684-8238-4.ch012

Modak, C., Ghosh, S. K., Sarkar, M. A. I., Sharif, M. K., Arif, M., Bhuiyan, M., Ahmed, M. P., Pabel, M. A. H., & Devi, S. (2024). Machine Learning Model in Digital Marketing Strategies for Customer Behavior: Harnessing CNNs for Enhanced Customer Satisfaction and Strategic Decision-Making. *Journal of Economics. Finance and Accounting Studies*, 6(3), 178–186.

Ramkumar, G., Othman, B., Malviya, B., Mohamma, A. J., Narayana, M. S., & Verma, D. (2022). A conceptual analysis on the impact of machine learning towards on digital marketing transformation. *2022 2nd International Conference on Advance Computing and Innovative Technologies in Engineering (ICACITE)*, 2274–2278.

Ramudu, K., Mohan, V. M., Jyothirmai, D., Prasad, D., Agrawal, R., & Boopathi, S. (2023). Machine Learning and Artificial Intelligence in Disease Prediction: Applications, Challenges, Limitations, Case Studies, and Future Directions. In *Contemporary Applications of Data Fusion for Advanced Healthcare Informatics* (pp. 297–318). IGI Global.

Ravisankar, A., Shanthi, A., Lavanya, S., Ramaratnam, M., Krishnamoorthy, V., & Boopathi, S. (2024). Harnessing 6G for Consumer-Centric Business Strategies Across Electronic Industries. In *AI Impacts in Digital Consumer Behavior* (pp. 241–270). IGI Global.

Sahebi, A. G., Kordheydari, R., & Aghaei, M. (2022a). A new approach in marketing research: Identifying the customer expected value through machine learning and big data analysis in the tourism industry. [AMT]. *Advancement in Management and Technology*, 2(3), 26–42.

Sahebi, A. G., Kordheydari, R., & Aghaei, M. (2022b). A new approach in marketing research: Identifying the customer expected value through machine learning and big data analysis in the tourism industry. [AMT]. *Advancement in Management and Technology*, 2(3), 26–42.

Somasundaram, R., Varalakshmi, S., Sanadi, H., Saini, R., Chinnusamy, S., & Boopaathi. (2024). Entrepreneurship in emerging markets and intrapreneurship within organizations. In *Advances in Business Strategy and Competitive Advantage* (pp. 291–322). IGI Global.

Van Chau, D., & He, J. (2024). Machine Learning Innovations for Proactive Customer Behavior Prediction: A Strategic Tool for Dynamic Market Adaptation. *Sage Science Review of Applied Machine Learning*, 7(1), 22–29.

Vennila, T., Karuna, M., Srivastava, B. K., Venugopal, J., Surakasi, R., & Sampath, B. (2022). New Strategies in Treatment and Enzymatic Processes: Ethanol Production From Sugarcane Bagasse. In *Human Agro-Energy Optimization for Business and Industry* (pp. 219–240). IGI Global.

Xiujuan, L., Kagita, M. K., & others. (2021). Machine Learning Techniques for Multi-media Communications in Business Marketing. *Journal of Multiple-Valued Logic & Soft Computing, 36.*

Yankovets, T., & Vyshnevska, M. (2019). Innovations and digital marketing: Current trends of development. *Evropský Časopis Ekonomiky a Managementu.*

Chapter 10
Role of Infinity in Shaping Financial Reality From a Quantum Finance Perspective:
A Bibliometric Analysis on Scopus

Miriam Toney
Christ University, India

V. V. Nandhita
Christ University, India

Ishaun Jason Crasta
Christ University, India

Gowtham Ramkumar
https://orcid.org/0000-0001-7885-9171
Christ University, India

ABSTRACT

In this literature survey, we seek after the manner in which the idea of boundlessness adjusts the universe of money. Utilizing bibliometric information of around 37 examination articles from the Scopus data set alongside different books on Quantum finance and the development of money, this survey reveals insight into the main writers, nations, organizations, outlets, articles, and subjects of different logical ways to deal with get into the quantum domain of money involving Vastness as the center base that gives us numerous ways of characterizing our ongoing economy and how it can change and adjust to the ongoing situation and how we can manage

DOI: 10.4018/979-8-3693-6225-9.ch010

future possibilities of reforming Money in general. Discoveries of this audit recommend that there is a roundabout connection among money and boundlessness. Future exploration headings for The Job of Endlessness in Molding Monetary Reality finish up this survey.

1.INTRODUCTION

"At any point can't help thinking about how things are esteemed and the way that they are valued, remembering the expected overflow?"

Monetary specialists concoct ideas in view of the ongoing business sector and there are endless choices to hop on. These choices are made up on an irregular premise and the best arbitrary will win and is additionally carried out given the ongoing situation and the unique climate. How our brain functions and how much it streams to find the ideal worth is the one of a kind methodology our psyche goes to accomplish a definitive objective.

This approach is an entirely different excursion and understanding this with the given information and conditions is what we might want to determine under the heading, to demonstrate this we might want to apply the idea of boundlessness which incorporates The CHAOS THEORY and FRACTAL GEOMETRY which are utilized to consolidate the idea of Infinity and Finance which will assist us with understanding the market better. Articles like ***Chaos and Nonlinear Forecastability in Economics and Finance*** How they are evaluated requires the extension of potential outcomes utilizing the creative mind of the modest number of individuals who get this particular information. The creative mind here being boundless, is the endless way to deal with one's creative mind. The idea of "infinity" and the universe of money are intrinsically inconsistent. " Infinity " suggests something unlimited, while finance works inside characterized frameworks and limited assets.

The impression of vastness isn't projected in stone, however, etched by social subtleties and authentic encounters. Inspecting how various social orders conceptualize "infinity" and how these viewpoints impact monetary ways of behaving can open sagacious roads.

Infinity, by its actual nature, challenges substantial estimation. Existing examination frequently moves inside the domain of hypothesis and story, attempting to make an interpretation of its ethereal impact into unmistakable numbers. Empirical research attempts to capture the elusive influence of infinity on market dynamics and human behavior, yielding only hints rather than conclusive evidence. The monetary scene is painted in shades of limited numbers, a sharp differentiation to the endless material of vastness. This jumble powers scientists to utilize intermediaries and roundabout measures, similar to shadows rather than the actual source. While these intermediaries offer significant bits of knowledge, the gamble of inclination and error hides like a concealed hunter, requesting wary understanding.

Figure 1. Evolution

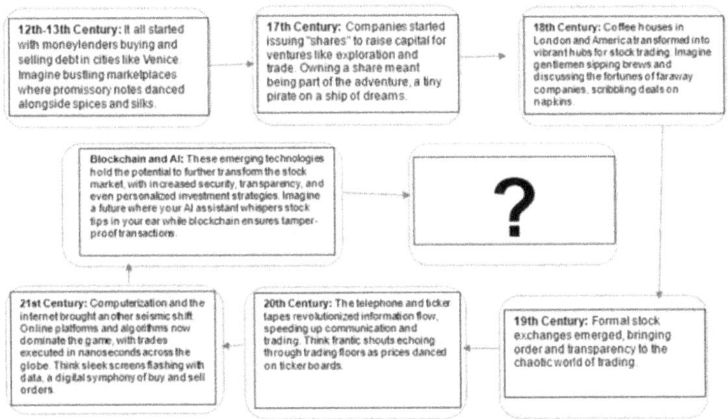

First of all, it has an origin and the way it evolves is because of various factors as mentioned in the above flowchart, Figure 1. These factors are interconnected and can interact in complex ways. Analyzing individual stocks necessitates considering all these influences and staying informed about the ever-evolving economic, political, and The journey to comprehend the infinite effect on finance is a continuous odyssey, full of difficulties however overflowing with potential. By recognizing the intricacies, embracing interdisciplinary joint effort, and focusing on moral contemplations, we can reveal insight into this enthralling problem and make ready for a more educated way to deal with exploring the immense, modifying monetary scene. Through this paper what we are trying to achieve is how we explore the infinite world of finance by merely focusing on key factors and the factors affecting it.

technological factors. While predicting the future is always challenging, understanding the driving forces behind stock evolution can equip you with valuable insights for making informed investment decisions. The above flowchart starts with the 12th century but does it end?

We could put an ending to it with the current data but we also know that it won't stop because it just won't. There are always going to be constant changes, that is just how the world works, and this is where evolution comes into play. The question mark indicates the next step that is unknown and when that next step is figured another will arise as well. Small differences in initial conditions can lead to drastically different outcomes in chaotic systems. This translates to the financial world, where seemingly identical investment scenarios can yield vastly different results depending on factors like entry timing, news triggers, and individual behavior.

2. LITERATURE REVIEW

To conduct this research, our idea mainly came from brainstorming into the alternate realm of finance where we see how infinity can influence our financial decisions.

Various studies are done to explore the application of chaos theory and the complex models which leads to unpredictability of the market movements. In a study by Klioutchnikov, I., Sigova, M., & Beizerov, N. (2017b). 'Chaos theory in finance. Procedia Computer Science', the sensitivity of the financial markets reduces the ability to make predictions accurately but sets a benchmark for future comparison. But it is proven in a study by (Levy, 2007) that tactical application of chaos theory and the chaotic system of industries does not allow forecasting long-term but makes a view for short-term predictions. Chaotic dynamics have the ability to bring in large movements which may appear normal but leave greater impacts than linear models.

The implications of the findings of a study by Hsieh (1991) points out that, there will be nonlinear dependence if they try to fit conditional density functions on stock returns. Also, to model the nonlinearity in a stock return, one should direct focus on conditional heteroskedasticity rather than conditional mean changes and it can provide conditional volatility forecasts if the flexible conditional heteroskedasticity model holds up under future analysis. At the same time, some studies relating to economic chaos are still weak and need further study in the future,("Chaos and Nonlinear Forecastability in Economics and Finance on JSTOR," n.d.).

3.METHODOLOGY

As the topic is taken in an exploratory format, we have started off by referring to the already existing concepts of finance and infinity by conducting immense research on both the topics individually and then finding the connection between them by using research papers, articles and a lot of books that were looked into, to plot our topic.

Philosophical perspectives by exploring how thinkers across history have conceptualized infinity and its relationship to human behavior and economic systems, psychological theories by examining how the perception of infinity influences risk-taking, decision-making, and financial behavior and considering the cognitive biases like the illusion of control and the availability heuristic and economic models by analyzing how mainstream economic models implicitly or explicitly rely on the assumption of infinite growth.

Quantifying the influence of infinity requires grappling with its unbound limits, subjective interpretations, and potential confounding variables in financial data. To navigate this landscape, researchers will need to rely on ingenious proxy indicators, such as measuring trends in risk-taking behavior or analyzing the prevalence of 'infinite growth' language in financial discourse.

3.1 Objectives of the Study

The present study was carried out with the following objectives:

1) To find out the research publications' growth in the Finance and Infinity
2) To know about the journals that contributed with the most number of articles during this period.
3) To identify the most impactful journals with the highest citations for their articles in the selected field and timeframe.
4) To review the most dominant institutions, authors, and articles of the selected field of research
5) To study the research trends by analyzing keywords during different phases of time.

The purpose of the study is to navigate the concept of "infinity" and the world of finance are inherently incompatible. "Infinity" implies something boundless and limitless, while finance operates within defined systems and finite resources. Financial experts come up with concepts based on the current market and there are infinite options to jump on and these options are made up on random, given the current scenario and the dynamic environment, the best random won.

While modern technologies and tools like the internet, mobile phones, email, etc., touch every aspect of our daily lives and we cannot progress without them, the underlying science becomes formidable.

In theory, infinite knowledge would encompass all past, present, and future financial data, along with a perfect understanding of economic principles, human behavior, and market dynamics.

This ideal scenario would allow for flawless predictions and optimal financial decisions in any circumstance.

While "infinite knowledge" might be an elusive ideal, the application of finance in reality benefits from a vast and ever-growing knowledge base. This continuous pursuit of knowledge leads to new advancements, improved financial decision-making, and a more efficient and inclusive financial system. Even with immense knowledge, the element of uncertainty will always remain in finance. The key lies in using the available knowledge effectively, adapting to changing circumstances, and making informed decisions within the confines of the real world

3.2 Data Collection

The study conducted a bibliometric analysis focusing on 40 articles related to quantum finance and infinity and their relevance to stable financial decision-making. The data was collected from the Scopus database, a comprehensive repository of scholarly literature encompassing various disciplines.

3.3. Selection Criteria

Articles included in the analysis met the following criteria:

Relevance: Articles were required to be directly related to the intersection of quantum finance and infinity, specifically addressing their applicability in fostering stable financial decision-making.
Timeframe: The selection was confined to a specific timeframe, ensuring that articles analyzed were published within this defined period.
Source: Articles were sourced exclusively from the Scopus database to maintain consistency and reliability in data collection.

3.4 Bibliometric Analysis

The study utilized the Bibliometrix package, a specialized tool for bibliometric analysis in R, to conduct the quantitative examination of the selected articles(Aria & Cuccurullo, 2017). Bibliometric analysis encompasses various metrics and techniques to explore patterns, trends, and relationships within scholarly literature. The following aspects were considered in the bibliometric analysis:

Research Publications Growth: The growth of research publications over time was examined to assess the evolving interest and activity in the field of quantum finance and infinity. This involved analyzing the number of articles published annually or within specific time intervals.
Journals Contribution Analysis: The study identified journals that contributed the most articles within the specified timeframe. This analysis provided insights into the publication outlets favored by researchers in the field.

Impactful Journals Identification: To determine the most impactful journals, citation data was examined to identify those with the highest number of citations for their articles. This metric reflects the influence and recognition of journals within the scholarly community.

Dominant Institutions, Authors, and Articles Review: The study reviewed dominant institutions, authors, and articles in the field of quantum finance and infinity. This involved analyzing author affiliations to identify institutions with significant contributions, as well as identifying prolific authors and articles that garnered notable attention or citations.

Research Trends Analysis: Trends in research topics and themes were analyzed by examining keywords associated with the selected articles. Keyword analysis over different time phases provided insights into the evolving research landscape and emerging areas of interest within the field.

3.5. Limitations

It is important to acknowledge potential limitations inherent in bibliometric analysis, including the reliance on available data sources, the exclusion of non-indexed publications, and the potential for biases in citation practices. Additionally, the selection of articles within a specific timeframe may not capture the entirety of research activity in the field. These limitations were considered in the interpretation of the study findings.

4. RESULTS

4.1. Most Influential Journals

4.1.1 Bradford's Law (Table 1)

According to Bradford's law, there exists a core set of journals that publish a significant portion of the most pertinent articles within a specific field of study. According to the law, a bigger number of journals will publish only a small number of relevant articles, while a smaller number of journals will publish a medium amount of relevant articles. A quantitative relationship between journals and the papers they publish is described by Bradford's Law Scattering. The so-called Bradford's Law has two more commonly accepted formulations: the graphical formulation, which is an empirical expression derived from a graphical survey of a distribution of periodicals, and the verbal formulation, which is derived from the verbal statement of Bradford's Conclusion.

Table 1. Core Sources by Bradford's Law

Source	Rank	Freq	cumFreq	Zone
Chaos, Solitons and Fractals	1	2	2	Zone 1
Educational Studies in Mathematics	2	2	4	Zone 1
Partial Differential Equations in Applied Mathematics	3	2	6	Zone 1
Physica A: Statistical Mechanics and its Applications	4	2	8	Zone 1
Accounting, Organizations and Society	5	1	9	Zone 1
Array	6	1	10	Zone 1
Automatica	7	1	11	Zone 1
Cogent Business and Management	8	1	12	Zone 1
Explorations In Economic History	9	1	13	Zone 1
Financial Analysts Journal	10	1	14	Zone 2
Futures	11	1	15	Zone 2
Housing Policy Debate	12	1	16	Zone 2
International Journal of Innovation Studies	13	1	17	Zone 2
International Journal of Pure And Applied Mathematics	14	1	18	Zone 2
International Review of Economics Education	15	1	19	Zone 2
International Review of Financial Analysis	16	1	20	Zone 2
Journal of Behavioral and Experimental Finance	17	1	21	Zone 2
Journal of Complexity	18	1	22	Zone 2
Journal of Economic Behavior And Organization	19	1	23	Zone 2
Journal of Economic Perspectives	20	1	24	Zone 2
Journal of Economic Surveys	21	1	25	Zone 2
Journal of Financial Stability	22	1	26	Zone 3
Journal of Open Innovation: Technology, Market, And Complexity	23	1	27	Zone 3
Law and Contemporary Problems	24	1	28	Zone 3
Matec Web of Conferences	25	1	29	Zone 3
Procedia Computer Science	26	1	30	Zone 3
Renewable and Sustainable Energy Reviews	27	1	31	Zone 3
Research in International Business and Finance	28	1	32	Zone 3
Reviews in Physics	29	1	33	Zone 3
Stochastic Processes and Their Applications	30	1	34	Zone 3
Strategic Management Journal	31	1	35	Zone 3
The Journal of Finance	32	1	36	Zone 3
World Bank Economic Review	33	1	37	Zone 3

4.1.2 Sources Local Impact- (Figure 2)

Looking at the publication years (1979-2023), we can see the data covers a period of 45 years. However, the distribution of publications seems uneven, with potentially fewer publications in the early years (1979-1990s) compared to later years. It is likely that the x-axis represents years. It covers the years 1979 to 2024. The number of publications is displayed on the y-axis, but the scale is not specified. The most noteworthy worth is around 37. Possible repercussions: The information could address the yearly distribution result of a particular diary, gathering, or examination establishment. The rising pattern proposes the source is distributing all the more often over the long haul. This could be because of a number of things, like: expansion in the area of study. Expanded research subsidizing. More researchers who are connected to the source Changes in distribution rehearse (e.g., open access diaries).

Figure 2. Sources Local Impact

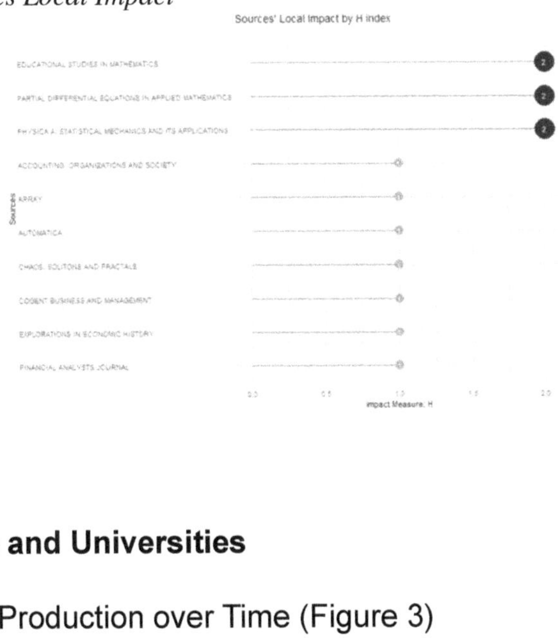

4.2. Authors and Universities

4.2.1 Author Production over Time (Figure 3)

The data in figure 3 provides us with top authors' production over time. It is to be noted that the bigger the circle is, the more articles have been published by the author in that year. The darker the circle is, the more citations have been received per year.

It can be inferred that Kachhia KB has the highest no. of articles produced from the year 1981 to 2001, and the dark blue dot denotes the highest number of citations as well with around numbers going up to 117 The next top two authors are Battison

S and Tirosh D also appears to have produced good no. of articles over time but the light blue color signifies low citations.

Writer: This probably alludes to the author(s) of an insightful distribution (article, gathering paper, and so forth.). Documents, or Articles, may indicate the number of articles to which each author has contributed. Articles Fractionalized (or Fragmentary Articles): This recommends a few reports might have various writers, and the worth here could demonstrate the writer's partial commitment (e.g., 1.0 for a sole writer, 0.5 for one of two co-writers). Creator's Watchwords (DE): These are logical catchphrases picked by the actual creators to portray their distributions. Catchphrases In addition to (ID): These may be watchwords relegated by the data set utilizing a controlled jargon or ordering framework. Investigation of Creator Commitments: Expecting "Articles" alludes to the complete number of articles each writer added to, then Kachchia KB has all the earmarks of being the most useful writer with 22 distributions. However, fractal articles suggest a contribution picture that is more nuanced. For example, Böttcher A with 10.125 in "Articles Fractionalized" may be a lead writer on less effective distributions.

Figure 3. Author's Production Over Time

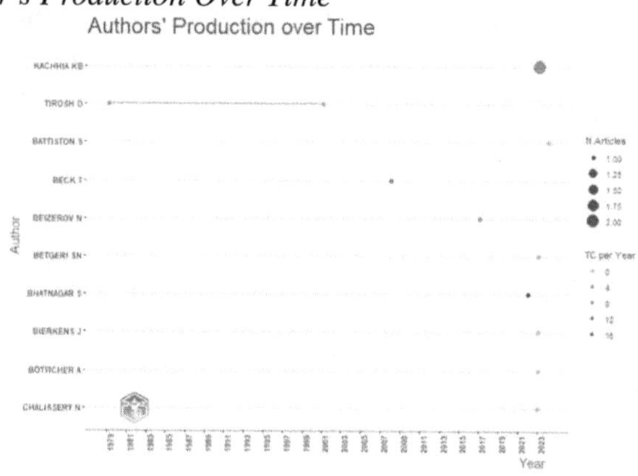

4.2.2 Most Relevant Affiliations and Affiliations over time - (Figure 4 and Figure 5)

Figure. 4 displays the top 10 relevant affiliations from which Journal of Documentation publications have been carried out. Germany was the dominant country in terms of a number of papersHunan University (4 publications): This university appears to be the most productive institution in this dataset, having contributed the most publications (4).

University of Toronto, University of Groningen, Tel Aviv University, and Charotar University of Science and Technology (CHARUSAT) (2 publications each): These four institutions seem to have a significant presence with two publications each. Affiliations with countless articles may be demonstrative of: Bigger exploration projects or divisions inside those foundations. a focus on those institutions' research. A productive gathering of specialists subsidiary with those establishments.

Figure 4. Most Relevant Affiliations

Figure 5. Affiliations' Production Over Time

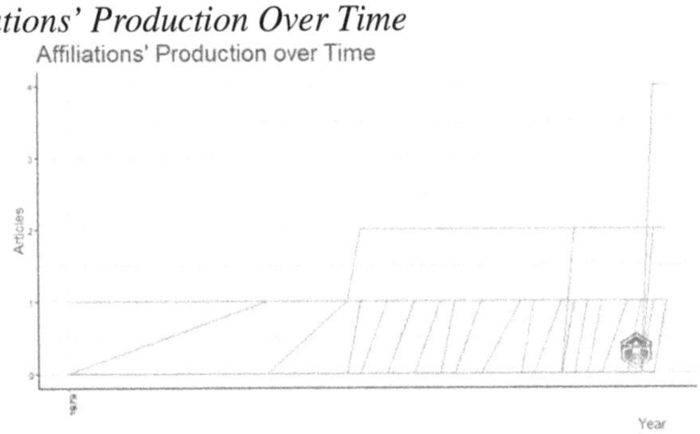

4.2.3 Lotka Law:

Lotka's Law is one of the most basic laws of bibliometrics, which deals with the frequency of publication of authors in a given field. The generalized form of Lotka's law can be expressed as Y = (C) Where Y is the number of authors with X articles, the exponent n and constant C are parameters to be estimated from a given set of author productivity data.

Figure 6 shows that around 85 authors have published exactly 1 article (with a frequency of 0.9770114943),2 have published exactly articles since the year 2019 and ranks second in highest no. of articles. Lotka's law is tested using Kolmogorov-Smirnov goodness-of-fit tests and Chi-square test. The present analysis reveals that Lotka's law is applicable to analyze this paper Both K-S and Chi-square have confirmed the applicability of Lotka's law and found that this law fits for a bibliometric analysis.

Figure 6. Lotka Law

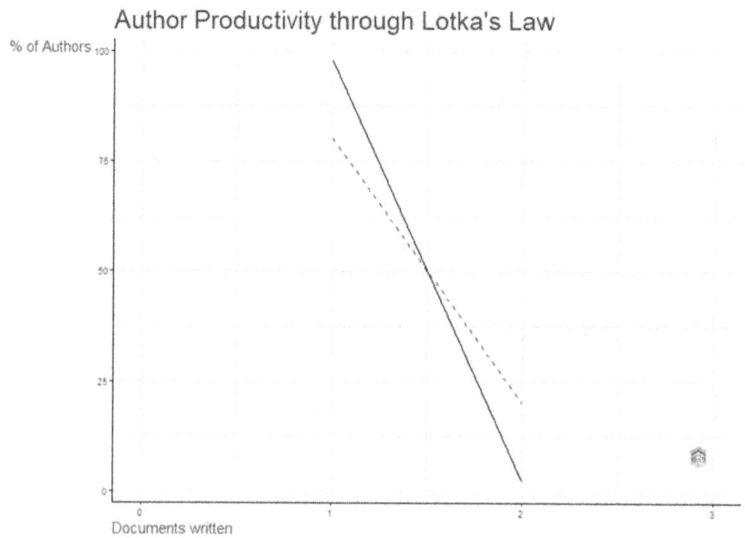

4.3 Network Analysis for Co-Authorship and Countries

4.3.1 Country Production over Time Figure

Figure 7 provides us with the country's production over time. It is to be noted that Germany has the highest production of all the countries along with being the country with steeper growth in production over the years. Following this, India is also seen to have a growing pace of production in articles since the year 2021 and ranks second in highest no. of articles. Netherlands ranks third after Germany and India and seems to have quite an impressive growth in the no. of articles produced over the years. USA is on the path of becoming better in production for the future years.

4.3.3 Most Cited Countries

Table 3 shows us the top 9 countries with the highest no. of citations in the articles. The country with the highest number of citations from all over the world is Germany. Germany leads the pack with an average of 105.7 citations per article, followed by USA (69.0), India (50.7), Spain (28.0), and the United Kingdom (23.8) with significantly lower citation averages.

Figure 7. Country Production over Time

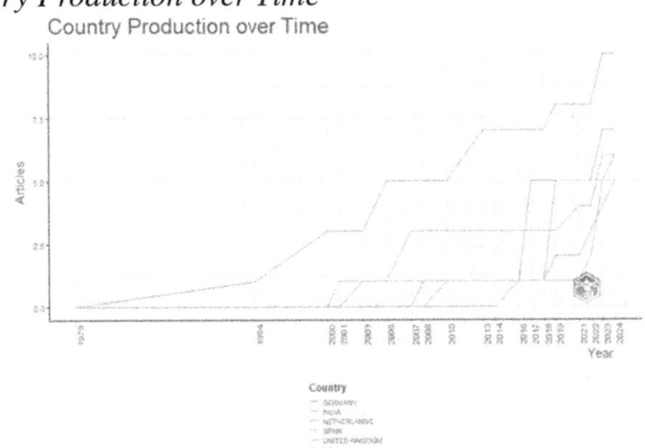

Table 2. Most Cited Countries

Country	TC	Average Article Citations
Germany	317	105.7
USA	152	50.7
India	95	23.8
Spain	69	69
United Kingdom	56	28
China	19	19
Israel	8	8
Austria	2	2
France	2	2
Japan	1	1
Canada	0	0
Finland	0	0
Netherlands	0	0

4.4. Analysis of Documents

4.4.1 Most Global Cited Documents (Figure 8)

Top Cited Documents:
1.HSIEH, DAVID A. (1991). Is the market for corporate control efficient? The Journal of Finance, 46(4), 1553-1573:640
2.LEVY, D. (1994). The paradox of quality management. Strategic Management Journal, 15(10), 633-643:330
3.ORÚS, R. (2019). Complexity and hidden symmetries in quantum many-body systems.Reviews of Physics, 1(2), 100028:235
Observations:

The most cited papers range from HSIEH's work on finance through LEVY's works on business management to ORÚS's exploration of physics. The documents written earlier—such as HSIEH's article published in1991 or LEVY'S paper released in 1994—have more citations than ORÚS'S publication dated at subsequent time i.e.,in 2019.

Apparently,the reason behind this is that previous articles have enjoyed more chances of being cited by others unlike newer ones which may not be equally exposed to the same. The most often quoted papers are published in a variety of fields, such as finance (HSIEH, 1991), business management (LEVY, 1994), and physics (ORÚS, 2019).

Compared to their later counterparts (2019), the former ones which were published between 1991 and 1994 have been cited higher by other researchers. This could be due to the fact that the earlier ones have had more time to become known.

4.4.2 Annual Citations per Year Figure

Figure 9 provides us with annual data of citations per year from 2017 to 2024. It can be noted that there is a significant increase in the mean total citations published between 2018 and 2020, followed by a decrease in 2021 and 2022. The average citations per year tend to fluctuate but generally increase over time, with 2020 showing the highest average (16.92). This suggests that the publications are gaining more traction over time.

Figure 8. Most Global Cited Documents

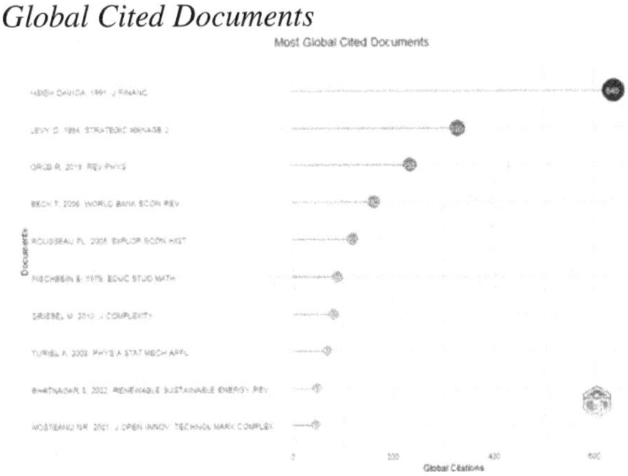

Figure 9. Annual Citations

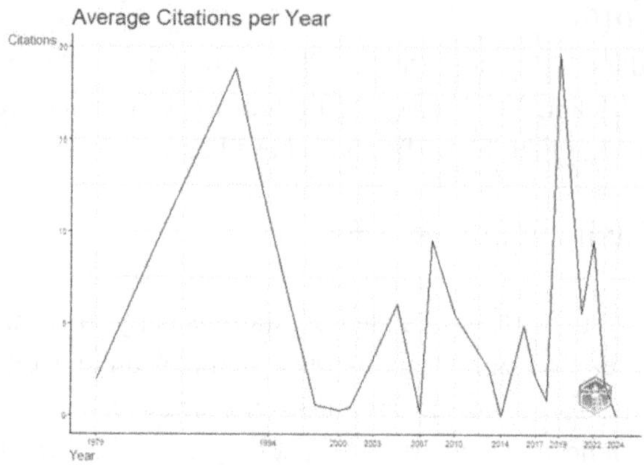

The early years, from 1979 to 1990, seem to have a low distribution rate. Somewhere in the range of 1980 and 1983, no articles were distributed, and 1979, 1984, 1985, 1986, 1987, 1988, and 1989 each saw one article distributed. Expansion of the Distributions (from the 1990s on): The distribution rate appears to have completely increased during the 1990s. Starting around 1990, something like one article has been distributed every year. Since 2010, at least two articles have been published annually, indicating a steady rate of publication.

4.5. Analysis and Co-Occurrence Network of Keywords

4.5.1 Factorial Analysis

A statistical technique called factor analysis is used to find underlying patterns in a dataset. It depends on the possibility that the noticed factors in a dataset are connected with fewer dormant or unseen factors.

Figure 10. Factorial Analysis

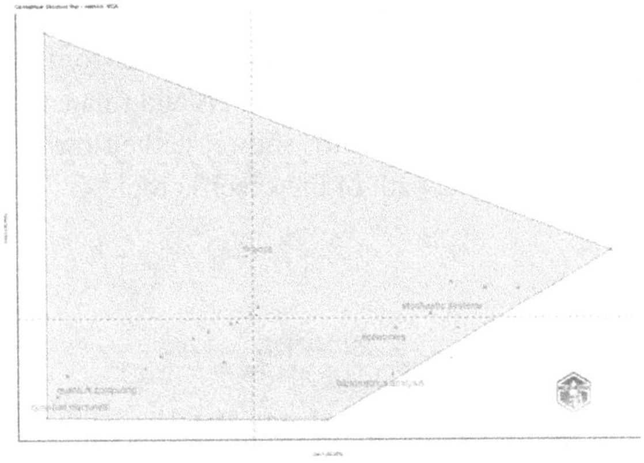

These dormant factors are known as elements and can be viewed as the "driving force" behind the noticed factors. Factor analysis is used in quantitative finance to simplify and comprehend intricate financial data. By distinguishing the hidden elements that impact monetary factors, we can more readily comprehend how the monetary framework functions and settle on additional educated choices. Finance, economics, mathematics, even physics, computer science, and environmental sustainability are all covered by the figures. Fractals and Fractal Examination (1.27, 1.33, 1.48): This proposes that fractals assume a critical part in the intricacy of monetary frameworks and markets. This indicates that one is interested in comprehending how deterministic systems can produce random-like behaviors that may have a connection to market oscillations (Chaos Theory and Complex Systems, 2.29). Machine Learning (1.33): This section tries to show how problems like risk assessment and market forecasting can be solved using machine intelligence techniques. Explicit Fractal Aspects: Monetary Business sectors (1.69): This condition might suggest having more mind boggling structure contrasted with the customary Euclidean framework (aspect 2). Fractal Functions and Interpolation (1.33): This shows that financial data could be modeled or approximated using fractal analysis. Hausdorff Aspect (1.48): It is a choice to box counting aspect which estimates by and large intricacy. Self-Comparative Fractals (1.48): This proposes searching for potential self-rehashing designs inside the monetary information.

4.5.3 Most Frequent Words and World Cloud

The most frequent words are listed in Figure 11. The word cloud from this list is shown in Figure 10. Finance, commerce, fractals and financial markets were the top four most frequent words. These words showcase the flow of the study and the importance of those terms in the path of the specific topic.

Figure 11. Word Cloud

Figure 12. Most Frequent Words

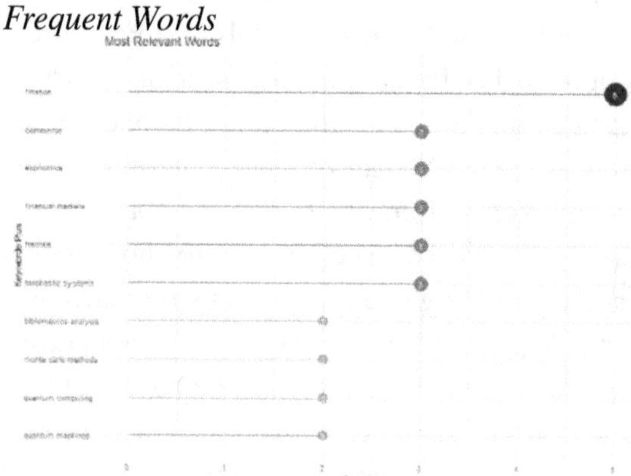

4.5.4 Word Frequency Over Time

Figure 12 provides us with the usage of most frequently used words over time from 2003 to 2024. The figure shows us a graph of usage of these words. It can be inferred from the graph, that the usage of the word “finance” has been uniformly increasing over the years while we see a steep increase in the usage of the word "evolution", especially from the year 2024. The word "quantum" also follows a similar pattern like the word "fractals" and is seen having a steep increase in usage since the year 2024.

It has been observed that the frequencies of the words "finance," "commerce," and "economics" are relatively constant from 2003 through to 2024. The implication is that there is an undeviating concentration on these few subjects contained in the data.

Figure 13. Word Frequency Over Time

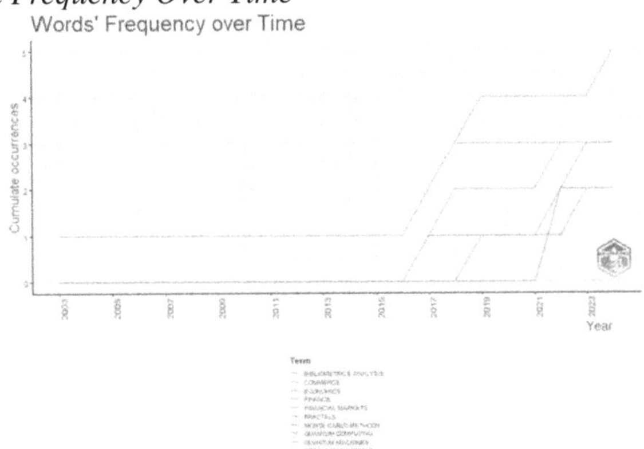

Starting from year 2017 we observe an increase in words related to particular methodologies and applications like "financial markets", "fractals", "stochastic systems", "bibliometrics analysis" and "Monte Carlo methods". This means that there is a growing interest among financial analysts who are using those techniques for financial research and calculations.

For instance, "quantum machines" and "quantum computing" appear for the first time in this database only in 2019 followed by slight increases in frequency thereafter. Thus it shows that quantum technologies may soon find applications in finance given these initials.

4.5.5 Tree Map

Treemap analysis uses layered rectangles to represent hierarchical data, providing a dynamic and user-friendly way to see information. The size of each rectangle indicates a quantitative characteristic, making it easier to quickly identify important groups or subsets.

Figure 14 highlights the combination of possible keywords.The word 'Finance' has a frequency of 4 ie; 7% of the 52 possible keywords. Then, Commerce has a frequency of 3 which is 5% of the possible keywords followed by employment and innovation with a frequency of 2 ie; 4% of the possible keywords. This pattern is followed by the rest of the possible keywords by a frequency of 1 which is 2% of the possible keywords.

4.5. 6 Thematic Map

Figure 14. Tree Map

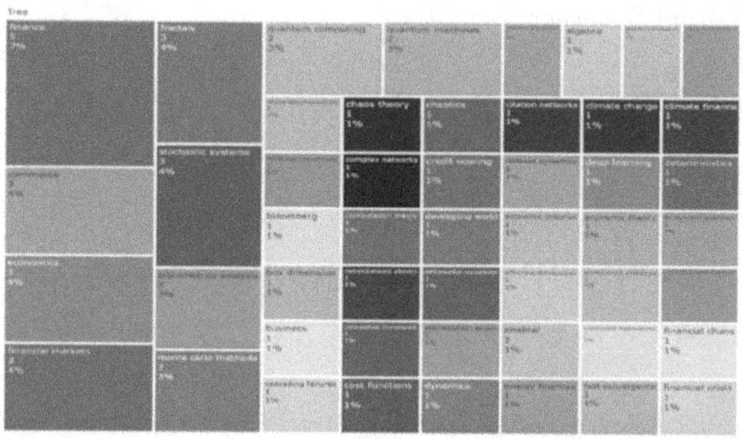

Figure 15. Thematic Map

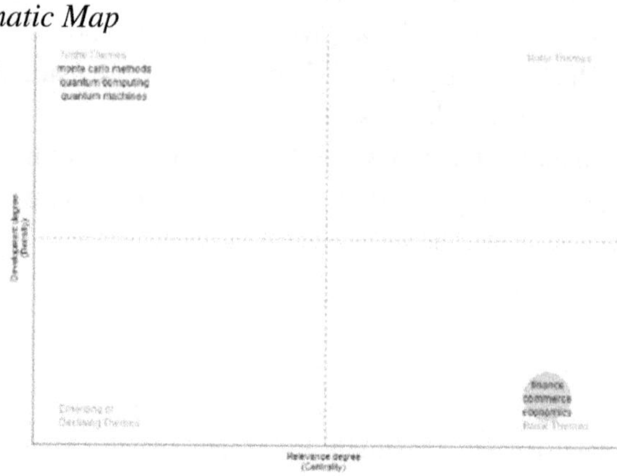

Figure 16. Keyword Co-occurrence

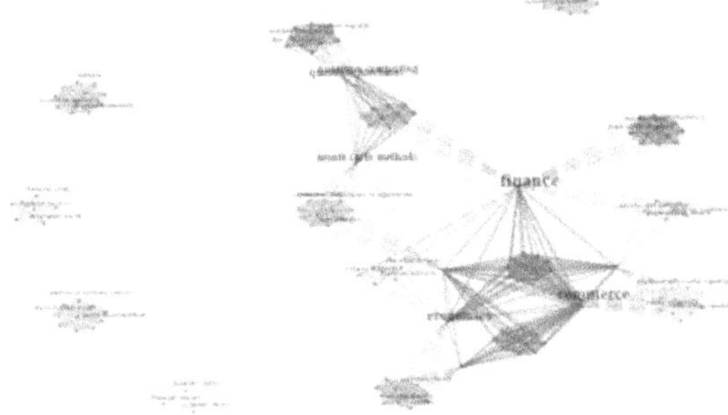

A thematic map analysis has shown the presence of only two clusters. Cluster 1 (which is labeled as "finance") comprises most finance, economics and business related words. These three centrality measures in cluster one including between centrality, closeness centrality and pagerank centrality have higher average values compared to cluster 2 (labeled "monte carlo methods"). This mainly implies that all words within cluster 1 are more central than those found in the other sub-network.

Cluster 2 (labeled "monte carlo methods"), include words related to computational techniques. The average centrality of this cluster is lower than what we observed for cluster 1. This implies that these words are not as connected or central to the overall network as those belonging to a different subset.

4.5.7 Dendrogram

Dendrogram represents the hierarchical order and the relationship between the keywords. The cut in the figure 17 and the vertical lines facilitate an investigation and interpretation of the different clusters.

Figure 17. Dendrogram

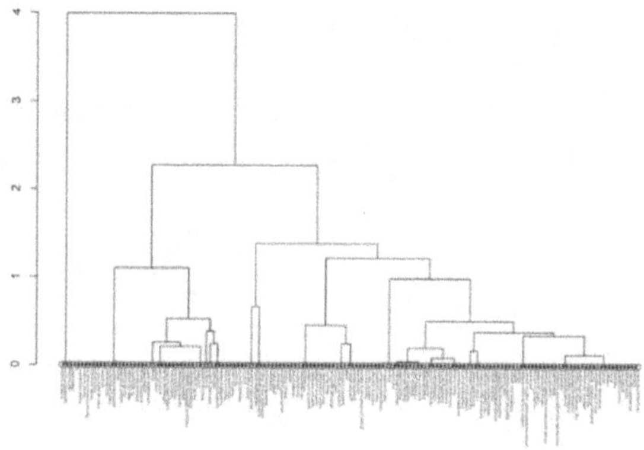

4.5.8 Most relevant authors

Assuming equal contribution: If we assume all authors contributed equally, then Kachchia KB, Tirosh D, and Battiston S appear to be the most relevant with 22, 20.83, and 10.33 articles respectively. Grouping by fractional articles: We could consider authors with a higher fractional contribution (e.g., Böthicher A at 10.125) as potentially more relevant than those with a full article at 10 (e.g., Beck T). This might indicate they were lead authors on a smaller number of impactful articles.

Figure 18. Most Relevant Authors

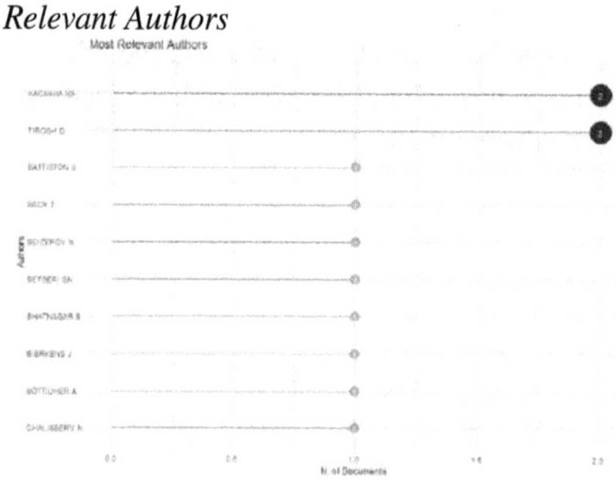

4.5.9 Country Scientific Production

The country collaboration network is based on co-occurrence frequencies. By default, the association strength is employed to normalize the network, this method has also been proven as one of the best. The clustering algorithm is based on a weighted and parameterized variant of the well-known modularity function of Newman and Girvan.

Figure 19. Country Scientific Production

This Figure shows the top 21 country collaboration networks of our retrieved bibliographic data. It can reflect the degree of communication between countries as well as the influential countries in this field. Netherlands (7 publications) and India (6 publications).

These top 3 countries account for nearly a third (32.8%) of the total publications (77). The United States, Netherlands and India are the leading countries in scientific production according to the data set.

Figure 20. Most Cited Countries

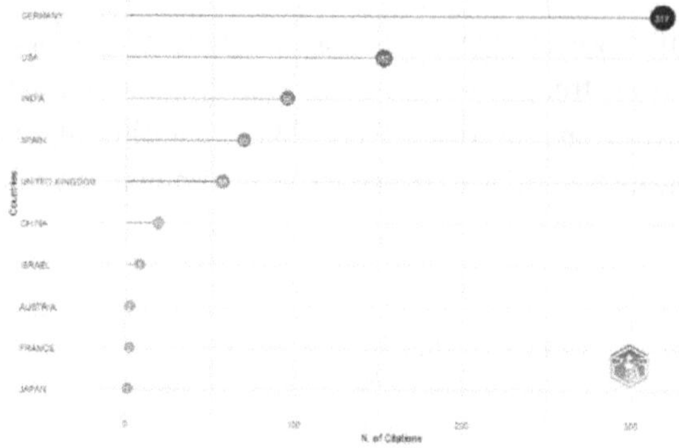

4.5.10 Most Cited Countries

Germany: Germany stands out with a critical typical reference count of 31,710.5 per article. This suggests that German research is influential and frequently cited by other researchers.

USA: The US follows intimately with a normal of 15,250.7 references per article, showing areas of strength for a powerful examination yield.

Hole Among Pioneers and Others: A critical hole exists between the main two nations (Germany and USA) and the rest. The average number of citations is significantly lower in countries like India (9,523.8), Spain (6,969), and the United Kingdom (5,628).

4.5.11 Average Citations Per Year

Figure 21. Average Citation Per Year

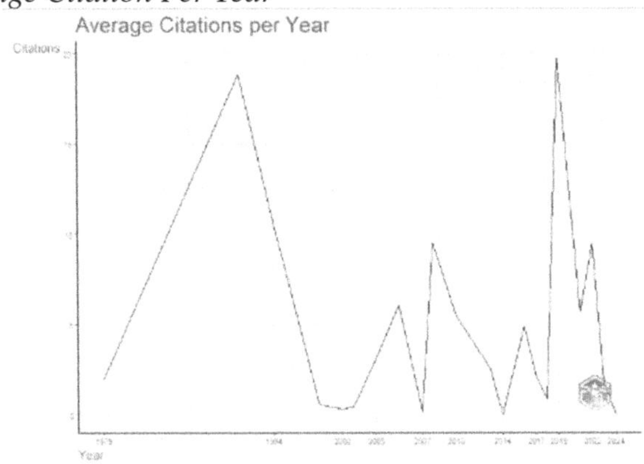

Although it appears that the data points only go back to 2015, the year is represented by the x-axis, which is labeled from 1958 to 2107. The y-pivot shows the quantity of articles distributed, named from 0 to 2100. The title at the highest point of the diagram is "Yearly Logical Creation."

There are a couple of things we can't decide from the picture alone: the specific nation to which the data pertain. The size of the y-pivot. It's reasonably not a direct scale, in light of the fact that the most elevated data of interest (around 2012) is a lot nearer to the x-hub than the least data of interest (1958). This recommends a more extreme expansion in distributions prior in the time period.

The wellspring of the information.Citation metrics for individual papers and journals are provided by bibliometric databases like Scopus and Web of Science. These measurements include:

- Influence Variable: These actions the typical number of references got per paper distributed in a diary in the beyond two years. (Stay focused on journals that might publish your research)
- h-Record: This considers both the quantity of distributions and their reference influence for a creator or diary.

4.5.12 CoWordNet

Figure 22. CoWord net

- Hubs: A few hubs, or logical watchwords or terms used in distributions (such as "business," "monetary business sectors," and "fractals," for example, are discussed in the information.
- Edge Loads: The qualities between hubs — for example, 11.5 for business monetary business sectors — may demonstrate the recurrence with which these terms show up together in reports. Better calibers show terms appearing together on a more standard premise.
- Values Excluded: Closeness and PageRank values are excluded. We'll have to decide how to respond to them (e.g., using a normal response or avoiding those hubs).
- Centrality Measures: In the event that the qualities are accessible, we can distinguish compelling terms inside the organization by working out centrality estimates like Group Betweenness and PageRank. High Gathering Betweenness suggests a term routinely interfaces different lots of terms. A term with a high PageRank indicates that it is frequently associated with other important terms.
- Localization: We are able to identify groups (networks) of terms that frequently co-occur, possibly revealing topical regions within the distributions.

5. CONCLUSION

It is very helpful to know these fundamentals, especially when dealing with money. The truth of finance from these essentials, we have now developed into a more complicated framework where rationale, common sense, and insightful abilities are utilized to shape the truth of money. Our understanding of the world and the universe would be drastically different without math. Math is central to numerous parts of our lives, from innovation and science to financial aspects and designing.

Without math, we wouldn't be able to evaluate, measure, or anticipate numerous peculiarities. While "endless information" may be great, the use of money truly profits by a tremendous and consistently developing information base. New developments, improved financial decision-making, and a financial system that is more effective and inclusive result from this ongoing pursuit of knowledge. The primary objective of this paper is the manner by which things are esteemed and the way that they are valued, remembering the likely overflow. How they are valued requires the extension of potential outcomes utilizing the creative minds of the modest number of individuals who get this particular information. Indeed, even with huge information, the component of vulnerability will constantly stay in finance.

The trick is to use the information you have to your advantage, change with the times, and make well-informed choices in the real world. By its very nature, infinity cannot be measured in any meaningful way. Existing examination frequently moves inside the domain of hypothesis and story, attempting to make an interpretation of its ethereal impact into unmistakable numbers.

Observational investigations wrestle with catching the subtle influence of vastness on human way of behaving and market elements, leaving us with glimpses, not absolutes. The monetary scene is painted in shades of limited numbers, a sharp differentiation to the endless material of boundlessness. Here's the reason a Bibliometric Analysis sticks out:

- Objectivity: It utilizes quantitative information like reference builds up to survey research influence, offering an apparently more unbiased methodology than emotional assessments.
- Large-scale analysis: It is able to look at huge amounts of data to find trends, patterns, and connections across entire research fields. This view of the big picture can be very helpful.
- Distinguishes intriguing issues and holes: Bibliometrics can uncover what regions are overall vigorously explored and where there may be a requirement for additional review.

In financial research, this paper has looked at the conflict between the vast amount of data and the need for specific metrics. Although having access to a pool of ever-expanding data presents a tremendous opportunity for new discoveries, converting this "endless information" into insights that can be implemented in the financial sector remains a challenge. Bibliometric analysis emerges as a useful tool in this situation. Large-scale analysis capabilities and objectivity, which rely on quantitative data like citation counts, are its strengths, allowing for the identification of research trends and potential gaps. Bibliometrics aids in navigating the information overload and prioritizes research efforts by highlighting areas that are receiving intense focus and those that may require additional investigation.

Researchers are forced to use proxies and indirect measures, such as shadows, rather than the source itself because of this mismatch. While these intermediaries offer significant experiences, the gamble of predisposition and error sneaks like a concealed hunter, requesting mindful translation. Notwithstanding, it is vital to recognize the constraints of bibliometrics. In addition, citation practices can vary significantly between fields, so citation counts alone may not always reflect groundbreaking work. Monetary examination, by its inclination, frequently manages mind boggling, multi-layered ideas that can't be completely caught through exclusively quantitative measurements. As a result, the approach that works best is a strategy that complements one another.

When it comes to determining the overall research landscape and identifying promising research avenues, bibliometrics can be of critical importance. Be that as it may, to genuinely comprehend the "reality of cash" in the entirety of its intricacy, a blend of quantitative and subjective techniques stays fundamental. This could include inside and out contextual investigations, master meetings, or even philosophical investigations close by the experiences gathered from bibliometric examination.

In the end, the interaction between a lot of information and the human capacity to find meaning and make informed decisions within its boundaries is what ultimately makes financial research successful. Successful examination devices like bibliometrics can enlighten the way ahead, however a solid portion of decisive reasoning and a nuanced comprehension of monetary truths are similarly important to explore the consistently developing scene of cash and worth.

REFERENCES

Beck, T., Demirgüç-Kunt, A., & World Bank. (2008). Access to Finance: an unfinished agenda. In THE WORLD BANK ECONOMIC REVIEW (Vols. 22–22, Issue 3, pp. 383–396). https://doi.org/DOI: 10.1093/wber/lhn021

Bhatnagar, S., & Sharma, D. (2022). Evolution of green finance and its enablers: A bibliometric analysis. *Renewable & Sustainable Energy Reviews*, 162, 112405. DOI: 10.1016/j.rser.2022.112405

Chalissery, N., Tabash, M. I., Nishad T, M., & Saleh Al-Faryan, M. A. (2022). A bibliometric analysis of socially responsible investment based on thematic clustering. *Cogent Business & Management*, 10(1), 2154057. Advance online publication. DOI: 10.1080/23311975.2022.2154057

("Chaos and Nonlinear Dynamics: Application of Financial Markets," n.d.)

Chaos and nonlinear forecastability in Economics and Finance on JSTOR. (n.d.-b). www.jstor.org. https://www.jstor.org/stable/54216

Chaos Theory and Strategy: Theory, Application, and Managerial Implications on JSTOR. (n.d.-b). www.jstor.org. https://www.jstor.org/stable/2486882

Cochrane, J. H. (2013). Finance: Function matters, not size. *The Journal of Economic Perspectives*, 27(2), 29–50. DOI: 10.1257/jep.27.2.29

Curtain, R. F., Zwart, H., & Iftime, O. (2017). A Kleinman–Newton construction of the maximal solution of the infinite-dimensional control Riccati equation. *Automatica*, 86, 147–153. DOI: 10.1016/j.automatica.2017.08.030

Cuthbertson, K., Nitzsche, D., & Hyde, S. (2007). MONETARY POLICY AND BEHAVIOURAL FINANCE. *Journal of Economic Surveys*, 21(5), 935–969. DOI: 10.1111/j.1467-6419.2007.00525.x

De Bettignies, J., & Ries, J. (2023). When less is more: Information and the financing of innovation. *Journal of Economic Behavior & Organization*, 214, 346–369. DOI: 10.1016/j.jebo.2023.07.038

Dobson, P., & Bierkens, J. (2023). Infinite dimensional Piecewise Deterministic Markov Processes. *Stochastic Processes and Their Applications*, 165, 337–396. DOI: 10.1016/j.spa.2023.08.010

Erokhin, S., & Roshka, O. (2018). Application of fractal properties in studies of financial markets. MATEC Web of Conferences, 170, 01074. https://doi.org/DOI: 10.1051/matecconf/201817001074

French, C. C. (n.d.). The Butterfly Effect in Interpreting Insurance Policies. Social Science Research Network. https://papers.ssrn.com/sol3/papers.cfm?abstract_id=3444910

Griebel, M., & Holtz, M. (2010). Dimension-wise integration of high-dimensional functions with applications to finance. *Journal of Complexity*, 26(5), 455–489. DOI: 10.1016/j.jco.2010.06.001

Hałaj, G., Martínez-Jaramillo, S., & Battiston, S. (2024). Financial stability through the lens of complex systems. *Journal of Financial Stability*, 71, 101228. DOI: 10.1016/j.jfs.2024.101228

Huber, C., & Kirchler, M. (2023). Experiments in finance: A survey of historical trends. *Journal of Behavioral and Experimental Finance*, 37, 100737. DOI: 10.1016/j.jbef.2022.100737

Kachhia, K. B. (2023c). Chaos in fractional order financial model with fractal–fractional derivatives. *Partial Differential Equations in Applied Mathematics : a Spin-Off of Applied Mathematics Letters*, 7, 100502. DOI: 10.1016/j.padiff.2023.100502

Kachhia, K. B. (2023d). Chaos in fractional order financial model with fractal–fractional derivatives. *Partial Differential Equations in Applied Mathematics : a Spin-Off of Applied Mathematics Letters*, 7, 100502. DOI: 10.1016/j.padiff.2023.100502

Kiliyanni, A. L., & Sivaraman, S. (2016). The perception-reality gap in financial literacy: Evidence from the most literate state in India. *International Review of Economics Education*, 23, 47–64. DOI: 10.1016/j.iree.2016.07.001

Klioutchnikov, I., Sigova, M., & Beizerov, N. (2017c). Chaos theory in finance. *Procedia Computer Science*, 119, 368–375. DOI: 10.1016/j.procs.2017.11.196

Michalski, T. (2021). Innovation, risk and finance paradigm from the polish perspective. *International Journal of Innovation Studies*, 5(3), 107–112. DOI: 10.1016/j.ijis.2021.07.002

Moşteanu, N. R., & Faccia, A. (2021). Fintech frontiers in quantum computing, fractals, and Blockchain Distributed ledger: Paradigm shifts and open innovation. *Journal of Open Innovation*, 7(1), 19. DOI: 10.3390/joitmc7010019

Mouck, T. (1998). Capital markets research and real world complexity: The emerging challenge of chaos theory. *Accounting, Organizations and Society*, 23(2), 189–215. DOI: 10.1016/S0361-3682(97)00004-4

Nishihara, M., Sawada, T., & Kato, H. (2023). Corporate investment, financing, and exit model with an earnings-based borrowing constraint. *International Review of Financial Analysis*, 85, 102456. DOI: 10.1016/j.irfa.2022.102456

Orús, R., Mugel, S., & Lizaso, E. (2019). Quantum computing for finance: Overview and prospects. *Reviews in Physics*, 4, 100028. DOI: 10.1016/j.revip.2019.100028

Quercia, R. G., Rohe, W. M., & Levy, D. (2000). A new look at creative finance. *Housing Policy Debate*, 11(4), 943–972. DOI: 10.1080/10511482.2000.9521393

Ren, Y., Ma, C., Chen, X., Lei, Y., & Wang, Y. (2023). Sustainable finance and blockchain: A systematic review and research agenda. *Research in International Business and Finance*, 64, 101871. DOI: 10.1016/j.ribaf.2022.101871

Rousseau, P. L., & Sylla, R. (2005). Emerging financial markets and early US growth. *Explorations in Economic History*, 42(1), 1–26. DOI: 10.1016/j.eeh.2004.03.004

Sanpedro, J. M. R., Lavana, U., & Miranda, E. M. (2014). SCHR\"ODINGER GROUP AND QUANTUM FINANCE. *International Journal of Pure and Applied Mathematics*, 90(3). Advance online publication. DOI: 10.12732/ijpam.v90i3.3

Smolyak, A., Levy, O., Shekhtman, L., & Havlin, S. (2018). Interdependent networks in Economics and Finance—A Physics approach. *Physica A*, 512, 612–619. DOI: 10.1016/j.physa.2018.08.089

Somefun, K., Perchet, R., Yin, C., & Leote de Carvalho, R. (2023). Allocating to thematic investments. *Financial Analysts Journal*, 79(1), 18–36.

Tall, D., Tall, D., & Tirosh, D. (2001). Infinity - The never-ending struggle. In Educational Studies in Mathematics (Vols. 48–48, pp. 199–238). https://wrap.warwick.ac.uk/475/1/WRAP_Tall_dot2001o-esm-intro-tirosh.pdf

The Intuition of Infinity on JSTOR. (n.d.). www.jstor.org. https://www.jstor.org/stable/3481965

Turiel, A., & Pérez-Vicente, C. J. (2003). Multifractal geometry in stock market time series. *Physica A*, 322, 629–649. DOI: 10.1016/S0378-4371(02)01830-7

Ukpabi, D. C., Karjaluoto, H., Bötticher, A., Nikiforova, A., Petrescu, D., Schindler, P., Valtenbergs, V., & Lehmann, L. (2023). Framework for understanding quantum computing use cases from a multidisciplinary perspective and future research directions. *Futures*, 154, 103277. DOI: 10.1016/j.futures.2023.103277

Vadyala, S. R., & Betgeri, S. N. (2023). General implementation of quantum physics-informed neural networks. *Array (New York, N.Y.)*, 18, 100287. DOI: 10.1016/j.array.2023.100287

Verma, S. K., & Kumar, S. (2024). Fractal dimension analysis of financial performance of resulting companies after mergers and acquisitions. *Chaos, Solitons, and Fractals*, 181, 114683. DOI: 10.1016/j.chaos.2024.114683

Vogl, M. (2022). Controversy in financial chaos research and nonlinear dynamics: A short literature review. *Chaos, Solitons, and Fractals*, 162, 112444. DOI: 10.1016/j.chaos.2022.112444

KEY TERMS AND DEFINITIONS

Finance: Finance is the study and management of money, investments, and other financial instruments. It involves the creation, oversight, and study of money, banking, credit, investments, assets, and liabilities. Finance is broadly divided into three categories: personal finance, corporate finance, and public finance. Key activities include budgeting, saving, investing, borrowing, and lending.

Infinity: Infinity refers to a concept in mathematics and philosophy that describes something without any limit. It is not a number but an idea that indicates an unending quantity. Infinity is often used in calculus, set theory, and other branches of mathematics to describe limits, infinite series, and the unbounded growth of functions.

Evolution: Evolution is the process by which different kinds of living organisms develop and diversify from earlier forms during the history of the earth. It is a central concept in biology, explaining how species adapt and change over generations through natural selection, genetic drift, mutations, and gene flow.

Fractal Geometry: Fractal geometry is a branch of mathematics that studies complex shapes and patterns that are self-similar across different scales. These shapes, known as fractals, can be found in nature (e.g., snowflakes, mountain ranges, lightning bolts) and are used in various fields, including computer graphics, nature modeling, and signal and image compression.

Chaos Theory: Chaos theory is a field of study in mathematics and physics that examines the behavior of dynamical systems that are highly sensitive to initial conditions. This sensitivity is popularly referred to as the "butterfly effect," where small changes in the initial state of a system can lead to significant and unpredictable differences in the later state. Chaos theory is applied in meteorology, engineering, economics, biology, and philosophy.

Commerce: Commerce is the activity of buying and selling, especially on a large scale. It encompasses various functions, including trade, marketing, sales, logistics, and finance. Commerce is essential for the economic development of nations, facilitating the exchange of goods and services, generating income, and contributing to the wealth and prosperity of societies.

Bibliometric Analysis: Bibliometric analysis is a research method used to measure and analyze the impact of scientific publications. It involves the quantitative assessment of academic literature, often using metrics such as citation counts, h-index, impact factor, and other indicators to evaluate the influence and reach of research articles, authors, and journals.

Financial Reality: Financial reality refers to the practical aspects of managing and dealing with finances in the real world. It encompasses the economic conditions, market behaviors, financial decisions, and practical constraints that individuals, businesses, and governments face in their financial activities.

Quantum Reality: Quantum reality is a concept in physics that describes the nature of reality at the quantum level. It involves the behavior and interactions of subatomic particles, which do not follow classical physical laws but are instead governed by the principles of quantum mechanics. Quantum reality challenges our traditional understanding of space, time, and causality.

Quantum Finance: Quantum finance applies the principles of quantum mechanics to financial markets and instruments. It explores the use of quantum computing and quantum theory to model complex financial systems, optimize trading strategies, and manage risk. Quantum finance is a cutting-edge field that seeks to leverage the computational power of quantum systems to solve problems that are intractable for classical computers.

Chapter 11
Using Quantum Fuzzy Neural Networks for Novel Structured Categorization of Images

N. Nithiyanandam
https://orcid.org/0000-0002-2729-1990
Department of Computing Technologies, SRM Institute of Science and Technology, Kattankulathur, India

G. K. Sandhia
Department of Computing Technologies, SRM Institute of Science and Technology, Kattankulathur, India

K. Vijiyakumar
Department of Computing Technologies, SRM Institute of Science and Technology, Kattankulathur, India

ABSTRACT

This research presents a new architecture for structured picture categorization problems called Hierarchical Fused Quantum Fuzzy Neural Network (HFQ-FNN). It combines the ideas of quantum computing with fuzzy logic and neural networks. With an accuracy of 84.04%, the suggested HFQ-FNN beats CNN and FDNN, two industry standards, on the Dirty-MNIST dataset, by a margin of 2.9% and 1.4%, respectively. Also, on the 15-Scene dataset, HFQ-FNN achieves an accuracy of 74.27% and shows a considerably higher F1 value, which is 3.0% better than DNN and 0.6% better than FDNN. The robustness analysis shows that HFQ-FNN is resilient against quantum noise, with a fidelity of 0.95 at a 0.1 noise probability. These

DOI: 10.4018/979-8-3693-6225-9.ch011

findings show that HFQ-FNN is a powerful tool for improving picture classification accuracy through the use of quantum computing, which could lead to major developments in the field of complicated data classification.

I. INTRODUCTION

The need for sophisticated machine learning methods has grown at an exponential rate in the modern day, thanks to the proliferation of massive data and intricate information systems. A state-of-the-art method that has recently gained a lot of interest is Quantum Fuzzy Neural Networks (Q-FNN), which combines the concepts of quantum computing with fuzzy logic and neural networks. The combination of neural networks' resilience in learning complex characteristics from data and fuzzy logic's ability to deal with ambiguity is made possible by the processing power and parallelism provided by quantum computing. In this introductory section, we lay the groundwork for investigating the unique use of Q-FNNs for structured picture classification, an area where conventional approaches frequently fail due to difficulties in dealing with ambiguity and extracting subtle patterns.

Machine learning has revolutionized numerous fields due to its ability to enable systems to learn from data autonomously, without the need for explicit programming (L'heureux, Grolinger, Elyamany, & Capretz, 2017). Inspired by the way the human brain works, neural networks have become the standard model in machine learning (Kasabov, 2019). Through repeated training, neural networks made up of interconnected "neurons" (connected circuits) may learn intricate patterns and correlations from given data (Sussillo & Abbott, 2009).

Classifying images is a fundamental task in the fields of computer vision and pattern recognition, which entails classifying images according to their content and characteristics (Liu, Zhang, Lu, & Ma, 2007). Due to factors such as noise, occlusions, lighting conditions, and large dimensionality of picture data, traditional machine learning methods frequently fail in picture classification tasks (Arif et al., 2022). Additionally, traditional deterministic models struggle to adequately deal with ambiguity and uncertainty that may be present in images (Al-Saidi, Ballagi, Hassen, & Saad, 2024).

Zadeh presented fuzzy logic in the 1960s (Zadeh, 2015). and it provides a mathematical foundation for handling input that is unclear or imprecise. Fuzzy logic provides for more nuanced transitions between true and false, indicating linguistic degrees of truth or membership, as opposed to the sharp operation of classical binary logic (Arfi, 2010). Fuzzy logic excels at representing the fuzziness and uncertainty found in real-world data because of this feature.

The concepts of quantum mechanics provide the basis of quantum computing, which uses quantum interference, superposition, and entanglement to conduct computations on a scale that classical computers just cannot match (Rieffel & Polak, 2000). Because quantum bits, or qubits, can exist in more than one state at once, quantum computers dramatically improve computing efficiency and parallelism (Tacchino, Chiesa, Carretta, & Gerace, 2020). There is great hope that this quantum advantage can speed up machine learning algorithms and help with computationally heavy challenges.

A unified framework that incorporates the strengths of quantum computing, fuzzy logic, and neural networks is the notion behind Quantum Fuzzy Neural Networks (Q-FNN) (Zhou, Li, Xu, Su, & Chen, 2023). The capabilities of neural networks for feature learning and pattern recognition are combined with those of fuzzy logic for uncertainty modelling, and the parallelism and processing power of quantum computing for Q-FNN (Patel, Bharill, Tiwari, & Prasad, 2019). This convergence paves the way for new, more accurate and resilient ways to handle complicated data analysis jobs.

Research into the use of Q-FNNs for structured picture classification is the focus of this article. The main goal is to come up with a new method that can handle the unpredictability and uncertainty in picture data better, so the classification results are more accurate and dependable. We hope to outperform both conventional approaches and current versions of Q-FNN in picture classification tasks by taking use of Q-FNN's hierarchical architecture, through the use of quantum neural networks, fuzzy membership functions are developed.

1.1 Recent Research on Convolutional Fuzzy Neural Networks and Image Classification

Recent years have witnessed substantial progress in the literature pertaining to Quantum Fuzzy Neural Networks. A number of Q-FNN designs, optimization methods, and domain-specific applications have been investigated by researchers. There is a lack of information in the literature about how to use Q-FNN for structured picture categorization, particularly in cases where there is a lot of ambiguity and complicated patterns.

Quantum computing has the ability to improve machine learning tasks, according to various research. One such task is image analysis and categorization. Improving the efficiency and accuracy of picture categorization algorithms has been demonstrated using quantum-enhanced feature extraction methods and algorithms influenced by quantum mechanics (Kharsa, Bouridane, & Amira, 2023).

In addition, there has been a lot of research into using neural networks with fuzzy logic to handle data-driven tasks with uncertainty and ambiguity. When faced with ambiguous data or situations requiring a nuanced assessment, fuzzy neural networks have shown to be a useful tool (Mitra & Hayashi, 2000).

Despite these developments, there is a dearth of literature on structured picture categorization challenges that integrates neural networks, fuzzy logic, and quantum computing. Our suggested method introduces a hierarchical fused Quantum Fuzzy Neural Network (HFQ-FNN) design optimized for picture classification in an effort to fill this need.

Figure 1. HFQ-FNN structure

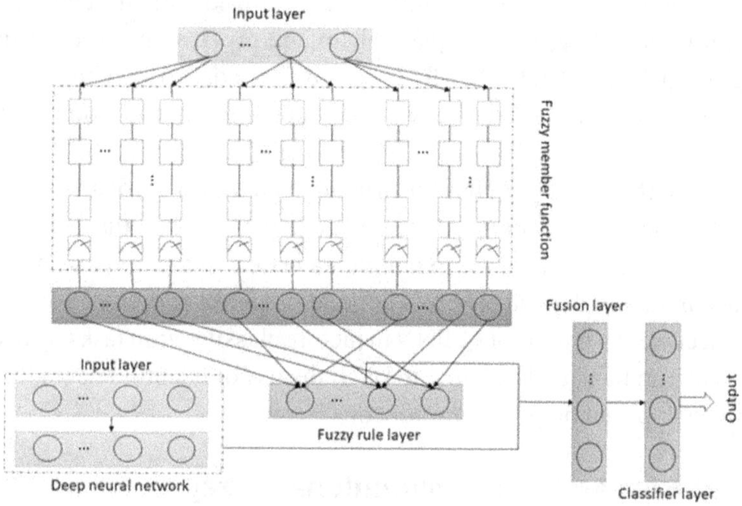

1.2 The Study's Goals

The following are the primary aims of the research:

- Create a new architecture for structured picture categorization using hierarchical fused Quantum Fuzzy Neural Networks (HFQ-FNNs).
- Find out how well HFQ-FNN deals with complicated patterns, uncertainty, and variability in picture data.
- Evaluate how well HFQ-FNN performs in comparison to more conventional image classification algorithms, current Q-FNN variations, and quantum-inspired techniques.

- Conduct virtual tests on benchmark picture datasets to verify that HFQ-FNN is robust and scalable.

Quantum Fuzzy Neural Networks (Q-FNN) are an exciting new development that combines quantum computing with fuzzy logic and neural networks. This could be a great step forward in solving the problems caused by complexity and uncertainty in data-driven processes. An innovative architecture for structured picture categorization is presented in this paper: the Hierarchical Fused Quantum Fuzzy Neural Network (HFQ-FNN). Our goal is to show that HFQ-FNN is better than other methods in managing ambiguous image input and getting accurate classification results through simulations and comparisons.

II. RELATED WORK

2.1 Classification of Images

Several fields, including deep learning, pattern recognition, and human-computer interaction, have investigated image classification. Many researchers are interested in it. In (Huang et al., 2023), the picture features are extracted so that the pictures may be categorized. Feature extraction is greatly affected by the picture composition mechanism, which is unusual for mid-level feature learning algorithms that usually focus on coding or pooling.

Using a hierarchical image decomposition approach efficiently achieves picture content exploration in feature extraction. Here, we dissect each picture into its component parts, or semantic features, such the structure and texture photos. Use one of many feature extraction approaches to match photos based on their semantic information, which includes things like structure and texture. When it comes to representing features associated with picture properties, there are two separate schemas. Automatic feature learning from raw pixels in a multistage network is the second schema, whereas the first uses hand-crafted features in a single tiered network.

Using a method motivated by biology, the author has investigated how to classify images of nature in reference (Li & Deng, 2022). It takes advantage of the well-known simultaneous improvements in the human brain's visual information processing and cognitive reasoning. Natural classification and image analysis are two of the most common applications of this method. A visual selective attention unit that draws inspiration from biology, a knowledge structuring unit, consisting of a visual information clustering unit, two primary components, and a whole system. It uses the inherent features of photos to automatically derive meaningful links between them. For more accurate picture categorization, based on what we can see with our eyes, the system works within those constraints.

The system is divided into two parts: the bottom-up saliency map module and the top-down selective attention module. The former uses low-level information from natural images to create a salient area, and the latter uses human interaction to make decisions about interesting stuff. These two parts are highly dependent on the human brain's visual dorsal and ventral pathways. The knowledge structuring unit now includes all of the components. Utilizing the results produced by the knowledge clustering unit—which employs a top-down, high-level paradigm for visual information perception and classification—permits visual information clustering to take place.

Spoof fingerprint identification with a Convolutional Neural Network (CNN) was previously discussed (in (Liu, Arunachalam, & Temme, 2021)). To fulfil the needs of certain applications, biometrics seeks to reliably distinguish between people using signals derived from traits like face, fingerprint, iris, voice, or written signature. Biometric technology has many advantages over older forms of security that depend on tangible objects, such as keys and cards, or on information that needs to be memorized, like PINs and passwords.

Every year There have been a variety of fingerprint detection algorithms introduced, including (Tiwari, Zhang, Qu, & Muhammad, 2024). Hardware and software algorithms are the two main classes into which these algorithms fall. The hardware for measuring human vital signs, including heart rate and blood pressure, consists of a specialized gadget coupled to a sensor device. In (Tiwari, Zhang, Qu, & Muhammad, 2024), a novel approach to recognizing complex facial photos with dynamic visual patterns is detailed for use in real-world applications. Feature extraction from images automatically using a training set, which includes both face and non-face photos, is also accomplished by means of CNN. All existing algorithms for face detection involve local facial features.

Over the past decade, numerous methods have been developed and evaluated for local facial feature analysis and image categorization based on the geometric model of the human face (; LeCun, Bottou, Bengio, & Haffner, 1998; Van Gemert, Geusebroek, Veenman, & Smeulders, 2008). Template matching strategies for recognizing specific photo sub-features are prioritized in other ways.

Finding human semi-frontal faces in large, complicated image databases, this method uses a classification algorithm. Depending on whether the photographs contain faces or not, it sorts them into two categories. To extract important information from images, CNN used to use automated methods. The fast processing is also automated by means of a series of simple convolutional and subsampling algorithms; thus, image pre-processing is unnecessary.

2.2 Classical Fuzzy Logic

There has been a recent uptick in interest in the feature points discovered by "corner" operators like the Plessey and interesting point operators like the one developed (Alshennawy & Aly, 2009). Classical operators classify a pixel as a specific type of feature point by performing a sequence of operations within a window that is centered on the pixel being examined. When there are noticeable variations in color or brightness inside the image's region of interest, the traditional operators work well. Pictured in Figure 1 are regions that may be simply thresholder into a binary image, making them ideal for use with classic operators. To further on the problems with conventional operators, consider how the classic edge detector fails to correctly identify edge pixels in many cases. This is especially true when the edge is clearly visible yet only causes a little shift in grayscale. Nevertheless, these borders are often visible without any special equipment. A feature point is a pixel in a local window whose value is related to the values of the pixels around it. Using neural Fuzzy Feature to build edge detectors has been the subject of recent study. For training, these detectors use a subset of the edges in example images that conventional edge detectors can identify. The original creators of this method (Yazdinejad, Dehghantanha, Parizi, & Epiphaniou, 2023), trained a neural network to provide fuzzy outputs similar to those of a normalized Sobel Operator. Though Bezdek's method is effective, the author and colleagues have shown that training neural network classifiers on sharp values is even better.

If one compares the neural fuzzy edge detector to its predecessor, the standard edge detector, it becomes immediately clear that the latter is inferior. Fuzzy inference systems (FIS) obtain their inputs according to the procedure described in references (Kak, 1995; Long, 2023), by passing the original image through three filters: a high-pass, a first-order edge detector filter (Sobel operator), and a low-pass (mean) filter. After that, everything is fine-tuned so that the structure may filter photographs to increase contrast and, in a separate problem, divide them into a specific number of input categories. What kind of filtering is required determines the fuzzy rules and membership functions.

2.3 Quantum Fuzzy Logic

The merging of quantum theory with fuzzy logic gives rise to quantum fuzzy logic. Theoretical evidence for the proposal that quantum logic might be seen as a type of fuzzy logic was given by Menichenko et al. in 2007. In theory, here is where quantum fuzzy logic is built. Quantum fuzzy logic was introduced by Tiwari et al.

in 2023 and used for multi-modal sentiment and sarcasm detection. Quantum fuzzy logic is an underexplored area that need more research.

The mentioned publications discuss picture classification, fuzzy logic, and quantum fuzzy logic, including its pros and cons. Hierarchical image decomposition captures structure and texture semantics and provides good feature extraction (Huang et al., 2023), however it depends on the composition approach and cannot be applied to different datasets. The biology-based architecture (Li & Deng, 2022) combines visual selective attention with knowledge structure and is effective at natural picture classification but struggles with computer complexity and domain adaption. Convolutional Neural Networks (CNNs) have showed promise in biometrics and facial recognition (Liu, Arunachalam, & Temme, 2021) and (Tiwari, Zhang, Qu, & Muhammad, 2024), but they confront computational problems and adversarial attacks. Traditional operators have trouble identifying edges, although classical fuzzy logic approaches (Alshennawy & Aly, 2009; Kak, 1995; Long, 2023; Yazdinejad, Dehghantanha, Parizi, & Epiphaniou, 2023) are simple and effective for greyscale picture fluctuations. However, they cannot handle complex edge cases. Neural fuzzy algorithms improve edge detection by using training data, but they are still susceptible to noise and require careful optimisation. Finally, quantum fuzzy logic (Melnichenko, 2010; Tiwari, Zhang, Qu, & Muhammad, 2024) offers a novel multi-modal analytical paradigm that has potential but hasn't been proven or tested adequately. Overall, these studies build strong footing, but they also demonstrate scalability, robustness, and practicality gaps that must be solved by future research.

III. PROPOSED METHOD

A fusion layer, a classifier layer, a representation of deep neural networks, and a quantum fuzzy logic representation make up the HFQ-FNN. Figure 1 shows the HFQ-FNN design. Two networks will be used to represent the input data: one will use quantum fuzzy logic, while the other will use deep neural networks. The data will be represented in fuzzy logic, and in neural networks, respectively. The aggregation module then combines the two components' characteristics. Last but not least, a classification neural network module takes the fused characteristics and uses them to sort the data into various groups.

A depiction of quantum fuzzy logic. A membership degree is assigned to each input variable for various fuzzy sets, an additional set of membership functions are connected to every input layer node. The input vector typically contains variables that are passed into the programme. To what extent does each input node belong to a given fuzzy set? That is what fuzzy membership functions determine. This is a mapping with respect to the k-th fuzzy membership function: $S \rightarrow [0,1]$ The membership function is chosen to be a Gaussian function with π as the mean and τ^2 as the variance in earlier studies (Lin, Lin, & Shen, 2001). This research suggests using the QNN as the membership function, as illustrated in Figure 2.

It was in 1995 when L.A. Zadeh initially introduced fuzzy sets (Zadeh, 1965). To put it simply, fuzzy sets are

$$B = \{(y, \pi_B(y)) | y \, \theta \, Y\} \quad (1)$$

Here, the membership function of the fuzzy set B is denoted as π_B, meaning that the target is transformed into its fuzzy representation. At its core, Y is the collection of all input variables. To represent a QNN, to be expressed as the membership function, which is usually accomplished with a parametrized quantum circuit.

$$\pi_B(y) = g_\vartheta(y) = \left(0|V^\dagger(y,\vartheta)NV(y,\vartheta)|0 + 1\right)/2 \quad (2)$$

In this context, $|0\rangle$ denotes the quantum computer's initial state, $V(y,\vartheta)$ is the input-dependent quantum circuit, y is the input, and ϑ is an adjustable parameter. We may observe N. It is possible to determine $g_\vartheta(y)$ by taking many measurements of the quantum circuit and then combining the results. Given that the expectation under the observable N is $0|V^\dagger(y,\vartheta)NV(y,\vartheta)|0$, we may deduce that $0|V^\dagger(y,\vartheta)NV(y,\vartheta)|0\epsilon[0,1]$. Consequently, $g_\vartheta(y)\epsilon[0,1]$ seems to be a function that determines membership.

In this case, as shown in Figure 2, we choose the $V(y,\vartheta)$ quantum circuit layout. The data re-uploading technique is used by this quantum circuit, which is composed of trainable circuit blocks and data encoding circuits with many layers.

Fig. 2 depicts a single-qubit quantum circuit that uses many levels of circuit blocks, at each level, which has both data-encoding and a circuit block that can be trained. Data encoding block is one such component, which employs the angle encoding technique—that is, a S_z gate—to encode the input data into a quantum state:

$$|y_j = S_z(y_j)\,|0 \quad (3)$$

Where

$$S_z(\vartheta) = \begin{bmatrix} cos\frac{\vartheta}{2} - & sin\frac{\vartheta}{2} \\ sin\frac{\vartheta}{2} & cos\frac{\vartheta}{2} \end{bmatrix} \quad (4)$$

Any qubit gate V, which is a b 2×2 unitary matrix, may be broken down into three rotation gates.

$$V = f^{j\beta} S_A(\gamma) S_z(\delta) S_A(\varepsilon) \tag{5}$$

S_A is the rotation gate around the Z-axis, and $f^{j\beta}$ is the global phase. The global phase factor is denoted by β.

$$S_A(\vartheta) = \begin{bmatrix} f^{-j\vartheta/2} & 0 \\ 0 & f^{j\vartheta/2} \end{bmatrix} \tag{6}$$

If we rotate the S_A, S_z, S_A gate at the corresponding angle, we may obtain any qubit state $|\omega$from any initial state $|\text{init}\rangle$, because the global phase cannot alter the quantum state.

$$|\omega = S_A(\beta) S_z(\gamma) S_A(\delta) \big| \text{init} \tag{7}$$

Then, the quantum circuit consisting of a single qubit can be written as

$$V_{single\_qubit} = \prod_{m} \left(S_A\left(\vartheta_m^3\right) S_z\left(\vartheta_m^2\right) S_A\left(\vartheta_m^1\right) S_z(y_j) \right) \tag{8}$$

m is the number of circuit layers, or the number of repetitions of the circuit block. The aforementioned quantum circuit is a single-qubit design that eschews

Figure 2. An implementation of quantum member function on a single-qubit circuit.

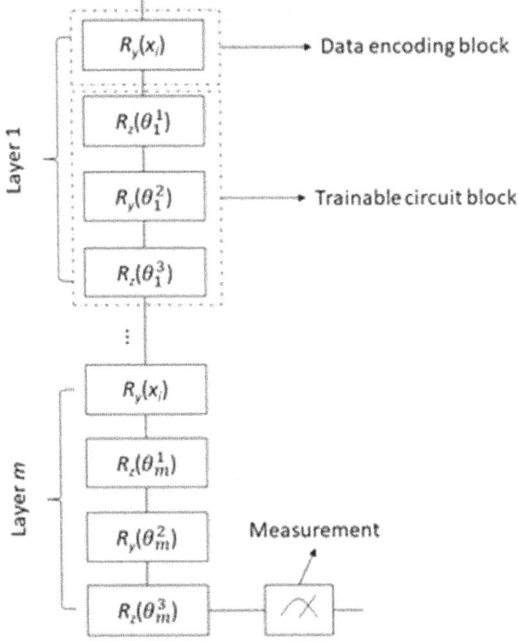

a gate with two qubits. Thus, it is especially well-suited to the present situation, in which resources for quantum computing are few.

Fuzzy degree is mapped to the l-th input node by this layer.

$$i_{j,k}^{(m)} = g_{\vartheta}^{j}(y_l), \forall_j \tag{9}$$

This is where the outcome of thej^{th} membership function's calculation is represented by $i_{j,k}^{(m)}$. Once the fuzzy membership function processing is complete, we go on to the fuzzy rule layer, which is symbolised by 'AND' fuzzy logic, defined as $i_j^{(m)} = \prod_l i_{j,l}^{(m-1)}$. The input is subsequently transformed into fuzzy degree.

Figure depicting a deep neural network. This neural representation will be acquired via the neural network's representation block. In such a setting, the neural representation of the input is usually extracted using a fully connected neural network. A fully connected neural network's m^th layer can be obtained in the following way.

$$iu_j^{(m)} = x_j^{(m)} i^{(m-1)} + c_j^{(m)} \tag{10}$$

The weights and bias that connect the $(m - 1)^{th}$ layer node to the mth layer j^{th} nodes are represented as $x_j^{(m)}$ and $c_j^{(m)}$, respectively. The next step is to use the ReLU activation function.

$$i_j^{(m)} = ReLU\left(i\,u_j^{(m)}\right) = \begin{cases} i_j^{(m)}, if\, i_j^{(m)} > 0 \\ 0, other \end{cases} \tag{11}$$

The result of the neural network with the mth layer is denoted as $i_j^{(m)}$. Each layer of a fully connected network can utilise the dropout method to avoid over-fitting the model, which improves performance. It is worth noting that different tasks call for different neural network architectures. A convolutional neural network (CNN) can outperform a fully connected neural network (FCN) in picture data categorization, for instance.

Fusion layer. In order to classify the input data, feature fusion uses the merged outputs of numerous neural networks to extract various characteristics, which are then used in the formation of neural features. This process is known as multi-modal fusion (Ngiam, Khosla, Kim, Nam, Lee, & Ng, 2011). Gathering the results from the neural representation module and the quantum fuzzy logic representation, we apply the identical aggregation approach as in (Deng, Ren, Kong, Bao, & Dai, 2016). These two representations are in charge of describing the data's fuzzy characteristics and neural features, correspondingly. In the first step, we merge the two attributes to obtain

$$i_{fus} = concat\left(i_{fuz}, i_{neu}\right) \tag{12}$$

Additionally, the features are fused using a fully connected neural network.

$$i_{fuz}^{(m)} = ReLU\left(x^{(m)} i_{fuz}^{(m-1)} + c^{(m)}\right) \tag{13}$$

The activation function is represented by ReLU, and the weight matrix and bias vector from the $(m - 1)^{th}$ layer node to the mth layer node are shown by, $x^{(m)}$and $c^{(m)}$, respectively. The output features are a combination of neural and deeply fused fuzzy features, obtained by a multi-layer fully connected network.

Classifier layer. The fused features are processed and categorized by the classifier layer. With the jth input sample, a l-dimensional output vector will be produced via the classifier layer, presuming that there are l total categories of data labels. Next, the predicted label is computed using a soft-max function.

$$\hat{z}_j = Softmax\left(z_j\right) = \frac{f^{z_j}}{\sum_l f^{z_{jl}}} \tag{14}$$

In which, $\widehat{z}_j = \left[\widehat{z}_{j1}, \widehat{z}_{j2}, \ldots, \widehat{z}_{jl}\right]$. The cross-entropy function is employed as the loss function in this paper. The cross-entropy loss function is computed for m training data sets in the following way:

$$D = \frac{1}{n}\sum_{j=1}^{n}\sum_{k=1}^{l} - z_{jk}\log\widehat{z}_{jk} - \left(1 - z_{jk}\right)log\left(1 - \widehat{z}_{jk}\right) \tag{15}$$

Consideration of the parameter optimization approach and the initialization of the model parameters are essential during the training phase of the model. Learning with deep neural networks relies heavily on parameter initialization. If the parameters are initialized properly, the model will be able to converge to a more optimal local minimum. Following the technique from (Glorot & Bengio, 2010) for initialization, we set the parameters of the classifier layer. When starting a fully connected neural network, it is standard practice to set the bias to 0 and the weights to 1 using the following guidelines.

$$x_{jk}^{(m)} \sim V\left[-\frac{1}{\sqrt{o^{(m-1)}}}, \frac{1}{\sqrt{o^{(m-1)}}}\right] \tag{16}$$

The sentence means that there are a certain number of nodes in the $(m-1)^{th}$layer and that V has a uniform distribution. We shall adjust the value of $o^{(m-1)}$ based on various learning assignments and do not strictly adhere to the principles mentioned earlier. For the rest of the network, we initialise the parameters using the Kaiming Uniform technique.

Before we can update the parameters using the conventional optimization approach, we must get the derivative of the loss function for each network parameter. This is the first step in the parameter optimization process. The gradient can be derived for the QNN portion, specifically for the membership function layer, by using the parameter shift approach.

Figure 3. Selections from the Dirty-MNIST database.

IV. EXPERIMENTS

4.1 Experiment Settings

4.1.1 Experiment Environment

Linux is the platform on which the experiment is run. While the Torch Quantum package is used to develop the quantum circuit component, PyTorch is used to generate classical neural networks.

4.1.2 Datasets

In order to ensure that the model was accurate, the experiment used the Dirty-MNIST and 15-Scene data sets.

The training set for Dirty-MNIST, which is a combination of MNIST and Ambiguously MNIST, contains sixty thousand sample-label pairings. Generating ambiguous MNIST samples with different entropies is what Ambiguous MNIST is all about. six thousand

Figure 4. Data from the 15-scene dataset used as samples.

Table 1. The model's hyperparameter parameters

Hyper-parameter	Value
Deep neural network	DNN/CNN
Batch size	128
Epochs	200
Qubits	1
Learning rate	0.01
Activation function	ReLU
Measurement	A basis
Quantum encoding gate	S_z

distinct samples, with ten labels apiece. For security reasons, acquisition algorithms cannot ignore "duplicates" and instead use the normalized dataset, which includes the addition of Gaussian noise to each sample with a standard deviation of 0.05. Items in Dirty-MNIST are displayed in Fig. 3.

The 15-Scene collection contains fifteen distinct urban and natural settings, including, but not limited to, beaches, city streets, woodlands, workplaces, kitchens, living spaces, and more. Figure 4 shows the fifteen-scene data collection. This dataset presents algorithms with significant hurdles, particularly in managing the diversity and complexity of the scenes, due to the variety of scene types it contains, which range from indoor situations to wild landscapes. Over 4,500 photographs of scenic landscapes make up this data set. As a training set, we select 100 photos from each category; the rest serve as a test set.

When testing the HFQ-FNN model, it is best to use benchmark datasets like the 15-Scene dataset or the Dirty-MNIST dataset. The described investigations made use of both of these databases. In addition to being diverse and hard, these datasets contain ambiguity, added noise, and varying degrees of complexity. Examining the model's performance on uncertain and noisy inputs is the goal of Dirty-MNIST, which uses ambiguous samples with Gaussian noise. In contrast, the 15-Scene dataset assesses the model's ability to handle complicated and diverse picture types with its diverse range of natural and urban landscapes. In order to accurately assess the model's ability to generalise and classify, the benchmark datasets designed for this framework should include complex scenarios, varying degrees of noise, and a wide range of image kinds.

4.1.3 Hyper-parameters

In this experiment, hyper-parameters from both QNNs and classical neural networks are used. Table 1 displays the suggested model's hyperparameter settings.

4.2 Evaluation Criteria

Common measures used to assess the efficacy of models in classification tasks include F1 score, recall, accuracy, and precision. We may learn about the model's performance in several areas with the use of these indicators. The following measures are described as

$$Precision = \frac{UQ}{UQ + GQ} \tag{17}$$

$$Recall = \frac{UQ}{UQ + GO} \tag{18}$$

$$Accuaracy = \frac{UQ + UO}{UQ + UO + GO + GQ} \tag{19}$$

$$G1 = \frac{2Precison \times Recall}{Precison + Recall} \tag{20}$$

There are five different variables that can be represented by these letters: *UQ* for true positive samples, *UO* for true negative samples, *GQ* for false positive samples, and *GO* for false negative samples.

Macro F1, macro accuracy, and macro recall are commonly used metrics in multi-class classification issues. To determine the macro precision, we must first compute and average the precision for each class independently. Averaging the memory across all categories also yields macro recall. With the precision and recall scores in hand, macro F1 is finally formed. Following is the formula for macro F1, macro recall, and macro precision in a multi-classification issue with l categories:

$$Macro\ Precision = \frac{1}{l} \sum_{j\epsilon\{1,\ldots,l\}} Precision_j, \tag{21}$$

$$Macro\ Recall = \frac{1}{l} \sum_{j\epsilon\{1,\ldots,l\}} Recall_j, \tag{22}$$

$$Macro\ F1 = \frac{2MacroPrecision \times MacroRecall}{MacroPrecision + MacroRecall} \tag{23}$$

Among these, $Precision_j$ stands for the accuracy rate and $Recall_j$ for each group. Similar to binary classification problems, multi-classification tasks use the ratio of properly predicted samples to total samples to calculate accuracy.

Figure 5. The Dirty-MNIST training convergent analysis.

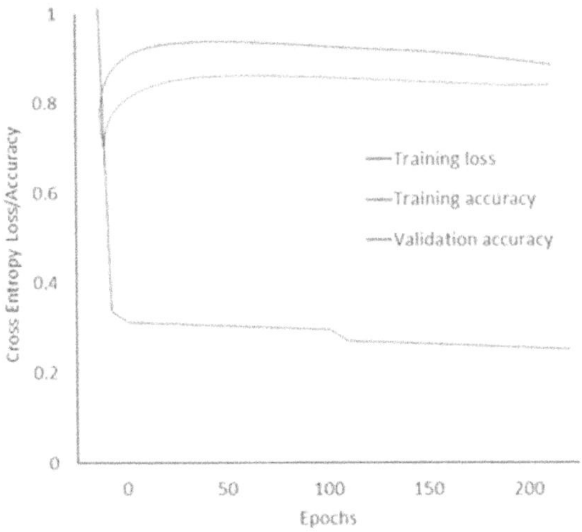

4.3 Evaluation of Performance

We employed CNN and FDNN as standards to evaluate the efficacy of the proposed method on the Dirty-MNIST dataset. For the proposed model, CNN stands in for the deep neural network. To further protect itself from competing DNNs, the FDNN's deep neural network is set up to CNN. Two layers—the convolutional and the pooling layers—make up the CNN network. Ten output channels are produced by setting the first layer's convolution kernel size to 5×5 with a stride of 1. Ten output channels are produced by the second layer's convolution kernel, which has a 5 × 5 size and a stride of 1. Furthermore, a pooling kernel of size 2 is used by each pooling layer, with a stride that is equal to the size of the pooling kernel. The final step in processing is to reduce the output to a one-dimensional vector. After that, information is mapped to 128-dimensional features by passing the data through a fully connected neural network. The CNN network, a model of a deep neural network, is an essential part of FDNN or HFQ-FNN. If the CNN model is to work autonomously, a classification layer must be added to the network to categorize the features of the hidden layer. Here, the 128-dimensional features are transformed into 10-dimensional ones.

Fig. 5 shows the training details that are necessary to see the convergence of HFQ-FNN. During the initial few model epochs, there is a noticeable decline in loss and a quick increase in both training and verification accuracy. With a loss of around 0.35, training accuracy of about 88.3%, and verification accuracy of about

81.5%, we reached the fifth epoch. Loss gradually diminishes with increasing epoch. Until the learning rate starts to degrade at 116th epoch, the loss is significantly reduced. After that, as time goes on, the loss curve becomes flatter, which means the model has converged.

In TABLE 2, we can see how well the suggested model worked on Dirty MNIST.

Table 2. Results on dirty-MNIST for the suggested model

Model	Accuracy	Recall	Precision	G1
CNN	83.84	84.84	85.49	85.08
FDNN	83.94	85.08	85.53	85.21
HFQ-FNN	84.04	85.1	85.71	85.33

The suggested model outperforms CNN and FDNN by 2.9 and 1.4 degrees, respectively, with a G1 value of 85.33%. This proves that the suggested model is capable of enabling QNNs to take part in training tasks and produce satisfactory outcomes. Compared to CNN and FDNN, the suggested model performs similarly in terms of accuracy. Compared to CNN and FDNN, the proposed model is 2.3 and 1.2 times more accurate, respectively. Instead of FDNN's fuzzy membership function, which is the Gaussian function, the suggested model employs QNN mapping to improve the accuracy of multi-class classification.

On the precision of multi-category classification. Figure 7 displays the DirtyMNIST confusion matrices for all three models. The classification performance for '7' is the poorest, whereas the three models have higher accuracy for '0', '1', '2', and '6'. For category '3', HFQ-FNN shows substantially improved classification accuracy when compared to the other two models.

To assess the suggested model's efficacy, we compare it to DNN and FDNN on the 15-Scene dataset. Following the procedure outlined in (Deng, Ren, Kong, Bao, & Dai, 2016), we begin by preprocessing the 15-Scene data. In particular, we extract the dense SIFT features from every single picture. The next step is to group the local features into 200 codewords. Lastly, the fundamental allocation technique assigns the SIFT features to codewords that are 200 bits long. Our choice for the DNN's hidden layer was a 256 × 256 fully connected neural network with three layers. Using a ReLU function, we activate all of the network layers, and we set the dropout probability to 40%. The FDNN model and the proposed model are identical in that they both employ deep neural networks. Figure 6 shows the convergence of the proposed model on the 15-Scene dataset. As the number of training and verification epochs increases, the cross entropy of the two sets decreases; the curve flattens out around 110 epochs and keeps going downhill from there. The model has achieved convergence when the cross entropy stops decreasing.

Table 3 displays the results of the suggested model. The suggested model outperforms DNN and HDNN by 3.0% and 0.6%o, respectively, with an accuracy of 74.27%. The suggested model outperformed DNN and FDNN by 3.7 and 1.8 standard deviations, respectively, in terms of F1 value, reaching 74.15%. Using the dataset consisting of fifteen scenery images,

Figure 6. The analysis of training convergence on 15-Scene.

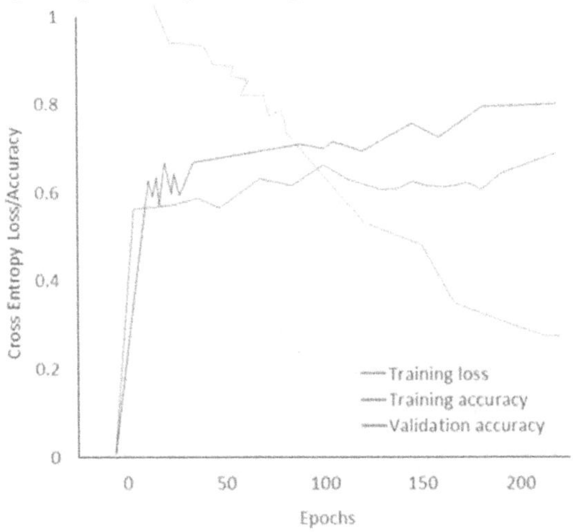

Table 3. A 15-Scene Performance Evaluation of the Proposed Model

Model	Accuracy	Recall	Precision	G1
DNN	73.99	72.13	73.06	71.96
FDNN	74.13	74.13	74.62	74.1
HFQ-FNN	74.27	74.27	74.9	74.15

Compared to DNN and FDNN, the suggested model outperforms them.

The goal of this research is to employ QNNs in the construction of fuzzy membership functions. One qubit is all that is needed by the suggested QNN. A quantum neural network (QNN) layer has a S_z gate for input data encoding and a S_A , S_z, S_A quantum gate with customisable parameters. There are three easily-findable parameters in a one-layer QNN. Parameters in this area of the network exhibit a linear growth pattern with increasing layer count. As opposed to the two-parameter (mean and variance) Gaussian membership function. The training difficulty of the suggested model grows in direct proportion to the QNN's layer count; however, the QNN gains the ability to learn a more appropriate fuzzy membership function.

Due to the possibility of quantum noise affecting the quantum component, the proposed fuzzy membership function does not construct its quantum circuit using two-qubit gates, such as the CNOT gate. The majority of quantum circuit noise comes from the CNOT gate because of its lengthy working duration. So, the quantum part is less noisy and easier to implement. What follows is a more in-depth analysis of quantum noise.

4.4 Robustness of Quantum Circuits

Environmental noise will influence the quantum system as it executes quantum circuits. The reliability of QNN is critically dependent on the quantum circuit's ability to withstand external noise. Consequently, we can state that a quantum circuit is robust if it is only slightly affected by external noise. Quantum circuits utilising a single qubit are the primary focus of this article. In quantum circuits, we shall model two kind of quantum noise—amplitude damping and depolarization noise:

Amplitude Damping (AD)

$$F_0 = \begin{pmatrix} 1 & 0 \\ 0 & \sqrt{1-\delta} \end{pmatrix} \quad F_1 = \begin{pmatrix} 1 & \sqrt{\delta} \\ 0 & 0 \end{pmatrix} \tag{24}$$

Depolarizing (DP)

$$F_0 = \sqrt{1-\delta}\begin{pmatrix} 1 & 0 \\ 0 & 1 \end{pmatrix} \quad F_1 = \sqrt{\frac{\delta}{3}}\begin{pmatrix} 0 & 1 \\ 1 & 0 \end{pmatrix}$$

$$F_2 = \sqrt{\frac{\delta}{3}}\begin{pmatrix} 1 & 0 \\ 0 & -1 \end{pmatrix} \quad F_3 = \sqrt{\frac{\delta}{3}}\begin{pmatrix} 0 & -j \\ j & 0 \end{pmatrix} \tag{25}$$

The dissipation of energy in quantum systems is described by amplitude damping. With a specific probability, depolarization noise explains how a quantum state can transition into a maximum mixed state ½. The quantum state is affected by noise with a probability denoted by δ.

As noise acts on quantum systems, operator-sum describes how this noise evolves:

$$\epsilon(q) = \sum_l F_l \sigma F_l^\dagger \tag{26}$$

where the evolved quantum system, denoted as $\{F_l\}$, is known as the Kraus operator and satisfies the equation $\sum_l F_l^\dagger F_l = J$. The modelling of noisy quantum circuits will be completed by applying a quantum noise behind each individual qubit gate.

When dealing with quantum circuits that incorporate noise, we can measure their noise tolerance using fidelity. The degree to which two quantum states are comparable is represented by fidelity:

$$G(\sigma,\tau) = U_s(\sqrt{\sqrt{\sigma\tau}\sqrt{\sigma}})^2 \quad (27)$$

In this case, we determine the degree of authenticity between the quantum states produced by the quantum circuit in the absence of quantum noise and those produced by the circuit when quantum noise is introduced. The quantum circuit's noise resistance improves as the fidelity approaches.

A real number between -1 and 1 is used as the input to the quantum circuit. We examined the impact of a 0.1 increase in the noise probability on 100 randomly selected input values ranging from -1 to 1. With respect to the quantum state of output.

Figure 7. Matrix confusions of various models on the Dirty-MNIST model.

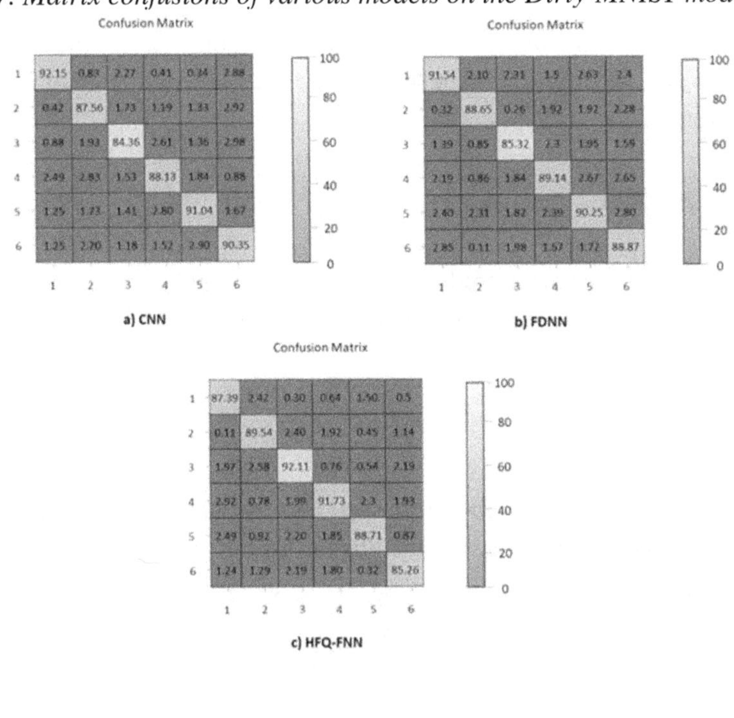

In Table 4, we display the quantum circuit fidelity for several noise probabilities: 0.01, 0.03, 0.05, 0.07, and 0.1. As the likelihood of noise rises, the quantum circuit's fidelity progressively declines. Despite a 0.1 chance of noise, the quantum circuit can still achieve a fidelity of 0.95. So, it's clear that the suggested HFQ-FNN is resistant to quantum noise.

Table 4. Reliability of a loud quantum circuit

γ	AD	DP
0.01	0.9964	0.995
0.03	0.9894	0.985
0.05	0.9823	0.975
0.07	0.9751	0.965
0.1	0.9644	0.95

V. DISCUSSION

5.1 Higher Qubit QNNs

In order to build a quantum circuit with more than one qubit, we use a multi-layer architecture that includes encoding and trainable blocks. Assuming there are o qubits, the S_z gate is utilised in the encoding block to encode the input element to the quantum state.

$$|y_j = \otimes_{r=1}^{o}\left(S_z(y_j)|0\square\right) \tag{28}$$

⊗ stands for the Kronecker product. A rotation layer and an entanglement layer make up the circuit of the trainable block. Each qubit has a S_z gate applied to it, making up the rotation layer.

$$V_{Rot}\left(\vartheta_m\right) = \otimes_{r=1}^{o} S_z\left(\vartheta_r^m\right) \tag{29}$$

Where $\vartheta_m = \left[\vartheta_{m'}^1, \vartheta_{m'}^2, \ldots, \vartheta_m^o\right]$. A pair of neighboring qubits are sequentially subjected to CNOT gates in the entanglement layer.

$$V_{Ent} = \prod_{r=1}^{o-1} CNOT_{(r,r+1)} \tag{30}$$

Where

$$CNOT = \begin{bmatrix} 1 & 00 & 0 \\ 0 & 10 & 0 \\ 0 & 00 & 1 \\ 0 & 01 & 0 \end{bmatrix}$$

. (31)

In CNOT, the number of qubits it affects is indicated by the subscript. Two labels are used to denote qubits: one for the control qubit and another for the target qubit. One way to describe the multi-qubit quantum circuit is as

$$V_{multi\_qubits} = \prod_{m} \left(V_{Ent} V_{Rot}(\vartheta_m) \otimes_{r=1}^{o} S_z(y_j) \right) \tag{32}$$

where the number of circuit layers is denoted by m. The expressive powers of multi-qubit quantum circuits are enhanced compared to single-qubit quantum circuits by including CNOT gates' entanglement and adding more spinning gates. It is possible to improve the model's accuracy by building multi-qubit QNNs.

5.2 Data Encoding Methods

This study presents an approach to quantum data encoding called angle encoding. To do this, one uses the classical data as the angle of rotation for a rotation gate, which then transforms the data into the corresponding quantum state. Further examples of popular encoding techniques are basis encoding and amplitude encoding. With just ⌈log[illegible]o ⌋qubits, the amplitude encoding method can encode a classical vector with o dimensions. With HFQ-FNN, the QNN's input is a real number, rendering amplitude encoding ineffective. Encoding data into the quantum state requires preparing binary integers 0 or 1 as $|0\rangle$ or $|1\rangle$, which is done by basis encoding. The article uses normalized data, which is a decimal value between -1 and 1, as its input. Before the data can be encoded into a quantum state, it must be translated to binary numbers. A huge number of qubits are needed for this method to encode data with a lot of decimal places. Despite the increased number of qubits, this approach has the potential to successfully extract data properties by capturing classical data discrepancies.

The ability of quantum algorithms to model and evaluate complex data linkages through superposition, entanglement, and interference makes quantum computing an ideal tool for neural networks and fuzzy logic. To be more precise, the created HFQ-FNN model uses parameterised quantum circuits, which stand for quantum fuzzy logic, to compute membership functions more accurately than traditional Gaussian-based functions. By utilising single-qubit circuits that incorporate several layers of trainable gates, it is feasible to convert inputs into quantum states. Data re-uploading is one method using this approach. Because of this, we can get better data representations and optimise more quickly. Using algorithms like the Parameter Shift Rule for gradient computing, quantum techniques differ from traditional approaches that rely on deterministic calculations. To meet the needs of quantum circuits, this algorithm was custom-made. Quantum fuzzy logic outperforms conventional neural networks in Dirty-MNIST and 15-Scene dataset classification tasks while also improving convergence efficiency. Challenges using both datasets have demonstrated that both methods provide more resilient handling of ambiguous or noisy datasets.

Hybrid system representation and classification are both enhanced by combining deep neural networks with quantum fuzzy logic, which addresses major shortcomings in existing approaches. For complicated, multi-modal datasets, traditional neural networks and fuzzy logic aren't up to the task of optimising performance or capturing subtle correlations in input that is unclear or noisy. A more accurate and versatile representation of input data may be achieved by HFQ-FNN with the help of quantum neural networks (QNNs) acting as fuzzy membership functions. Outperforming standard models in accuracy, convergence, and robustness, the HFQ-FNN architecture offers a robust framework for diverse datasets, including Dirty-MNIST and 15-Scene, through the neural and fuzzy feature fusion. By combining conventional and quantum computing, this innovative method has the ability to enhance multi-class categorisation.

6. CONCLUSION

An efficient and reliable method for structured picture classification tasks is offered by the Hierarchical Fused Quantum Fuzzy Neural Network (HFQ-FNN) design. A state-of-the-art framework for dealing with complicated data uncertainties, HFQ-FNN integrates quantum computing with fuzzy logic and neural networks. The fusion layer, classifier layer, and representation blocks of quantum fuzzy logic and deep neural networks collaborate to collect and combine key features for precise classification. Results from experiments on the Dirty-MNIST and 15-Scene datasets demonstrate that HFQ-FNN performs better. With an accuracy of 84.04% and the capacity to add quantum membership functions for better accuracy, HFQ-FNN outperformed CNN and FDNN on the Dirty-MNIST dataset by 2.9% and 1.4% in terms of G1 value, respectively. In a similar vein, HFQ-FNN achieved a far higher F1 value and an accuracy of 74.27% on the 15-Scene dataset, outperforming DNN and FDNN by 3.0% and 0.6%, respectively. In addition, we proved that HFQ-FNN is resilient to quantum noise; we achieved a fidelity of 0.95 with a 0.1 probability of noise. These findings provide credence to HFQ-FNN's ability to improve picture categorization accuracy with the use of quantum computing, and they suggest that this method could be useful in solving complicated data categorization problems across several fields.

REFERENCES

Al-Saidi, M., Ballagi, Á., Hassen, O. A., & Saad, S. M. (2024). Cognitive Classifier of Hand Gesture Images for Automated Sign Language Recognition: Soft Robot Assistance Based on Neutrosophic Markov Chain Paradigm. *Computers, 13*(4), 106. DOI: 10.3390/computers13040106

Alshennawy, A. A., & Aly, A. A. (2009). Edge detection in digital images using fuzzy logic technique. *International Journal of Computer and Information Engineering, 3*(3), 540-548. Zadeh, L. A. (1965). Fuzzy sets. *Information and Control, 8*(3), 338–353.

Arfi, B. (2010). *Linguistic fuzzy logic methods in social sciences* (Vol. 253). Springer. DOI: 10.1007/978-3-642-13343-5

Arif, Z. H., Mahmoud, M. A., Abdulkareem, K. H., Mohammed, M. A., Al-Mhiqani, M. N., Mutlag, A. A., & Damaševičius, R. (2022). Comprehensive review of machine learning (ML) in image defogging: Taxonomy of concepts, scenes, feature extraction, and classification techniques. *IET Image Processing, 16*(2), 289–310. DOI: 10.1049/ipr2.12365

Deng, Y., Ren, Z., Kong, Y., Bao, F., & Dai, Q. (2016). A hierarchical fused fuzzy deep neural network for data classification. *IEEE Transactions on Fuzzy Systems, 25*(4), 1006–1012. DOI: 10.1109/TFUZZ.2016.2574915

Glorot, X., & Bengio, Y. (2010, March). Understanding the difficulty of training deep feedforward neural networks. In *Proceedings of the thirteenth international conference on artificial intelligence and statistics* (pp. 249-256). JMLR Workshop and Conference Proceedings.

Howard, A. G., Zhu, M., Chen, B., Kalenichenko, D., Wang, W., Weyand, T., . . . Adam, H. (2017). Mobilenets: Efficient convolutional neural networks for mobile vision applications. *arXiv preprint arXiv:1704.04861.*

Huang, H. L., Xu, X. Y., Guo, C., Tian, G., Wei, S. J., Sun, X., Bao, W.-S., & Long, G. L. (2023). Near-term quantum computing techniques: Variational quantum algorithms, error mitigation, circuit compilation, benchmarking and classical simulation. *Science China. Physics, Mechanics & Astronomy, 66*(5), 250302. DOI: 10.1007/s11433-022-2057-y

Kak, S. C. (1995). Quantum neural computing. *Advances in Imaging and Electron Physics, 94*, 259–313. DOI: 10.1016/S1076-5670(08)70147-2

Kasabov, N. K. (2019). *Time-space, spiking neural networks and brain-inspired artificial intelligence*. Springer Berlin Heidelberg. DOI: 10.1007/978-3-662-57715-8

Kharsa, R., Bouridane, A., & Amira, A. (2023). Advances in Quantum Machine Learning and Deep Learning for Image Classification: A Survey. *Neurocomputing*, *560*, 126843. DOI: 10.1016/j.neucom.2023.126843

L'heureux, A., Grolinger, K., Elyamany, H. F., & Capretz, M. A. (2017). Machine learning with big data: Challenges and approaches. *IEEE Access : Practical Innovations, Open Solutions*, *5*, 7776–7797. DOI: 10.1109/ACCESS.2017.2696365

LeCun, Y., Bottou, L., Bengio, Y., & Haffner, P. (1998). Gradient-based learning applied to document recognition. *Proceedings of the IEEE*, *86*(11), 2278–2324. DOI: 10.1109/5.726791

Li, W., & Deng, D. L. (2022). Recent advances for quantum classifiers. *Science China. Physics, Mechanics & Astronomy*, *65*(2), 220301. DOI: 10.1007/s11433-021-1793-6

Lin, F. J., Lin, C. H., & Shen, P. H. (2001). Self-constructing fuzzy neural network speed controller for permanent-magnet synchronous motor drive. *IEEE Transactions on Fuzzy Systems*, *9*(5), 751–759. DOI: 10.1109/91.963761

Liu, Y., Arunachalam, S., & Temme, K. (2021). A rigorous and robust quantum speed-up in supervised machine learning. *Nature Physics*, *17*(9), 1013–1017. DOI: 10.1038/s41567-021-01287-z

Liu, Y., Zhang, D., Lu, G., & Ma, W. Y. (2007). A survey of content-based image retrieval with high-level semantics. *Pattern Recognition*, *40*(1), 262–282. DOI: 10.1016/j.patcog.2006.04.045

Long, G. L. (2023). Enhanced universality in quantum neural networks with fewer qubits and reduced circuit depth. *Science China. Physics, Mechanics & Astronomy*, *66*(7), 270361. DOI: 10.1007/s11433-023-2144-9

Melnichenko, G. (2010). Energy discriminant analysis, quantum logic, and fuzzy sets. *Journal of Multivariate Analysis*, *101*(1), 68–76. DOI: 10.1016/j.jmva.2009.04.011

Mitra, S., & Hayashi, Y. (2000). Neuro-fuzzy rule generation: Survey in soft computing framework. *IEEE Transactions on Neural Networks*, *11*(3), 748–768. DOI: 10.1109/72.846746 PMID: 18249802

Ngiam, J., Khosla, A., Kim, M., Nam, J., Lee, H., & Ng, A. Y. (2011). Multimodal deep learning. In *Proceedings of the 28th international conference on machine learning (ICML-11)* (pp. 689-696).

Patel, O. P., Bharill, N., Tiwari, A., & Prasad, M. (2019). A novel quantum-inspired fuzzy based neural network for data classification. *IEEE Transactions on Emerging Topics in Computing*, *9*(2), 1031–1044. DOI: 10.1109/TETC.2019.2901272

Rieffel, E., & Polak, W. (2000). An introduction to quantum computing for non-physicists. *ACM Computing Surveys*, *32*(3), 300–335. DOI: 10.1145/367701.367709

Sussillo, D., & Abbott, L. F. (2009). Generating coherent patterns of activity from chaotic neural networks. *Neuron*, *63*(4), 544–557. DOI: 10.1016/j.neuron.2009.07.018 PMID: 19709635

Tacchino, F., Chiesa, A., Carretta, S., & Gerace, D. (2020). Quantum computers as universal quantum simulators: State-of-the-art and perspectives. *Advanced Quantum Technologies*, *3*(3), 1900052. DOI: 10.1002/qute.201900052

Tiwari, P., Zhang, L., Qu, Z., & Muhammad, G. (2024). Quantum Fuzzy Neural Network for multimodal sentiment and sarcasm detection. *Information Fusion*, *103*, 102085. DOI: 10.1016/j.inffus.2023.102085

Van Gemert, J. C., Geusebroek, J. M., Veenman, C. J., & Smeulders, A. W. (2008). Kernel codebooks for scene categorization. In *Computer Vision–ECCV 2008: 10th European Conference on Computer Vision, Marseille, France, October 12-18, 2008* [Springer Berlin Heidelberg.]. *Proceedings*, *10*(Part III), 696–709.

Yazdinejad, A., Dehghantanha, A., Parizi, R. M., & Epiphaniou, G. (2023). An optimized fuzzy deep learning model for data classification based on NSGA-II. *Neurocomputing*, *522*, 116–128. DOI: 10.1016/j.neucom.2022.12.027

Zadeh, L. A. (1965). Fuzzy sets. *Information and Control*, *8*(3), 338–353. DOI: 10.1016/S0019-9958(65)90241-X

Zadeh, L. A. (2015). Fuzzy logic—A personal perspective. *Fuzzy Sets and Systems*, *281*, 4–20. DOI: 10.1016/j.fss.2015.05.009

Zhou, H., Li, Y., Xu, H., Su, Y., & Chen, L. (2023). A self-organizing fuzzy neural network modeling approach using an adaptive quantum particle swarm optimization. *Applied Intelligence*, *53*(11), 13569–13592. DOI: 10.1007/s10489-022-04133-8

Chapter 12
Insights on Building Quantum Convolutional Neural Networks

S. Sony Priya
https://orcid.org/0000-0002-8069-9223
SRM Institute of Science and Technology, India

R. I. Minu
SRM Institute of Science and Technology, India

ABSTRACT

The convolutional neural network (CNN) is a widely recognized model in computer vision due to its capability to utilize data correlation effectively. However, CNNs often face challenges when training on large datasets or dimensions. To address this, the Quantum Convolutional Neural Network (QCNN) introduces an innovative solution for CNN-based problems, specifically within quantum computing frameworks. By integrating CNN architecture into quantum environments, QCNN enhances the model's overall efficiency and functionality. This approach marks an initial effort to propose a solution for classification challenges in quantum physics and chemistry. Furthermore, the study highlights a computational method utilizing the Multi-scale Entanglement Renormalization Ansatz (MERA) with logarithmic depth O(log(n)). Experiments conducted using the TensorFlow Quantum platform on the MNIST dataset demonstrate that QCNNs can achieve faster learning compared to conventional CNNs.

DOI: 10.4018/979-8-3693-6225-9.ch012

INTRODUCTION

Convolutional Neural Networks (CNNs) have emerged as a cornerstone in modern artificial intelligence applications, particularly in domains such as computer vision, audio processing, and face recognition. Their ability to automatically recognize and extract significant features from data without manual intervention is a testament to their design efficiency. CNNs achieve this through key mechanisms such as parameter sharing, convolution operations, and pooling, which reduce computational complexity compared to fully connected networks. This makes CNNs adaptable and versatile for deployment across a wide range of devices and platforms LeCun et al. (1998). However, as the scale and dimensionality of datasets grow, classical CNNs face critical limitations. The computational demands of classical CNNs scale dramatically with data size and complexity, leading to inefficiencies in both training and inference. This challenge is further exacerbated by the dependency on vast amounts of labeled data, which requires substantial effort to curate, and the need for high-performance computational infrastructure. Such requirements make it challenging to deploy classical CNNs efficiently in large-scale, real-world applications LeCun et al. (1998), Goodfellow et al. (2016).

As datasets grow, classical CNNs often struggle with the curse of dimensionality, where computational costs increase exponentially due to the high number of parameters and layers. Additionally, training large models on high-dimensional data requires significant memory and computational power, often resulting in bottlenecks in scalability and real-time performance. To overcome these challenges, researchers have turned to quantum computing, a paradigm that leverages the principles of quantum superposition, entanglement, and parallelism to achieve exponential speedups for certain computational tasks Nielsen & Chuang (2010).

Superposition, a core quantum mechanical concept, allows a quantum system to exist in multiple states concurrently. Unlike traditional bits that represent either 0 or 1, quantum bits (qubits) can exist in a superposition of both states. This enables Quantum Convolutional Neural Networks (QCNNs) to investigate numerous computational paths simultaneously, resulting in significant acceleration of data processing and model training Nielsen & Chuang (2010). For instance, in QCNNs, superposition enables concurrent exploration of feature spaces, leading to faster convergence during learning. Entanglement, another crucial quantum property, describes the correlation between quantum particles where the state of one particle is instantly linked to another, regardless of spatial separation. In QCNNs, entanglement aids in encoding complex relationships between data features, improving the model's capacity to identify intricate patterns in high-dimensional datasets Bell (1964).

By harnessing quantum properties like superposition for parallel exploration of computational pathways and entanglement for encoding complex data relationships, QCNNs can process high-dimensional datasets more efficiently. These quantum mechanisms decrease training times and improve scalability, addressing the computational limitations faced by classical CNNs. Superposition allows QCNNs to evaluate a vast number of computational states concurrently, optimizing feature space exploration. Entanglement enhances the model's ability to learn intricate data correlations by linking multiple features simultaneously. Collectively, these principles provide QCNNs with distinct computational advantages over classical CNNs, particularly when dealing with large-scale and complex data.

A notable advancement at the intersection of quantum computing and machine learning is the QCNN. QCNNs modify the architecture of classical CNNs for a quantum environment, leveraging quantum properties to enhance computational efficiency and performance. By utilizing the parallel computation capabilities of quantum systems, QCNNs can process high-dimensional data more effectively than their classical counterparts. This integration has created new opportunities for addressing the scalability issues inherent in classical machine learning models.

The main benefit of QCNNs lies in their ability to exploit quantum properties such as superposition and entanglement to decrease both learning and computation time. These properties allow QCNNs to assess multiple computational paths concurrently, enabling faster convergence during training. Moreover, QCNNs are particularly well-suited for processing high-dimensional data, where classical CNNs often struggle with inefficiencies. By incorporating classical CNN operations within a quantum framework, QCNNs enhance feature extraction and generalization capabilities, even in scenarios with limited resources.

A critical advancement in QCNNs is the integration of the Multi-scale Entanglement Renormalization Ansatz (MERA), which introduces a hierarchical structure with logarithmic depth . This design combines hierarchical quantum states with Quantum Error Correction, allowing for effective encoding and processing of extensive datasets. The hierarchical structure of MERA compresses quantum states efficiently, capturing essential features across multiple scales while reducing computational complexity. This enables QCNNs to achieve faster convergence and scalability compared to traditional architectures.

Despite these advantages, current quantum hardware imposes significant constraints. The size of quantum simulators remains inadequate to support large-scale QCNN implementations, currently limiting their practical applicability (Schuld et al., 2014). To tackle these issues, researchers have developed innovative QCNN structures, each employing distinct strategies to enhance efficiency and scalability. For example, Cong et al. (2019) created a QCNN framework based on MERA, facilitating hierarchical reduction of data dimensions while preserving crucial features, thus decreasing computational complexity.

In a separate advancement, MacCormack et al. (2022) introduced the branching QCNN (bQCNN) to overcome limitations in conventional QCNNs, such as the "dying ReLU" issue. The bQCNN structure incorporates mid-circuit measurements that dynamically influence subsequent quantum operations based on intermediate results. This adaptive mechanism enhances the flexibility and expressiveness of QCNN models by introducing a broader set of trainable parameters. The branching feature also improves the model's resilience, making it applicable to a wider range of uses.

Another notable contribution is the introduction of quanvolutional layers by Parisi et al. (2022). These layers apply localized quantum operations to input data using random quantum circuits, similar to classical convolutional filters. However, unlike their classical counterparts, quanvolutional layers utilize quantum phenomena such as entanglement and superposition to improve feature extraction. This method has shown potential in enhancing the representational power of quantum models while maintaining computational efficiency.

Lastly, LaRose and Coyle (2020) proposed an innovative approach to filter construction in QCNNs, aimed at minimizing quantum gate complexity. By optimizing the design of quantum filters, their architecture reduces resource requirements without sacrificing performance. This development addresses one of the key obstacles in scaling QCNNs for practical applications.

The progress in QCNN architectures has significant implications for both theoretical research and practical applications. In quantum physics, QCNNs offer a powerful tool for simulating complex quantum systems and analyzing entangled states. For instance, the MERA-based QCNN architecture has been applied to study many-body quantum systems, providing insights into their hierarchical structures and correlations (Cong et al., 2019). Similarly, in quantum chemistry, QCNNs show promise for accelerating simulations of molecular structures and chemical reactions, which are computationally demanding on classical systems.

Beyond quantum domains, QCNNs also demonstrate potential in traditional machine learning applications. Their ability to efficiently process high-dimensional data makes them suitable for tasks such as image classification, speech recognition, and natural language processing. Furthermore, the integration of quanvolutional layers and branching mechanisms could lead to more robust and adaptive models for real-world deployment. As quantum hardware continues to improve, the scalability and applicability of QCNNs are expected to increase, paving the way for breakthroughs in fields such as cryptography, optimization, and artificial intelligence.

To validate the potential of QCNNs, this study implements a QCNN architecture on the MNIST dataset, demonstrating its effectiveness in achieving comparable accuracy to traditional CNNs while offering enhanced computational efficiency. The results underscore the viability of QCNNs in real-world applications and highlight their promise for future advancements in quantum machine learning.

Preliminaries

Convolutional Neural Network

A primary benefit of CNNs is its capacity to autonomously recognize and extract the essential features from the images without requiring manual intervention. This process begins by feeding an image into the CNN, where a sequence of convolutional and pooling operations is applied. The resulting output from these layers is passed through a fully connected layer to perform classification. By utilizing an optimizer, the model's performance is further refined by minimizing the loss function.CNNs face challenges when dealing with high-dimensional inputs or extensive datasets, as their learning effectiveness decreases. Moreover, the computational complexity rises with an increase in the number of neurons. To tackle these issues, Quantum-MachineLearning has emerged as a promising solution, offering efficient methods for handling large-scale data and reducing computational burden.

Figure 1. CNN Architecture

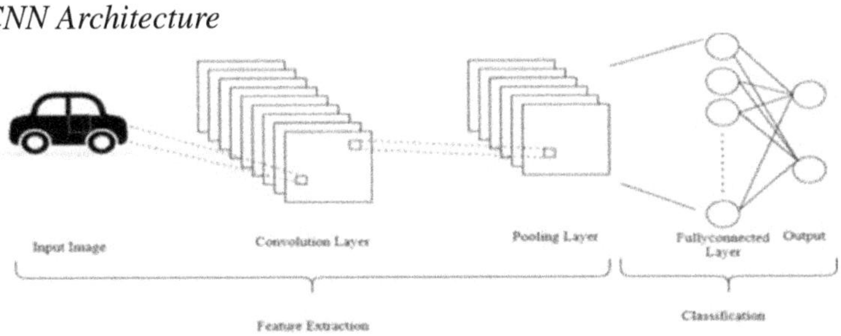

Quantum basis:

A bit is the fundamental unit of information in a classical computer, capable of holding a value of either 0 or 1. In contrast, a qubit is a quantum computer's basic unit of information. Unlike a bit, a qubit can hold a value of $|0\rangle$ or $|1\rangle$ or something in between these values known as superposition. An n-qubit quantum computer exists in a superposition of 2^n states. A single qubit is mathematically represented as:

$$q = \alpha|0\rangle + \beta|1\rangle \tag{1}$$

Here α and β are referred to as amplitudes, which is a complex number and satisfies $\alpha^2+\beta^2=1$. The quantum states $|0\rangle$ and $|1\rangle$ are represented by bra-ket notation or Dirac notation which uses angle brackets ⟨, ⟩, and a vertical bar | and its vector representations are:

$$|0\rangle=\begin{pmatrix}1\\0\end{pmatrix}\ |1\rangle=\begin{pmatrix}0\\1\end{pmatrix} \tag{2}$$

In quantum computing, quantum algorithms operate by executing quantum operations called quantum gates on a selection of qubits. A quantum circuit represents a quantum algorithm through the use of gates. Commonly used quantum gates along with their matrix representations and the notation required for constructing quantum circuits are illustrated in Table 1.

Table 1. Quantum gates

Gate	Equation	Input	Output	Matrix	Notation
X (Pauli-X)	$X=\|0\rangle\langle 1\|+\|1\rangle\langle 0\|$	$\|0\rangle$ $\|1\rangle$	$\|1\rangle$ $\|0\rangle$	$x=\begin{bmatrix}0&1\\1&0\end{bmatrix}$	X
Y (Pauli-Y)	$Y=-i\|0\rangle\langle 1\|+i\|1\rangle\langle 0\|$	$\|0\rangle$ $\|1\rangle$	$i\|1\rangle$ $-i\|0\rangle$	$y=\begin{bmatrix}0&-i\\i&0\end{bmatrix}$	Y
Z (Pauli-Z or phase-flip)	$Z=\|0\rangle\langle 0\|-\|1\rangle\langle 1\|$	$\|0\rangle$ $\|1\rangle$	$\|0\rangle$ $-\|1\rangle$	$z=\begin{bmatrix}1&0\\0&-0\end{bmatrix}$	Z
I (Identity gate)	$I=\|0\rangle\langle 0\|+\|1\rangle\langle 1\|$	$\|0\rangle$ $\|1\rangle$	$\|0\rangle$ $\|1\rangle$	$I=\begin{bmatrix}1&0\\0&1\end{bmatrix}$	I
R_x	$R_x(\theta)=\cos(\theta/2)\ I-i\sin(\theta/2)\ X$		Rotates qubit along x axis by θ radians	$R_x(\theta)=\begin{pmatrix}\cos(\theta/2)&-j\sin(\theta/2)\\-j\sin(\theta/2)&\cos(\theta/2)\end{pmatrix}$	R_x
R_y	$R_y(\theta)=\cos(\theta/2)\ I-i\sin(\theta/2)\ Y$		Rotates qubit along y axis by θ radians	$R_y(\theta)=\begin{pmatrix}\cos(\theta/2)&-\sin(\theta/2)\\\sin(\theta/2)&\cos(\theta/2)\end{pmatrix}$	Ry
R_z	$R_z(\phi)=\cos(\phi/2)\ I-i\sin(\phi/2)\ Z$		Rotates qubit along z axis by ϕ radians	$R_z(\phi)=\begin{pmatrix}e^{-i\phi/2}&0\\0&e^{i\phi/2}\end{pmatrix}$	Rz
CNOT	$CNOT=\|0\rangle\langle 0\|\oplus I+\|1\rangle\langle 1\|\oplus X$	$\|00\rangle$ $\|01\rangle$ $\|10\rangle$ $\|11\rangle$	$\|00\rangle$ $\|10\rangle$ $\|11\rangle$ $\|01\rangle$	$CNOT=\begin{pmatrix}1&0&0&0\\0&1&0&0\\0&0&0&1\\0&0&1&0\end{pmatrix}$	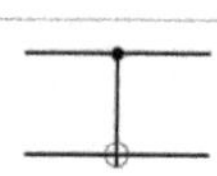
H (Hadamard Gate)	$H=\frac{\|0\rangle+\|1\rangle}{\sqrt{2}}\langle 0\|+\frac{\|0\rangle-\|1\rangle}{\sqrt{2}}\langle 1\|$	$\|0\rangle$ $\|1\rangle$	$\frac{1}{\sqrt{2}}(\|0\rangle+\|1\rangle)$ $\frac{1}{\sqrt{2}}(\|0\rangle-\|1\rangle)$	$H=\frac{1}{\sqrt{2}}\begin{pmatrix}1&1\\1&-1\end{pmatrix}$	H

Quantum Convolutional Neural Network:

Building on the principles of conventional CNNs, QCNN is composed of three key components: the quantum convolutional layer, the quantum pooling layer, and the fully connected layer (Zheng et al., 2023). The quantum convolutional layer is designed using multiple two-qubit universal gates. Similar to classical CNNs, QCNN incorporates local connections and parameter sharing. These features are achieved by implementing the quantum convolutional layer with several two-qubit gates, facilitating interactions between neighboring qubits while maintaining a consistent set of parameters across all qubits.

Before convolution operations can be performed, conventional input data must be transformed into quantum data through a process known as quantum state preparation or data encoding (Schuld, M et al., 2015). This process translates classical information into quantum states within a Hilbert space using a quantum feature map. Several data encoding methods are available to achieve this goal (Ranga et al., 2024).

Data Encoding Methods

Basis encoding. In basis encoding, the real number i.e., the input X is converted into binary number $b_{n-1} \ldots\ldots b_1 b_0$, then this binary number is transformed into quantum state $| b_{n-1} \ldots b_1 b_0 \rangle$. Figure 2 shows an example of basis encoding.

Figure 2. Basis encoding

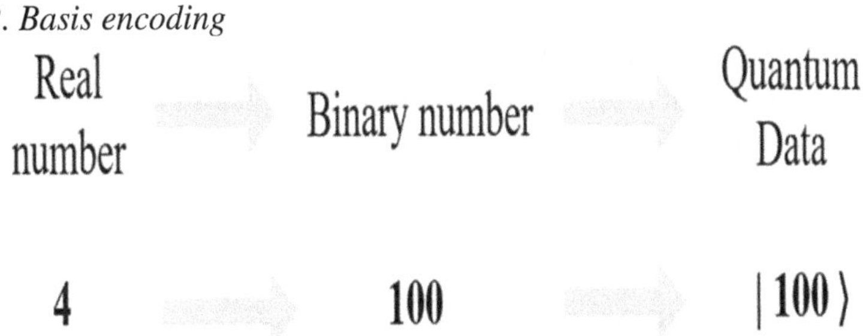

Amplitude Encoding. Amplitude encoding conveys information via the amplitudes of a quantum state. This approach is also referred to as Wavefunction Encoding (LaRose R & Coyle B,2020). It maps an Input vector v of length n, n must be power of two, into amplitudes of an N-qubit quantum state. The required number of qubits is given by $N=\lceil \log_2(n) \rceil$.

$$|\Psi\rangle=\sum_{i}^{n} v_i |i\rangle \quad (3)$$

AngleEncoding. Angle Encoding is commonly referred to as tensor product encoding or qubit encoding. This method involves encoding data by applying x- or y-axis gate rotation to the value to be encoded. Here, x_i denotes the feature vector.

$$|\Psi\rangle = \otimes_{i=1}^{N} \cos(x_i)|0\rangle + \sin(x_i)|1\rangle \tag{4}$$

Quantum Random Access Memory (QRAM) encoding. This encoding technique works based on classical RAM.QRAM takes superposition of 2 addresses as input and produces output as superposition of addresses and the values in the corresponding addresses. This is explained in figure 3.

Figure 3. QRAM encoding

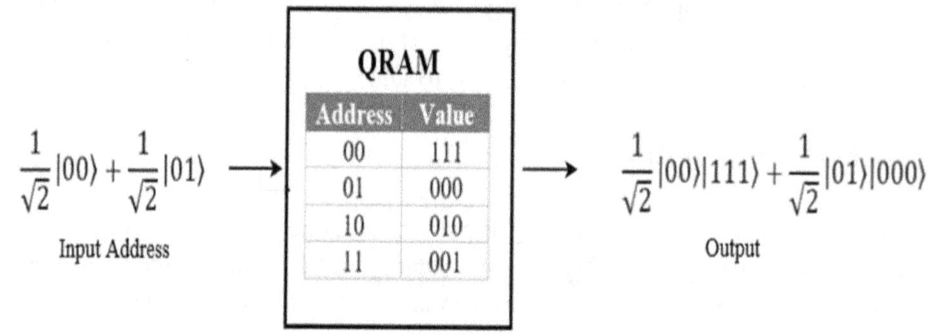

Quantum Associative memory (QuAM) Encoding. QuAM encoding technique gets n data points encoded using basis encoding and outputs a superposition of these n data points in a qubit register.

$$|\Psi\rangle = \sum_{i=1}^{n} \frac{1}{\sqrt{n}} |x_i\rangle \tag{5}$$

Quantum Convolutional Layer

Following the encoding process, the resulting quantum representation is passed to the convolutional layer.This layer consists of several universal two-qubit gates (U_i) that facilitate interactions between adjacent qubits while sharing the same parameter. Similar to classical CNNs, QCNN exhibits local connections and parameter sharing. During the convolution operation, the input is convolved with a set of kernels or filters to extract critical features. For the *h*-th layer, consider the input as X^h and the kernel as k^h, with the convolution operation output represented as $X^h * k^h$, which is referred to as feature map.

The integration of Convolutional Neural Networks (CNNs) into quantum computing environments leverages unique quantum properties, such as superposition, entanglement, parameter sharing, and measurement-based data reduction. Quantum computing allows for parallelism through superposition, faster extraction via entanglement, and reduced computational complexity through parameter sharing. In QCNNs, measurements serve both as activation functions and data reducers, while shallow quantum circuits mitigate gradient vanishing issues, enabling efficient learning.

Multi-Scale Entanglement Renormalization Ansatz (MERA)

The Multi-scale Entanglement Renormalization Ansatz (MERA) (Cong et al., 2019) introduces a hierarchical structure with logarithmic depth O(log(n)), enabling QCNNs to efficiently compress and process quantum states. This hierarchical reduction mitigates the computational complexity typically associated with high-dimensional data, allowing for faster convergence during training. For example, consider a dataset represented as a quantum state that encodes correlations between data points at multiple scales. MERA's hierarchical design systematically disentangles short-range correlations at each level while preserving long-range correlations. This process reduces the size of the dataset progressively while retaining critical features necessary for accurate learning.

Unlike traditional convolutional approaches, where computational costs scale linearly with data size, MERA's logarithmic depth allows it to handle high-dimensional data more efficiently. By capturing multi-scale entanglement and compressing data hierarchically, MERA significantly reduces the number of operations needed for feature extraction, making it more scalable for complex datasets. This capability is particularly advantageous in quantum environments, where resource constraints are more pronounced than in classical systems.

Quantum Pooling Layer

The quantum pooling layer succeeds the quantum convolutional layer. This layer, akin to conventional neural networks, reduces the feature map dimensions using controlled gates and quantum measurements. Common quantum gates include $\{R_y, R_z, R_y^{\dagger}, R_z^{\dagger}\}$, which can be utilized for controlled operations. Rotational gates are typically employed in constructing fully connected layers. The final step involves applying measurements to extract essential information and transforming quantum data into classical data during this stage.

In Quantum CNN, measurement acts as an activation function, similar to classical CNNs. Additionally, backpropagation and optimization are carried out as in conventional models. A significant restriction of QNNs is the potential for the gradient to diminish exponentially with an increase in the number of qubits. In Classical Deep Neural Networks (CDNNs), the gradient may similarly decline exponentially as the number of layers increases. To resolve this, shallow circuits utilizing a limited number of qubits are utilized (Cerezo et al., 2021). Figure 4 illustrates the general architecture of QCNN.

Figure 4. QCNN Architecture

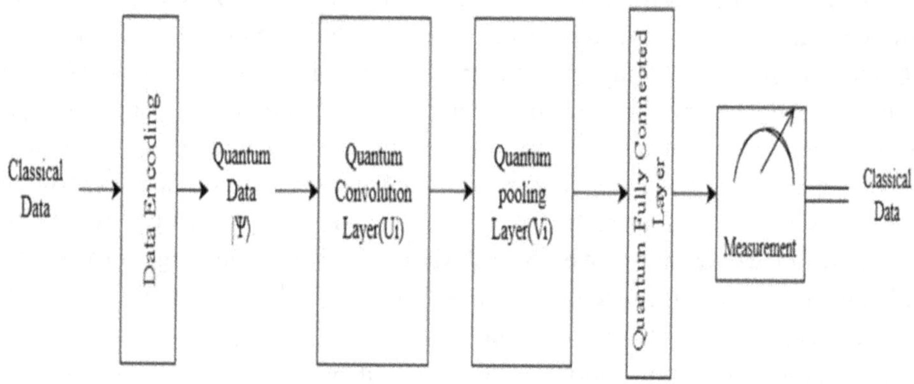

IMPLEMENTATION

This study utilizes the MNIST dataset(LeCun, Y et al., 1998) to assess the effectiveness of the QCNN model in comparison to the conventional CNN. A dataset of 60,000 handwritten numbers from 0 to 9 is used for training and 10,000 for testing. Each image is represented as a 28×28 grayscale picture.The classification capabilities of both CNN and QCNN models were assessed using this dataset. For the experiments, images were resized to 10×10 inches, ensuring an equal number of layers in both models. The QCNN model used in this study is depicted in Figure 5. All experiments were conducted using IBM's Qiskit quantum environment. The sparse categorical cross-entropy loss function, used to measure prediction errors, was employed, while the Adam optimizer, designed to efficiently minimize the loss, was chosen for optimization

Figure 5. QCNN Model

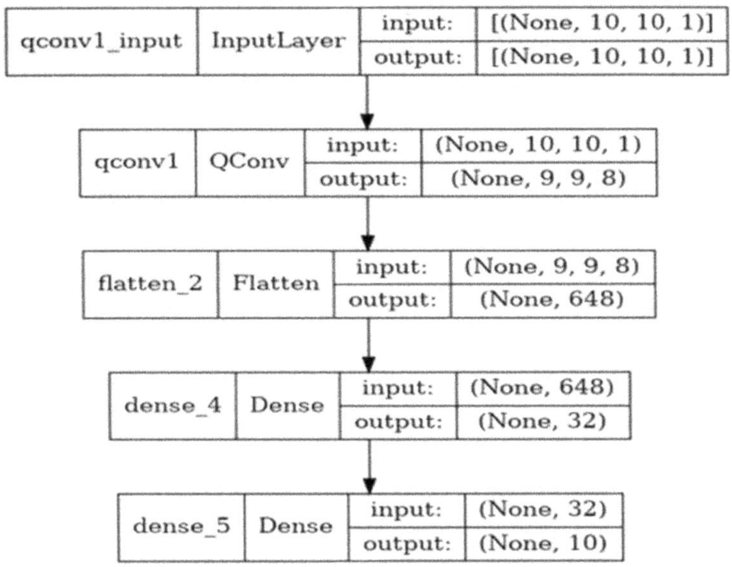

The training process for this model exceeds five hours. The CNN model demonstrates an accuracy of 95.70%, while the QCNN model achieves 95.32%. Figure 6 illustrates a comparison of the validation loss and validation accuracy of the CNN and QCNN models over multiple epochs.

Figure 6. Validation Loss and Accuracy Comparison Between CNN and QCNN

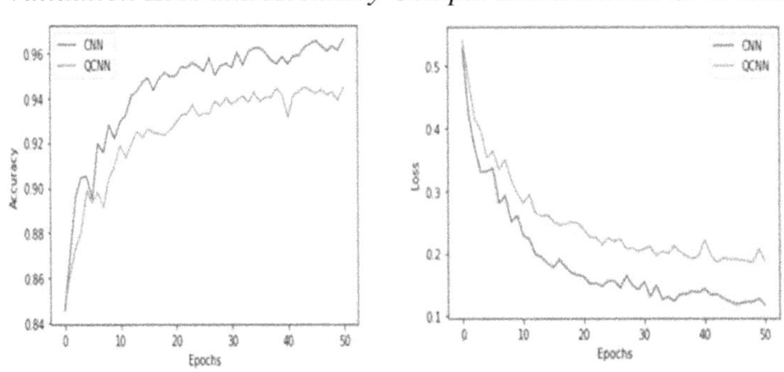

CONCLUSION

This study introduces a QCNN architecture for standard machine learning classification problems.The network structure and initialization methods significantly affect overall effectiveness. Optimizing the performance of the learning model can be achieved through the meticulous design of internal quantum circuits. The calculation of quantum gradients during backpropagation necessitates extensive quantum circuit evaluations, with computational demands varying based on circuit depth or width. The proposed QCNN model shows its ability to effectively categorize visual information from the MNIST dataset, achieving accuracy levels comparable to those of traditional CNNs. Future investigations could expand this QCNN framework to tackle additional challenges across diverse fields.

REFERENCES

Bell, J. S. (1964). On the einstein podolsky rosen paradox. *Physics Physique Fizika*, 1(3), 195–200. DOI: 10.1103/PhysicsPhysiqueFizika.1.195

Cerezo, M., Sone, A., Volkoff, T., Cincio, L., & Coles, P. J. (2021). Cost function dependent barren plateaus in shallow parametrized quantum circuits. *Nature Communications*, 12(1), 1–12. DOI: 10.1038/s41467-021-21728-w PMID: 33741913

Chalumuri, A., Kune, R., Kannan, S., & Manoj, B. S. (2021). Quantum-enhanced deep neural network architecture for image scene classification. *Quantum Information Processing*, 20(11), 1–21. DOI: 10.1007/s11128-021-03314-7

Cong, I., Choi, S., & Lukin, M. D. (2019). Quantum convolutional neural networks. *Nature Physics*, 15(12), 1273–1278. DOI: 10.1038/s41567-019-0648-8

Goodfellow, I., Bengio, Y., & Courville, A. (2016). *Deep Learning*. MIT Press.

LaRose, R., & Coyle, B. (2020). Robust data encodings for quantum classifiers. *Physical Review. A*, 102(3), 032420. DOI: 10.1103/PhysRevA.102.032420

LeCun, Y., Bottou, L., Bengio, Y., & Haffner, P. (1998). Gradient-based learning applied to document recognition. *Proceedings of the IEEE*, 86(11), 2278–2324. DOI: 10.1109/5.726791

MacCormack, I., Delaney, C., Galda, A., Aggarwal, N., & Narang, P. (2022). Branching quantum convolutional neural networks. *Physical Review Research*, 4(1), 013117. DOI: 10.1103/PhysRevResearch.4.013117

McClean, J. R., Boixo, S., Smelyanskiy, V. N., Babbush, R., & Neven, H. (2018). Barren plateaus in quantum neural network training landscapes. *Nature Communications*, 9(1), 1–6. DOI: 10.1038/s41467-018-07090-4 PMID: 30446662

Nielsen, M. A., & Chuang, I. L. (2010). *Quantum computation and quantum information*. Cambridge university press.

Parisi, L., Neagu, D., Ma, R., & Campean, F. (2022). Quantum ReLU activation for Convolutional Neural Networks to improve diagnosis of Parkinson's disease and COVID-19. *Expert Systems with Applications*, 187, 115892. DOI: 10.1016/j.eswa.2021.115892

Ranga, D., Rana, A., Prajapat, S., Kumar, P., Kumar, K., & Vasilakos, A. V. (2024). Quantum Machine Learning: Exploring the Role of Data Encoding Techniques, Challenges, and Future Directions. *Mathematics*, 12(21), 3318. DOI: 10.3390/math12213318

Schuld, M., Sinayskiy, I., & Petruccione, F. (2014). The quest for a quantum neural network. *Quantum Information Processing*, 13(11), 2567–2586. DOI: 10.1007/s11128-014-0809-8

Schuld, M., Sinayskiy, I., & Petruccione, F. (2015). An introduction to quantum machine learning. *Contemporary Physics*, 56(2), 172–185. DOI: 10.1080/00107514.2014.964942

Zheng, J., Gao, Q., Lü, J., Ogorzałek, M., Pan, Y., & Lü, Y. (2023). Design of a quantum convolutional neural network on quantum circuits. *Journal of the Franklin Institute*, 360(17), 13761–13777. DOI: 10.1016/j.jfranklin.2022.07.033

Compilation of References

Adikari, A., Burnett, D., Sedera, D., De Silva, D., & Alahakoon, D. (2021). Value co-creation for open innovation: An evidence-based study of the data driven paradigm of social media using machine learning. *International Journal of Information Management Data Insights*, 1(2), 100022. DOI: 10.1016/j.jjimei.2021.100022

Ahmadi, A. (2023). Quantum Computing and Artificial Intelligence: The Synergy of Two Revolutionary Technologies. *Asian Journal of Electrical Sciences*, 12(2), 15–27. DOI: 10.51983/ajes-2023.12.2.4118

Ahmed, R. G. (2018). Hyperthy and renal disorders. [DOI]. *Animal and Veterinary Sciences*, 6(1), 1–10. PMID: 29301274

Ahn, D., Lee, J., Kim, M. S., & Hwang, S. W. (2002). SelfConsistent non-Markovian theory of a quantum-state evolution for quantum-information-processing. *Physical Review A*, 66(1), 012302. DOI: 10.1103/PhysRevA.66.012302

Ajagekar, A., & You, F. (2019). Quantum computing for energy systems optimization: Challenges and opportunities. *Energy*, 179, 76–89. DOI: 10.1016/j.energy.2019.04.186

Akman, G., Yorur, B., Boyaci, A. I., & Chiu, M.-C. (2023). Assessing innovation capabilities of manufacturing companies by combination of unsupervised and supervised machine learning approaches. *Applied Soft Computing*, 147, 110735. DOI: 10.1016/j.asoc.2023.110735

Alet, F., Hanada, M., Jevicki, A., & Peng, C. (2021). Entanglement and confinement in coupled quantum systems. *The Journal of High Energy Physics*, 2021(2), 1–31. DOI: 10.1007/JHEP02(2021)034

Alexeev, Y., Bacon, D., Brown, K. R., Calderbank, R., Carr, L. D., Chong, F. T., DeMarco, B., Englund, D., Farhi, E., Fefferman, B., Gorshkov, A. V., Houck, A., Kim, J., Kimmel, S., Lange, M., Lloyd, S., Lukin, M. D., Maslov, D., Maunz, P., & Thompson, J. (2021). Quantum computer systems for scientific discovery. *PFX Quantum : a Physical Review Journal*, 2(1), 017001. DOI: 10.1103/PRXQuantum.2.017001

Aliferis, P., Gottesman, D., & Preskill, J. (2008). Accuracy threshold for Quantum Computation. *Quant. Inf. Proc.*, 8, 181–244.

Al-Saidi, M., Ballagi, Á., Hassen, O. A., & Saad, S. M. (2024). Cognitive Classifier of Hand Gesture Images for Automated Sign Language Recognition: Soft Robot Assistance Based on Neutrosophic Markov Chain Paradigm. *Computers*, 13(4), 106. DOI: 10.3390/computers13040106

Alshennawy, A. A., & Aly, A. A. (2009). Edge detection in digital images using fuzzy logic technique. *International Journal of Computer and Information Engineering, 3*(3), 540-548. Zadeh, L. A. (1965). Fuzzy sets. *Information and Control*, 8(3), 338–353.

Altmann, P., Sünkel, L., Stein, J., Müller, T., Roch, C., & Linnhoff-Popien, C. (2023). Sequent: Towards traceable quantum machine learning using sequential quantum enhanced training. *arXiv Preprint arXiv:2301.02601*. DOI: 10.5220/0011772400003393

Anbazhagu, U., Priyadharshini, K., Deepajothi, S., Haripriya, M., & Banu, E. A. (2025). Quantum Computing in Healthcare Using AI-Driven Medical Technologies. In *Modern SuperHyperSoft Computing Trends in Science and Technology* (pp. 367–398). IGI Global Scientific Publishing.

Arasu, B. S., Seelan, B. J. B., & Thamaraiselvan, N. (2020). A machine learning-based approach to enhancing social media marketing. *Computers & Electrical Engineering*, 86, 106723. DOI: 10.1016/j.compeleceng.2020.106723

Arfi, B. (2010). *Linguistic fuzzy logic methods in social sciences* (Vol. 253). Springer. DOI: 10.1007/978-3-642-13343-5

Arif, Z. H., Mahmoud, M. A., Abdulkareem, K. H., Mohammed, M. A., Al-Mhiqani, M. N., Mutlag, A. A., & Damaševičius, R. (2022). Comprehensive review of machine learning (ML) in image defogging: Taxonomy of concepts, scenes, feature extraction, and classification techniques. *IET Image Processing*, 16(2), 289–310. DOI: 10.1049/ipr2.12365

Arshad, M. W., Murtza, I., & Arshad, M. A. (2023). Applications of Quantum Computing in Health Sector. Journal of Data Science and Intelligent Systems.

Arute, F., Arya, K., Babbush, R., Bacon, J., Bardin, J. C., Barends, R., Biswas, R., Boixo, S., Brandao, F. G. S. L., Buell, D. A., Burkett, B., Chen, Y., Chen, Z., Chiaro, B., Collins, R., Courtney, W., Dunsworth, A., Farhi, E., Foxen, B., & Martinis, J. M. (2022). Quantum supremacy using a programmable superconducting processor. *Nature*, 574(7779), 505–510. DOI: 10.1038/s41586-019-1666-5 PMID: 31645734

Arya, A., Devadas, M. S., Lakshmi, T. H., Yogeesh, N., & Maaliw, R. R.III (2024). Quantum-Inspired Optimization in AI for Healthcare Networks. In *Quantum Networks and Their Applications in AI* (pp. 197–213). IGI Global. DOI: 10.4018/979-8-3693-5832-0.ch013

Aspuru-Guzik, A., Whitfield, J. D., Gidney, C., & Neven, H. (2023). Quantum computing for chemistry: A review. *Nature Reviews. Chemistry*, 7(1), 1–20. 10.1038/s41570-022-00400-0 PMID: 37117828

Awan, U., Hannola, L., Tandon, A., Goyal, R. K., & Dhir, A. (2022). Quantum computing challenges in the software industry. A fuzzy AHP-based approach. *Information and Software Technology*, 147, 106896. DOI: 10.1016/j.infsof.2022.106896

Awaysheh, A., Wilcke, J., Elvinger, F., Rees, L., Fan, W., & Zimmerman, K. L. (2019). Review of medical decision support and machine-learning methods. *Veterinary Pathology*, 56(4), 512–525. DOI: 10.1177/0300985819829524 PMID: 30866728

Babu, C. S., Sudhir, M., & Kumar, S. (2024). Application of Support Vector Machine Algorithm in Automated Lending Protocols for Decentralized Finance Platforms. In *Decentralized Finance and Tokenization in FinTech* (pp. 1–20). IGI Global.

Bacon, D. (2006). Operator Quantum Error-Correcting Subsystems for self-correcting quantum memories. *Physical Review A*, 73(1), 012340. DOI: 10.1103/PhysRevA.73.012340

Bacon, D. (2008). Stability of quantum concatenated-code Hamiltonians. [DOI]. *Physical Review A*, 78(4), 042310. DOI: 10.1103/PhysRevA.78.042324

Baek, C., Ostuka, T., Tarucha, S., & Choi, B. S. (2018). Density-matrix simulation of logical qubit using 3-qubit quantum error correction code. *arXiv*. https://doi.org//arXiv.1807.06767DOI: 10.48550

Balki, I., Amirabadi, A., Levman, J., Martel, A. L., Emersic, Z., Meden, B., Garcia-Pedrero, A., Ramirez, S. C., Kong, D., Moody, A. R., & Tyrrell, P. N. (2019). Sample-size determination methodologies for machine learning in medical imaging research: A systematic review. *Canadian Association of Radiologists Journal*, 70(4), 344–353. DOI: 10.1016/j.carj.2019.06.002 PMID: 31522841

Barrett, S. D., & Milburn, G. J. (2003). Measuring the Decoherence rate in a semiconductor charge qubit. *Physical Review B: Condensed Matter*, 68(15), 155307. DOI: 10.1103/PhysRevB.68.155307

Basán, N. P., Cóccola, M. E., Dondo, R. G., Guarnaschelli, A., Schweickardt, G. A., & Méndez, C. A. (2020). A reactive-iterative optimization algorithm for scheduling of air separation units under uncertainty in electricity prices. [DOI]. *Computers & Chemical Engineering*, 141, 107050. DOI: 10.1016/j.compchemeng.2020.107050

Bayerstadler, A., Becquin, G., Binder, J., Botter, T., Ehm, H., Ehmer, T., Erdmann, M., Gaus, N., Harbach, P., Hess, M., Klepsch, J., Leib, M., Luber, S., Luckow, A., Mansky, M., Mauerer, W., Neukart, F., Niedermeier, C., Palackal, L., & Winter, F. (2021). Industry quantum computing applications. *EPJ Quantum Technology*, 8(1), 25. DOI: 10.1140/epjqt/s40507-021-00114-x

Beck, T., Demirgüç-Kunt, A., & World Bank. (2008). Access to Finance: an unfinished agenda. In THE WORLD BANK ECONOMIC REVIEW (Vols. 22–22, Issue 3, pp. 383–396). https://doi.org/DOI: 10.1093/wber/lhn021

Bell, J. S. (1964). On the einstein podolsky rosen paradox. *Physics Physique Fizika*, 1(3), 195–200. DOI: 10.1103/PhysicsPhysiqueFizika.1.195

Bertels, K. O. E. N., Sarkar, A., Hubregtsen, T., Serrao, M., Mouedenne, A. A., Yadav, A., Krol, A., Ashraf, I., & Almudever, C. G. (2020). Quantum computer architecture toward full-stack quantum accelerators. *IEEE Transactions on Quantum Engineering*, 1, 1–17. DOI: 10.1109/TQE.2020.2981074

Bhaskar, S., Bradley, S., Sakhamuri, S., Moguilner, S., Chattu, V. K., Pandya, S., Schroeder, S., Ray, D., & Banach, M. (2020).. . *Frontiers in Public Health*.

Bhatnagar, S., & Sharma, D. (2022). Evolution of green finance and its enablers: A bibliometric analysis. *Renewable & Sustainable Energy Reviews*, 162, 112405. DOI: 10.1016/j.rser.2022.112405

Bhatta, S., & Dang, J. (2024). Quantum-enhanced machine learning technique for rapid post-earthquake assessment of building safety. *Computer-Aided Civil and Infrastructure Engineering*, 39(21), 3188–3205. DOI: 10.1111/mice.13291

Bhatt, V. K. (2021). Assessing the significance and impact of artificial intelligence and machine learning in placement of advertisements. *2021 IEEE International Conference on Technology Management, Operations and Decisions (ICTMOD)*, 1–6. DOI: 10.1109/ICTMOD52902.2021.9739228

Bhowmik, T. K., Parui, S. K., & Roy, U. (2008). Discriminative HMM training with GA for handwritten word recognition. In *2008 19th International Conference on Pattern Recognition*. DOI DOI: 10.1109/ICPR.2008.4761830

Biamonte, J., Wittek, P., Pancotti, N., Rebentrost, P., Wiebe, N., & Lloyd, S. (2017). Quantum machine learning. *Nature*, 549(7671), 195–202. DOI: 10.1038/nature23474 PMID: 28905917

Blomster, M., & Koivumäki, T. (2022). Exploring the resources, competencies, and capabilities needed for successful machine learning projects in digital marketing. *Information Systems and e-Business Management*, 20(1), 123–169. DOI: 10.1007/s10257-021-00547-y

Blunt, N. S., Camps, J., Crawford, O., Izsák, R., Leontica, S., Mirani, A., Moylett, A. E., Scivier, S. A., Sünderhauf, C., Schopf, P., Taylor, J. M., & Holzmann, N. (2022). Perspective on the current state-of-the-art of quantum computing for drug discovery applications. *Journal of Chemical Theory and Computation*, 18(12), 7001–7023. DOI: 10.1021/acs.jctc.2c00574 PMID: 36355616

Bombin, H. (2011). Clifford Gates by Code Deformation. *New Journal of Physics*, 13(4), 043005. DOI: 10.1088/1367-2630/13/4/043005

Boopathi, S. (2023). Deep Learning Techniques Applied for Automatic Sentence Generation. In *Promoting Diversity, Equity, and Inclusion in Language Learning Environments* (pp. 255–273). IGI Global. DOI: 10.4018/978-1-6684-3632-5.ch016

Boopathi, S. (2024). Digital HR Implementation for Business Growth in Industrial 5.0. In *Convergence of Human Resources Technologies and Industry 5.0* (pp. 1–22). IGI Global. DOI: 10.4018/979-8-3693-1343-5.ch001

Boopathi, S., Gavaskar, T., Dogga, A. D., Mahendran, R. K., Kumar, A., Kathiresan, G., N., V., Ganesan, M., Ishwarya, K. R., Ramana, G. V., & others. (2021, August 4). *Emergency medicine delivery transportation using unmanned aerial vehicle (Patent Grant)*.

Boopathi, S. (2022). Experimental investigation and multi-objective optimization of cryogenic Friction-stir-welding of AA2014 and AZ31B alloys using MOORA technique. *Materials Today. Communications*, 33, 104937. DOI: 10.1016/j.mtcomm.2022.104937

Boopathi, S., & Kanike, U. K. (2023). Applications of Artificial Intelligent and Machine Learning Techniques in Image Processing. In *Handbook of Research on Thrust Technologies' Effect on Image Processing* (pp. 151–173). IGI Global. DOI: 10.4018/978-1-6684-8618-4.ch010

Boopathi, S., & Khang, A. (2023). AI-Integrated Technology for a Secure and Ethical Healthcare Ecosystem. In *AI and IoT-Based Technologies for Precision Medicine* (pp. 36–59). IGI Global. DOI: 10.4018/979-8-3693-0876-9.ch003

Boopathi, S., Myilsamy, S., & Sukkasamy, S. (2021). *Experimental Investigation and Multi-Objective Optimization of Cryogenically Cooled Near-Dry Wire-Cut EDM Using TOPSIS Technique*. IJAMT PREPRINT.

Boretti, A. (2024). Technical, economic, and societal risks in the progress of artificial intelligence driven quantum technologies. *Discover Artificial Intelligence*, 4(1), 67. DOI: 10.1007/s44163-024-00171-y

Born, M., & Oppenheimer, R. (2000). On the quantum theory of molecules. In *Quantum Chemistry* (pp. 1–24). Classic Scientific Papers. DOI: 10.1142/9789812795762_0001

Bova, F., Goldfarb, A., & Melko, R. G. (2021). Commercial applications of quantum computing. *EPJ Quantum Technology*, 8(1), 1–8. DOI: 10.1140/epjqt/s40507-021-00091-1 PMID: 33569545

Braunstein, S. L. (1998). Error Correction for continuous quantum variables. *Physical Review Letters*, 80(18), 4084–4087. DOI: 10.1103/PhysRevLett.80.4084

Bravyi, S., Cross, A. W., Gambetta, J. M., Maslov, D., Rall, P., & Yoder, T. J. (2024). High-threshold and low-overhead fault-tolerant quantum memory. *Nature*, 627(8005), 778–782. DOI: 10.1038/s41586-024-07107-7 PMID: 38538939

Bravyi, S., Dial, O., Gambetta, J. M., Gil, D., & Nazario, Z. (2022). The future of quantum computing with superconducting qubits. *Journal of Applied Physics*, 132(16), 160902. DOI: 10.1063/5.0082975

Broughton, M., Verdon, G., McCourt, T., Martinez, A. J., Yoo, J. H., Isakov, S. V., Massey, P., Halavati, R., Niu, M. Y., Zlokapa, A., & Associates. (2020). Tensorflow quantum: A software framework for quantum machine learning. *arXiv Preprint arXiv:2003.02989.*

Brun, T., Devetak, I., & Hsieh, M. H. (2006). Correcting quantum errors with entanglement. science, 314(5798), 436-439.

Buffoni, L., & Caruso, F. (2021). New trends in quantum machine learning (a). *Europhysics Letters*, 132(6), 60004. DOI: 10.1209/0295-5075/132/60004

Campbell, E. (2024). A series of fast-paced advances in Quantum Error Correction. *Nature Reviews. Physics*, 6(3), 160–161. DOI: 10.1038/s42254-024-00706-3

Carrasquilla, J. (2020). Machine learning for quantum matter. *Advances in Physics: X*, 5(1), 1797528. DOI: 10.1080/23746149.2020.1797528

Cerezo, M., Sone, A., Volkoff, T., Cincio, L., & Coles, P. J. (2021). Cost function dependent barren plateaus in shallow parametrized quantum circuits. *Nature Communications*, 12(1), 1–12. DOI: 10.1038/s41467-021-21728-w PMID: 33741913

Chalissery, N., Tabash, M. I., Nishad T, M., & Saleh Al-Faryan, M. A. (2022). A bibliometric analysis of socially responsible investment based on thematic clustering. *Cogent Business & Management*, 10(1), 2154057. Advance online publication. DOI: 10.1080/23311975.2022.2154057

Chalumuri, A., Kune, R., Kannan, S., & Manoj, B. S. (2021). Quantum-enhanced deep neural network architecture for image scene classification. *Quantum Information Processing*, 20(11), 1–21. DOI: 10.1007/s11128-021-03314-7

Chandra, S., Ghule, G., Bilfaqih, S. M., Thiyagarajan, A., Sharmila, J., & Boopathi, S. (2024). Adaptive Strategies in Online Marketing Using Machine Learning Techniques. In *Digital Transformation Initiatives for Agile Marketing* (pp. 67–100). IGI Global., DOI: 10.4018/979-8-3693-4466-8.ch004

Chandrasekaran, A., Kamal, D., Batra, R., Kim, C., Chen, L., & Ramprasad, R. (2019). Solving the electronic structure problem with machine learning. npj Computational Materials, 5(1), 22.

Chan, S., & Siegel, E. L. (2019). Will machine learning end the viability of radiology as a thriving medical specialty? *The British Journal of Radiology*, 92(1094), 20180416. DOI: 10.1259/bjr.20180416 PMID: 30325645

Chaos and nonlinear forecastability in Economics and Finance on JSTOR. (n.d.-b). www.jstor.org. https://www.jstor.org/stable/54216

Chaos Theory and Strategy: Theory, Application, and Managerial Implications on JSTOR. (n.d.-b). www.jstor.org. https://www.jstor.org/stable/2486882

Chen, C.-S., Chen, S. Y.-C., Tsai, A. H.-W., & Wei, C.-S. (2024). Qeegnet: Quantum machine learning for enhanced electroencephalography encoding. *2024 IEEE Workshop on Signal Processing Systems (SiPS)*, 153–158. DOI: 10.1109/SiPS62058.2024.00035

Cheng, J., Wang, J., Tan, Z., & Wu, S. (2021). Theoretical Study of Photoassociation of Alkali-Metal Dimers. *Russian Journal of Physical Chemistry A. Focus on Chemistry*, 95(S2, Suppl 2), S396–S405. DOI: 10.1134/S0036024421150061

Chen, J. (2021, April). Review on quantum communication and quantum computation. [). IOP Publishing.]. *Journal of Physics: Conference Series*, 1865(2), 022008. DOI: 10.1088/1742-6596/1865/2/022008

Chintala, S. (2021). Explore the impact of emerging technologies such as AI, machine learning, and blockchain on transforming retail marketing strategies. *Webology (ISSN: 1735-188X), 18*(1).

Chipidza, W., Li, Y., Mashatan, A., Turetken, O., & Olfman, L. (2023). Quantum computing and IS - Harnessing the opportunities of emerging technologies. *Communications of the Association for Information Systems*, 52, 480–499. DOI: 10.17705/1CAIS.05219

Choi, J., Oh, S., & Kim, J. "The Useful Quantum Computing Techniques for Artificial Intelligence Engineers," *2020 International Conference on Information Networking (ICOIN)*, Barcelona, Spain, 2020, pp. 1-3, DOI: 10.1109/ICOIN48656.2020.9016555

Ciliberto, C., Herbster, M., Ialongo, A. D., Pontil, M., Rocchetto, A., Severini, S., & Wossnig, L. (2018). Quantum machine learning: A classical perspective. *Proceedings - Royal Society. Mathematical, Physical and Engineering Sciences*, 474(2209), 20170551. DOI: 10.1098/rspa.2017.0551 PMID: 29434508

Cochrane, J. H. (2013). Finance: Function matters, not size. *The Journal of Economic Perspectives*, 27(2), 29–50. DOI: 10.1257/jep.27.2.29

Cong, I., Choi, S., & Lukin, M. D. (2019). Quantum convolutional neural networks. *Nature Physics*, 15(12), 1273–1278. DOI: 10.1038/s41567-019-0648-8

Curtain, R. F., Zwart, H., & Iftime, O. (2017). A Kleinman–Newton construction of the maximal solution of the infinite-dimensional control Riccati equation. *Automatica*, 86, 147–153. DOI: 10.1016/j.automatica.2017.08.030

Cusumano, M. A. (2018). The business of quantum computing. *Communications of the ACM*, 61(10), 20–22. DOI: 10.1145/3267352

Cuthbertson, K., Nitzsche, D., & Hyde, S. (2007). MONETARY POLICY AND BEHAVIOURAL FINANCE. *Journal of Economic Surveys*, 21(5), 935–969. DOI: 10.1111/j.1467-6419.2007.00525.x

Dash, S., Shakyawar, S. K., Sharma, M., & Kaushik, S. (2019). Big data in healthcare: Management, analysis and future prospects. *Journal of Big Data*, 6(1), 1–25. DOI: 10.1186/s40537-019-0217-0

De Bettignies, J., & Ries, J. (2023). When less is more: Information and the financing of innovation. *Journal of Economic Behavior & Organization*, 214, 346–369. DOI: 10.1016/j.jebo.2023.07.038

De la Hoz Domínguez, E. J., Herrera, T. J. F., & Mendoza, A. A. M. (2020). Machine Learning and SMEs: Opportunities for an improved deci-sion-making process. *Investigación e Innovación En Ingenierías*, 8(1), 21–36.

de Leon, N. P., Itoh, K. M., Kim, D., Mehta, K. K., Northup, T. E., Paik, H., Palmer, B. S., Samarth, N., Sangtawesin, S., & Steuerman, D. W. (2021). Materials challenges and opportunities for quantum computing hardware. *Science*, 372(6539), eabb2823. Advance online publication. DOI: 10.1126/science.abb2823 PMID: 33859004

Deibuk, V., & Yuriychuk, I. "Noisy Multiple-Control Fredkin Gate in Nuclear Spin Based Qubits Chain." *2020 IEEE Third International Conference on Data Stream Mining & Processing (DSMP)*. IEEE, 2020. DOI: 10.1109/DSMP47368.2020.9204263

Deng, Y., Ren, Z., Kong, Y., Bao, F., & Dai, Q. (2016). A hierarchical fused fuzzy deep neural network for data classification. *IEEE Transactions on Fuzzy Systems*, 25(4), 1006–1012. DOI: 10.1109/TFUZZ.2016.2574915

Devitt, S. J., Munro, W. J., & Nemoto, K. (2013). Quantum error correction for beginners. *Reports on Progress in Physics*, 76(7), 076001.

DiVincenzo, D. P., & Aliferis, P. (2007). Effective FaultTolerant Quantum Computation with slow measurement. *Physical Review Letters*, 98(2), 020501. DOI: 10.1103/PhysRevLett.98.020501 PMID: 17358588

Dobson, P., & Bierkens, J. (2023). Infinite dimensional Piecewise Deterministic Markov Processes. *Stochastic Processes and Their Applications*, 165, 337–396. DOI: 10.1016/j.spa.2023.08.010

Endo, S., Benjamin, S. C., & Li, Y. (2018). Practical quantum error mitigation for near future applications. *Physical Review X*, 8(3), 031027. DOI: 10.1103/PhysRevX.8.031027

Erokhin, S., & Roshka, O. (2018). Application of fractal properties in studies of financial markets. MATEC Web of Conferences, 170, 01074. https://doi.org/DOI: 10.1051/matecconf/201817001074

Fernández-Caramés, T. M. (2020, July). From Pre-Quantum to Post-Quantum IoT Security: A Survey on Quantum-Resistant Cryptosystems for the Internet of Things. *IEEE Internet of Things Journal*, 7(7), 6457–6480. DOI: 10.1109/JIOT.2019.2958788

Feynman, R.P. (1985). "Quantum mechanical computers." Optics news 11.2 11-20

Fredkin, E., & Toffoli, T. (1982). Conservative logic. *International Journal of Theoretical Physics*, 21(3), 219–253.

Fredström, A., Parida, V., Wincent, J., Sjödin, D., & Oghazi, P. (2022). What is the market value of artificial intelligence and machine learning? The role of innovativeness and collaboration for performance. *Technological Forecasting and Social Change*, 180, 121716. DOI: 10.1016/j.techfore.2022.121716

French, C. C. (n.d.). The Butterfly Effect in Interpreting Insurance Policies. Social Science Research Network. https://papers.ssrn.com/sol3/papers.cfm?abstract_id=3444910

Fritsche, L. (1986). Generalized Kohn-Sham theory for electronic excitations in realistic systems. *Physical Review. B*, 33(6), 3976–3989. DOI: 10.1103/PhysRevB.33.3976 PMID: 9938813

Gardiner, C. W., & Zoller, P. (2000). Quantum noise, Vol. 56 of Springer series in synergetics. Springer–Verlag, Berlin, 97, 98.

Garodia, A. (n.d.). *Transforming Healthcare and Pharmaceutical Operations through AI-Based Automation Solutions*.

Gaviria, J. F., Narváez, G., Guillen, C., Giraldo, L. F., & Bressan, M. (2022). Machine learning in photovoltaic systems: A review. *Renewable Energy*, 196, 298–318. DOI: 10.1016/j.renene.2022.06.105

Gerke, S., Babic, B., Evgeniou, T., & Cohen, I. G. (2020). The need for a system view to regulate artificial intelligence/machine learning-based software as medical device. *NPJ Digital Medicine*, 3(1), 53. DOI: 10.1038/s41746-020-0262-2 PMID: 32285013

Gill, S. S. (2021). Quantum and blockchain based Serverless edge computing: A vision, model, new trends and future directions. *Internet Technology Letters*, •••, 275.

Gill, S. S., Kumar, A., Singh, H., Singh, M., Kaur, K., Usman, M., & Buyya, R. (2022). Quantum computing: A taxonomy, systematic review and future directions. *Software, Practice & Experience*, 52(1), 66–114. DOI: 10.1002/spe.3039

Gill, S. S., Xu, M., Ottaviani, C., Patros, P., Bahsoon, R., Shaghaghi, A., Golec, M., Stankovski, V., Wu, H., Abraham, A., Singh, M., Mehta, H., Ghosh, S. K., Baker, T., Parlikad, A. K., Lutfiyya, H., Kanhere, S. S., Sakellariou, R., Dustdar, S., & Uhlig, S. (2024).. . *Software, Practice & Experience*.

Glady, J. B. P., D'Souza, S. M., Priya, A. P., Amuthachenthiru, K., Vikram, G., & Boopathi, S. (2024). A Study on AI-ML-Driven Optimizing Energy Distribution and Sustainable Agriculture for Environmental Conservation. In *Harnessing High-Performance Computing and AI for Environmental Sustainability* (pp. 1–27). IGI Global., DOI: 10.4018/979-8-3693-1794-5.ch001

Glorot, X., & Bengio, Y. (2010, March). Understanding the difficulty of training deep feedforward neural networks. In *Proceedings of the thirteenth international conference on artificial intelligence and statistics* (pp. 249-256). JMLR Workshop and Conference Proceedings.

Goodfellow, I., Bengio, Y., & Courville, A. (2016). *Deep Learning*. MIT Press.

Goswami, S., & Sharma, S. (2024). Artificial Intelligence, Quantum Computing and Cloud Computing Enabled Personalized Medicine in Next Generation Sequencing Bioinformatics. *2024 IEEE International Conference on Interdisciplinary Approaches in Technology and Management for Social Innovation (IATMSI), 2*, 1–5. DOI: 10.1109/IATMSI60426.2024.10502533

Goto, T., Tran, Q. H., & Nakajima, K. (2021). Universal approximation property of quantum machine learning models in quantum-enhanced feature spaces. *Physical Review Letters*, 127(9), 090506. DOI: 10.1103/PhysRevLett.127.090506 PMID: 34506199

Gouveia, A., & Correia, M. (2020a). Towards quantum-enhanced machine learning for network intrusion detection. *2020 IEEE 19th International Symposium on Network Computing and Applications (NCA)*, 1–8.

Gouveia, A., & Correia, M. (2020b). Towards quantum-enhanced machine learning for network intrusion detection. *2020 IEEE 19th International Symposium on Network Computing and Applications (NCA)*, 1–8.

Griebel, M., & Holtz, M. (2010). Dimension-wise integration of high-dimensional functions with applications to finance. *Journal of Complexity*, 26(5), 455–489. DOI: 10.1016/j.jco.2010.06.001

Gujju, Y., Matsuo, A., & Raymond, R. (2024). Quantum machine learning on near-term quantum devices: Current state of supervised and unsupervised techniques for real-world applications. *Physical Review Applied*, 21(6), 067001. DOI: 10.1103/PhysRevApplied.21.067001

Guo, C., Liang, F., Lin, J., Xu, Y., Sun, L., Liu, W., Liao, S., & Peng, C. (2019, July). Control and Readout Software for Superconducting Quantum Computing. *IEEE Transactions on Nuclear Science*, 66(7), 1222–1227. DOI: 10.1109/TNS.2019.2920337

Gupta, H., Varshney, H., Sharma, T. K., Pachauri, N., & Verma, O. P. (2022). Comparative performance analysis of quantum machine learning with deep learning for diabetes prediction. *Complex & Intelligent Systems*, 8(4), 3073–3087. DOI: 10.1007/s40747-021-00398-7

Gupta, M., & Nene, M. J. "Quantum Computing: An Entanglement Measurement," *2020 IEEE International Conference on Advent Trends in Multidisciplinary Research and Innovation (ICATMRI)*, Buldhana, India, 2020, pp. 1-6, DOI: 10.1109/ICATMRI51801.2020.9398441

Gururaj, V., Umadi, K. R., Kumar, M., Shankar, S. P., & Varadam, D. (2022, March). Comprehensive Survey of different Machine Learning Algorithms used for Software Defect Prediction. In *2022 International Conference on Decision Aid Sciences and Applications (DASA)* (pp. 425-430). IEEE.

Gutnik, S. (2021). Application of data mining and machine learning methods to enhance the effectiveness of digital marketing strategies. *Digital Strategies in a Global Market: Navigating the Fourth Industrial Revolution*, 131–144.

Gyongyosi, L., & Imre, S. (2019). A survey on quantum computing technology. *Computer Science Review*, 31, 51–71. DOI: 10.1016/j.cosrev.2018.11.002

Hałaj, G., Martínez-Jaramillo, S., & Battiston, S. (2024). Financial stability through the lens of complex systems. *Journal of Financial Stability*, 71, 101228. DOI: 10.1016/j.jfs.2024.101228

Haribalaji, V., Boopathi, S., & Asif, M. M. (2021). Optimization of friction stir welding process to join dissimilar AA2014 and AA7075 aluminum alloys. *Materials Today: Proceedings*, 50, 2227–2234. DOI: 10.1016/j.matpr.2021.09.499

Harrison, C. J., & Sidey-Gibbons, C. J. (2021). Machine learning in medicine: A practical introduction to natural language processing. *BMC Medical Research Methodology*, 21(1), 158. DOI: 10.1186/s12874-021-01347-1 PMID: 34332525

Hartree, D. R. (1927). Bozman, AM, Denmark, AE, and Trickey, EM Elementary Mathematics.

Hassija, V., Chamola, V., Goyal, A., Kanhere, S. S., & Guizani, N. (2020). Forthcoming applications of quantum computing: Peeking into the future. *IET Quantum Communication*, 1(2), 35–41. DOI: 10.1049/iet-qtc.2020.0026

Hassija, V., Chamola, V., Saxena, V., Chanana, V., Parashari, P., Mumtaz, S., & Guizani, M. (2020). The present landscape of quantum computing. *IET Quantum Communication*, 1(2), 42–48. DOI: 10.1049/iet-qtc.2020.0027

Hdaib, M., Rajasegarar, S., & Pan, L. (2024). Quantum deep learning-based anomaly detection for enhanced network security. *Quantum Machine Intelligence*, 6(1), 26. DOI: 10.1007/s42484-024-00163-2

Hema, N., Krishnamoorthy, N., Chavan, S. M., Kumar, N., Sabarimuthu, M., & Boopathi, S. (2023). A Study on an Internet of Things (IoT)-Enabled Smart Solar Grid System. In *Handbook of Research on Deep Learning Techniques for Cloud-Based Industrial IoT* (pp. 290–308). IGI Global. DOI: 10.4018/978-1-6684-8098-4.ch017

Henry, E. (2024). *Integrating Quantum Model Computing With Machine Learning Quantum Algorithms For Accelerating Ai Model Training.*

Herman, D., Googin, C., Liu, X., Galda, A., Safro, I., Sun, Y., . . . Alexeev, Y. (2022). A survey of quantum computing for finance. arXiv preprint arXiv:2201.02773.

Hermsmeier, R., Kłos, J., Kotochigova, S., & Tscherbul, T. V. (2021). Quantum spin state selectivity and magnetic tuning of ultracold chemical reactions of triplet alkali-metal dimers with alkali-metal atoms. *Physical Review Letters*, 127(10), 103402. DOI: 10.1103/PhysRevLett.127.103402 PMID: 34533330

Holevo, A. S. (2019). *Quantum systems, channels, information: A mathematical introduction*. Walter de Gruyter GmbH & Co KG. DOI: 10.1515/9783110642490

Houssein, E. H., Abohashima, Z., Elhoseny, M., & Mohamed, W. M. (2022). Machine learning in the quantum realm: The state-of-the-art, challenges, and future vision. *Expert Systems with Applications*, 194, 116512. DOI: 10.1016/j.eswa.2022.116512

Howard, A. G., Zhu, M., Chen, B., Kalenichenko, D., Wang, W., Weyand, T., . . . Adam, H. (2017). Mobilenets: Efficient convolutional neural networks for mobile vision applications. *arXiv preprint arXiv:1704.04861.*

How, M.-L., & Cheah, S.-M. (2023). Business Renaissance: Opportunities and challenges at the dawn of the Quantum Computing Era. *Businesses*, 3(4), 585–605. DOI: 10.3390/businesses3040036

Hu, L., & Ni, Q. "Quantum Automated Object Detection Algorithm," 2019 25th International Conference on Automation and Computing (ICAC), Lancaster, UK, 2019, pp. 1-4, DOI: 10.23919/IConAC.2019.8895167

Huang, H. L., Xu, X. Y., Guo, C., Tian, G., Wei, S. J., Sun, X., Bao, W.-S., & Long, G. L. (2023). Near-term quantum computing techniques: Variational quantum algorithms, error mitigation, circuit compilation, benchmarking and classical simulation. *Science China. Physics, Mechanics & Astronomy*, 66(5), 250302. DOI: 10.1007/s11433-022-2057-y

Huber, C., & Kirchler, M. (2023). Experiments in finance: A survey of historical trends. *Journal of Behavioral and Experimental Finance*, 37, 100737. DOI: 10.1016/j.jbef.2022.100737

Huggins, W., Patil, P., Mitchell, B., Whaley, K. B., & Stoudenmire, E. M. (2019). Towards quantum machine learning with tensor networks. *Quantum Science and Technology*, 4(2), 024001. DOI: 10.1088/2058-9565/aaea94

Huhtanen, S. (2024). *Bachelor's thesis, Faculty of Engineering and Natural Sciences*. Tampere University. DOI

Ingle, R. B., Swathi, S., Mahendran, G., Senthil, T., Muralidharan, N., & Boopathi, S. (2023). Sustainability and Optimization of Green and Lean Manufacturing Processes Using Machine Learning Techniques. In *Circular Economy Implementation for Sustainability in the Built Environment* (pp. 261–285). IGI Global. DOI: 10.4018/978-1-6684-8238-4.ch012

Jabbari, T., & Friedman, E. G. (2020). Global interconnects in VLSI complexity single flux quantum systems. *Proceedings of the Workshop on System-Level Interconnect: Problems and Pathfinding Workshop*, 1–7. DOI: 10.1145/3414622.3431911

Jackson, N. E., Savoie, B. M., Statt, A., & Webb, M. A. (2023). Introduction to machine learning for molecular simulation. *Journal of Chemical Theory and Computation*, 19(14), 4335–4337. DOI: 10.1021/acs.jctc.3c00735 PMID: 37489106

Jendoubi, I., Essefi, E., & Hendeoui, H. (2025). Quantum Computing of Computational Chemistry: Applications of Molecular Quantum Dynamics. In The Quantum Evolution (pp. 292-305). CRC Press.

Jendoubi, I., Berriche, H., Ben Ouada, H., & Gadéa, F. X. (2012). Structural and spectroscopic study of the LiRb molecule beyond the Born–Oppenheimer approximation. *The Journal of Physical Chemistry A*, 116(11), 2945–2960. DOI: 10.1021/jp209106w PMID: 22360282

Jensen, F. (2017). *Introduction to computational chemistry*. John wiley & sons.

Jiang, L., Chen, L., Giannetsos, T., Luo, B., Liang, K., & Han, J. (2019). Toward practical privacy-preserving processing over encrypted data in IoT: An assistive healthcare use case. *IEEE Internet of Things Journal*, 6(6), 10177–10190. DOI: 10.1109/JIOT.2019.2936532

Joel, O. T., & Oguanobi, V. U.Oloruntosin Tolulope JoelVincent Ugochukwu Oguanobi. (2024). Navigating business transformation and strategic decision-making in multinational energy corporations with geodata. *International Journal of Applied Research in Social Sciences*, 6(5), 1–15. DOI: 10.51594/ijarss.v6i5.1103

Kachhia, K. B. (2023c). Chaos in fractional order financial model with fractal–fractional derivatives. *Partial Differential Equations in Applied Mathematics : a Spin-Off of Applied Mathematics Letters*, 7, 100502. DOI: 10.1016/j.padiff.2023.100502

Kak, S. C. (1995). Quantum neural computing. *Advances in Imaging and Electron Physics*, 94, 259–313. DOI: 10.1016/S1076-5670(08)70147-2

Kalaiselvi, T., Saravanan, G., Haritha, T., Babu, A. V. S., Sakthivel, M., & Boopathi, S. (2024). A Study on the Landscape of Serverless Computing: Technologies and Tools for Seamless Implementation. In *Serverless Computing Concepts, Technology and Architecture* (pp. 260–282). IGI Global. DOI: 10.4018/979-8-3693-1682-5.ch016

Kamepalli, S., & Rao, B. S. (2019). Recent applications of machine learning: A survey. *International Journal of Innovative Technology and Exploring Engineering*, 8(6), 263–267.

Kandala, A., Temme, K., Córcoles, A. D., Mezzacapo, A., Chow, J. M., & Gambetta, J. M. (2019). Error mitigation extends the computational reach of a noisy quantum processor. *Nature*, 567(7749), 491–495. DOI: 10.1038/s41586-019-1040-7 PMID: 30918370

Kaplan, A., Cao, H., FitzGerald, J. M., Iannotti, N., Yang, E., Kocks, J. W., Kostikas, K., Price, D., Reddel, H. K., Tsiligianni, I., Vogelmeier, C. F., Pfister, P., & Mastoridis, P. (2021). Artificial intelligence/machine learning in respiratory medicine and potential role in asthma and COPD diagnosis. *The Journal of Allergy and Clinical Immunology. In Practice*, 9(6), 2255–2261. DOI: 10.1016/j.jaip.2021.02.014 PMID: 33618053

Karn, A. K., Sinha, P., Kaur, S., & Bansal, H. (2024). Quantum-Enhanced Strategies for Optimizing Disaster Response: A Machine Learning Approach. In *The Rise of Quantum Computing in Industry 6.0 Towards Sustainability* (pp. 193–204). Springer. DOI: 10.1007/978-3-031-73350-5_12

Kasabov, N. K. (2019). *Time-space, spiking neural networks and brain-inspired artificial intelligence*. Springer Berlin Heidelberg. DOI: 10.1007/978-3-662-57715-8

Kaur, H., Pannu, H. S., & Malhi, A. K. (2019). A systematic review on imbalanced data challenges in machine learning: Applications and solutions. *ACM Computing Surveys*, 52(4), 1–36.

Kavitha, S. S. (2024). Quantum support vector machines: A comparative study with classical SVMs. *International Journal of Applied Research in Social Sciences*, 6(5), 1–15. 10.51594/ijarss.v6i5.1103

Kedi, W. E., Ejimuda, C., Idemudia, C., & Ijomah, T. I. (2024). Machine learning software for optimizing SME social media marketing campaigns. *Computer Science & IT Research Journal*, 5(7), 1634–1647. DOI: 10.51594/csitrj.v5i7.1349

Kendon, V. (2020). Quantum computing using continuous-timeevolution. *Interface Focus*, 10(6), 20190143. DOI: 10.1098/rsfs.2019.0143 PMID: 33178417

Khan, A. A., Laghari, A. A., & Awan, S. A. (2021). Machine learning in computer vision: A review. *EAI Endorsed Transactions on Scalable Information Systems*, 8(32), e4–e4.

Khang, A. (2024). *AI-Driven Innovations in Digital Healthcare: Emerging Trends, Challenges, and Applications: Emerging Trends, Challenges, and Applications.*

Khan, T. M., & Robles-Kelly, A. (2020). Machine learning: Quantum vs classical. *IEEE Access : Practical Innovations, Open Solutions*, 8, 219275–219294. DOI: 10.1109/ACCESS.2020.3041719

Kharsa, R., Bouridane, A., & Amira, A. (2023). Advances in Quantum Machine Learning and Deep Learning for Image Classification: A Survey. *Neurocomputing*, 560, 126843. DOI: 10.1016/j.neucom.2023.126843

Kiliyanni, A. L., & Sivaraman, S. (2016). The perception-reality gap in financial literacy: Evidence from the most literate state in India. *International Review of Economics Education*, 23, 47–64. DOI: 10.1016/j.iree.2016.07.001

Kim, D., Kang, J., Kim, T. W., Pan, Y., & Park, J. H. (2021). The future of quantum information: Challenges and vision. *Journal of Information Processing Systems*, 17(1), 151–162.

Kim, Y., Lee, J., & Ahn, J. (2019). Innovation towards sustainable technologies: A socio-technical perspective on accelerating transition to aviation biofuel. *Technological Forecasting and Social Change*, 145, 62–73. DOI: 10.1016/j.techfore.2019.04.002

Klimov, P. V., Bengtsson, A., Quintana, C., Bourassa, A., Hong, S., Dunsworth, A., & Neven, H. (2024). Optimizing quantum gates towards the scale of logical qubits. *Nature Communications*, 15(1), 2442.

Klioutchnikov, I., Sigova, M., & Beizerov, N. (2017c). Chaos theory in finance. *Procedia Computer Science*, 119, 368–375. DOI: 10.1016/j.procs.2017.11.196

Krishnamoorthy, V., Chandra, S., Rajesha, S., Bhattacharjee, S., Murugan, G., & Sampath, B. (2024). Emerging Startups in the Evolving Industry Landscape by Empowering Entrepreneur Growth: An Agile Marketing Practice. In *Digital Transformation Initiatives for Agile Marketing* (pp. 455–484). IGI Global. DOI: 10.4018/979-8-3693-4466-8.ch017

Kruize, J. W., Robbemond, R. M., Scholten, H., Wolfert, J., & Beulens, A. J. M. (2013).. . *Computers and Electronics in Agriculture.*

Kumar, M., Kumar, K., Sasikala, P., Sampath, B., Gopi, B., & Sundaram, S. (2023). Sustainable Green Energy Generation From Waste Water: IoT and ML Integration. In *Sustainable Science and Intelligent Technologies for Societal Development* (pp. 440–463). IGI Global.

Kumar, R., Kumar, P., & Kumar, Y. (2020). Time series data prediction using IoT and machine learning technique. *Procedia Computer Science*, 167, 373–381. DOI: 10.1016/j.procs.2020.03.240

Kumar, Y., Kaur, K., & Singh, G. (2020). Machine learning aspects and its applications towards different research areas. *2020 International Conference on Computation, Automation and Knowledge Management (ICCAKM)*, 150–156. DOI: 10.1109/ICCAKM46823.2020.9051502

Kumar, Y., Koul, A., Sisodia, P. S., Shafi, J., Verma, K., Gheisari, M., & Davoodi, M. B. (2021). Heart failure detection using quantum-enhanced machine learning and traditional machine learning techniques for internet of artificially intelligent medical things. *Wireless Communications and Mobile Computing*, 2021(1), 1616725. DOI: 10.1155/2021/1616725

Kushwah, J. S., Gupta, M., Shrivastava, S., Saxena, N., Saini, R., & Boopathi, S. (2024). Psychological Impacts, Prevention Strategies, and Intervention Approaches Across Age Groups: Unmasking Cyberbullying. In *Change Dynamics in Healthcare, Technological Innovations, and Complex Scenarios* (pp. 89–109). IGI Global.

L'heureux, A., Grolinger, K., Elyamany, H. F., & Capretz, M. A. (2017). Machine learning with big data: Challenges and approaches. *IEEE Access : Practical Innovations, Open Solutions*, 5, 7776–7797. DOI: 10.1109/ACCESS.2017.2696365

Landauer, R. (1961). Irreversibility and heat generation in the computing process. *IBM Journal of Research and Development*, 5(3), 183–191. DOI: 10.1147/rd.53.0183

LaRose, R., & Coyle, B. (2020). Robust data encodings for quantum classifiers. *Physical Review. A*, 102(3), 032420. DOI: 10.1103/PhysRevA.102.032420

LeCun, Y., Bottou, L., Bengio, Y., & Haffner, P. (1998). Gradient-based learning applied to document recognition. *Proceedings of the IEEE*, 86(11), 2278–2324. DOI: 10.1109/5.726791

Li, K., Zhao, P., Dai, S., Zhu, A., Hong, B., Liu, J., ... & Zhang, Y. (2024). Exploring the impact of quantum computing on machine learning performance.

Li, C., Hou, S., & Xie, C. (2023). Constructing diabatic potential energy matrices with neural networks based on adiabatic energies and physical considerations: Toward quantum dynamic accuracy. *Journal of Chemical Theory and Computation*, 19(11), 3063–3079. DOI: 10.1021/acs.jctc.2c01074 PMID: 37216273

Lin, F. J., Lin, C. H., & Shen, P. H. (2001). Self-constructing fuzzy neural network speed controller for permanent-magnet synchronous motor drive. *IEEE Transactions on Fuzzy Systems*, 9(5), 751–759. DOI: 10.1109/91.963761

Liu, N., Huang, T., Gao, J., Xu, Z., Wang, D., & Li, F. (2021). Quantum-enhanced deep learning-based lithology interpretation from well logs. *IEEE Transactions on Geoscience and Remote Sensing*, 60, 1–13.

Liu, Y., Arunachalam, S., & Temme, K. (2021). A rigorous and robust quantum speed-up in supervised machine learning. *Nature Physics*, 17(9), 1013–1017. DOI: 10.1038/s41567-021-01287-z

Liu, Y., Zhang, D., Lu, G., & Ma, W. Y. (2007). A survey of content-based image retrieval with high-level semantics. *Pattern Recognition*, 40(1), 262–282. DOI: 10.1016/j.patcog.2006.04.045

Li, W., & Deng, D. L. (2022). Recent advances for quantum classifiers. *Science China. Physics, Mechanics & Astronomy*, 65(2), 220301. DOI: 10.1007/s11433-021-1793-6

Long, G. L. (2023). Enhanced universality in quantum neural networks with fewer qubits and reduced circuit depth. *Science China. Physics, Mechanics & Astronomy*, 66(7), 270361. DOI: 10.1007/s11433-023-2144-9

Luckow, A., Klepsch, J., & Pichlmeier, J. (2021). Quantum computing: Towards industry reference problems. *Digitale Welt*, 5(2), 38–45. DOI: 10.1007/s42354-021-0335-7

Lu, W., Lu, Y., Li, J., Sigov, A., Ratkin, L., & Ivanov, L. A. (2024). Quantum Machine Learning: Classifications, Challenges, and Solutions. *Journal of Industrial Information Integration*, 42, 100736. DOI: 10.1016/j.jii.2024.100736

MacCormack, I., Delaney, C., Galda, A., Aggarwal, N., & Narang, P. (2022). Branching quantum convolutional neural networks. *Physical Review Research*, 4(1), 013117. DOI: 10.1103/PhysRevResearch.4.013117

Maheswari, B. U., Imambi, S. S., Hasan, D., Meenakshi, S., Pratheep, V., & Boopathi, S. (2023). Internet of things and machine learning-integrated smart robotics. In *Global Perspectives on Robotics and Autonomous Systems: Development and Applications* (pp. 240–258). IGI Global. DOI: 10.4018/978-1-6684-7791-5.ch010

Makino, M., Yoshimoto, R., Ono, M., Itoko, T., Katsuki, T., Koseki, A., Kudo, M., Haida, K., Kuroda, J., Yanagiya, R., Saitoh, E., Hoshinaga, K., Yuzawa, Y., & Suzuki, A. (2019). Artificial intelligence predicts the progression of diabetic kidney disease using big data machine learning. *Scientific Reports*, 9(1), 11862. DOI: 10.1038/s41598-019-48263-5 PMID: 31413285

Malathi, J., Kusha, K., Isaac, S., Ramesh, A., Rajendiran, M., & Boopathi, S. (2024). IoT-Enabled Remote Patient Monitoring for Chronic Disease Management and Cost Savings: Transforming Healthcare. In *Advances in Explainable AI Applications for Smart Cities* (pp. 371–388). IGI Global.

Manan, I., Rehman, F., Sharif, H., Riaz, N., Atif, M., & Aqeel, M. (2022, December). Quantum computing and machine learning algorithms-a review. In 2022 3rd International Conference on Innovations in Computer Science & Software Engineering (ICONICS) (pp. 1-6). IEEE. DOI: 10.1109/ICONICS56716.2022.10100452

Mandadapu, P. (2024). Exploring Quantum-Enhanced Machine Learning for Computer Vision: Applications and Insights on Noisy Intermediate-Scale Quantum Devices. *arXiv Preprint arXiv:2404.02177.*

Mangini, S., Tacchino, F., Gerace, D., Bajoni, D., & Macchiavello, C. (2021). Quantum computing models for artificial neural networks. *Europhysics Letters*, 134(1), 10002. DOI: 10.1209/0295-5075/134/10002

Manikandan, S. K. (2021). Equidistant quenches in few-level quantum systems. *Physical Review Research*, 3(4), 043108. DOI: 10.1103/PhysRevResearch.3.043108

Manzalini, A. (2020). Quantum communications in future networks and services. [DOI]. *Quantum Reports*, 2(1), 221–232. DOI: 10.3390/quantum2010014

Martinez, J. E., Fuentes, P., Crespo, P. M., & Garcia-Frias, J. (2020). Approximating decoherence processes for the design and simulation of quantum error correction codes on classical computers. *IEEE Access : Practical Innovations, Open Solutions*, 8, 206469–206477. DOI: 10.1109/ACCESS.2020.3025619

Martin, K. D., & Murphy, P. E. (2017).. . *Journal of the Academy of Marketing Science.*

Maslov, D., Dueck, G. V., & Miller, D. M. (2005). Synthesis of Fredkin-Toffoli reversible networks. *IEEE Transactions on Very Large Scale Integration (VLSI) Systems*, 13(6), 765–769. DOI: 10.1109/TVLSI.2005.844284

McClean, J. R., Boixo, S., Smelyanskiy, V. N., Babbush, R., & Neven, H. (2018). Barren plateaus in quantum neural network training landscapes. *Nature Communications*, 9(1), 1–6. DOI: 10.1038/s41467-018-07090-4 PMID: 30446662

McKay, D. C., Wood, C. J., Sheldon, S., Chow, J. M., & Gambetta, J. M. (2017). Efficient Z gates for quantum computing. *Physical Review. A*, 96(2), 022330. DOI: 10.1103/PhysRevA.96.022330

Mehdiyev, N., & Fettke, P. (2020). *Local post-hoc explanations for predictive process monitoring in manufacturing. arXiv*. DOI.

Melnichenko, G. (2010). Energy discriminant analysis, quantum logic, and fuzzy sets. *Journal of Multivariate Analysis*, 101(1), 68–76. DOI: 10.1016/j.jmva.2009.04.011

Melnikov, A., Kordzanganeh, M., Alodjants, A., & Lee, R.-K. (2023). Quantum machine learning: From physics to software engineering. *Advances in Physics: X*, 8(1), 2165452. DOI: 10.1080/23746149.2023.2165452

Michalski, T. (2021). Innovation, risk and finance paradigm from the polish perspective. *International Journal of Innovation Studies*, 5(3), 107–112. DOI: 10.1016/j.ijis.2021.07.002

Miklosik, A., & Evans, N. (2020). Impact of big data and machine learning on digital transformation in marketing: A literature review. *IEEE Access : Practical Innovations, Open Solutions*, 8, 101284–101292. DOI: 10.1109/ACCESS.2020.2998754

Minssen, T., Gerke, S., Aboy, M., Price, N., & Cohen, G. (2020). Regulatory responses to medical machine learning. *Journal of Law and the Biosciences*, 7(1), lsaa002. DOI: 10.1093/jlb/lsaa002 PMID: 34221415

Mitra, S., & Hayashi, Y. (2000). Neuro-fuzzy rule generation: Survey in soft computing framework. *IEEE Transactions on Neural Networks*, 11(3), 748–768. DOI: 10.1109/72.846746 PMID: 18249802

Modak, C., Ghosh, S. K., Sarkar, M. A. I., Sharif, M. K., Arif, M., Bhuiyan, M., Ahmed, M. P., Pabel, M. A. H., & Devi, S. (2024). Machine Learning Model in Digital Marketing Strategies for Customer Behavior: Harnessing CNNs for Enhanced Customer Satisfaction and Strategic Decision-Making. *Journal of Economics. Finance and Accounting Studies*, 6(3), 178–186.

Mohanraj, G., Krishna, K. S., Lakshmi, B. S., Vijayalakshmi, A., Pramila, P. V., & Boopathi, S. (2024). Optimizing Trust and Security in Healthcare 4.0: Human Factors in Lightweight Secured IoMT Ecosystems. In *Lightweight Digital Trust Architectures in the Internet of Medical Things (IoMT)* (pp. 52–72). IGI Global. DOI: 10.4018/979-8-3693-2109-6.ch004

Mondal, A., & Parhi, K. K. (2024). Optimization of Quantum Circuits for Stabilizer Codes. IEEE Transactions on Circuits and Systems I: Regular Papers.

Mori, T. (2023). Floquet states in open quantum systems. *Annual Review of Condensed Matter Physics*, 14(1), 35–56. DOI: 10.1146/annurev-conmatphys-040721-015537

Morita, M., Kendrick, B. K., Kłos, J., Kotochigova, S., Brumer, P., & Tscherbul, T. V. (2023). Signatures of Non-universal Quantum Dynamics of Ultracold Chemical Reactions of Polar Alkali Dimer Molecules with Alkali Metal Atoms: Li (2S)+ NaLi (a 3Σ+)→ Na (2S)+ Li2 (a 3Σ u+). *The Journal of Physical Chemistry Letters*, 14(14), 3413–3421. DOI: 10.1021/acs.jpclett.3c00159 PMID: 37001115

Moşteanu, N. R., & Faccia, A. (2021). Fintech frontiers in quantum computing, fractals, and Blockchain Distributed ledger: Paradigm shifts and open innovation. *Journal of Open Innovation*, 7(1), 19. DOI: 10.3390/joitmc7010019

Mouck, T. (1998). Capital markets research and real world complexity: The emerging challenge of chaos theory. *Accounting, Organizations and Society*, 23(2), 189–215. DOI: 10.1016/S0361-3682(97)00004-4

Mummadi, S., & Fathima, S. (2024, June). A Comprehensive Study on Quantum Key Distribution Protocols. In 2024 15th International Conference on Computing Communication and Networking Technologies (ICCCNT) (pp. 1-8). IEEE.

Mummadi, S., & Udari, G. C. (2023, July). Design and Implementation of Low Quantum Cost Reversible Universal Shift Register. In 2023 14th International Conference on Computing Communication and Networking Technologies (ICCCNT) (pp. 1-7). IEEE.

Mummadi, S., & Rudra, B. (2023). Fundamentals of Quantum Computation and Basic Quantum Gates. In *Handbook of Research on Quantum Computing for Smart Environments* (pp. 1–24). IGI Global. DOI: 10.4018/978-1-6684-6697-1.ch001

Mummadi, S., & Rudra, B. (2023). Practical demonstration of quantum key distribution protocol with error correction mechanism. *International Journal of Theoretical Physics*, 62(4), 86.

Muthukumar, R., Pratheep, V. G. G., Sultanuddin, S. J., Kunduru, K. R., Kumar, P., & Boopathi, S. (2024). Leveraging Fuel Cell Technology With AI and ML Integration for Next-Generation Vehicles: Empowering Electric Mobility. In A Sustainable Future with E-Mobility: Concepts, Challenges, and Implementations (pp. 312-337). IGI Global.

Nakahara, M. (2012). Frank Gaitan: Quantum error correction and fault-tolerant quantum computing. [DOI]. *Quantum Information Processing*, 11(5), 1279–1282. DOI: 10.1007/s11128-011-0287-1

Namdeo, S., Khurana, S., & Nene, M. J. (2024). Quantum-Enhanced Cognitive Systems: Harnessing Parameterized Quantum Circuits for Advanced Machine Learning Applications. *International Conference on Innovations and Advances in Cognitive Systems*, 257–271. DOI: 10.1007/978-3-031-69201-7_20

Neumann, N., Phillipson, F., & Versluis, R. (2019). Machine learning in the quantum era. *Digitale Welt*, 3(2), 24–29. DOI: 10.1007/s42354-019-0164-0

Ngiam, J., Khosla, A., Kim, M., Nam, J., Lee, H., & Ng, A. Y. (2011). Multimodal deep learning. In *Proceedings of the 28th international conference on machine learning (ICML-11)* (pp. 689-696).

Nguyen, T., Sipola, T., & Hautamäki, J. (2024). Machine Learning Applications of Quantum Computing: A Review. *arXiv Preprint arXiv:2406.13262*.

Nielsen, M. A., & Chuang, I. L. (2010). *Quantum computation and quantum information.* Cambridge university press.

Nishihara, M., Sawada, T., & Kato, H. (2023). Corporate investment, financing, and exit model with an earnings-based borrowing constraint. *International Review of Financial Analysis*, 85, 102456. DOI: 10.1016/j.irfa.2022.102456

Olorunsogo, T., Jacks, B. S., & Ajala, O. A. (2024). Leveraging quantum computing for inclusive and responsible AI development: A conceptual and review framework. *Computer Science & IT Research Journal*, 5(3), 671–680. DOI: 10.51594/csitrj.v5i3.927

Ortolano, G., Napoli, C., Harney, C., Pirandola, S., Leonetti, G., Boucher, P., Losero, E., Genovese, M., & Ruo-Berchera, I. (2023). Quantum-enhanced pattern recognition. *Physical Review Applied*, 20(2), 024072. DOI: 10.1103/PhysRevApplied.20.024072

Orús, R., Mugel, S., & Lizaso, E. (2019). Quantum computing for finance: Overview and prospects. *Reviews in Physics*, 4, 100028. DOI: 10.1016/j.revip.2019.100028

Pachiappan, K., Anitha, K., Pitchai, R., Sangeetha, S., Satyanarayana, T., & Boopathi, S. (2024). Intelligent Machines, IoT, and AI in Revolutionizing Agriculture for Water Processing. In *Handbook of Research on AI and ML for Intelligent Machines and Systems* (pp. 374–399). IGI Global.

Pakela, J. (2021). Quantum Inspired Machine Learning Algorithms for Adaptive Radiotherapy (Doctoral dissertation).

Palle, R. R. (2018).. . *International Journal of Intelligent Automation and Computing*, 1(1), 33–40. https://research.tensorgate.org/index.php/IJIAC/article/view/101

Pal, S., Bhattacharya, M., Lee, S.-S., & Chakraborty, C. (2023).. . *Molecular Biotechnology*.

Parisi, L., Neagu, D., Ma, R., & Campean, F. (2022). Quantum ReLU activation for Convolutional Neural Networks to improve diagnosis of Parkinson's disease and COVID-19. *Expert Systems with Applications*, 187, 115892. DOI: 10.1016/j.eswa.2021.115892

Patel, O. P., Bharill, N., Tiwari, A., & Prasad, M. (2019). A novel quantum-inspired fuzzy based neural network for data classification. *IEEE Transactions on Emerging Topics in Computing*, 9(2), 1031–1044. DOI: 10.1109/TETC.2019.2901272

Paudel, H. P., Syamlal, M., Crawford, S. E., Lee, Y. L., Shugayev, R. A., Lu, P., Ohodnicki, P. R., Mollot, D., & Duan, Y. (2022). Quantum computing and simulations for energy applications: Review and perspective. *ACS Engineering Au*, 2(3), 151–196. DOI: 10.1021/acsengineeringau.1c00033

Peral-García, D., Cruz-Benito, J., & García-Peñalvo, F. J. (2024). Systematic literature review: Quantum machine learning and its applications. *Computer Science Review*, 51, 100619. DOI: 10.1016/j.cosrev.2024.100619

Peres, A. (1985). Reversible logic and quantum computers. *Physical review A*, 32(6), 3266.

Perifanis, N.-A., & Kitsios, F. (2023). Investigating the influence of artificial intelligence on business value in the digital era of strategy: A literature review. *Information (Basel)*, 14(2), 85. DOI: 10.3390/info14020085

Petschnigg, C., Brandstötter, M., Pichler, H., Hofbaur, M., & Dieber, B. (2019). Quantum computation in robotic science and applications. In *2019 International Conference on Robotics and Automation (ICRA)* (pp. 803–810). https://doi.org/DOI: 10.1109/ICRA.2019.8793768

Picton, P. D. (1994). Modified Fredkin gates in logic design. *Microelectronics Journal*, 25(6), 437–441. DOI: 10.1016/0026-2692(94)90068-X

Pirandola, S., Braunstein, S. L., & Lloyd, S. (2023). Advances in quantum cryptography and post-quantum security. *Quantum Science and Technology*, 8(2), 238–260. DOI: 10.1088/2058-9565/ace432

Pitchai, R., Guru, K. V., Gandhi, J. N., Komala, C. R., Kumar, J. R. D., & Boopathi, S. (2024). Fog Computing-Integrated ML-Based Framework and Solutions for Intelligent Systems: Digital Healthcare Applications. In *Technological Advancements in Data Processing for Next Generation Intelligent Systems* (pp. 196–224). IGI Global. DOI: 10.4018/979-8-3693-0968-1.ch008

Potter, K., & Stilinski, D. (2024). *Quantum Machine Learning: Exploring the Potential of Quantum Computing forAI Applications.*

Prabha, C. (2024). Future Perspective and Emerging Trends in Computational Intelligence. *Intelligent Data Analytics for Bioinformatics and Biomedical Systems*, 381–396.

Pramila, P., Amudha, S., Saravanan, T., Sankar, S. R., Poongothai, E., & Boopathi, S. (2023). Design and Development of Robots for Medical Assistance: An Architectural Approach. In *Contemporary Applications of Data Fusion for Advanced Healthcare Informatics* (pp. 260–282). IGI Global.

Prasad, M. S. C., Dhanalakshmi, M., Mohan, M., Somasundaram, B., Valarmathi, R., & Boopathi, S. (2024). Machine Learning-Integrated Sustainable Engineering and Energy Systems: Innovations at the Nexus. In *Harnessing High-Performance Computing and AI for Environmental Sustainability* (pp. 74–98). IGI Global. DOI: 10.4018/979-8-3693-1794-5.ch004

Quercia, R. G., Rohe, W. M., & Levy, D. (2000). A new look at creative finance. *Housing Policy Debate*, 11(4), 943–972. DOI: 10.1080/10511482.2000.9521393

Ramezani, S. B., Sommers, A., Manchukonda, H. K., Rahimi, S., & Amirlatifi, A. (2020). Machine learning algorithms in quantum computing: A survey. *2020 International Joint Conference on Neural Networks (IJCNN)*, 1–8. DOI: 10.1109/IJCNN48605.2020.9207714

Ramkumar, G., Othman, B., Malviya, B., Mohamma, A. J., Narayana, M. S., & Verma, D. (2022). A conceptual analysis on the impact of machine learning towards on digital marketing transformation. *2022 2nd International Conference on Advance Computing and Innovative Technologies in Engineering (ICACITE)*, 2274–2278.

Ramudu, K., Mohan, V. M., Jyothirmai, D., Prasad, D., Agrawal, R., & Boopathi, S. (2023). Machine Learning and Artificial Intelligence in Disease Prediction: Applications, Challenges, Limitations, Case Studies, and Future Directions. In *Contemporary Applications of Data Fusion for Advanced Healthcare Informatics* (pp. 297–318). IGI Global.

Ranga, D., Rana, A., Prajapat, S., Kumar, P., Kumar, K., & Vasilakos, A. V. (2024). Quantum Machine Learning: Exploring the Role of Data Encoding Techniques, Challenges, and Future Directions. *Mathematics*, 12(21), 3318. DOI: 10.3390/math12213318

Ranjan, A., Arya, A. K. S., & Ravinder, M. "Quantum Techniques for Image Processing," 2020 2nd International Conference on Advances in Computing, Communication Control and Networking (ICACCCN), Greater Noida, India, 2020, pp. 1035-1039, DOI: 10.1109/ICACCCN51052.2020.9362910

Raparthi, M., Nimmagadda, V. S. P., Sahu, M. K., Gayam, S. R., Pattyam, S. P., Kondapaka, K. K., & Kasaraneni, B. P. (2022). Quantum machine learning: A new frontier in data science. *Journal of Quantum Information Science*, 12(3), 123–145. 10.4236/jqis.2022.123009

Raussendorf, R. (2012). Key ideas in quantum error correction. *Philosophical Transactions of the Royal Society A: Mathematical, Physical and Engineering Sciences, 370*(1975), 4541–4565. DOI

Ravi, G. S., Smith, K. N., Gokhale, P., & Chong, F. T. (2021, November). Quantum Computing in the Cloud: Analyzing job and machine characteristics. In *2021 IEEE International Symposium on Workload Characterization (IISWC)* (pp. 39-50). IEEE. DOI: 10.1109/IISWC53511.2021.00015

Ravisankar, A., Shanthi, A., Lavanya, S., Ramaratnam, M., Krishnamoorthy, V., & Boopathi, S. (2024). Harnessing 6G for Consumer-Centric Business Strategies Across Electronic Industries. In *AI Impacts in Digital Consumer Behavior* (pp. 241–270). IGI Global.

Rayhan, A., & Rayhan, S. (2023). *Quantum Computing and AI: A Quantum Leap in Intelligence*.

Ren, Y., Ma, C., Chen, X., Lei, Y., & Wang, Y. (2023). Sustainable finance and blockchain: A systematic review and research agenda. *Research in International Business and Finance*, 64, 101871. DOI: 10.1016/j.ribaf.2022.101871

Rieffel, E., & Polak, W. (2000). An introduction to quantum computing for non-physicists. *ACM Computing Surveys*, 32(3), 300–335. DOI: 10.1145/367701.367709

Riera-Campeny, A., Moreno-Cardoner, M., & Sanpera, A. (2020). Time crystallinity in open quantum systems. *Quantum : the Open Journal for Quantum Science*, 4, 270. DOI: 10.22331/q-2020-05-25-270

Rousseau, P. L., & Sylla, R. (2005). Emerging financial markets and early US growth. *Explorations in Economic History*, 42(1), 1–26. DOI: 10.1016/j.eeh.2004.03.004

Saeedi, M., & Markov, I. L. (2013). Synthesis and optimization of reversible circuits—A survey. *ACM Computing Surveys*, 45(2), 1–34.

Sahebi, A. G., Kordheydari, R., & Aghaei, M. (2022a). A new approach in marketing research: Identifying the customer expected value through machine learning and big data analysis in the tourism industry. [AMT]. *Advancement in Management and Technology*, 2(3), 26–42.

Sanpedro, J. M. R., Lavana, U., & Miranda, E. M. (2014). SCHR\"ODINGER GROUP AND QUANTUM FINANCE. *International Journal of Pure and Applied Mathematics*, 90(3). Advance online publication. DOI: 10.12732/ijpam.v90i3.3

Saravanan, S., Khare, R., Umamaheswari, K., Khare, S., Krishne Gowda, B. S., & Boopathi, S. (2024). AI and ML Adaptive Smart-Grid Energy Management Systems: Exploring Advanced Innovations. In *Principles and Applications in Speed Sensing and Energy Harvesting for Smart Roads* (pp. 166–196). IGI Global. DOI: 10.4018/978-1-6684-9214-7.ch006

Satav, S. D., Hasan, D. S., Pitchai, R., Mohanaprakash, T., Sultanuddin, S., & Boopathi, S. (2023). Next generation of internet of things (ngiot) in healthcare systems. In *Sustainable Science and Intelligent Technologies for Societal Development* (pp. 307–330). IGI Global.

Satuluri, V. R., & Ponnusamy, V. (2021). Quantum-enhanced machine learning. *2021 Smart Technologies, Communication and Robotics (STCR)*, 1–6.

Schaefer, H. H., & Schaefer, H. H. (1971). *Locally convex topological vector spaces*. Springer New York. DOI: 10.1007/978-1-4684-9928-5

Schrödinger, E. (1926). An undulatory theory of the mechanics of atoms and molecules. *Physical Review*, 28(6), 1049–1070. DOI: 10.1103/PhysRev.28.1049

Schuld, M., & Petruccione, F. (2021). *Machine learning with quantum computers* (Vol. 676). Springer. DOI: 10.1007/978-3-030-83098-4

Schuld, M., Sinayskiy, I., & Petruccione, F. (2014). The quest for a quantum neural network. *Quantum Information Processing*, 13(11), 2567–2586. DOI: 10.1007/s11128-014-0809-8

Schuld, M., Sinayskiy, I., & Petruccione, F. (2015). An introduction to quantum machine learning. *Contemporary Physics*, 56(2), 172–185. DOI: 10.1080/00107514.2014.964942

Schuld, M., Sinayskiy, I., & Petruccione, F. (2022). Quantum machine learning for supervised and unsupervised algorithms. *Nature*, 610(1), 1–15. DOI: 10.1038/s41586-022-04589-5

Seino, J., Kageyama, R., Fujinami, M., Ikabata, Y., & Nakai, H. (2019). Semi-local machine-learned kinetic energy density functional demonstrating smooth potential energy curves. *Chemical Physics Letters*, 734, 136732. DOI: 10.1016/j.cplett.2019.136732

Sekhar, K. C., Ranganathan, L., Bathrinath, S., Premnath, D., Yuvasri, B., & Boopathi, S. (2024). Cloud Computing Adoption for Small and Medium Enterprises in Mechanical Engineering. In *Advances in Web Technologies and Engineering* (pp. 219–247). IGI Global. DOI: 10.4018/979-8-3693-1487-6.ch011

Sengeni, D., Padmapriya, G., Imambi, S. S., Suganthi, D., Suri, A., & Boopathi, S. (2023). Biomedical waste handling method using artificial intelligence techniques. In *Handbook of Research on Safe Disposal Methods of Municipal Solid Wastes for a Sustainable Environment* (pp. 306–323). IGI Global. DOI: 10.4018/978-1-6684-8117-2.ch022

Sequeira, A. M. R. (2021). *Quantum-enhanced reinforcement learning* [PhD Thesis].

Shah, A., Shah, M., & Kanani, P. "Leveraging Quantum Computing for Supervised Classification," 2020 4th International Conference on Intelligent Computing and Control Systems (ICICCS), Madurai, India, 2020, pp. 256-261, DOI: 10.1109/ICICCS48265.2020.9120975

Shaikh, T. A., & Ali, R. (2016, December). Quantum computing in big data analytics: A survey. In 2016 IEEE international conference on computer and information technology (CIT) (pp. 112-115). IEEE.

Sharma, S. (2020). Qeml (quantum enhanced machine learning): Using quantum computing to enhance ml classifiers and feature spaces. *arXiv Preprint arXiv:2002.10453*.

Sharma, N., & Ketti Ramachandran, R. (2021). The emerging trends of quantum computing towards data security and key management. *Archives of Computational Methods in Engineering*, •••, 1–14.

Shehab, M., Abualigah, L., Shambour, Q., Abu-Hashem, M. A., Shambour, M. K. Y., Alsalibi, A. I., & Gandomi, A. H. (2022). Machine learning in medical applications: A review of state-of-the-art methods. *Computers in Biology and Medicine*, 145, 105458. DOI: 10.1016/j.compbiomed.2022.105458 PMID: 35364311

Shutaywi, M., & Kachouie, N. N. (2021). Silhouette analysis for performance evaluation in machine learning with applications to clustering. *Entropy (Basel, Switzerland)*, 23(6), 759. DOI: 10.3390/e23060759 PMID: 34208552

Smolyak, A., Levy, O., Shekhtman, L., & Havlin, S. (2018). Interdependent networks in Economics and Finance—A Physics approach. *Physica A*, 512, 612–619. DOI: 10.1016/j.physa.2018.08.089

Somasundaram, R., Varalakshmi, S., Sanadi, H., Saini, R., Chinnusamy, S., & Boopaathi. (2024). Entrepreneurship in emerging markets and intrapreneurship within organizations. In *Advances in Business Strategy and Competitive Advantage* (pp. 291–322). IGI Global.

Somefun, K., Perchet, R., Yin, C., & Leote de Carvalho, R. (2023). Allocating to thematic investments. *Financial Analysts Journal*, 79(1), 18–36.

Sreedhar, P. S. S., Sujay, V., Rani, M. R., Melita, L., Reshma, S., & Boopathi, S. (2024). Impacts of 5G Machine Learning Techniques on Telemedicine and Social Media Professional Connection in Healthcare. In *Advances in Medical Technologies and Clinical Practice* (pp. 209–234). IGI Global. DOI: 10.4018/979-8-3693-1934-5.ch012

Steane, A. M. (1996). Error correcting codes in quantum theory. *Physical Review Letters*, 77(5), 793–797. DOI: 10.1103/PhysRevLett.77.793 PMID: 10062908

Steane, A. M. (1996). Multiple particle interference and quantum error correction. *Proceedings - Royal Society. Mathematical, Physical and Engineering Sciences*, 452(1954), 2551–2577. DOI: 10.1098/rspa.1996.0136

Straube, D.F.C.(2023).Quantumcomputingasanenablingtechnologyforthenextbusiness cycle.

Subha, S., Inbamalar, T., Komala, C., Suresh, L. R., Boopathi, S., & Alaskar, K. (2023). A Remote Health Care Monitoring system using internet of medical things (IoMT). *IEEE Explore*, 1–6.

Sultana, F., Bhardwaj, R., Kumar, R. N., Gaur, R., Shankar, S. P., & Bharadwaj, A. (2024, April). Smart Traffic Management System for Efficient Mobility and Emergency Response. In *2024 International Conference on Knowledge Engineering and Communication Systems (ICKECS)* (Vol. 1, pp. 1-5). IEEE. DOI: 10.1109/ICKECS61492.2024.10616800

Sun, G. "Splicing ET (error-tolerant) Quantum Computing System," 2019 18th International Conference on Optical Communications and Networks (ICOCN), Huangshan, China, 2019, pp. 1-3, DOI: 10.1109/ICOCN.2019.8934156

Suresh Babu, C. V. Sathiya Narayana S. (2024). Navigating Uncharted Waters: Overcoming Challenges in Integrating Machine Learning and Deep Learning for Enhanced Clinical Risk. In H. Liu, R. Tripathy, & P. Bhattacharya (Eds.), Clinical Practice and Unmet Challenges in AI-Enhanced Healthcare Systems (pp. 289-310). IGI Global. DOI: 10.4018/979-8-3693-2703-6.ch015

Sussillo, D., & Abbott, L. F. (2009). Generating coherent patterns of activity from chaotic neural networks. *Neuron*, 63(4), 544–557. DOI: 10.1016/j.neuron.2009.07.018 PMID: 19709635

Swathi, M., & Rudra, B. (2021, January). Implementation of reversible logic gates with quantum gates. In 2021 IEEE 11th annual computing and communication workshop and conference (CCWC) (pp. 1557-1563). Ieee.

Swathi, M., & Rudra, B. (2022, April). A novel architecture for binary code to gray code converter using quantum cellular automata. In Edge Analytics: Select Proceedings of 26th International Conference—ADCOM 2020 (pp. 43-61). Singapore: Springer Singapore.

Swathi, M., & Rudra, B. (2022, January). Novel encoding method for quantum error correction. In 2022 IEEE 12th Annual Computing and Communication Workshop and Conference (CCWC) (pp. 1001-1005). IEEE.

Swathi, M., & Rudra, B. (2022). *"Experimental analysis of a quantum encoder in various quantum systems." 2022 IEEE 13th Annual Ubiquitous Computing, Electronics & Mobile Communication Conference (UEMCON)*. IEEE.

Swathi, M., & Rudra, B. (2022). A novel approach for asymmetric quantum error correction with syndrome measurement. *IEEE Access : Practical Innovations, Open Solutions*, 10, 44669–44676. DOI: 10.1109/ACCESS.2022.3170039

Swathi, M., & Rudra, B. (2022). An efficient approach for quantum entanglement purification. *International Journal of Quantum Information*, 20(04), 2250004.

Tacchino, F., Chiesa, A., Carretta, S., & Gerace, D. (2020). Quantum computers as universal quantum simulators: State-of-the-art and perspectives. *Advanced Quantum Technologies*, 3(3), 1900052. DOI: 10.1002/qute.201900052

Taghandiki, K. (2024). Quantum Machine Learning Unveiled: A Comprehensive Review. *Journal of Engineering and Applied Research*, 1(2), 29–48.

Taherdoost, H., & Madanchian, M. (2023). AI Advancements: Comparison of Innovative Techniques. *AI*, 5(1), 38–54. DOI: 10.3390/ai5010003

Tall, D., Tall, D., & Tirosh, D. (2001). Infinity - The never-ending struggle. In Educational Studies in Mathematics (Vols. 48–48, pp. 199–238). https://wrap.warwick.ac.uk/475/1/WRAP_Tall_dot2001o-esm-intro-tirosh.pdf

Thapliyal, H., & Muñoz-Coreas, E. (2019). Design of quantum computing circuits. *IT Professional*, 21(6), 22–26.

The Intuition of Infinity on JSTOR. (n.d.). www.jstor.org. https://www.jstor.org/stable/3481965

Tiwari, P., Zhang, L., Qu, Z., & Muhammad, G. (2024). Quantum Fuzzy Neural Network for multimodal sentiment and sarcasm detection. *Information Fusion*, 103, 102085. DOI: 10.1016/j.inffus.2023.102085

Tripathi, S. M., Upadhyay, H., & Soni, J. (2024). Advanced Cardiovascular Health in a Quantum AI-driven Healthcare Framework. *Authorea Preprints*. DOI: 10.36227/techrxiv.171207460.05729698/v1

Turiel, A., & Pérez-Vicente, C. J. (2003). Multifractal geometry in stock market time series. *Physica A*, 322, 629–649. DOI: 10.1016/S0378-4371(02)01830-7

Tyagi, A. K., & Chahal, P. (2020). Artificial intelligence and machine learning algorithms. In *Challenges and applications for implementing machine learning in computer vision* (pp. 188–219). IGI Global. DOI: 10.4018/978-1-7998-0182-5.ch008

Tyagi, S., Pathak, S., Raj, V. H., Laxminarayanamma, K., Singh, N., & Dhanraj, J. A. (2025). Quantum Network Applications in AI-Driven Risk Management. In *Multidisciplinary Applications of AI and Quantum Networking* (pp. 289–308). IGI Global.

Ukpabi, D. C., Karjaluoto, H., Bötticher, A., Nikiforova, A., Petrescu, D., Schindler, P., Valtenbergs, V., & Lehmann, L. (2023). Framework for understanding quantum computing use cases from a multidisciplinary perspective and future research directions. *Futures*, 154, 103277. DOI: 10.1016/j.futures.2023.103277

Unruh, W. G. (1995). Maintaining Coherence in Quantum Computers. *Physical Review A*, 51(2), 992–997. DOI: 10.1103/PhysRevA.51.992 PMID: 9911677

Upadhyaya, A. N., Saqib, A., Devi, J. V., Rallapalli, S., Sudha, S., & Boopathi, S. (2024). Implementation of the Internet of Things (IoT) in Remote Healthcare. In *Advances in Medical Technologies and Clinical Practice* (pp. 104–124). IGI Global. DOI: 10.4018/979-8-3693-1934-5.ch006

Upama, P. B., Faruk, M. J. H., Nazim, M., Masum, M., Shahriar, H., Uddin, G., . . . Rahman, A. (2022, June). Evolution of quantum computing: A systematic survey on the use of quantum computing tools. In 2022 IEEE 46th Annual Computers, Software, and Applications Conference (COMPSAC) (pp. 520-529). IEEE. DOI: 10.1109/COMPSAC54236.2022.00096

Ur Rasool, R., Ahmad, H. F., Rafique, W., Qayyum, A., Qadir, J., & Anwar, Z. (2023). Quantum computing for healthcare: A review. *Future Internet*, 15(3), 94. DOI: 10.3390/fi15030094

Vadyala, S. R., & Betgeri, S. N. (2023). General implementation of quantum physics-informed neural networks. *Array (New York, N.Y.)*, 18, 100287. DOI: 10.1016/j.array.2023.100287

Vallero, M., Casagranda, G., Vella, F., & Rech, P. (2024). On the efficacy of surface codes in compensating for radiation events in superconducting devices. *arXiv*. https://doi.org//arXiv.2310.15555DOI: 10.1109/SC41406.2024.00075

Van Chau, D., & He, J. (2024). Machine Learning Innovations for Proactive Customer Behavior Prediction: A Strategic Tool for Dynamic Market Adaptation. *Sage Science Review of Applied Machine Learning*, 7(1), 22–29.

Van Gemert, J. C., Geusebroek, J. M., Veenman, C. J., & Smeulders, A. W. (2008). Kernel codebooks for scene categorization. In *Computer Vision–ECCV 2008: 10th European Conference on Computer Vision, Marseille, France, October 12-18, 2008* [Springer Berlin Heidelberg.]. *Proceedings*, 10(Part III), 696–709.

van Loock, P. (2010). A note on quantum error correction with continuous variables. *Journal of Modern Optics*, 57(19), 1965–1971.

Van Nieuwenhuizen, C. (2024). Quantum-enhanced Optimization-Applications and Challenges: Analyzing applications and challenges of quantum-enhanced optimization algorithms for solving large-scale optimization problems in various domains. *Journal of Artificial Intelligence Research and Applications*, 4(1), 296–306.

Varadam, D., Shankar, S. P., Hegde, P., Shobitha, V., Sunidhi, M., & Sanjana, N. (2024). Intelligent Techniques for Detection and Diagnosis of Neurodegenerative Diseases. In AI-Driven Alzheimer's Disease Detection and Prediction (pp. 293-319). IGI Global. DOI: 10.4018/979-8-3693-3605-2.ch020

Varadam, D., Shankar, S. P., Shankar, A., Narayan, A., & Kumar, T. N. (2024). Application of AI and Blockchain Technologies in the Medical Domain. AI and Blockchain Applications in Industrial Robotics, 200-225.

Varadam, D., Shankar, S. P., Bharadwaj, A., Saxena, T., Agrawal, S., & Dayananda, S. (2024). Enhancing industrial robotics performance and security with AI and blockchain technologies. In *AI and blockchain applications in industrial robotics* (pp. 58–81). IGI Global.

Varsha, T., Shekar, Y. C., Shankar, S. P., Bharadwaj, A., Varadam, D., & Supriya, M. S. (2023, July). On Campus Student Recruitment Analysis using Machine Learning techniques. In *2023 IEEE International Conference on Electronics, Computing and Communication Technologies (CONECCT)* (pp. 1-6). IEEE. DOI: 10.1109/CONECCT57959.2023.10234797

Vasudevan, D. P., Lala, P. K., Di, J., & Parkerson, J. P. (2006). Reversible-logic design with online testability. *IEEE Transactions on Instrumentation and Measurement*, 55(2), 406–414. DOI: 10.1109/TIM.2006.870319

Veeranjaneyulu, R., Boopathi, S., Narasimharao, J., Gupta, K. K., Reddy, R. V. K., & Ambika, R. (2023). Identification of Heart Diseases using Novel Machine Learning Method. *IEEE- Explore*, 1–6.

Venkateswaran, N., Kunduru, K. R., Ashwin, N., Sundar Ganesh, C. S., Hema, N., & Boopathi, S. (2024). Navigating the Future of Ultra-Smart Computing Cyberspace: Beyond Boundaries. In *Advances in Computational Intelligence and Robotics* (pp. 170–199). IGI Global. DOI: 10.4018/979-8-3693-2399-1.ch007

Venkateswaran, N., Vidhya, R., Naik, D. A., Raj, T. M., Munjal, N., & Boopathi, S. (2023). Study on Sentence and Question Formation Using Deep Learning Techniques. In *Digital Natives as a Disruptive Force in Asian Businesses and Societies* (pp. 252–273). IGI Global. DOI: 10.4018/978-1-6684-6782-4.ch015

Vennila, T., Karuna, M., Srivastava, B. K., Venugopal, J., Surakasi, R., & Sampath, B. (2022). New Strategies in Treatment and Enzymatic Processes: Ethanol Production From Sugarcane Bagasse. In *Human Agro-Energy Optimization for Business and Industry* (pp. 219–240). IGI Global.

Verma, S. K., & Kumar, S. (2024). Fractal dimension analysis of financial performance of resulting companies after mergers and acquisitions. *Chaos, Solitons, and Fractals*, 181, 114683. DOI: 10.1016/j.chaos.2024.114683

Vilas, N. B., Hallas, C., Anderegg, L., Robichaud, P., Winnicki, A., Mitra, D., & Doyle, J. M. (2022). Magneto-optical trapping and sub-Doppler cooling of a polyatomic molecule. *Nature*, 606(7912), 70–74. DOI: 10.1038/s41586-022-04620-5 PMID: 35650357

Vogl, M. (2022). Controversy in financial chaos research and nonlinear dynamics: A short literature review. *Chaos, Solitons, and Fractals*, 162, 112444. DOI: 10.1016/j.chaos.2022.112444

Wallman, J. J., & Emerson, J. (2016). Noise tailoring for scalable quantum computation via randomized compiling. *Physical Review. A*, 94(5), 052325. DOI: 10.1103/PhysRevA.94.052325

Wang, S., Pei, Z., Wang, C., & Wu, J. (2021). Shaping the future of the application of quantum computing in intelligent transportation system. *Intelligent and Converged Networks*, 2(4), 259–276. DOI: 10.23919/ICN.2021.0019

Wang, X., Lin, Z., Che, L., Chen, H., & Lu, D. (2022). Experimental Quantum-Enhanced Machine Learning in Spin-Based Systems. *Advanced Quantum Technologies*, 5(8), 2200005. DOI: 10.1002/qute.202200005

Wang, Y., & Liu, H. (2022). Quantum computing in a statistical context. *Annual Review of Statistics and Its Application*, 9(1), 479–504. DOI: 10.1146/annurev-statistics-042720-024040

Wang, Y., Yu, Y., Zhang, G., & Sheng, X. (2012). Fuzzy auto-adjust PID controller design of brushless DC motor. [DOI]. *Physics Procedia*, 24, 1577–1582.

Weder, B., Breitenbücher, U., Leymann, F., & Wild, K. (2020). IEEE/ACM 13th International Conference on Utility and Cloud Computing (UCC)

Weder, B., Breitenbücher, U., Leymann, F., & Wild, K. "Integrating Quantum Computing into Workflow Modeling and Execution," 2020 IEEE/ACM 13th International Conference on Utility and Cloud Computing (UCC), Leicester, UK, 2020, pp. 279-291, DOI: 10.1109/UCC48980.2020.00046

Wehner, S., Elkouss, D., & Hanson, R. (2022). Quantum internet: A vision for the future. *Science*, 362(6416), 1–10. DOI: 10.1126/science.aar7938

Westermayr, J., & Marquetand, P. (2020). Machine learning for electronically excited states of molecules. *Chemical Reviews*, 121(16), 9873–9926. DOI: 10.1021/acs.chemrev.0c00749 PMID: 33211478

Winker, T., Groppe, S., Uotila, V., Yan, Z., Lu, J., Franz, M., & Mauerer, W. (2024). Quantum machine learning: Foundations, new techniques, and opportunities for database research. *ACM Transactions on Database Systems*, 49(1), 1–30. 10.1145/3555041.3589404

Xia, Q., Xie, H., & Yang, L. (2024). Analysis of Maximum Threshold and Quantum Security for Fault-Tolerant Encoding and Decoding Scheme Base on Steane Code. arXiv preprint arXiv:2403.04297.

Xiong, J., Fischer, W. M., Inoue, K., Nakahara, M., & Bauer, C. E. (2000). Molecular evidence for the early evolution of photosynthesis. science, 289(5485), 1724-1730.

Xiujuan, L., Kagita, M. K., & others. (2021). Machine Learning Techniques for Multi-media Communications in Business Marketing. *Journal of Multiple-Valued Logic & Soft Computing, 36*.

Yankovets, T., & Vyshnevska, M. (2019). Innovations and digital marketing: Current trends of development. *Evropský Časopis Ekonomiky a Managementu.*

Yazdinejad, A., Dehghantanha, A., Parizi, R. M., & Epiphaniou, G. (2023). An optimized fuzzy deep learning model for data classification based on NSGA-II. *Neurocomputing*, 522, 116–128. DOI: 10.1016/j.neucom.2022.12.027

Yingngam, B., & Khang, A. (2024). Quantum Computing in Drug Discovery. In *The Quantum Evolution* (pp. 242–275). CRC Press. DOI: 10.1201/9781032642079-11

Yovanof, G. S., & Hazapis, G. N. (2008). Disruptive technologies, services, or business models? *Wireless Personal Communications*, 45(4), 559–574. DOI: 10.1007/s11277-008-9486-1

Zadeh, L. A. (1965). Fuzzy sets. *Information and Control*, 8(3), 338–353. DOI: 10.1016/S0019-9958(65)90241-X

Zadeh, L. A. (2015). Fuzzy logic—A personal perspective. *Fuzzy Sets and Systems*, 281, 4–20. DOI: 10.1016/j.fss.2015.05.009

Zheng, J., Gao, Q., Lü, J., Ogorzałek, M., Pan, Y., & Lü, Y. (2023). Design of a quantum convolutional neural network on quantum circuits. *Journal of the Franklin Institute*, 360(17), 13761–13777. DOI: 10.1016/j.jfranklin.2022.07.033

Zhou, H., Li, Y., Xu, H., Su, Y., & Chen, L. (2023). A self-organizing fuzzy neural network modeling approach using an adaptive quantum particle swarm optimization. *Applied Intelligence*, 53(11), 13569–13592. DOI: 10.1007/s10489-022-04133-8

Zhu, S., Gilbert, M., Chetty, I., & Siddiqui, F. (2022). The 2021 landscape of FDA-approved artificial intelligence/machine learning-enabled medical devices: An analysis of the characteristics and intended use. *International Journal of Medical Informatics*, 165, 104828. DOI: 10.1016/j.ijmedinf.2022.104828 PMID: 35780651

About the Contributors

R.I. Minu, a distinguished scholar and ACMW Chair in computer science and engineering, has forged an impressive path in academia, marked by unwavering passion for knowledge and innovation. Graduating with a B.E. in Electronics and Communication Engineering from Bharathidasan University in 2004, Dr. Minu quickly demonstrated promise in the field. She continued her academic journey, earning an M.E. in Computer Science and Engineering and later a Ph.D. from Anna University in 2007 and 2015, respectively. Her commitment to advancing knowledge led her to a Post Doc in Quantum Deep Learning Algorithm for Image Recognition at the University of Louisiana at Lafayette, USA, in 2022 and 2023. Currently serving as a Faculty Member at the Department of Computer Science and Engineering, School of Computing, SRM Institute of Science and Technology, Kattankulathur, India, Dr. Minu is a prominent figure in academia. Her research interests span a spectrum of cutting-edge technologies, including Computer Vision, Machine Vision, IoT, 5G, Edge/Fog Computing, Artificial Intelligence, Machine Learning, and Semantic Web. Dr. Minu's scholarly impact is evident in her extensive publication record, featuring over 40 research papers in esteemed peer-reviewed journals and three comprehensive books. Beyond her publications, she actively explores and advances emerging technologies such as IoT, Edge/Fog Computing, Artificial Intelligence, Data Science, Blockchain, Digital Twin, and 5G. As ACMW Chair, Dr. R.I. Minu continues to inspire and lead in the academic and professional realms, contributing significantly to the growth and evolution of computer science and engineering.

G. Nagarajan, a distinguished academician and IEEE Member, boasts a formidable background in Electrical and Electronics Engineering, Applied Electronics, and Computer Science and Engineering. His academic journey began with a B.E. degree from MS University, followed by M.E. degrees in Applied Electronics from Anna University and Computer Science and Engineering from

Sathyabama University. Dr. Nagarajan's quest for knowledge culminated in a Ph.D. in Computer Science and Engineering from Sathyabama University in 2015. His dedication to advancing research led him to pursue a Post Doc in Quantum-Inspired Blockchain-Based Trust Management System for Medical IoT Devices at the University of Louisiana at Lafayette, USA, in 2022 and 2023. Presently serving as a Faculty Member at the Department of Computer Science and Engineering, School of Computing, Sathyabama Institute of Science and Technology in Chennai, India, Dr. Nagarajan is known for his unwavering commitment to education and research. His research interests span an array of cutting-edge domains, including Computer Vision, IoT, 5G, Edge/Fog Computing, Artificial Intelligence, Machine Learning, and Wireless Sensor Networks. Dr. Nagarajan's scholarly impact is evident through his prolific publication record, featuring over 120 research papers in prestigious peer-reviewed journals such as IEEE, ACM, Springer-Verlag, Inderscience, and Elsevier. Additionally, he has authored 20 book chapters and has authored and edited three comprehensive books, solidifying his position as a thought leader in emerging technologies. His current endeavors focus on exploring and advancing emerging technologies such as IoT, Edge/Fog Computing, Artificial Intelligence, Data Science, Blockchain, Digital Twin, and 5G. Dr. Nagarajan's dedication to research excellence and his significant contributions to the academic community underscore his prominence in the field of computer science and engineering.

Martin Margala, PhD joined the School of Computing and Informatics as Professor and Director in August 2021. Before joining UL Lafayette, from September 2011 to July 2021, Dr. Margala was Professor and Chair of the Electrical and Computer Engineering Department at the University of Massachusetts Lowell and a Co-Director of the Center for Smart Cyber-Physical Systems (SCyPS). He received his PhD degree in Electrical and Computer Engineering from the University of Alberta, Canada (#61 in Global Ranking in North America region; #13 in Global subject specific ranking Electrical and Electronic Engineering in North America region USNews) in the spring of 1998. He is a senior member of ACM, IEEE, and SPIE with more than 50 journal and 200 peer reviewed conference publications in the areas of Design for Testability for Energy Efficient Architectures and Systems, High-Performance Reliable Low-Power Architectures and Reconfigurable Secure Architectures and Systems. Dr. Margala has directed 22 PhD students and 19 MS students, many of whom now hold leading positions in academia and industry. He has served on numerous program committees of international conferences and on workgroups (such as the International Technology Roadmap for Semiconductors) that have a great impact on the future direction of academia and industry.

Siva Shankar S is a highly accomplished individual with a multifaceted career in academia. Born and raised in India, Dr. Siva Shankar S has pursued a rigorous educational journey, earning a Bachelor's degree in Technology (B.Tech.), followed by a Master's degree (M.Tech.) and a Doctorate (Ph.D.) in his field of expertise. With a passion for advancing knowledge and pushing the boundaries of technology, Dr. Siva Shankar S has dedicated himself to the field of Computer Science and Engineering. His academic achievements have been recognized by prestigious institutions, and his contributions to research have earned him accolades, including being listed in the India Book of Records. As an educator, Dr. Siva Shankar S has served as an Associate Professor at KG Reddy College of Engineering and Technology in Telangana, India. In addition to teaching, he has taken on leadership roles within the department, serving as the Dean of Foreign Affairs. In this capacity, he has played a vital role in fostering international collaborations and promoting cross-cultural exchange within the academic community. Throughout his career, Dr. Siva Shankar S has demonstrated a commitment to excellence, innovation, and global engagement. His work continues to inspire students, colleagues, and researchers in the field of Computer Science and Engineering, leaving a lasting impact on the academic community and beyond.

E.Logashanmugam graduated from Madurai Kamaraj University in 1991 with Electronics and Communication Engineering as his major and subsequently acquired his Post Graduation in the same field from Madras Institute of Technology; Anna University .He had done his research in Video Signal Processing domain and received his Doctoral Degree from Sathyabama University. Having great aptitude and passion for teaching, he started his humble beginning and career at Sathyabama in 1995 as a Lecturer and has been growing professionally along with the Institution over these twenty-five years in various Academic and Administration Capacities such as Professor, Faculty Head, Dean and Administration Director. As a Dynamic Researcher, Academician and scholar, Dr.E.Logashanmugam is deeply associated with many Research Organisations such as IGCAR, BRFST, and BRNS etc. He plays an imperative and pivotal role as Principle Investigator and as such attracted a number of research projects from many scientific funding agencies of Government of India to this forerunning premier Institution and to his credit also. He had been the nodal officer in developing a Centre for Advance Electronic Testing in association with QMax Technologies, Chennai and trained more than four hundred students belonging to circuit branches which turned out to be instrumental for their Placements. In recognition of his merits and achievements Dr.E.Logashanmugam has been honoured and conferred with various awards and rewards such as Best Faculty Award from SATHYABAMA and Best Mentor award from Cognizant Technology Solutions. He has chaired many number of technical sessions in Conferences and successfully conducted a large number of short-term courses for students, Faculty Development Programs in Embedded Systems, Speech, Signal and Image Processing. He has contributed a lot in the fields of Video signal Processing, Image Processing, Intelligent Computing, Magnetic Bearing and control, Smart Antenna, DMD based Single Pixel camera coupled with more than 110 publications in reputed research journals and presentations in Conference Proceedings. Dr.E.Logashanmugam is a Life Member of various professional Chapters. He has a solid track record of mentoring more than 100 Graduate students over the Years. He has produced six Doctorates and at present supervising five Ph.D scholars. The Students mentored by him are now well placed in various reputed National and International organisations and research Institutions. He is currently working on the editorial boards appointed for reviewing peer journals in the field of Embedded System, Image Processing and Micro Electronic devices.

***

Aryan Bharadwaj is a passionate student, interested in research in artificial intelligence and machine learning. Growing up in Bangalore, Aryan was fascinated by the potential of technology to transform the world. He pursued his undergraduate degree in computer science, at Ramaiah University of Applied Sciences. During his studies, Aryan excelled in AI, natural language processing, and data mining courses. Apart from studies he has published several papers about AI.

G.K. SANDHIA, Working as an Associate Professor in the department of Computing Technologies, SRM Institute of Science and Technology, Kattankulathur, Chengalpattu, India. She has 17 years of experience in the field of Teaching. She completed her B.Tech – Information Technology in the year 2005 at Kamban Engineering College, Anna University, and she completed her M.E – CSE in the year 2007 at Arunai Engineering College, Anna University, and She completed her PhD in the year 2021 at SRM Institute of Science and Technology, Kattankulathur. She has interested in the following areas as Cryptography and Network Security, Cloud Computing, Machine Learning, Quantum Cryptography.

Ibtissem Jendoubi obtained his PhD in Physics from the Faculty of Sciences of Monastir in 2015 titled 'theoretical prediction of the formation of cold and ultra-cold molecules'

K.Vijiyakumar is an Assistant professor in Department of Computing Technologies, School of computing,SRM Institute of Science and Technology, Kattankalathur, Chennai. He completed his M.Tech degree (CSE) in the year 2010 from Pondicherry Engineering College. He completed his PhD degree in Pondicherry Technological University, Puducherry. His research area includes computer vision, Image processing, deep learning and machine learning.

R. I. Minu received the B.E. degree in Electronics and Communication Engineering from Bharathidasan University in 2004, and the M.E. and Ph.D. degrees in Computer Science and Engineering from Anna University in 2007 and 2015, respectively. She is currently a Professor in the Department of Computing Technologies, School of Computing, SRM Institute of Science and Technology, Kattankulathur, India.She has published more than 50 research articles in peer-reviewed journals, including those from Elsevier, Springer-Verlag, Taylor & Francis, and IEEE conferences. Her research focuses on emerging technologies, such as the Internet of Things (IoT), edge/fog computing, artificial intelligence (AI), data science, blockchain, digital twin, 5G, and Quantum Machine Learning.

N. Nithiyanandam, working as an Assistant Professor in the department of Computing Technologies, SRM Institute of Science and Technology, Kattankulathur, Chengalpattu, India.He has 15 years of experience in the field of Teaching and 3 years of experience in the field of Industry. He completed his B.Tech Information Technology in the year 2004 at Sri Venkateshwara College of Engineering, Sriperumbudur, Madras University, and he completed his M.E Computer Science and Engineering in the year 2013 at Vels University, Chennai, and He completed his PhD in the year 2021 at Pondicherry University, Puducherry. He is interested in Network Security, Cloud Computing, Quantum Computing and Machine Learning.

Sahana. P. Shankar completed her B.E in Information Science and Engineering and MTech in Software Engineering from Ramaiah Institute of Technology, Bangalore. She is a third rank holder in B.E and a first rank holder with gold medal in MTech. She has worked with Unisys as an Associate Engineer for three years. She holds a US Patent in the field so software testing. She has worked with RIT as a Teaching Assistant for 6 months under the TEQIP-II scholarship program. She has published papers in various international journals and conferences. She has also authored several book chapters. She is an ISTQB certified software tester. She is pursuing her PhD from VTU, Belgaum. She is currently working with Ramaiah University of Applied Sciences, Bangalore as an Assistant Professor in the Department of Computer Science and Engineering since 2018.

Gowtham. R is working as an Assistant Professor in the Department of Commerce, School of Commerce, Finance and Accountancy, Christ (Deemed to be University), Bangalore. He completed his Doctorate of Philosophy in Commerce, especially Taxation, in the Department of Commerce, SRM Institute of Science and

Technology, Kattankulathur, Chennai. He also worked as Assistant Professor at the Department of Commerce, Madras Christian College.

S.Sony Priya received the B.E and M.E. degree in Computer Science and Engineering from Anna University in 2007 and 2013, respectively. She is currently a Research Scolar in the Department of Computing Technologies, School of Computing, SRM Institute of Science and Technology, Kattankulathur, India. Her research focuses on artificial intelligence (AI) and Quantum Machine Learning.

C.V. Suresh Babu is a pioneer in content development. A true entrepreneur, he founded Anniyappa Publications, a company that is highly active in publishing books related to Computer Science and Management. Dr. C.V. Suresh Babu has also ventured into SB Institute, a center for knowledge transfer. He holds a Ph.D. in Engineering Education from the National Institute of Technical Teachers Training & Research in Chennai, along with seven master's degrees in various disciplines such as Engineering, Computer Applications, Management, Commerce, Economics, Psychology, Law, and Education. Additionally, he has UGC-NET/SET qualifications in the fields of Computer Science, Management, Commerce, and Education. Currently, Dr. C.V. Suresh Babu is a Professor in the Department of Information Technology at the School of Computing Science, Hindustan Institute of Technology and Science (Hindustan University) in Padur, Chennai, Tamil Nadu, India.

Gnaneshwarachary Udary received his Master's degree in 2009 in VLSI Systems Design from Jawaharlal Nehru Technological University Hyderabad. He is currently working as an Assistant Professor in B. V. Raju Institute of Technology. Pursuing Ph.D in Koneru Lakshmaiah University (KLEF). He had 14 years of teaching experience. His research interests include CMOS Analog design, VLSI system design, Quantum Computing.

Deepak Varadam holds a Masters Degree in Microsystems Engineering from Heriot-Watt University, Edinburgh (Scotland), U.K. and P.G.Diploma in ECE from Napier University, U.K. He worked as a Postgraduate Masters Research Scientist under Biomedical Microengineering Group (BMG) at Heriot-Watt University. He is currently working as an Assistant Professor in Faculty of Engineering and Technology, Computer Science and Engineering Department at Ramaiah University of Applied Sciences (RUAS) since 2010. He has been actively participating in delivering corporate trainings, seminars and have publications in national, international journals and conferences. His research interests is in MEMS, Embedded Systems, Software Engineering, Computer Graphics, AI, Blockchain, and IoT. He is currently an ExeCom Member of the IEEE RUAS Student Chapter.

Index

A

B

C

D

E

F

G

H

I

M

N

O

P

Q

S

T

www.ingramcontent.com/pod-product-compliance
Lightning Source LLC
LaVergne TN
LVHW081344300926
849161LV00008B/2063